Strategic Nuclear Targeting

CORNELL STUDIES IN SECURITY AFFAIRS

edited by Robert J. Art *and* Robert Jervis

Strategic Nuclear Targeting

EDITED BY

DESMOND BALL

AND

JEFFREY RICHELSON

Cornell University Press

ITHACA AND LONDON

First published 1986 by Cornell University Press.

International Standard Book Number 0–8014–1898–4
Library of Congress Catalog Card Number 85–48195
Printed in the United States of America
*Librarians: Library of Congress cataloging information
appears on the last page of the book.*

*The paper in this book is acid-free and meets the guidelines for permanence
and durability of the Committee on Production Guidelines for
Book Longevity of the Council on Library Resources.*

Contents

[6]

Preface

Targeting is central to any serious discussion of nuclear strategy. What targets do the United States, the Soviet Union, Great Britain, and France plan to attack in the event of a strategic nuclear war? What are the strategic rationales for these targeting plans and for the selection of particular targets? What national priorities and strategic concepts inform the target planning process, how are they developed, and how closely are they matched operationally in the war plans of nations? By what mechanisms are weapons allocated to the selected targets? How are words transformed into action?

Despite the centrality of such matters, however, the subject has gone virtually unaddressed in the public literature. Strategic debate has tended to focus almost entirely on general arguments about alternative concepts and doctrines, such as Minimum Deterrence, Massive Retaliation, Counterforce, Assured Destruction, Damage Limitation, Flexible Response, and Controlled Escalation; and on arguments about weapons acquisition, such as the types, characteristics, basing modes, and numbers of intercontinental ballistic missiles, submarine-launched ballistic missiles, and long-range strategic bombers which should be procured.

Since the mid-1970s, however, recognition has begun to increase of the need for a more informed public debate on the subject of strategic nuclear targeting. Declassified U.S. nuclear war plans of the late 1940s and early 1950s showed that the target planning process had frequently been arbitrary and inefficient and sometimes irrational. Debates over weapons acquisition have been found wanting, moreover, because of a failure adequately to relate the weapons themselves to the policies for their use in nuclear war. More recent concerns about developments in strategic nuclear technology, the state of the global strategic balance, and the requirements of successful deterrence have also demanded a better understanding of targeting policies and plans. In the United States, targeting policy even became a partisan political issue during the 1980 presidential election, when in July 1980 the Carter administration made public the general contents and rationale of a new presidential directive, PD–59, on nuclear weapons employment policy.

This is the first book designed to bring together in one volume a comprehensive collection of critiques, analyses, and assessments of targeting questions and associated public concerns. PD–59 was based on a two-year review of U.S. targeting policy which involved more than a dozen government and contractor reports on a wide variety of targeting issues. This volume provides a consideration of some of the same issues, but from a broader set of perspectives. The promulgation of PD–59 and the increasing public attention to targeting issues which it stimulated also resulted in the first tentative and isolated discussions of targeting issues by nuclear strategists in the professional military and strategic studies journals. The best of these articles have also been included in this book. However, they fall short of providing comprehensive coverage of all the important targeting issues, and hence more than half of the chapters in this volume were specially prepared to address the full range of relevant issues. This book, then, is the most comprehensive discussion of all the important targeting issues, prepared by leading strategic analysts in various fields, yet to be made publicly available. It will permit a fully informed and wide-ranging public debate of this neglected but crucial subject.

Some of the contributions to this volume have been published previously, although in most cases these have been revised and updated. Much of the material in Chapter 2, by David Alan Rosenberg, was published in a somewhat different form in "The Origins of Overkill: Nuclear Weapons and American Strategy, 1945–1960," *International Security 7*, no. 4 (Spring 1983), 3–71. Much of the material in Chapter 3 originally appeared as the second and third chapters of Desmond Ball, *Targeting for Strategic Deterrence* (Adelphi Paper no. 185, International Institute for Strategic Studies, London, Summer 1983), 8–25. Chapter 7, by Jeffrey Richelson, was originally published under the same title in *Comparative Strategy 2*, no. 3 (1980), 223–37. Chapter 8, by Colin S. Gray, was originally published as *Targeting Problems for Central War* by the Hudson Institute (Croton-on-Hudson, New York, HI–3086–P, October 1979) and then as an article under the same title in the *Naval War College Review* 33, no. 1 (January–February 1980), 3–21. Chapter 9, by Michael Kennedy and Kevin N. Lewis, was originally published in much longer form as *On "Keeping Them Down" or, Why Do Recovery Models Recover So Fast?* (Rand Corporation, Santa Monica, California, P–6531, June 1981). Some of the material in Chapter 13 was originally published by George C. Quester in "Ethnic Targeting: A Bad Idea Whose Time Has Come" in

Journal of Strategic Studies 5, no. 2 (June 1982), 228–35. These contributions are reproduced here by permission.

DESMOND BALL AND JEFFREY RICHELSON

Canberra
Washington, D.C.

Glossary

ACDA	Arms Control and Disarmament Agency
AEC	Atomic Energy Commission
AFSATCOM	Air Force Satellite Communications System
ALCS	Airborne Launch Control System
ASAT	Antisatellite Weapon
ASW	Antisubmarine Warfare
BMD	Ballistic Missile Defense
CBW	Chemical-Biological Weapons
CEP	Circle of Equal Probability
CMC	Cruise Missile Carrier
COPRA	Comparative Postwar Recovery Analysis
CPSU	Communist Party of the Soviet Union
CRS	Constant Returns to Scale
C³I	Command, Control, Communications, and Intelligence
DE	Damage Expectancy
DGZ	Desired Ground Zero
DOD	Department of Defense (U.S.)
DSTP	Director, Strategic Target Planning
FBM	Fleet Ballistic Missile
FEMA	Federal Emergency Management Agency
FPA	Federal Preparedness Agency
FY	Fiscal Year
GOSPLAN	State Planning Commission (USSR)
IRBM	Intermediate Range Ballistic Missile
JCS	Joint Chiefs of Staff
JSCP	Joint Strategic Capabilities Plan
JSOP	Joint Strategic Objectives Plan
JSTPS	Joint Strategic Target Planning Staff
KGB	Committee for State Security (USSR)
LNO	Limited Nuclear Option
LOA	Launch on Assessment
LOW	Launch on Warning
LUA	Launch under Attack
MAD	Mutual Assured Destruction
MAO	Major Attack Option
MCP	Memorandum of Conference with the President
MIRV	Multiple Independently Targeted Re-entry Vehicle

MRV	Multiple Re-entry Vehicle
MVD	Ministry of Internal Affairs (USSR)
NCA	National Command Authority
NESC	Net Evaluation Sub Committee
NIE	National Intelligence Estimate
NSC	National Security Council
NSDD	National Security Decision Directive
NSDM	National Security Decision Memorandum
NSSM	National Security Study Memorandum
NSTAP	National Strategic Targeting and Attack Policy
NSTDB	National Strategic Target Data Base
NSTL	National Strategic Target List
NTPR	Nuclear Targeting Policy Review
NUWEP	Nuclear Weapons Employment Policy
ODM	Office of Defense Mobilization
OMT	Other Military Targets
OSD	Office of the Secretary of Defense (U.S.)
PD	Presidential Directive
PGMRV	Precision Guided Maneuvering Re-entry Vehicle
PLA	People's Liberation Army (China)
PRM	Presidential Review Memorandum
RSFSR	Russian Socialist Federated Soviet Republic
RV	Re-entry Vehicle
SAC	Strategic Air Command
SACEUR	Supreme Allied Commander, Europe
SAGA	Studies Analysis and Gaming Agency
SAM	Surface-to-Air Missile
SAMOS	Satellite and Missile Observation System
SAO	Selective Attack Option
SIGINT	Signals Intelligence
SIOP	Single Integrated Operational Plan
SLBM	Submarine Launched Ballistic Missile
SSBN	Nuclear Powered Ballistic Missile Submarine
TANDEM	Tactical Nuclear Damage Effects Model
TVD	Teatr Voyennykh Deystviy (Theater of Military Operations)
USD(P)	Under Secretary of Defense (Policy)
VGK	Supreme High Command (USSR)
VPK	Military Industrial Commission (USSR)

PART I

INTRODUCTION

[1]

Toward a Critique of
Strategic Nuclear Targeting

Desmond Ball

Questions of targeting are central to any serious discussion of nuclear strategy. What are the targets that the United States, the Soviet Union, Great Britain, and France plan to attack in the event of a strategic nuclear war? What are the strategic rationales for these targeting plans and for the selection of particular targets? What are the various relevant sets of national guidance and the strategic concepts and doctrines that inform the target planning process, how are they developed, and how closely are they matched operationally in the war plans? What is the relationship between extant targeting policies and plans and particular notions of deterrence?

Despite their centrality, there was little explicit discussion of these targeting issues until the mid-1970s. Strategic discourse rarely proceeded beyond general arguments concerning concepts such as Minimum Deterrence, Massive Retaliation, No-Cities Counterforce, Assured Destruction, Damage Limitation, Flexible Response, and Controlled Escalation; issues relating to the actual employment of nuclear weapons in pursuance of these various concepts and doctrines were addressed only infrequently.

Over the past decade, however, there has been increasing recognition of the need for a better understanding of the considerations that attend the target planning process and for a more informed public debate on this crucial subject. This appreciation has derived from a number of developments.

Perhaps the most important of these have been developments in strategic nuclear technology and in the global strategic nuclear balance. With respect to strategic nuclear technology, there have been extraordinary improvements in the accuracies of ballistic missile systems (both ICBMs and SLBMs), which, according to some strategic analysts, have made possible a larger and more variegated set of targeting options, including more discriminating options designed to provide decision makers with the ability to undertake limited or selective nuclear strikes. Developments in strategic command, control, communications, and intelligence (C³I) systems also offer the promise of controlling the escalation process in such a way that limits might be maintained on a nuclear exchange.

With respect to the global strategic balance, the loss of clear and unequivocal nuclear superiority by the United States by the mid-1970s forced U.S. policy makers to pay greater attention to the weapons allocation process. During the period of U.S. superiority, it was possible to avow a declaratory policy of Assured Destruction at one level in the confidence that extant capabilities allowed for the pursuit of a wide range of strategic options in the event of an actual nuclear exchange. A looser rein could also be given to bureaucratic/political machinations in the weapons acquisition process, since the requirements of cost-effectiveness were less stringent. As Harold Brown acknowledged in January 1979: "It would be inefficient to base [U.S. strategic nuclear] forces on such a conservative definition of the assured-destruction mission that it would provide us with a surplus of warheads in most circumstances (but perhaps of the wrong types) for use against non-urban targets."[1]

With the loss of U.S. superiority, U.S. strategic decision makers have been forced to be much more consistent and efficient with respect to the alignment of weapons acquisition policy, declaratory policy, and nuclear weapons employment policy.[2]

The loss of U.S. superiority also forced American policy makers to consider the development of targeting policies that might be more credible than the threat of large-scale attacks in deterring Soviet conventional aggression in Western Europe and Southwest Asia and the Middle East. In particular, following the crisis in Jordan in September 1970, considerable attention was accorded the development of regional nuclear options (RNOs) which could be employed in "non-central campaigns."[3]

These changes in the strategic environment generated an active interest in U.S. targeting policy and plans by both governmental and private strategic analysts, with each group being influenced by and in turn influencing the other. The public discussion of limited nuclear options (LNOs) by Secretary of Defense James Schlesinger in early 1974 was especially important in taking consideration of targeting issues outside the official realm and in joining dialogue between the private and governmental analysts.

In August 1977, President Jimmy Carter directed that a Nuclear Targeting Policy Review (NTPR) be conducted to refine and codify U.S. strategic nuclear targeting policy. Numerous supporting studies were commissioned from within government, and from consulting agencies and academia, on such topics as the history of U.S. targeting plans, Soviet and Chinese views on nuclear war and nuclear weapons employment policies, the possibility of targeting the Soviet population, targeting economic and political recovery assets, regionalization of the Soviet Union, the C³I constraints on escalation control, and the question of war termination. Sanitized versions of many of these studies were subsequently published in academic and professional journals.

The primary result of the NTPR was Presidential Directive (PD) 59, titled *Nuclear Weapons Employment Policy* and signed by President Carter on 25 July 1980, which directed that increased emphasis be accorded the targeting of Soviet military and political assets (as against economic and industrial assets) as well as the capability to fight a prolonged nuclear war. The NTPR also led to the institutionalization of the targeting review process with the creation of the Nuclear Targeting Policy Review Group within the Office of the Under Secretary of Defense for Policy (USD(P)), which is responsible for maintaining continuous and critical review of U.S. strategic nuclear targeting policies and plans.

The strategic policy embodied in PD-59 was reaffirmed by President Ronald Reagan in National Security Decision Directive (NSDD) 13, signed in October 1981. Although previous presidential guidance had directed that the United States should be able to initiate the limited or selective use of strategic nuclear weapons, to engage in a prolonged or protracted nuclear conflict, and to control the escalation process in such a way that the United States would "prevail" in this conflict, the rhetoric used by officials of the Reagan administration in their discussions of these aspects of U.S. strategic nuclear employment policy has engendered widespread and serious public concern. This concern cannot be alleviated without an informed public debate.

Such debate has been inhibited in the past by the failure in most discussions of U.S. strategic nuclear policy to differentiate the substance of employment or action policy—or how the United States would actually employ nuclear weapons in the event of a nuclear exchange—from the rhetoric of declaratory policy, which is generally designed for a variety of strategic and bureaucratic-political purposes sometimes quite unrelated to the demands of extant action policy.

The history of U.S. strategic nuclear policy has been characterized by James Schlesinger as "shifting sands."[4] The policy of Massive Retaliation which was developed early in the Eisenhower administration was rejected in 1961 for being suicidal and incredible, providing the United States with only a single choice—humiliation or holocaust. Interest then developed in Damage Limitation and strategies of coercion. This was short-lived, however, and the emphasis passed to Assured Destruction—with, as Schlesinger pointed out, "little attention [being] paid to

[17]

the suicidal implications found so distressing in prior years."[5] The interest in Damage Limitation and coercion—and, indeed, in nuclear war fighting—was revived in the early 1970s and, despite widespread controversy, has continued to the present day. Throughout these shifting rationales, however, U.S. doctrines and plans have remained remarkably resilient, at least with respect to the general categories and particular types of targets. This resilience becomes readily apparent in the historical review of U.S. targeting doctrine and plans, which follows in chapters 2 and 3.

In Chapter 2 David Alan Rosenberg describes the U.S. strategic nuclear war plans of the late 1940s and the 1950s, which typically invoked the strategic rationale of the destruction of "Soviet war-making capacity"—involving attacks on Soviet nuclear capabilities (which in 1950 became the first priority in U.S. target plans), other Soviet military capabilities, and Soviet cities in order to destroy war-sustaining industry, governmental control, and the civil morale necessary to maintain a war effort. However, the growth of U.S. nuclear capability during this period was a far more significant determinant of U.S. targeting policies and plans than any strategic rationale. In fact, U.S. capabilities and target plans had their own interconnected dynamism which had little relationship to any avowed national strategic policy. The expansion of target lists demanded increased capabilities, which in turn determined targeting objectives. The development of the first Single Integrated Operational Plan in 1960 (SIOP-62) offered an opportunity to impose some limits on the target generation process and to relate target planning to national strategic policy, but the dynamics of the operational planning process proved too strong.

Desmond Ball describes the development of the SIOP since 1960 in chapter 3. This begins with an account of the development of new strategic guidance in 1961–62, which served as the basis for a major revision of SIOP-62. The new SIOP, designated SIOP-63, contained a number of targeting options, including most especially the no-cities option of withholding attacks from Soviet population centers. The chapter continues with a description of the studies and analyses undertaken during the Nixon administration, studies which resulted in National Security Decision Memorandum (NSDM) 242 of 17 January 1974, the promulgation of the Nuclear Weapons Employment Policy (NUWEP) on 4 April 1974, and the development of SIOP-5. It then describes the developments in targeting policy undertaken during the Carter administration—including, most particularly, Presidential Directive (PD) 59 of 25 July 1980 and a second NUWEP, designated NUWEP-80, signed in October 1980. It also describes the recent developments in targeting policy un-

[18]

dertaken by the Reagan administration, including National Security Decision Directive (NSDD) 13 signed by President Reagan in October 1981, a new NUWEP (NUWEP-82) promulgated in July 1982, and the development of a new SIOP, designated SIOP-6, which took effect on 1 October 1983. These developments of the last decade have resulted in an extremely comprehensive and varied targeting structure, which provides the U.S. National Command Authorities (NCA) with a wide range of nuclear weapons employment options and a machinery for their flexible execution in the event of a nuclear exchange with the USSR.

The strategic nuclear target planning process in the United States has now become extremely sophisticated, but the question must remain as to how realistic much of this planning really is. For one thing, the concept of Escalation Control requires that U.S. strategic nuclear forces be supported by a survivable C³I system with sufficient endurance to maintain control through some extended period of protracted conflict. However, strategic C³I systems are necessarily subject to certain critical vulnerabilities that impose quite debilitating physical constraints on the situations in which escalation might be controlled, the time period over which control might be maintained, and the proportion of the SIOP forces that could be employed in a controlled fashion. The boundary of control in any militarily significant exchange (as compared to demonstration strikes) is unlikely to lie beyond either a few days or a few tens of detonations![6]

Nuclear weapons possess only problematical utility as instruments of communication and intrawar bargaining and negotiation. Much of the discrimination that has been programmed into U.S. nuclear war plans in recent years is probably significant only to U.S. target planners themselves; it is most unlikely to be unmistakably obvious to the adversary.

Any strategic policy that involves notions of control and limitation requires that all the participants in the conflict be willing and have the capability to exercise restraint—in weapons, in targets, and in political objectives. However, strategic policy makers and planners in no other country with strategic nuclear weapons capabilities have proved willing to seriously entertain the imposition of such restraints on their employment policies and plans.

In the case of the Soviet Union, William T. Lee shows in chapter 4 that the development of Soviet strategic nuclear capabilities has clearly and carefully matched the demands of Soviet targeting doctrine for full coverage of all forces and installations which if destroyed or damaged would affect the outcome of a nuclear exchange and the relative postwar strengths of the Soviet Union and its adversaries. In the event of a nuclear exchange, Soviet forces would be used massively and simultaneously against U.S. nuclear forces, other military forces, the U.S. and

Allied military-industrial base, and the U.S. and Allied military, political, and administrative control centers—in all geographic Theaters of Military Operations (TVDs).

In the case of both British and French targeting, there are clear disjunctions between the requirements of their respective national employment policies and the actual capabilities of their strategic nuclear forces. In the British case, as Lawrence Freedman describes in chapter 5, the acceptance of the NATO doctrine of Flexible Response in the 1960s coincided with the phaseout of the V-bomber force and the move to total reliance on the SSBN force of four Polaris submarines, which greatly reduced the target coverage and employment flexibility of the British posture. More recently, the planned acquisition of five Trident submarines equipped with D-5 SLBMs (each capable of carrying eight to fourteen MIRV warheads) will increase British strategic nuclear capabilities, in terms of both coverage and flexibility, far beyond those required by the relatively simple demands of the employment policy and plans. As Freedman concludes, "this extra flexibility and scope was not sought and seems to have been acquired without any clear sense of how it should be employed."

In the French case, the disjunction arises from a reverse situation—that is, a deficiency in French strategic nuclear capabilities as compared to the requirements of the new and rather broader *oeuvres vives* or "enlarged anticities doctrine." As David S. Yost argues in chapter 6, "France's strategic capabilities are barely sufficient to carry out declaratory doctrine today, and planned improvements cannot obscure the fact that the technical credibility of France's deterrent largely depends on a benign strategic environment."

These differences between the British and French strategic nuclear employment policies are relatively insignificant, however, when compared to their common attribute of urban-industrial targeting and the propensity of this to invalidate U.S. employment policies. Given that one of the most likely scenarios leading to a strategic nuclear exchange between the United States and the Soviet Union is a Warsaw Pac–NATO conflict in Europe, it is also likely that the British and French nuclear forces would be employed against Soviet urban-industrial centers (including Moscow) before U.S. capabilities for escalation control could be exercised.

Part 3 of this collection is concerned with the discussion of a wide range of targeting issues that have been considered by U.S. strategic analysts over the past decade. Taken together, they provide a remarkable critique of the strategic logic and viability of the critical elements of current U.S. strategic nuclear employment policy.

As described in chapter 3, current U.S. target plans cover some fifty thousand potential target installations, which are divided into four principal categories: the Soviet nuclear forces, other military targets (OMT), the Soviet military and political leadership centers, and the Soviet economic and industrial base. Unfortunately, there are grave difficulties, some of which are operationally insurmountable, associated with the execution of strikes against each of these target categories.

In the case of an attack on the strategic nuclear forces of the Soviet Union, for example, there is the obvious point that such an attack could only be successful if the United States were to initiate a massive first strike or "disarming" action, which is disavowed by official U.S. policy. In any event, the success of the strike would depend on the Soviet Union not launching its weapons on receipt of warning of the U.S. attack—a condition that seems discounted by Soviet employment doctrine.[7]

There are two related strategic issues involved in targeting the Soviet nuclear forces which derive from the wide geographical dispersion of the Soviet ICBM force. The first is that the geographic spread of Soviet ICBM sites suggests possible difficulties with strategic policies that attempt to control escalation and rely, at least in part, on Soviet attack assessment capability. Unlike the United States, which has deployed its ICBMs generally in the center of the country, the Soviet ICBMs extend across virtually the entire USSR. A Soviet attack limited to U.S. ICBM sites would fall completely east of 115°W longitude and west of the Mississippi River, and would be less difficult for U.S. early-warning and attack assessment systems to differentiate from an attack involving the major U.S. population and industrial centers and the national capital. A U.S. retaliatory strike against the Soviet ICBM fields, on the other hand, must cover nearly the entire geographic expanse of the Soviet Union, including the more heavily populated and industrialized area west of the Urals. Processing data on some one thousand to two thousand warheads and other objects such as penetration aids and booster fragments targeted over this vast region might pose insuperable problems for the Soviet attack assessment system. This is especially the case with respect to the three or four ICBM fields in the Moscow areas.[8]

The second, related concern arises from the possibility of extensive collateral damage attending a U.S. strike against the Soviet ICBM fields. In the U.S. case, the separation of the ICBM fields from major urban areas means that the collateral impact on population of a Soviet counter-ICBM attack would be relatively small, although casualties in St. Louis and Kansas City might be significant, depending on the prevailing winds, pursuant to an attack on the 150 Minuteman II ICBMs at Whiteman Air Force Base, Missouri. On the other hand, with about half of the Soviet ICBM fields west of the Urals and several of them located near some of the most densely populated areas of the USSR, the Soviet casualty figures following a counter-ICBM attack could be quite high, depending very much on the nature of the attack and the prevailing wind directions at the time. At the least, the relative location of the Soviet ICBM fields increases the difficulties of persuading the Soviet leadership to accept the notion of limited counterforce nuclear warfare.

The principal issues relating to the targeting of the Soviet leadership are discussed by Jeffrey Richelson and Colin S. Gray in chapters 7 and 8. Although both these articles were written in the late 1970s and were only lightly updated, the issues they discuss are still relevant today— as what were then apparent changes in targeting policy have become confirmed changes.

There is at the outset the problem of defining the bounds of what is, potentially at least, an extremely large target set, and then of identifying the individuals and facilities that comprise this set. Both the CIA and the Pentagon estimate that the Soviet leadership (excluding the military command) numbers about 110,000 people, made up of some 5,000 party and government officials at the national and republic level, 63,000 party and government leaders at kray, oblast, city, and urban rayon level, 2,000 managers of key economic and industrial installations, and about 40,000 other essential personnel.[9] Targeting the CPSU headquarters and other governmental and administrative buildings in Moscow, the republic capitals, and the oblasts, krays, and major cities, as well as military headquarters and command posts and KGB centers throughout the Soviet Union, could require many thousands of weapons.

There is also the problem that the locations of many leadership assets, and particularly the relocation sites for use during a nuclear exchange, are not known. This is a tacit admission in the following statement by Secretary of Defense Harold Brown in his Fiscal Year 1981 Posture Statement: "Hardened command posts have been constructed near Moscow and other cities. For the some 100,000 people we define as the Soviet leadership, there are hardened underground shelters near places of work, and at relocation sites outside the cities. *The relatively few leadership shelters we have identified* would be vulnerable to direct attack."[10] Even where facilities have been identified, it would be difficult (if not impossible) to know exactly which elements of the leadership had dispersed to which facilities.

A further complication in targeting these facilities is that many of them have been substantially hardened against blast and other nuclear effects. Some of the underground centers for the governmental and military leadership in the Moscow area are several hundred feet underground and capable of withstanding 1,000 psi blast overpressure.[11] According to testimony of the secretary of the air force in 1977, the Soviet Union has also built "thousands of hardened military command posts, communications antennas and associated control facilities,"[12] many of which are hardened to greater than 600 psi.[13]

Moreover, the destruction of the political control facilities does not necessarily mean the destruction of the political control personnel. KGB officers are less likely to be in KGB buildings than dispersed among the population they are tasked with monitoring and controlling.

Indeed, this points to a larger problem. Many of the political and military leadership centers are located in or near major urban areas, particularly Moscow and the republic capitals. It would be difficult to destroy any extensive segment of the Soviet leadership without causing large numbers of civilian casualties. Although Colin Gray is the most persuasive advocate of targeting the Soviet political control system, he is in no sense oblivious to this and other difficulties associated with counterleadership operations. As he has observed elsewhere, "It is an unfortunate fact that the United States cannot wage a surgical war against the Communist Party of the Soviet Union and the KGB. A knockout blow against the control structure, leaving Soviet society essentially untouched, is simply not feasible, even with new technologies for very precise weapon delivery."[14]

Large-scale attacks on the Soviet leadership would be virtually indistinguishable from countercity attacks. Escalation control would be difficult to pursue following such attacks.

In fact, such attacks would probably mean the end of escalation control. As Gray points out in chapter 8, "Once executed, a very large strike against the Soviet political and administrative leadership would mean that the United States had 'done its worst.' If the Soviet government, in the sense of a National Command Authority, were still able to function, it is likely that it would judge that it had little, if anything, left to fear."

Finally, a counter-political-leadership strike would make it impossible for the Soviets to negotiate war termination.

Other military targets (OMT) are military targets other than strategic counterforce and military and political leadership targets. This target set includes approximately half of the fifty thousand potential targets in the current SIOP and comprises a wide variety of types of targets, including Soviet conventional military forces, military bases and airfields (including large civilian airfields that could be used by military aircraft in wartime), chemical and biological weapons (CBW) capabilities, Soviet space facilities, and installations and capabilities that do not fit clearly into the other three principal target sets. Given the miscellaneous nature of this target set, it is extremely difficult to envisage any comprehensive attack against it of the sort that could well be undertaken against the Soviet leadership, nuclear forces, or economic-industrial base. Rather, partic-

[23]

ular elements of the set would be selected for attack as determined by the circumstances at the time. In the case of a limited nuclear strike, for example, it is most unlikely that either Soviet leadership capabilities or economic-industrial centers would be prime targets, and in some scenarios care might be taken to avoid the Soviet nuclear forces. The initial use of nuclear weapons by the United States is likely to be directed at targets relevant to the crisis at hand, such as the Soviet ground forces and naval bases that comprise the Soviet capability for force projection. Because of the Soviet antisatellite (ASAT) threat to U.S. space-based communications and intelligence capabilities, the Soviet ASAT facilities might be regarded as lucrative targets. Some of these installations and capabilities might of course be targeted in a general nuclear war as well, though here they would have to compete with the other three target sets for attention by the SIOP forces.

In the case of some of the Limited and Regional Nuclear Options, there is an important issue of strategic policy concerning the choice of weapons to be allocated by the SIOP planners. With regard to the European theater, for example, the OMT category includes "literally thousands of Warsaw Pact targets of major military importance,"[15] and in recent years there has been much attention devoted to "such promising concepts as targeting Soviet Second Echelon forces so as to delay reinforcement and disrupt the timing of a Soviet attack."[16] The problem is that the Minuteman ICBMs are the only SIOP weapons with the necessary accuracy, flight time, command and control, and retargeting flexibility to be employed in this mission. But there are much higher priority requirements for Minuteman capabilities elsewhere, and, in any case, to use a U.S.-based weapon in a theater conflict would conflict with the policy guidelines for escalation control.

In the case of a general nuclear war, the critical operational issue is that of selecting which of the twenty-five thousand targets in the OMT category are of sufficient importance to warrant the use of a nuclear weapon against them. In the case of the Soviet surface-to-air missile (SAM) system, which consists of more than ten thousand launchers at some one thousand two hundred sites, each of which must be given an appropriate Desired Ground Zero (DGZ) by the SIOP planners, it is obvious that only those sites covering bomber routes to the primary bomber targets would actually ever be attacked themselves—with the determination of the specific SAM sites being dependent upon several last-minute considerations (chiefly involving the B-52 and F-111 final flight profiles). In the case of attacks on Soviet airfields, army camps, and naval bases and ports, which would primarily be the responsibility of the SLBM force, there would be difficult operational problems involved in ascertaining which of them was currently hosting interesting forces and then communicating the appropriate attack messages to the fleet ballistic missile (FBM) submarines.

There are five hundred major air bases in the Soviet Union, and in an emergency the Soviet air force would also have available numerous smaller strips (i.e., those less than 4,000 feet in length) and "sodstrip" contingency airfields. Targeting this force is extremely demanding. Aircraft are quite vulnerable to nuclear effects while on the ground, since blast overpressures as low as 3 psi can cause severe damage (requiring major maintenance before the aircraft can fly), but their ability to quickly become airborne and to disperse can often effectively negate this vulnerability. Aircraft munitions, fuel, and maintenance supplies and personnel are not so easily or rapidly moved, but to attack every air base could well require more weapons than are available. A potentially more effective threat might be to strike the divisional and regimental headquarters of the Soviet air force, but this raises problems concerning leadership targeting.

The United States is in some ways disadvantaged compared to the Soviet Union with respect to capabilities for OMT attacks. To begin with, the Soviet OMT set is much larger than its U.S. counterpart. There is an asymmetry in intelligence because the Soviet Union is a much more closed society than the United States. The Soviet Union also places much greater emphasis on the defense of its conventional forces—both actively, as evinced by its enormous air defense capabilities, and passively, through concealment, dispersion, and hardening. Further, the United States has few nuclear weapons specifically tailored for the OMT mission. Hence, the implementation of that part of U.S. targeting guidance concerning OMT may not be feasible.

With regard to economic targeting, the fundamental issue concerns the determination of the objective: Is it simply to destroy some fraction of Soviet industrial capacity or to negate some fraction of Soviet economic activity? Is it to deny economic and industrial support of the Soviet war effort in order to obstruct Soviet military operations in the event of a large-scale conventional war or a protracted nuclear war? Or is it to impede Soviet postattack economic recovery in order to ensure U.S. dominance in the postwar world?

It is clear that the principal objective of the U.S. war plans of the late 1940s was the destruction of critical war-supporting industries in order to affect Soviet battlefield operations, the longer-term ability of the Soviet economy to support combat, and the Soviet will to continue the conflict.[17] In the late 1960s, however, under the ascription of the Assured Destruction doctrine, the requirement became to simply destroy one-half to two-thirds of Soviet industrial capacity; the rationale, as stated by Secretary of Defense Robert McNamara in February 1965, was that such a level of destruction "would certainly represent intolerable punishment to any industrialized nation and thus should serve as an effective deterrent."[18] For this purpose, it did not matter whether the industrial capacity destroyed consisted of machine goods or rolling stock, tank factories or garment factories, bakeries or toy factories. Various studies completed in the early 1970s argued strongly that the obstruction of Soviet economic recovery should be the primary objective of economic targeting, and this was endorsed in the NSDM-242 of 17 January 1974 and the NUWEP of 4 March 1974. This prompted much analytic work within the American defense community on the development of Cobb-Douglas models and input-output tables of the Soviet economy designed to assess the Soviet Union's postattack powers of recuperation and to elucidate critical interdependencies and vulnerabilities for targeting purposes. Fertilizer plants became one of the more celebrated target sets in SIOP-5 because analysis indicated the critical role these would play in Soviet agricultural recovery. The NUWEP of October 1980 directed that less emphasis be accorded economic targeting, but it also directed that dual objectives be pursued—the disruption of economic recovery remained, but the destruction of war-supporting industry was reemphasized as a targeting objective.

Having determined the objective, a methodological issue arises as to how best to achieve it—the "bottleneck" approach or the Congreve approach. The notion of attacking bottlenecks—or target systems that contain only a relatively few installations whose destruction would have immediate and disproportionate effects, such as transportation systems and some specialized industries such as ball-bearing factories—is superficially very appealing. However, debilitating imprecision in both intelligence and models of Soviet economic activity, as well as in weapons delivery capabilities, make the bottleneck approach difficult to implement successfully in practice. An alternative is the Congreve approach, suggested by Ambrose Congreve in 1942, according to which industrial plants are bombed with the objective of destroying capital goods.[19] The larger the plant in terms of output of goods, the more important it ranks as a target; the type of goods produced is much less important than the estimated value of the goods destroyed. The weakness of this approach is that little distinction is made between types of capital goods—machine tools or haberdashery machinery, metal processing equipment or food processing plant. It is probable, at least with respect to the Soviet Union, that some integration of bottleneck and Congreve theories provides the best strategy.

Chapter 9 by Michael Kennedy and Kevin N. Lewis provides a critique of the economic models used to assess the efficacy of targeting Soviet economic recovery capabilities. These models typically indicate that the

Soviet Union could recover from an all-out U.S. nuclear attack involving several thousand warheads in perhaps only four or five years, and probably no more than fifteen years at the outside. This seemingly optimistic assessment is basically a consequence of the assumptions concerning the homogeneity and hence "shiftability" of new capital investment, the ability of the leadership to "prioritize" postwar economic activity, and the substitutability of labor and capital resources. More realistic assumptions would generally produce much longer recovery periods.

The analysis by Kennedy and Lewis tends to support the bottleneck approach to economic targeting, even though the authors appreciate that uncertainities in the identification of industrial plant and in the models of the Soviet economy make such a strategy difficult to devise in practice.

A further difficulty with the bottleneck approach is suggested by Frederic S. Nyland's analysis of "exemplary industrial targets" in chapter 10. His analysis indicates not only that economic choke points are probably few and far between but also that, even if they could be found, they probably could not be effectively attacked within the constraints imposed by policy guidance with respect to escalation control.

One of the more interesting changes in U.S. targeting policy over the past decade has been the exemption of 'population *per se*' as a target objective. This exemption was first announced by Secretary of Defense Elliot Richardson, who testified in April 1973: "We do not in our strategic planning target civilian population *per se*."[20] And the chairman of the Joint Chiefs of Staff explained in 1976: "We do not target population *per se* any longer. We used to. What we are now doing is targeting a war recovery capability."[21]

However, as Jeffrey Richelson points out in chapter 11, the significance of this change is not easy to discern in practice since the U.S. continues to target the major Soviet cities. In the *Annual Report* to Congress on the F.Y. 1979 defense budget on 2 February 1978, Secretary of Defense Harold Brown stated: "It is essential that we retain the capability at all times to inflict an unacceptable level of damage on the Soviet Union, including destruction of a minimum of 200 major Soviet cities."[22] In January 1979, in the *Annual Report* on the F.Y. 1980 defense budget, Secretary Brown stated: "To have a true countervailing strategy, our forces must be capable of covering, and being withheld from, a substantial list of targets. Cities cannot be excluded from such a list, not only because cities, population, and industry are closely linked, but also because it is essential at all times to retain the option to attack urban-industrial targets—both as a deterrent to attacks on our own cities and as a final retaliation if that particular deterrent should fail."[23] According to a report of the U.S. Arms Control and Disarmament Agency, all 200 of the largest Soviet

[27]

cities and 80 percent of the 886 Soviet cities with populations above twenty-five thousand are included in U.S. target plans simply by virtue of associated industrial and military targets.[24] Large-scale U.S. attacks against these targets would probably kill from 50 to 100 million people.[25] Hence, as Richelson concludes, the injunction against population targeting "can be taken only as a statement of targeting mechanics rather than a meaningful description of the effects (relative or absolute) of such a strategy."

A critical factor in determining the state of the postexchange environment and the prospects for recovery is whether or not nuclear power plants and their support facilities (such as fuel fabrication facilities, reprocessing plants, and waste storage centers) are attacked. As Bennett Ramberg points out in chapter 12, energy production plants have figured as prime targets in most major wars in the past four decades and have been included in U.S. nuclear war plans since the late 1940s. Attacks on nuclear power plants and their support facilities, however, would create unique hazards. Large reservoirs of radioactive material, including some particularly long-lived sources (such as cesium 137), would be dispersed, adding significantly to both the immediate and the longer-term effects of the conflict. For example, attacks on the forty power reactors in the Soviet Union could well render some fifty thousand square miles of territory in some of the most densely populated areas of the European part of the USSR uninhabitable for at least fifty years.

One of the inevitable but nevertheless unfortunate consequences of the more widespread and institutionalized (and also increasingly lucrative) discussion of strategic nuclear targeting issues is that it has encouraged the consideration of some targeting "options" that would otherwise and more properly have remained unappreciated. A community of strategic analysts has now been established whose primary raison d'être is the generation of "new" approaches to the employment of strategic nuclear forces. Many of these approaches have been extremely naïve in their appreciation of the technical aspects of target planning and of the escalatory dynamics that would likely pervade any strategic nuclear exchange and essentially determine their scale and character. Some of the proposed options are quite fanciful.

Two related notions that were the subject of serious and high-level consideration during the NTPR were those of "ethnic targeting" and "regionalization of the Soviet Union." These notions, which are discussed by David Cattell and George T. Quester in chapter 13, have been described by Cattell and Quester as "bad ideas whose time has come." It is not that these notions lack any worthy rationale. From the point of view of deterrence, the threat of attacks that promise to undermine the control of the Kremlin's great Russian oligarchy over its Soviet empire—

that is, attacks designed to kill Russians and spare non-Russians and thus denude the ethnic power base of this oligarchy, and attacks designed to physically separate the outer republics from Moscow—could provide a powerful restraint on any prospective Soviet aggression. And if deterrence were to fail, it would be morally wrong for the U.S. to attack "captive peoples" who would be innocent of any responsibility for the war.

On the other hand, there are serious moral and practical problems with these notions. Any strategy that involves plans to kill certain peoples (and save others) on the basis of racial or ethnic differences has inherent genocidal connotations, particularly when many Russians are no more "guilty" or no less "captive" than their Lithuanian, Ukrainian, Armenian, Kazak, or Uzbek brothers and sisters. In any case, both Quester and Cattell show that, despite the remarkable accuracy with which nuclear weapons can now be delivered, they cannot be employed so precisely as to kill Russian troops stationed in the non-Russian republics without also killing numerous ethnic peoples. Indeed, the detonation of U.S. nuclear weapons on or near Vilnius, or Kiev, or Yerevan, or Alma-Ata, or Tashkent is far more likely to make the inhabitants of these cities antagonistic toward the United States than it is to incite them to rebel against Moscow. Cattell and Quester cite a quotation from Bernard Brodie that is worth recitation:

> The person preoccupied with dodging enemy missiles does not find much time to think about other matters which might otherwise disturb him. He is unlikely to be brooding on the historic sins and errors of a government to which he can scarcely conceive an alternative. He is politically apathetic, and his apathy may look a good deal better to those whose job it is to control him than did the discouraged restlessness that perhaps preceded it. Besides, if he has been bombed out of house and home, he is grateful for small offerings, and he may acquire a more favourable attitude toward the régime merely from being given coffee at the refugee station.[26]

These notions can perhaps best be regarded as examples of some of the less impractical approaches to the development of plans that would allow the use of nuclear weapons in other than indiscriminate and massive ways.

The final chapter in part 3, by George Quester, is concerned with war termination. The employment of force should be related to clear and discrete political objectives, most—if not all—of which should be achievable short of total exhaustion of the strategic forces or total destruction of the economy and policy. However, whether or not the U.S. force employment plans are adequate for terminating the conflict of an all-out strategic exchange is problematic. As Quester notes, there is "no

[29]

shortage of paradox in the sorting of choices that has to be made [if the U.S. was] . . . striving to terminate a nuclear war as soon as possible after deterrence has failed." In particular, there is an unavoidable tension between the demands of *ex ante bellum* deterrence, which require the devotion of extensive resources to countervalue capabilities, and the capabilities required for intrawar bargaining and deterrence—which might in turn conflict with the requirements for deterrence in the postexchange environment. In addition, any planning for war termination requires a much clearer appreciation of the dynamics of the escalation process than that which currently exists.

The technical and politico-strategic problems associated with war termination are extremely formidable. The principal technical system that has officially been identified with facilitating war termination is a direct communications line between the respective U.S. and Soviet national command authorities—the so-called hot line between Moscow and Washington.[27] However, despite this system's critical importance to war termination, no special measures have been taken to protect it from the collateral effects of a nuclear exchange. The satellite ground stations are naturally quite soft (less than 5 psi) and could well be incidental casualties of strikes against nearby targets. As Gerald Dinneen, assistant secretary of defense for command, control, communications, and intelligence (C^3I), testified in March 1979: "The ground terminals, of course, are here in Washington, so most likely they are not going to be there. Unless we have some way of getting into that hotline from the Airborne Command Post, then you would have to assume that after the first impact on Washington that hotline is not available."[28]

The termination of a nuclear exchange also requires the strictest NCA control over the strategic forces themselves. Communications with FBM submarines attempting to launch their missiles in the face of enemy antisubmarine warfare (ASW) activity, or with Strategic Air Command (SAC) bombers flying at low altitudes within Soviet air space, could be very difficult, and, at least in these situations, the ability to countermand orders or to disengage forces could be very tenuous. The deployment of UHF Air Force Satellite Communications (AFSATCOM) terminals on SAC B-52s and FB-111s will considerably improve the situation with respect to the bombers; but ICBMs and SLBMs, once launched, obviously cannot be recalled and lack any mechanism for destruction in flight.[29] It is possible to imagine an intrawar pause or armistice being nullified by such deficiencies in the mechanics of disengagement.

The politico-strategic problems could prove to be even more intractable. Limited war in the nuclear age is not so much concerned with military objectives as with being a means of communication, but nuclear weapons may not be very useful media. They are not suited to signaling any precise and unambiguous message but, on the contrary, are supremely capable of degrading the whole environment of communications.

The decision-making structures and processes of large national security establishments are quite unsuited to negotiating early war termination. To begin with, intramural bureaucratic negotiations in Washington and Moscow must produce agreement before serious negotiation could proceed between the two. These intramural negotiations are likely to result in compromise positions that lack coherence, are unclear to the adversary, and are insufficiently stable to support a negotiated end to the conflict.[30] Robert Jervis has noted that "when people spend a great deal of time drawing up a plan or making a decision, they tend to think that the message about it they wish to convey will be clear to the receiver," whereas the reality is generally quite different.[31]

There are other conceptual problems. How can policy objectives be translated into certain levels of force employment such that they can be achieved only by those levels—not by less and, most critically, not by more? There probably is no single, discrete, salient relationship. Rather, there are generally a variety of objectives, not all of which are equally apparent, some of which may be determined by factors (such as domestic imperatives) beyond the control of the national leaderships, and some of which may change as the war proceeds. Moreover, if both adversaries are going to be sufficiently rational to agree at some point in a nuclear exchange that a fair and acceptable impasse has been reached, then it is difficult to see why they would have initiated the exchange at the outset.

These problems are critical to efforts at war termination, and hence to the efficacy of any rational strategic force employment policy, but they have not received the attention they warrant. As Colin Gray argues in chapter 8, there is little point in planning "set[s] of very selective targeting building blocks for prospective rounds one, two and three of strategic force application" while rounds four and five entail massive urban-industrial strikes. Without appropriate planning for war termination, the execution of any of the limited or selective nuclear options in the U.S. SIOP would probably amount "in practice, to suicide on the installment plan."

Any large-scale use of nuclear weapons would be catastrophic. An all-out strategic nuclear exchange could well result in about a quarter of a billion fatalities in the United States and the Soviet Union from just the direct blast, fire, and prompt radiation effects, together with another quarter billion in Europe and Asia from the same effects. In addition, it is likely that numerous multiple detonations would produce radical environmental and biological consequences. In particular, a large-scale nuclear war could produce a significant decrease in normal atmospheric temperatures—the "Nuclear Winter" phenomenon—which could in turn "lead to effects of equal or more significance than the horrific devastation associated with the short-term effects."[32] However, it would be premature to suggest major changes to targeting doctrines and policies at this stage. The calculations supporting the nuclear winter thesis contain numerous gross uncertainties; the global circulation models used to assess the atmospheric and climatic effects remain primitive; and the strategic scenarios on which the calculations have so far been based are generally fairly unrealistic. It would be prudent to give further consideration to targeting strategies that avoid attacks on military, leadership, and economic/industrial targets in urban areas, since these attacks create a greater risk of climatic effects. Whether or not the nuclear winter phenomenon is probable, the other consequences of any large-scale nuclear exchange would clearly be sufficient to ensure that no combatant could possibly "prevail."

PART II

Targeting Policies and Plans

[2]

U.S. Nuclear War Planning, 1945–1960

David Alan Rosenberg

Between 1945 and 1960, the United States developed and institutionalized a rigid, tightly coordinated approach to nuclear war planning. That process climaxed in August 1960, when President Dwight D. Eisenhower designated the commander in chief of the Strategic Air Command (SAC) as director of strategic target planning, with responsibility for preparing a National Strategic Target List (NSTL) and a Single Integrated Operational Plan (SIOP) for massive, coordinated attack on a combination of target systems—counterforce, military, industrial, and governmental—within the Soviet Union, China, and the satellite nations, planned for the first twenty-four hours of a general war.[1]

Within two weeks, the new Joint Strategic Target Planning Staff (JSTPS) headed by Gen. Thomas S. Power, the SAC commander, was at work in Omaha, manned by 219 SAC personnel (who also retained their SAC staff jobs), 29 navy, 10 army, 8 air force, and 3 marine officers. Their work was guided by a National Strategic Targeting and Attack Policy (NSTAP), prepared by the Joint Chiefs of Staff (JCS) and approved by Secretary of Defense Thomas Gates. Still classified, it appears to have called for a plan that "will provide for the optimum integration of committed forces for the attack of a minimum list of targets." Soviet strategic nuclear capability was assigned first priority, followed by "primary military and government control centers of major importance." The guidance also called for a 90-percent probability of severe damage to at least 50 percent of industrial floor space in urban-industrial targets. The assurance of delivery factor in each case was to be at least 75 percent.[2]

By November, the first NSTL and SIOP were ready. The JSTPS selected 2,600 separate installations for attack, out of a target data base of 4,100. This translated into an NSTL of approximately 1,050 Desired Ground Zeros (DGZs) for nuclear weapons, including 151 urban-industrial targets. Given sufficient warning, the United States would launch its entire strategic force carrying 3,500 nuclear weapons against the Soviet Union, Communist China, and the satellite nations. At the very least, an "alert force" composed of 880 bombers and missiles would attack some 650 DGZs (including 170 defense suppression targets) with over 1,400 weapons having a total yield of 2,100 megatons. The SIOP aimed for an assurance of delivery factor of 97 percent for the first 200 DGZs, and 93 percent for the next 400, well above the goals established by the JCS.[3]

This paper describes the events and decisions within the United States government which led from the advent of the atomic bomb in 1945 through the first SIOP. It addresses nuclear strategy not as an exercise in conceptualization but as a complex endeavor, partly intellectual and partly bureaucratic. It focuses specifically on the strategic and operational planning process for nuclear war—the most rudimentary level of nuclear strategy—and how that process related to dynamics such as high-policy guidance, strategic theory, and technological development which should have served to control and regulate it. This is essentially a study in the failure of regulation.

During the 1945–60 period, American nuclear strategy was developed at three separate levels of government. At the highest level, the National Security Council (NSC), with the approval of the president, defined national security objectives and promulgated policy guidance concerning nuclear weapons in foreign affairs and military strategy. The secretary of defense, the secretary of state, and the chairman of the Atomic Energy Commission (AEC) were the most important actors in NSC decisions on such matters as the expansion of nuclear production, the deployment of nuclear weapons in the United States and abroad, and the sharing of nuclear weapons information with allies. Although the secretary of defense was the primary link between the military and the president, most defense secretaries during this period, with the notable exceptions of James Forrestal and Thomas Gates, did not take the initiative in advising the president on fundamental questions of nuclear strategy.[4]

It was the president himself, by virtue of his constitutional authority as commander in chief of the armed forces and his statutory responsibility under the Atomic Energy Acts of 1946 and 1954, who had the ultimate say on nuclear weapons. Because of the compartmentalized secrecy surrounding these weapons, analysis of high policy in the Truman and Eisenhower years often comes down to the question Senator Howard Baker focused on during the Watergate hearings of 1973: What did the president know, and when did he know it? Equally important, how well did he understand the information he was provided with.

At the second level of nuclear strategy were the military planners who attempted to translate high-policy guidance into strategic plans and concepts. From 1948 on, the Joint Chiefs of Staff produced a series of strategic plans, usually on an annual basis. Those most directly concerned with nuclear conflict were the Joint Outline Emergency War Plan, which in 1952 became the Joint Strategic Capabilities Plan (JSCP), and the Joint Mid-Range War Plan, which in 1952 became the Joint Strategic Objectives Plan (JSOP). The JSCP covered global war planning for the immediate future, while the JSOP had a four-to-six-year time horizon. The targeting and damage criteria set by the JCS for the immediate use of nuclear weapons were contained in Annex C to the JSCP.

The guidance developed by the JCS was in turn translated into target lists and operational plans. Through the mid-1950s, the Air Intelligence Production Division (later Air Targets Division) of the Air Force Directorate of Intelligence prepared the target lists. The Strategic Air Command had primary responsibility for operational planning. At this level, nuclear strategy was a pragmatic exercise in problem solving. The challenge confronting SAC was how best to employ available nuclear resources to achieve the objectives contained in the JSCP.[5]

SAC occupied a unique position with regard to operational planning, being both a separate major air force command and a specified command within the JCS national unified and specified command structure. As a specified command, SAC prepared its own annual war plans and submitted them directly to the JCS for review and approval. The army and navy did not prepare their own nuclear war plans because their nuclear forces fell under the operational control of the unified commanders in Europe, the Atlantic, and the Pacific. Nevertheless, both services had a real interest in SAC's nuclear targeting and attack plans and sought to influence the content and direction of those plans through the JCS review process.

Three external dynamics influenced the development of nuclear strategy in this era. The first was technological change, which created new strategic challenges and options while setting real, though expanding, limits on how nuclear weapons could be employed.

The second was the work of strategic theorists, both inside and outside the government, who engaged in critical and speculative inquiry into the possibilities and dangers of the nuclear era. Although such conceptual work was important in shaping public perceptions, and occasionally influenced the thinking of high policy makers or strategic planners, it generally had little relevance in the 1945–60 period to the pragmatic concerns of operational planners.[6]

The third and most significant variable was intelligence estimates. The Central Intelligence Agency (CIA) controlled most U.S. intelligence resources, but it had to battle the air force (and SAC), which had official responsibility for air intelligence, for such significant assets as the U-2 high-altitude reconnaissance aircraft which began overflights in 1956, and the first reconnaissance satellites launched in 1960. All of these assets were far from perfect in providing completely accurate and timely information, and finished intelligence estimates based on them often contained, in their appendixes and footnotes, bureaucratic disputes over conclusions. Targeting estimates, prepared by air force analysts in Washington and Omaha, were subject to less dispute. The JCS and the services had neither the time nor the staff to challenge such estimates in detail, and the lists grew unchecked as additional intelligence suggested new possibilities.[7]

The foundations of postwar nuclear strategy established in the Truman years were characterized by ambiguity. Harry Truman viewed the atomic bomb as the ultimate terror weapon: a weapon of last resort. He was unwilling or unable to provide clear policy guidance regarding how it should be integrated into war planning. Through 1948, the only formal policies of the United States with regard to nuclear weapons were civilian control at home and a declared commitment to the goal of international control through the United Nations.

Nuclear war planning was further inhibited by the extreme secrecy surrounding nuclear weapons information. From 1945 until the spring of 1947, even the president was not formally briefed on the size of the nuclear stockpile, and military planners and policy makers were no better informed. The JCS did not formally consider any war plan calling for the use of nuclear weapons until late 1947, and in the spring of 1948 Truman ordered them to concentrate on non-nuclear war planning, out of concern that the American people would not permit atomic bombs to be used for "aggressive purposes" and in hopes that his declared policy of international control of atomic energy might yet bear fruit.[8]

In the absence of specific policy guidance, the most critical determinant in strategic and operational nuclear planning was capability. From 1945 through 1948, the vaunted era of American nuclear monopoly, the nation's stockpile and delivery capability were extremely limited. There were only two weapons in the stockpile at the end of 1945, nine in July 1946, thirteen in July 1947, and fifty in July 1948. None of these weapons was assembled. They were all Mark 3 "Fat Man" implosion bombs, each weighing ten thousand pounds; they were relatively inefficient in their use of fissionable material and took thirty-nine men more than two days to assemble. Because the bombs were so large and heavy, they could only be loaded on their bombers by installing a special hoist in a twelve-by-fourteen-by-eight-foot-deep pit, trundling the bomb into the pit, rolling the aircraft over it, and then hoisting the weapon into the specifically modified bomb bay. Through 1948, there were only about thirty B-29s in the Strategic Air Command modified to drop atomic bombs, all in the 509th Bomb Group based in Roswell, New Mexico.[9]

In the summer of 1948, the Berlin crisis forced foreign policy makers to think more seriously about the deployment of nuclear weapons. On 16 September 1948 the NSC approved NSC-30, "Policy on Atomic Warfare," which finally authorized the military to plan for the use of nuclear weapons in war but reserved to the president alone the responsibility for deciding when and if they would be used. This policy statement, which endorsed a potentially troublesome split between planners and policy makers, remained the nation's basic high-policy paper on nuclear warfare through at least 1959. On 23 November the NSC approved a statement of U.S. objectives vis-à-vis the Soviet Union, NSC-20/4, which laid out basic goals in the event of general war but did not address questions of strategy. The very general war objectives contained in NSC-20/4 were all the guidance the military would receive under the Truman administration and prefaced all war plans through 1954.[10]

By the time the JCS were formally authorized to proceed with nuclear war planning, U.S. nuclear capability had increased substantially, and the strategic nuclear offensive had emerged as the most critical element in the nation's strategy for general war. Technological developments confirmed by the Sandstone nuclear weapons tests in the spring of 1948 suggested that the "doctrine of scarcity," which had been assumed as the basis of planning for the use of nuclear weapons up to that point, might no longer apply. Equally important, President Harry Truman's ceiling on the Fiscal Year 1950 defense budget effectively forced reliance on the strategic air offensive by placing more costly conventional alternatives out of reach. Finally, in October 1948, Lt. Gen. Curtis LeMay was named commanding general of SAC.[11]

LeMay was an outstanding operational commander and a dynamic leader. He was determined to build SAC, which had been organized in 1946 but largely neglected since that time, into a "cocked weapon" capable of delivering at least 80 percent of the nation's nuclear stockpile in a single devastating blow "telescoping mass and time." In December 1948, the air force high command endorsed LeMay's position that delivery of the SAC offensive should be the highest priority mission of the air force, and from that time on his budgetary and programming requirements were given top priority.[12]

SAC faced a military challenge unprecedented in American history. Visionaries since the advent of the airplane had anticipated a time when vast air armies could lay waste to an enemy country at the beginning of a war. SAC's problem was that no one had ever done it before. In addition, the Soviet Union was very large and virtually unknown, and intelligence resources for planning the air offensive were poor. In the

1940s these consisted primarily of captured German aerial photographs, and pre–World War II and even czarist era maps. Beginning in the late 1940s, reconnaissance missions were flown along the borders of the Soviet Union, and occasionally CIA operatives were sent to the interior to check out particular targets of interest. The air force also participated in the CIA-sponsored "Moby Dick" program, which sent balloons equipped with high-altitude cameras drifting across the Soviet Union from Europe to Japan. The recovered pictures, however, were often difficult to interpret since it was impossible to tell precisely where the balloons had been. The bulk of air force basic intelligence on the USSR between 1949 and 1953 came from the interrogation of thousands of repatriated prisoners of war.[13]

World War II experience had convinced air force planners that attacks on specific target systems, such as transportation networks and petroleum and electric power industries were militarily more effective than the indiscriminate bombing of population centers. But the lack of weapons and inadequate intelligence prevented preparation of this type of plan. By the fall of 1947, one hundred urban centers had been identified for atomic attack, and some air force planners were beginning to talk about "bonus effects and industrial capital" and "what was a city besides a collection of industry?" From 1947 through 1949, the separate target systems within the Soviet Union grew less important in SAC plans, while governmental control centers and "urban industrial concentrations" became primary objectives.[14]

In August 1950, the JCS formally organized targeting categories and priorities for nuclear war. First priority was assigned to the "destruction of known targets affecting the Soviet capability to deliver atomic bombs." Second priority was assigned to fixed targets affecting the mobility of Soviet ground forces in Western Europe. Third priority was given to attacks on the Soviet liquid fuel, electric power, and atomic energy industries. These categories were subsequently codenamed BRAVO, ROMEO, and DELTA, for blunting, retardation, and the disruption/destruction of war-making capacity respectively. With some changes, particularly a broadening of the industrial targets category, they formed a basic framework for U.S. nuclear targeting for nearly a decade.[15]

When a target list was prepared which reflected this set of categories, however, it met with strong opposition from the Strategic Air Command. In January 1951, LeMay met with a high-level air staff target panel to explain the unacceptable operational demands it would place on his command. Visual prestrike reconnaissance would be required for a disproportionately large number of targets; isolated target complexes like electric power stations would be difficult for air crews to locate visually or with radar in unfamiliar and hostile terrain; and such isolation would reduce opportunities for "bonus damage." Given the small size of the U.S. stockpile and delivery force, LeMay was convinced that "we should concentrate on industry itself which is located in urban areas"; so even if a bomb missed its target, "a bonus will be derived from the use of the bomb."[16]

The air staff panel agreed to take these considerations into account in preparing future target lists and to submit such lists to SAC before sending them to the JCS for approval. The JCS subsequently concurred, and in the spring of 1951 formally rejected the proposed target list. SAC's influence in target planning was compounded in 1952, when the air force abolished the jointly staffed Air Intelligence Production Division and incorporated its functions into the overall Air Force Directorate of Intelligence. Although in May 1953 a new "joint" arrangement was agreed to whereby the navy and army assigned representatives to the Estimates and Targets divisions of the Intelligence Directorate, the influence of the other services in nuclear target planning was nominal from this time on.[17]

By the end of the Truman administration, the basic elements of postwar nuclear strategy were in place. In 1949, 1950, and 1952, Truman had responded to the urgings of his military advisors by approving three separate increases in nuclear production capacity. These approved increases, which may have been the most substantive and important nuclear policy decisions of his entire administration, launched the United States into an era of nuclear plenty and generated a construction program that would be adequate to support all subsequent expansion of the nation's nuclear weapons stockpile. The stockpile grew from approximately one thousand weapons in 1953 to nearly eighteen thousand by the end of the decade.[18]

Nuclear weapons had also grown increasingly sophisticated and powerful in the last years of the Truman administration. The "nominal" twenty-kiloton yield of the Mark 3 bomb was multiplied more than twenty-five times as a result of innovations perfected between 1948 and 1952. These included advances in the design, composition, stability, and power of the high explosives used to detonate a fission core as well as improvements in the mechanics, structure, and composition of the fissile "pit," including exploitation of the "levitation" concept, which resulted in higher yields and increased efficiency in the use of fissionable material.[19]

By 1952, atomic weapons were being mass produced, and the various fission cores were interchangeable among the weapons assemblies then being manufactured. The technology of "boosted" weapons, which employed a small amount of fusion fuel within a "hollow implosion" core to further increase efficiency and yield, was first tested in April 1951 and appears to have been capable of producing yields approaching one megaton. In prospect were "true" thermonuclear weapons. The first of these was tested in October 1952. A twenty-one-ton, cryogenically cooled, liquid-fueled monster, it yielded 10.4 megatons but could not be delivered against Soviet-bloc targets. Development of "dry"-lithium-deuteride-fueled fusion bombs weighing between four thousand and forty thousand pounds was already under way, and "emergency" delivery capability in SAC B-36s was ready by 1953.[20]

Growth of the stockpile was linked to expansion of the target lists, and both were used to justify expansion of SAC. By 1952, the air force was estimating that there were as many as five to six thousand Soviet targets that would have to be struck, and that many more bombs and bombers would be needed to do the job. This line of argument was labeled "bootstrapping" by critics in the other services.[21] Air-force-generated target lists were used to justify increases in the stockpile, which were then used to justify increases in SAC appropriations. As the air force chief of staff Hoyt Vandenberg explained in 1951:

> In the event of war, there will be concurrent requirements for the destruction of Soviet atomic delivery capability, direct atomic attack on Soviet ground and tactical air forces, and destruction of the critical components of the enemy's war sustaining resources. It must be pointed out that if we do not provide an air force tactically strong enough to deliver atomic weapons on target with a high degree of reliability (and we thereby run out of delivery capability while appropriate targets and unexpended bombs remain) we will have committed a military blunder which will defy logical explanation to the American people. We will have failed to make provision to exploit our one major military advantage over the USSR.[22]

Such air force arguments succeeded in convincing the JCS to assign primacy to the buildup of SAC within the general rearmament program mandated by the NSC in response to the Korean conflict. The Fiscal Year 1953 defense budget was based on an air force objective for June 1954 of 143 wings. President Truman cut this goal to 133 wings by the end of Fiscal Year 1954, but the air force retained its priority position, receiving over 40 percent of the military budget.[23]

Not only was nuclear capability rapidly expanding by the end of the Truman years, American war planning was being conducted on a routine basis with a regularity and intensity unprecedented in peacetime. In the summer of 1952, the JCS authorized creation of a new "family" of war plans to institutionalize short- and long-range planning: the Joint Strategic Capabilities Plan to deal with military situations in the current fiscal year; the Joint Strategic Objectives Plan which established force and mobilization requirements for the next three to five years; and the Joint Long Range Strategic Estimate, which looked ahead five years or more. All three plans were to be prepared annually, although in practice the latter two appeared somewhat more irregularly.

The JSCP and the operational plans it guided, including the SAC Emergency War Plan, were prepared consistently on an annual basis. They fostered a process of debate and analysis that, in the absence of real global conflict, served as a kind of "surrogate war" for generating and testing forces and concepts. Each new planning effort built on the experience gained in the preceding "war," thereby creating a dynamic that tended to discourage radical changes.[24]

Finally, by the time Truman left office, the JCS had formalized a system of targeting that, as discussed above, placed high priority on preemption of Soviet nuclear capability. Equally important, the Strategic Air Command, as a result of its operational requirements and the powerful voice of its commander, had gained near veto power over target selection and had firmly established "bonus damage" as a major criterion in U.S. nuclear war planning.

It is not clear that President Truman fully understood the implications of JCS targeting priorities and SAC strike plans. NSC-68 of April 1950 explicitly ruled out preventive war ("a military attack not provoked by a military attack on us or our allies") but left the door open for preemption is response to an imminent Soviet strike. To what extent Truman endorsed the preemptive strategy that emerged during his administration is unknown. He left office without ever establishing a basic framework of national policy to guide the development of nuclear strategy and nuclear war planning.[25]

Dwight D. Eisenhower was far better prepared than Harry S Truman, both by experience and inclination, to deal with issues of nuclear strategy. As army chief of staff from 1945 to 1948, acting chairman of the JCS in 1949, and supreme allied commander in Europe from 1950 to 1952, he became aware of the reality and the promise of the ongoing technological revolution in nuclear weapons and chose to rely on those weapons for as many military uses as possible.[26] Where Truman viewed the atomic bomb as a weapon of last resort, Eisenhower viewed it as an integral part of the American arsenal and essentially a weapon of first resort. Shortly after taking office, he began to dismantle Truman's structure for civilian control of the atomic weapons stockpile and to disperse and deploy nuclear weapons, both to reduce stockpile vulnerability and to improve military readiness. By 1961, over 90 percent of the nation's nuclear weapons were under military control.[27]

The Eisenhower administration's basic national security policy was spelled out in NSC-162/2 of October 1953 and was reflected in the three-year defense program approved that December. High priority was given to SAC's strategic striking power as the mainstay of the policy of "massive retaliation." The development and deployment of tactical nuclear weapons was also encouraged. NSC-162/2 established the policy that nuclear weapons would be considered "as available for use as other munitions" and encouraged the military to plan to employ them in limited as well as general war. Finally, NSC-162/2 stressed the need to protect the nation's mobilization base and marked the beginning of an intensive, long-term effort to develop early warning and continental defense systems.[28]

Anxiety over the growing Soviet nuclear threat, represented by the Soviet test of a three-to-four-hundred-kiloton boosted fission weapon in August 1953, raised the spectre of preventive war.[29] This possibility was seriously discussed in 1953–54 by some high-level Eisenhower foreign policy advisers, the Advance Study Group of the JCS, and the air force air staff. President Eisenhower himself wondered whether an American commitment to maintaining a margin of superiority in destructive power over the Soviet Union might not prove so costly that "we would be forced to consider whether or not our duty to future generations did not require us to initiate war at the most propitious moment we could designate." By the fall of 1954, however, the president and the NSC chose to formally reject as policy options not only preventive war but also "acts intended to provoke war."[30]

If preventive war was ruled out, preemption was not. In this era before ballistic missiles, preemption appeared to be both militarily and constitutionally feasible. Because of the time needed to prepare Soviet bomber forces and bases for strikes on the United States, it was anticipated that there would be a period of days or even weeks of strategic warning before an attack. Even if the United States were taken by surprise, significant preemption was still considered possible because the USSR would need up to thirty days to complete delivery of its nuclear stockpile. In accord with the policy of massive retaliation, Eisenhower anticipated that if war broke out in Europe, the United States would use tactical nuclear weapons to hold the line while SAC was launched as a "first priority" to "blunt the enemy's initial threat." After "averting disaster," the United States would go on to mobilize to win the war over a possibly extended period.[31]

By 1954, SAC was preparing to launch a simultaneous, massive, integrated strike against a combination of target systems in the Soviet Union. In order to overwhelm Soviet air defenses, SAC planned to have the entire strike force of up to 735 bombers hit enemy early warning screens simultaneously. Targeting categories and priorities set by the JCS were blurred in the interests of getting all the bombers into and out

[44]

of Soviet air space as quickly as possible. There was no calculated strategy for war winning or termination beyond that of producing as much destruction in multiple Soviet target systems as possible in a single, devastating blow. Increasing emphasis was placed on utilizing high-yield weapons to cause bonus damage and destroy multiple targets simultaneously. This was facilitated by the entry into the American stockpile after the spring of 1954 of readily deliverable fusion weapons with yields ranging as high as fifteen megatons.[32]

Opposition to plans for the strategic air offensive was voiced by a number of critics, including physicists and strategists at the Rand Corporation and the scientists who had explored the tactical utility of nuclear weapons in the defense of Western Europe in Project VISTA in 1953.[33] Such opposition was effectively countered by two highly secret analyses by the Weapons Systems Evaluation Group in 1953 and 1955. Each showed, first, that an air offensive against Soviet industry would be needed in order to prevent the Soviet Union from supporting protracted campaigns in Western Europe and, second, that SAC would have to significantly increase the scale of its planned offensive in order to successfully preempt and neutralize the growing Soviet nuclear threat to the continental United States.[34]

Within the Joint Chiefs of Staff there was also considerable disagreement about the wisdom and impact of the proposed SAC offensive. Two successive army chiefs of staff, Matthew Ridgway and Maxwell Taylor, were particularly outspoken critics of the policy of relying on the strategic air offensive as the centerpiece of American war planning and the consequent reduction of resources for conventional forces and limited war. By the mid-1950s, however, the JCS were exercising only minimal control over SAC war planning. Curtis LeMay did not submit his basic war plan for JCS review from 1951 until 1955, when he was formally requested to do so by air force chief of staff Nathan Twining. Even then LeMay only agreed to provide the JCS with a briefing and summary overview. Not long after, SAC gained virtual control over its target selection as well. In the summer of 1955, the army proposed the creation of a joint Target Selection and Evaluation Group to replace the "joint" arrangement in the air force Air Intelligence Directorate. A joint staff report that fall, however, concluded that the increasing complexity of target planning made a joint process unworkable and recommended that the JCS formally delegate authority for target selection, consistent with JCS-approved criteria, to the unified and specified commands, including SAC. This recommendation was approved by the JCS in November.[35]

By early 1956, the NSC was estimating that the United States was on the threshold of achieving the capability to carry out a "decisive strike" against the Soviet Union, one that would require only hours or days to complete, as compared to the weeks or months that would have been needed in the late 1940s or early 1950s. Taking advantage of improved intelligence, SAC could effectively eliminate Soviet ability to strike back and could reduce Soviet civil, political, and social life to a "condition of chaos."[36]

The achievement of decisive nuclear capability, however, proved to be a chimera. By 1956, the United States was on the verge of the ballistic missile era and was facing the prospect of an unprecedented threat not only to its people and mobilization base but to its strategic striking force. In February 1955, the Technological Capabilities Panel of the Office of Defense Mobilization (ODM) Science Advisory Committee, chaired by James R. Killian, Jr., the president of M.I.T., presented President Eisenhower with its report titled "Meeting the Threat of Surprise Attack." The Killian Report attempted to project a "sense of urgency without despair," while laying out a timetable of changes that could be expected over the next decade or more as the Soviet Union approached the United States in thermonuclear capability. It strongly recommended that the United States take steps to protect its striking force through improved intelligence, early warning, and defensive measures and to begin or accelerate development of intermediate range and intercontinental ballistic missiles in order to preserve and prolong the relative strategic advantage that the nation currently enjoyed.[37]

This report made a deep impression on President Eisenhower. He had great confidence in the objectivity and analytical ability of the Killian panel, which was composed almost entirely of civilian businessmen and scientists with no prior commitment to promoting any particular defense program. From this time on, the timetable and conceptual framework spelled out in the Killian Report appears to have served as a yardstick for Eisenhower's own analysis of strategic issues and the shifting balance of power. Most of the specific recommendations of the report were supported by the president and subsequently approved by the NSC, including a high-priority program to develop and deploy ballistic missiles.[38]

The prospective development of comparatively small, high-yield thermonuclear weapons suitable for missile warheads greatly facilitated the development of such weapons by permitting relaxation of accuracy requirements and ushered in an era of profound strategic innovation and intensive reevaluation of American defense. Since such missiles could travel at speeds approaching eighteen thousand miles an hour, there would be little tactical warning of an enemy strike. Strategic warning would be dependent on knowing the location of missile bases and would involve determining and tracking preparations necessary to ready the missile warhead, guidance system, and propulsion systems for launch.

Although such characteristics could greatly enhance U.S. strategic capability, they appeared even more dangerous when viewed in the hands of a prospective enemy.

Even without missiles, the Soviet nuclear threat by this time was judged to be extremely serious. In November 1955, the Soviet Union exploded its first true, multimegaton, thermonuclear bomb. In January 1956, the Net Evaluation Subcommittee (NESC) of the NSC, which had been preparing annual reports on the balance between U.S. and Soviet nuclear capabilities since 1953, reported that by 1958 the Soviet bomber force would probably be able to carry out a surprise attack on the United States that would result in "practically total" economic and governmental collapse. Even with a month's strategic warning, the United States would be unable to take defensive measures that would substantially reduce the appalling level of damage.[39]

The projections of a possible bomber gap, which emerged as a major political issue in the spring of 1956, further complicated this problem. Although most Americans perceived the bomber gap as a technological or numerical challenge, for President Eisenhower and his advisers it had another dimension as well. Expansion of Soviet nuclear delivery capability, particularly in view of the hundreds of airfields available for dispersion of mid- and long-range bombers, meant that the United States might not even be able to preempt an impending Soviet attack without major expansion of the SAC bomber force. Moreover, Soviet achievement of true thermonuclear capability greatly reduced the value of partial preemption or defense. If even a few Soviet bombers armed with the new megaton weapons escaped destruction on the ground and eluded U.S. air defenses, they could inflict insupportable levels of damage on U.S. cities. The problem of how to maintain an adequate and secure preemptive capability was from this time on a major consideration in shaping U.S. force level and operational planning.[40]

When the advent of ballistic missiles was taken into account, the United States appeared to be confronting a situation of extreme jeopardy. In 1957, the Security Resources Panel of the ODM's Science Advisory Committee prepared a report titled "Deterrence and Survival in the Nuclear Age" which was briefed to the president on 4 November. It concluded that "by 1959, the U.S.S.R. may be able to launch an attack with ICBMs carrying megaton warheads against which SAC will be almost completely vulnerable under present programs." The so-called Gaither Report stressed the need for a better early warning system and recommended acceleration of ballistic missile programs and current active and passive air defense efforts. Several members of the committee proposed reconsideration of the preventive war option as the only feasible course of action, but they proved to be in the minority.[41]

President Eisenhower reacted to the frightening projections of the NESC and the Gaither committee by reinforcing, not reconsidering, his policy of massive retaliation. In the winter and spring of 1956, he undertook a concerted effort to bring national policy and strategic planning into line with the concept of instantaneous nuclear response to a Soviet attack against the United States or its allies. The NSC statement of basic national security policy was revised to confirm U.S. determination to use nuclear weapons in the event of general war, at the discretion of the president, and, despite strenuous objections by army chief of staff Maxwell Taylor, JCS guidance for short- and midrange planning was clarified to exclude the possibility that nuclear weapons might be withheld in favor of conventional response to a major conflict in Europe.[42]

During the 1956 review of basic national security policy, the president also requested and received NSC confirmation of his right to preauthorize the use of nuclear weapons in order to facilitate rapid response. In the spring of 1956, he issued such a preauthorization for the use of nuclear armed air defense missiles, scheduled to be deployed within the year. In 1957, he took steps toward preauthorizing other uses of nuclear weapons as well. The still-classified directives dealing with this subject were forwarded to all unified and specified commanders, after extensive review and discussion within the departments of Defense and State, in 1959 and 1960.[43]

By 1956, SAC had begun to prepare for the threat of Soviet bomber attack by instituting ground alert procedures that would ensure at least some of its aircraft could be launched with little warning. The inadequacy of these procedures was highlighted by R. C. Sprague, the director of the Security Resources Panel Steering Committee, who prepared a highly secret report for Eisenhower in conjunction with the Gaither Report. Sprague told the president that he had checked on SAC's current readiness on a randomly selected day and had found that "not a single plane could have left the ground within six hours except for a few that were by chance in the air" at the time. He estimated that the United States would probably be able to get off only 50 to 150 large weapons in the face of a surprise attack and that, given improved Soviet air defenses, a substantial number of these would not reach their targets.[44]

SAC response time was significantly improved in the next few years, in part because of the new "sealed pit" nuclear weapons technology, which permitted the prolonged, safe, in-plane storage and transport of preassembled thermonuclear weapons.[45] By 1959, "Fail Safe" procedures were in place which would permit the swift launching of the strike force under "positive control" without risk of unauthorized attack, and plans had been debated and approved in principle by the JCS to enable SAC, if so directed by the president, to maintain a portion of its force on airborne alert. SAC also sought to improve the security of its forces on the ground by dispersing its bombers and tankers to additional bases in the continental United States.[46]

Other passive and active airfield defense systems recommended by the Gaither committee, however, were assigned a low priority, as air force leaders continued to focus on the problem of preempting, rather than merely surviving, a Soviet nuclear attack. Growth of target lists proceeded very rapidly in the late 1950s as additional targets related to Soviet nuclear strike capability and air defense were identified. The bootstrapping dynamic, whereby these lists were used to justify continued production of nuclear weapons along with the bombers and missiles needed to deliver them, continued unabated. In 1955, SAC's target data base had grown to where it was necessary to acquire an IBM 704 computer system to perform all the calculations necessary to analyze and prioritize it. Beginning in 1956, the identification of additional potential targets was facilitated by the initiation of the CIA's U-2 overflight program, although intelligence remained severely limited. Even though SAC had formally been relieved of the ROMEO (retardation) mission in 1956, its basic war plan target list contained 2,997 separate installations at the end of the year. By early 1957, that number had risen to 3,261. By 1959, SAC had screened and analyzed over 20,000 possible target installations in the Soviet bloc, selecting the most significant and grouping them into Desired Ground Zeros consistent with the blast radii of high-yield weapons.[47]

In May 1959, the chief of staff of the air force approved a force structure objective that specified the numbers of bombers and missiles required through 1970. A target estimate prepared in support of this objective concluded that by 1963 there would be 8,400 specific Soviet targets requiring destruction, and that by the end of the decade there would be 10,400. Since multiple weapons would have to be assigned to each DGZ in order to achieve the 90 percent assurance of destruction factor expected in air force war plans, a missile force including 3,000 Minuteman, 150 Atlas, and 110 Titan Intercontinental Ballistic Missiles (ICBMs) would be needed by 30 June 1968, as well as a combined total of nearly 900 B-52, B-58, B-70, and nuclear-powered bombers.[48]

The Air Intelligence Directorate was subsequently asked to prepare a more detailed target analysis to justify the proposed force structure. The estimate produced was somewhat more conservative although still quite ambitious. The three largest groups of targets on the list were those concerned with suppressing Soviet air defenses and stopping atomic attacks on the United States and its allies. A fourth group, apparently earmarked for tactical air forces, was concerned with halting Soviet land and sea operations, while the fifth and smallest group was concerned with disrupting the war support and recuperation capability of Soviet industry. The target planners estimated that there would be a total of 3,560 targets in 1960, 6,300 in 1965, and 6,955 in 1970. These could be grouped into 1,450, 3,100, and 3,800 DGZs, respectively. A footnote explained that the sharp increase in the first half of the decade was based on a projected increase in missile sites, each of which would require its own DGZ.[49]

Opposition to SAC's planned strategic air offensive had been steadily growing within the JCS. In 1956, a serious split developed over air force requirements for large-yield weapons. A critique was prepared that, based on excessive overlapping of large-yield weapons on individual targets, charged the air force with overstating its requirements. President Eisenhower, called in to settle the dispute, agreed that the critique had merit. Although he approved the goals for weapons production based on the air force estimate, he directed the JCS to review the target plans in question to see if large weapons were not being assigned inappropriately and to make any necessary revisions.[50]

In the spring of 1957, following up on this concern, the army and navy undertook a thorough analysis of the damage that would result from implementation of the SAC war plan. For this exercise, codenamed Project BUDAPEST, analysts from the two services were for the first time granted access to a complete nuclear target list. On 28 August 1957 their devastating critique, demonstrating that fallout and radiation would be excessively and dangerously high due to excessive redundant targeting, was presented to the JCS. Blast radii were huge, and there were as many as seventeen overlaps on a single target. Duplicate weapons were assigned in profusion, even when the supplemental damage they would achieve was known to be minimal. The air force chief of staff was incensed by this indictment and ridiculed the idea that SAC should seek to do any less than maximum damage. Every gallon of fuel oil destroyed, Gen. Thomas White declared, could otherwise help carry another Russian bomber toward the United States.[51]

The most significant debates of the late 1950s, however, focused on an issue even more basic than overkill. If the United States had ruled out preventive war and would not receive enough warning of an impending attack to be able to achieve any significant degree of preemption, what was the justification for SAC's proposed combined attack on counterforce and countervalue targets? If the United States was planning for retaliation, should it not seek to ensure, first, that its delivery forces could survive a surprise attack and, second, that it would not be launching the bulk of its retaliatory strike against deserted airfields and empty missile silos?

The most articulate military spokesman for this point of view was the chief of naval operations, Adm. Arleigh Burke. The navy's carrier task forces had long been counted as part of the U.S. "offensive striking power," but the navy had never seen itself in competition for the SAC mission, being skeptical of the efficacy of strategic bombing and far more concerned with the problems of sea control and limited war. During the mid-1950s, navy leaders had joined army leaders with increasing frequency in criticizing the emphasis placed on the strategic nuclear offensive and the SAC bomber force.[52]

In 1956–57, as the Polaris-submarine-launched ballistic missile system began to take shape, the navy found itself with a weapons system that could make a unique contribution to nuclear strategy. Long concerned that the United States was placing all of its nuclear retaliatory "eggs" in SAC's land-based "basket," and recognizing the opportunities inherent in Polaris, Burke officially proclaimed it to be not just a navy weapon for use against targets of naval interest but a national deterrent system.[53]

The unique characteristic of the submarine-launched ballistic missile was its relative invulnerability. It could hide from a surprise attack and carry out retaliatory strikes with both deliberation and discrimination. It could safely be withheld to allow time for decision making, thereby reducing the danger of general war through miscalculation. During an era of mutual deterrence, Polaris could serve as a backup to, and possibly eventually become a replacement for, the strategic forces of SAC. Savings realized through cutbacks in land-based strategic forces could then be channeled into upgrading conventional forces for limited war.

The Polaris system generated its own strategic theory: finite deterrence. Burke believed that the United States should identify a limited second-strike target list tailored to retaliation after a surprise attack. The list would include military and governmental command and control centers, urban industrial centers, and all readily identifiable remaining Soviet nuclear capability. The finite deterrence target list would contain far fewer counterforce targets than the SAC list, since the Soviet ballistic missile forces not already launched were likely to be disguised or mobile and therefore impossible to locate and destroy. Weapons requirements would be further reduced by not assigning multiple weapons to targets beyond the point where the damage expectancy curve began to flatten out. As Burke explained it: "You very seldom see a cowboy, even in the movies, wearing three guns. Two is enough."[54]

In late 1957, Burke and army chief of staff Maxwell Taylor introduced concurrent proposals in the JCS calling for an "alternative undertaking" to be included in Annex C to the JSCP, which established target and damage criteria for nuclear war. Burke and Taylor argued that the existing criteria were intended for a situation in which the United States had the initiative and that, after a surprise attack, there might be inadequate forces remaining to implement the planned offensive with any degree of success. They proposed that an alternative list of a limited number of high-priority targets be developed to provide for the possibility that war might begin under such "disadvantageous" circumstances.

Some time during the winter or spring of 1958, after a long and heated paper debate, the JCS approved an additional alternative set of guidance for inclusion in the JSCP. It called for a retaliatory strike that would accord first priority to the destruction of any remaining Soviet nuclear capability "to the extent profitable," and to "the destruction of government controls and population centers in the U.S.S.R. to the extent necessary to neutralize the capability of the U.S.S.R. to carry on the war." The army and navy leaders both hoped that the required target lists, which were not completed for more than two years, would lay the groundwork for a serious reconsideration of the massive strategic offensive still identified as the "primary" undertaking.[55]

In November 1958, Eisenhower's special assistant for national security affairs, Gordon Gray, proposed that the 1959 Net Evaluation Subcommittee be instructed to undertake a special study of alternative targeting systems, in support of a reevaluation of American war objectives then under way. Gray pointed out that the question of how to achieve effective deterrence could not be separated from the question of war objectives, and that neither could be considered independently of targeting plans.[56] President Eisenhower agreed, and the NESC was tasked with preparing a special appraisal "of the relative merits, from the point of view of effective deterrence, of alternative retaliatory efforts directed toward (1) primarily a military target system, or (2) an optimum mix of a combined military-urban industrial target system."[57]

The JCS, as the custodians of the targeting information that would be used for this study, were asked to provide the basic frames of reference. Because of disagreements between the chiefs of staff, instructions to the NESC were not ready until February 1959, when a compromise was worked out by JCS chairman Nathan Twining, a former air force chief of staff, in consultation with Gray and Secretary of Defense Neil McElroy. Three alternative target systems would be considered instead of two: primarily military, primarily urban-industrial (proposed by the army and navy), and an "optimum mix" of the two. Each system would be analyzed in terms of the effort that would be required not simply to deter war but to achieve "the objective of prevailing in general war." After defining the minimum target list necessary in each system, one of the three lists would be chosen as the pattern for future planning.[58] Because the study was considered so sensitive, it was assigned to the NESC staff, under the direction of Lieutenant General Thomas Hickey of the army, bypassing the regular committee.

The Hickey committee took more than a year to complete its report, and its conclusions are still classified. It is known, however, that the committee recommended an optimum-mix target system and adopted basic SAC methods of analysis in preparing its recommended target list. That list consisted of a total of 2,021 targets, comprising an unknown number of DGZs, but consisting of 121 ICBM sites, 140 air defense bases, 200 bomber bases, 218 military and governmental control centers, and 124 other military targets, including naval bases and nuclear weapons production facilities and storage sites. Most of the remaining target installations were located within 131 urban centers in the Soviet Union and Communist China. When President Eisenhower was briefed on the Hickey Report in February 1960, he authorized that it be used by the JCS as guidance for the preparation of all future target lists.[59]

The Hickey committee study marked a serious attempt by the Eisenhower administration to find ways of limiting the proposed strategic nuclear air offensive without abandoning the objective of defending the American homeland by preempting an impending Soviet strike. Although Eisenhower had grown increasingly pessimistic about the devastation the United States would inevitably suffer in a nuclear exchange, he never altered his commitment to responding rapidly and in strength to a Soviet attack, in hopes of averting disaster. He never accepted or fully understood the navy's argument for a strategy of pure deterrence and did not see Polaris as an alternative to SAC. The Polaris system, he stated in May 1960, would be useful primarily for knocking out enemy defenses to pave the way for SAC bomber strikes.[60]

The prospective deployment of Polaris, augured by the successful test firing of a Polaris missile from a submerged submarine in July 1960, posed a potentially serious problem of command and control. In the spring of 1959, the air force had proposed that a single strategic command should be created, under SAC, to integrate the planning and operations of all U.S. strategic forces, including Polaris. This proposal was strenuously resisted by both navy and army leaders, who argued that the JCS should reestablish their direct control over target planning and should provide whatever coordination was needed between the strategic forces of the various services.[61]

The question of target planning and command and control produced an irreconcilable split within the JCS, which could only be resolved, JCS chairman Twining was convinced, by a "command decision." In August 1959 Twining prepared a long memorandum for Secretary of Defense McElroy laying out the issues in question and proposing a solution. He recommended that the navy be allowed to retain operational control over Polaris for the time being but that SAC be assigned responsibility as an "agent" of the JCS for preparing a national strategic target list and a single integrated operational plan.[62]

Twining's proposal had no immediate impact but was passed on to Thomas Gates, who assumed the post of secretary of defense in January 1960. Frustrated in his efforts to resolve the deep splits among the JCS, Gates proposed to President Eisenhower the following July that a compromise be imposed along the lines suggested by Twining. Eisenhower reluctantly agreed to abandon efforts to reach consensus among the service chiefs but stressed the importance of involving all the services, not just SAC, in the joint target and operational planning organization. In August, Gates submitted a formal proposal for creation of a Joint Strategic Target Planning Staff, with SAC in a position of dominance but not formal control, to prepare the proposed NSTL and SIOP.[63]

"This is not a compromise," Burke told the president during the heated two-hour discussion that followed the presentation of Gates's proposal on 11 August 1960. "This proposal is a radical departure from previous practice. I am fearful that if the responsibility and authority for making a single operation plan is delegated to a single commander [then] the JCS will have lost control over operations at the beginning of a general war."[64] Burke argued that the JCS should retain "not only basic responsibility for directing effort in general war, but the means for generating the basic plans and for controlling the development of these plans." Putting the NSTL and SIOP under SAC would undermine JCS authority, restrict the military options available to U.S. unified theater commanders, alarm NATO allies, and give SAC excessive influence in determining atomic weapons requirements and allocations, force levels and deployments, and military budgets. Coordination should be achieved by assigning retaliatory tasks—"not in specific detail"—to the unified commanders, including SAC, with the JCS directing implementation.[65]

Eisenhower rejected Burke's arguments. "This whole thing," he stressed, "has to be on a completely integrated basis. It must be firmly laid on. The initial strike must be simultaneous." It must utilize both navy and air force nuclear capability, for "if we put large forces outside of the plan, we defeat the whole concept of retaliatory effort, which takes priority over everything else." The only question, as the president saw it, was who should develop the plan. He was inclined to agree with Gates that SAC had the best resources to do so. He therefore approved preparation of an initial NSTL and SIOP as proposed, although, at Burke's request, he agreed that the JCS should be given an opportunity to review the completed plan and recommend changes in procedure. A final decision would have to be made by December 1960, Eisenhower remarked, so that he would not "leave his successor with the monstrosity" of uncoordinated, unintegrated forces now in prospect.[66]

During the following months, navy leaders were active in critiquing

[54]

the emerging SIOP. They pointed out that it was not an objectives plan but a capabilities plan, aimed at utilizing all available forces to achieve maximum destruction. The Joint Strategic Target Planning Staff had failed to determine the minimum force necessary to achieve military objectives and had failed to leave an adequate reserve for follow-up strikes. They strongly objected to the excessively high damage and assurance criteria and to SAC's failure to consider the secondary effects of blast, fire, and radiation in projecting damage.[67] One navy estimate noted that according to SAC's criteria, the damage caused by a thirteen-kiloton bomb on Hiroshima could only be assured by assigning three hundred to five hundred kilotons of weapons to a similar target.[68] Such inefficient, redundant targeting would also cause unmanageable levels of radioactive fallout. Adm. Harry Felt worried that if the whole SIOP were executed, his Pacific command might have to be "more concerned about residual radiation damage resulting from our own weapons than from those of the enemy."[69] Another navy message noted that executing just the alert force portion of the SIOP, "and assuming only one weapon delivered to each DGZ, the fallout already exceeds JCS limits for points such as Helsinki, Berlin, Budapest, Northern Japan, and Seoul."[70]

Even more important, the SIOP was not tailored to either retaliation or preemption. As Burke observed: "counterforce receives higher precedence than is warranted for a retaliatory plan, and less precedence than is warranted for an initiative plan."[71] He urged that plans be made for each option under consideration as well as for discriminating between Soviet targets and those in satellite nations.

Burke communicated navy concern through various channels to Eisenhower, who in early November dispatched his science advisor, Harvard professor George B. Kistiakowsky, to Omaha. Kistiakowsky came away convinced that the SAC/JSTPS "damage criteria and the directives to the planners are such as to lead to unnecessary and undesirable overkill."[72] He found that many judgments made in preparing the plans were arbitrary and that SAC's vaunted computer procedures were in some cases "sheer bull." The SIOP itself, made up from a "background of plenty" in weapons and delivery systems, made a virtue of excess: "I believe that the alert force is probably all right, but not the follow-on forces which carry megatons to kill 4 and 5 times over somebody who is already dead."[73]

Kistiakowsky presented his evaluation to the president on the morning of 25 November. The presentation, Eisenhower confided to his naval aide, Capt. E. P. "Pete" Aurand, "frighten[ed] the devil out of me." The sheer numbers of targets, the redundant targeting, and the enormous overkill surprised and horrified him. Kistiakowsky, a scientist who represented no parochial service interest, had made the president realize that the SIOP might not be a rational instrument for controlling nuclear planning but rather an engine generating escalation force requirements. He wondered whether a better strategy might not be to reserve the Polaris force as a backup and let SAC "have just one whack—not ten whacks" at each target, relying on Polaris, with the aid of reconnaissance satellites, "to clean up what isn't done." We have got to set limits, he told Aurand. "We've got to get this thing right down to the deterrence."[74]

For the Eisenhower administration, however, it was too late to turn back. The question of whether the United States could or should plan to blunt or preempt an impending Soviet nuclear strike remained unresolved. The problem of adjusting U.S. nuclear strategy to the ballistic missile era, which had barely opened by the time Eisenhower left office, would fall to the succeeding administration. The Hickey committee study, which had been intended to define a means of controlling escalating force requirements, had proved an inadequate restraint, reflecting the persistent difficulty of imposing high-policy controls on the dynamics of operational planning.

In December 1960, despite navy criticisms and President Eisenhower's own misgivings, the JCS approved the first SIOP as the nation's nuclear war plan for Fiscal Year 1962. This action effectively ended a period of conflict and opportunity in U.S. nuclear strategy. The alternative undertaking, which had promised to demonstrate how limits could be placed on the strategic air offensive, became a moot exercise. The SIOP concretized, for the indefinite future, patterns of nuclear strategy that had emerged on the basis of operational requirements and the dynamics of operational planning during the preceding fifteen years.

[3]

The Development of the SIOP,
1960–1983

DESMOND BALL

The most recent version of the U.S. Single Integrated Operational Plan (SIOP), formally designated SIOP-6, officially came into effect on 1 October 1983—just twenty-three years after the preparation of the first SIOP, formally designated SIOP-62, which was completed in December 1960 and officially came into effect at the beginning of Fiscal Year 1962 on 1 July 1961. The developments in the U.S. strategic nuclear posture during these twenty-three years have been numerous and in many instances dramatic. In the first place, there has been a threefold increase in the number of bombs and warheads in the SIOP forces—from about 3,200 in December 1960, which, except for 12 Atlas D ICBMs and 32 Polaris SLBMs, were all deployed on B-47 and B-52 strategic bombers and of which some two-thirds were not maintained on alert, to some 11,000 bombs and warheads, of which more than 2,000 are deployed on ICBMs and nearly 5,000 on SLBMs, and of which some two-thirds are maintained on full alert. In addition, the U.S. SIOP forces now have much greater flexibility than they had in 1960–61, partly because of the much greater variety of delivery systems and warheads now available, together with their much improved accuracies, and partly because of the enhanced capabilities of the strategic command, control, communications, and intelligence (C³I) systems that support the SIOP forces.

On the other hand, there has been relatively little change since the early 1960s in the overall structure of the SIOP, the basic categories of targets the SIOP contains, the general priorities established for the allocation of warheads to these target categories, the techniques and procedures by which warheads are actually allocated to specific targets, and the machinery developed for the provision of basic national strategic guidance to inform the strategic nuclear target planning process. Although the president, the National Security Council (NSC), the Office of the Secretary of Defense (OSD), and the Organization of the Joint Chiefs of Staff (OJCS) have all been integrally involved in every change to the SIOP since the preparation of SIOP-62, at least with respect to basic policy guidance, the construction of the SIOP is very much the domain of the Joint Strategic Target Planning Staff (JSTPS) located at the headquarters of the Strategic Air Command (SAC) at Offutt Air Force Base in Omaha, Nebraska.

THE ESTABLISHMENT OF THE JSTPS AND
THE PREPARATION OF SIOP-62

As David Rosenberg has pointed out in the previous chapter, it had become apparent by the end of the 1950s that new organizational structures and planning procedures were necessary for the development of U.S. targeting plans.

First, problems of coordinating the nuclear operations of SAC and navy commanders had already proved difficult to resolve. During the 1950s, each JCS unified and specified commander who had nuclear delivery forces (such as land- or carrier-based tactical bombers) assigned to him drew up his own atomic target annex, or list. This annex was supposed to include only those targets of unique importance to his particular theater of responsibility. However, the targets considered vital by one commander were often considered vital by the commander of an adjacent theater, or by the SAC commander as part of the general strategic offensive. Consequently, targets were frequently covered in two or more separate target annexes. For example, at one time, 115 airfields and 40 industrial complexes in the Far Eastern theater had been targeted by two separate commanders, and 37 airfields and 7 industrial complexes by three; in the European theater, 121 airfields were targeted by two commanders and 31 airfields by three.[1] In 1952, the JCS published a directive that, among other things, led to a series of worldwide coordination conferences in which representatives from the various commands met to examine the composition of their respective target annexes and to resolve any conflicts. The process was described by Gen. Curtis LeMay as simply "to co-ordinate targets so we would not destroy the same target twice."[2] This approach apparently achieved some success in reducing unnecessary overlapping target coverage. However, considerable strain existed within the coordination system, particularly since individual commanders were inclined to emphasize the needs of their own commands over the objective of attack synchronization.[3]

Second, the imminent introduction of ICBMs and, most particularly, submarine-launched ballistic missiles (SLBMs) was bound to compound these problems. It was apparent both that these ballistic missiles required different targeting arrangements to those of bombers and also that, at least through the early 1960s, the number of SLBMs becoming operational would exceed that of ICBMs. (The first Polaris submarine, *George Washington*, became operational in July 1960; until mid-1962 the number of SLBMs that were operational did in fact exceed the number of ICBMs.)

In 1958, the SAC commander, Gen. Thomas S. Power, recommended that SAC exercise centralized control over all ballistic missile systems, including the Polaris submarines. He was sharply critical of the "committee" approach, suggesting that the coordination process would become far more complex as nuclear delivery forces increased in number, variety, speed, and range. Similar points were made by the secretary of the air force, James Douglas. Bureaucratic as well as operational considerations were at play in this instance. The air force had always viewed the navy's acquisition of atomic weapons as a usurpation of the air force's primary responsibility for the strategic bombing mission. The deployment of fleet ballistic missile (FBM) submarines would give the navy even more of a role in this area. The creation of a unified "strategic command" would allow the air force to maintain its primacy, particularly since the SAC commander would be the most logical candidate for the unified commander position. The navy officials not surprisingly objected to this suggestion, arguing that the navy had developed the Polaris system and that therefore no air force officer was qualified to exercise final control over its operations.[4]

To defuse the situation, the secretary of defense, then Thomas Gates, produced a compromise that satisfied air force concerns about target coordination yet maintained navy control over the FBM submarines. On 16 August 1960 he directed the formation of a full-time Joint Strategic Target Planning Staff (JSTPS) to ensure the coordination of the nuclear targets of all commanders. The JSTPS was to be located at SAC headquarters in Omaha, Nebraska, headed by the SAC commander. A navy flag officer was to serve as deputy director, and representatives from each command with nuclear weapons (and, after 1963, from NATO) were attached to the staff. The JSTPS was to report directly to the JCS (see fig. 3.1).[5]

The JSTPS performs two primary functions: the first is to maintain the National Strategic Target List (NSTL), which contains data on all the targets that might need to be attacked in a nuclear strike; the second is to prepare the SIOP. The SIOP assigns targets to all strategic weapon systems, including "bombers, fighter bombers, intercontinental ballistic and air-launched missiles . . . and missile submarines." In formulating the SIOP, the JSTPS examines such matters as the type of weapons to be allocated against a particular target, the aircraft routings and positive

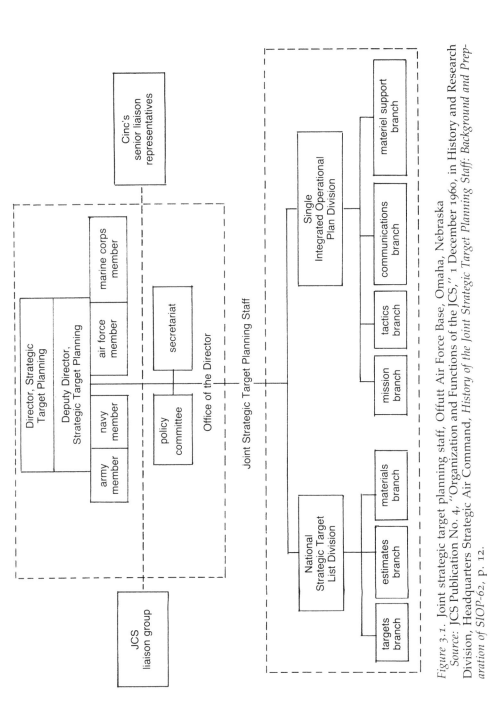

Figure 3.1. Joint strategic target planning staff, Offutt Air Force Base, Omaha, Nebraska
Source: JCS Publication No. 4, "Organization and Functions of the JCS," 1 December 1960, in History and Research Division, Headquarters Strategic Air Command, *History of the Joint Strategic Target Planning Staff: Background and Preparation of SIOP-62*, p. 12.

control points necessary to obtain an objective, and the prevention of interference between weapons.[6]

The proposed organization of the JSTPS was approved by the JCS on 1 September 1960. The staff was then assembled in great haste since Secretary Gates had ordered that both the first NSTL and the first SIOP should be completed by 14 December 1960.[7]

The general policy guidance for the preparation of SIOP-62 was contained in two basic documents—*National Strategic Targeting and Attack Policy* (NSTAP) and *Guidance for the Preparation of the Single Integrated Operational Plan for Strategic Attack*.[8] These directed the JSTPS to prepare a plan that "will provide for the optimum integration of committed forces" against several target categories, including Soviet strategic nuclear capability as the first priority, followed by "primary military and government control centers of major importance," and then Soviet urban-industrial centers.[9]

The concept of the "optimum mix" had been developed in a study entitled NESC 2009, which had been undertaken by the Net Evaluation Sub Committee (NESC) of the NSC, under the direction of Lt. Gen. Thomas Hickey, in response to an NSC decision of 20 November 1958. This decision, approved by President Dwight D. Eisenhower on 1 December 1958, requested the NESC staff to examine alternative targeting strategies and to appraise "the relative merits, from the point of view of effective deterrence, of alternative retaliatory efforts directed toward 1) primarily a military target system, or 2) an optimum mix of a combined military-urban industrial target system."[10]

The NESC 2009 study argued for an optimum mix of both counterforce targets and (so long as "all known elements of Soviet nuclear capabilities and support systems" had been covered) countervalue targets, reflecting the conclusion that both the Soviet nuclear strike capability and industrial base would have to be destroyed if the United States were to prevail in a general war. The study argued that U.S. targeting policy in the event of a nuclear war should involve a series of "sequential options," consisting of such target sets as "central strategic systems, theater threats, and countervalue targets";[11] it produced a Comprehensive Strategic Target List consisting of a total of 2,021 targets, including 121 ICBM sites, 140 air defense bases, 200 bomber bases, 218 military and governmental control centers, and 124 other military targets (including naval bases and nuclear weapons production facilities and storage sites), with most of the remaining target installations located within 131 urban centers in the Soviet Union and China.[12] In February 1960, President Eisenhower authorized the use of NESC 2009 as guidance for the preparation of all future target lists, and hence it became the basis of the first NSTL and the first SIOP.[13]

The SIOP of December 1960 contained only one "plan," under which the United States would launch all its strategic nuclear delivery vehicles immediately upon the initiation of nuclear war with the USSR. The single target list predominantly included Soviet, Chinese, and satellite cities—whether by virtue of their value as urban-industrial targets or because of the location of numerous military and government control centers, as well as airfields and other military bases and facilities, within or on the outskirts of these cities. No strategic reserves were planned, and there was no provision for the preservation of command and control capabilities. As Daniel Ellsberg has observed, "If the SIOP [of 1960] were activated, we would have hit every city in the Soviet Union and China in addition to all military targets."[14] Expected Soviet, Chinese, and satellite fatalities were estimated by the JCS at 360 to 425 million people.[15]

THE 1962 SIOP (SIOP-63)

The Kennedy administration, which came into office on 20 January 1961, began with a complete and unequivocal rejection of the Eisenhower administration's basic national strategic policy of Massive Retaliation, which it chose to interpret as a wholly inflexible doctrine. One of its first acts was to order the revision of the December 1960 SIOP in order to provide the president with various options from which he could choose in the event of a nuclear exchange with the Soviet Union.[16]

Within the first week of taking office, Secretary of Defense Robert McNamara was given a formal briefing by William Kaufmann on a series of studies undertaken by the Rand Corporation and the air staff during 1959–60 which pointed to the strategic utility of counterforce strikes that held attacks on cities and population to a minimum. McNamara was an immediate convert to this particular "no cities" version of counterforce strategy.

On 1 March 1961, McNamara assigned a wide range of projects (the so-called 96 Trombones) to the senior Pentagon staff. The first of these was given to the chairman of the JCS (Gen. Lyman Lemnitzer) and the assistant secretary of defense for international security affairs (Paul Nitze) to prepare a draft memorandum revising basic national security policies relating to nuclear weapons, "including the assumptions relating to 'counterforce' strikes and the initiation of the use of tactical nuclear weapons." The section on objectives and general war, the first draft of which was completed by 7 April 1961 and the final draft by mid-May, was prepared by Daniel Ellsberg and stressed the necessity of providing the president with a variety of options from which to choose in the event of nuclear war. The second project required the JCS to examine and prepare a "doctrine" that, if accepted, "would permit controlled response and negotiating pauses in the event of themonuclear war." The Joint Staff paper for this project, prepared by Lt. Col. Robert P. Lukeman, argued in favor of flexibility and graduated options in the use of strategic nuclear forces.

The Ellsberg and Lukeman papers were then embodied in the Pentagon's *Guidelines for Planning*, which included a draft *Policy Guidance on Plans for Central War*, which in turn became the basis of the 1961 revision of the SIOP.

The new strategic policy developed under these guidelines had a number of novel features:

1. China and the satellite countries were separated from the USSR for targeting purposes.
2. Soviet strategic forces were separated from Soviet cities on U.S. target lists.
3. Strategic reserves were to be held by the United States in accordance with the concept of intrawar deterrence.
4. U.S. command and control systems were to be protected to allow "controlled response."
5. Soviet command and control was to be preserved, at least in the initial stages of any nuclear exchange.

The U.S. SIOP was given five options, plus various suboptions, with U.S. attacks against the USSR to proceed along the following spectrum: (1) Soviet strategic nuclear delivery forces, including missile sites, bomber bases, and submarine tenders; (2) other elements of Soviet military forces and military resources, located away from cities, for example, air defenses covering U.S. bomber routes; (3) Soviet military forces and military resources near cities; (4) Soviet command and control centers and systems; (5) if necessary, all-out urban-industrial attack. Suboptions included use of air-/ground-burst weapons, clean/dirty bombs, larger/smaller warheads, civil defense/evacuation. There was also provision that options (1) and (2) be exercised in preemptive fashion in response to unequivocal strategic warning of an impending major Sino-Soviet bloc attack on the United States or its allies.[17]

Initial work on the national guidance for the revision of the SIOP, done mainly by Daniel Ellsberg and Frank Trinkl under the direction of Alain Enthoven (all Rand alumni), was completed by late summer of 1961. It was then taken up by Henry Rowen and Gen. Maxwell Taylor and formalized that autumn. The JCS studied and approved the strategic change in late 1961, and the change was officially adopted in January 1962. To provide the USSR with the option of fighting a controlled nuclear war, Moscow was specifically separated out from the other targets on the NSTL in late 1961. Final approval was given to specific targets, ground-zero areas marked, and specific bombs and missiles allocated to the targets—all prepared by the JSTPS—at a meeting in the last week of June 1962 between McNamara, his deputy Roswell L. Gilpatric, and the most senior U.S. military officers at SAC headquarters.

In January 1962, McNamara's Fiscal Year 1963 defense budget statement revealed, for the first time from an official in public, that the first steps toward the no-cities version of the counterforce strategy were being taken. On the question of counterforce, McNamara said in his prepared statement that "A major mission of the strategic retaliatory forces is to deter war by their capability to destroy the enemy's war-making capabilities."[18] In subsequent testimony he stated that U.S. strategic weapons were being placed in a configuration such that cities could be either spared or destroyed.

A month later, in Chicago on 17 February 1962, McNamara described the flexibility of the new U.S. nuclear war-fighting strategy:

> Our forces can be used in several different ways. We may have to retaliate with a single massive attack. Or, we may be able to use our retaliatory forces to limit damage done to ourselves, and our allies, by knocking out the enemy's bases before he has had time to launch his second salvos. We may seek to terminate a war on favorable terms by using our forces as a bargaining weapon—by threatening further attack. In any case, our large reserve of protected firepower would give an enemy an incentive to avoid our cities and to stop a war. Our new policy gives us the flexibility to choose among several operational plans.[19]

On 5 May 1962, McNamara described the no-cities strategy at a secret session of NATO in Athens:

> The United States has come to the conclusion that to the extent feasible, basic military strategy in general nuclear war should be approached in much the same way that more conventional military operations have been regarded in the past. That is to say, our principal military objectives, in the event of nuclear war . . . *should be the destruction of the enemy's military forces* while attempting to preserve the fabric as well as the integrity of allied society. Specifically, our studies indicate that a strategy which targets nuclear forces only against cities or a mixture of civil and military targets has serious limitations for the purpose of deterrence and for the conduct of general nuclear war.[20]

Then, on 16 June 1962, he distilled his Athens speech into his landmark commencement address at the University of Michigan at Ann Arbor, in which he reiterated that the "principal military objectives, in the event of a nuclear war stemming from a major attack on the Alliance, should be the destruction of the enemy's military forces, not of his civilian population. . . . We are giving a possible opponent the strongest imaginable incentive to refrain from striking our own cities."[21]

The adoption of the no-cities version of counterforce strategy was supported by two strategic developments of the early 1960s. One was the development in 1960–61 of photographic reconnaissance satellites, which by September 1961 had provided essentially complete photographic coverage of the USSR. Two U.S. satellite programs were involved. The best known is the air force's Satellite and Missile Observation System (SAMOS), which involved the radio transmission of photographs from the satellites to several ground stations around the world. The first of these satellites, SAMOS II, was successfully launched on 31 January 1961. However, the resolution of the photographs obtained in this way was relatively poor, and in any case SAMOS II was only operational for about three weeks, which was not sufficient to cover the USSR fully. (The next successful SAMOS was not launched until 22 December 1961.) The much more important program was that of the CIA, which launched a series of satellites under cover of the air force's Discoverer biosatellite program. These CIA satellites used recoverable capsules for retrieving the photographic intelligence that, together with the lower altitudes at which the satellites were orbited, provided much higher resolution. The first of these satellites was launched on 19 August 1960 and recovered the next day; subsequent successful recoveries were made from satellites launched on 12 November and 7 December 1960, and 16 June, 7 July, 30 August, and 12 September 1961, by which time the missile gap myth of 1958–61 had finally been laid to rest. The National Intelligence Estimate (NIE) of 21 September 1961 (NIE 11-8/1-61) estimated that the USSR had less than ten ICBMs operational.

These satellites provided the first fully comprehensive mapping of the Soviet Union—the ICBM and intermediate-range ballistic missile (IRBM) bases, submarine ports, air defense sites, army and air force bases, and so forth—without which the no-cities version of counterforce strategy could not have been implemented.

The second development was the acknowledged attainment of clear and overwhelming U.S. strategic superiority—to which the satellite photographs directly certified. At the end of 1961, when the strategic basis of the 1962 SIOP was completed and accepted by the JCS, the Soviet Union had only 4 SS-6 ICBMs operational, whereas the United States had 54 ICBMs and 5 FBM submarines with 80 Polaris SLBMs. At the end of 1962, the respective figures were 30 Soviet ICBMs as against 200 U.S. ICBMs and 144 U.S. SLBMs. Moreover, the NIEs of late 1961 and

Table 3.1. Soviet Bloc Target List

	Number of Targets	Number of Weapons Assigned
Strategic Nuclear High Urgency		
Soft Targets		
Primary bomber, dispersal, and		
fighter control bases	200	400
ICBM-soft	125	220
MRBM/IRBM	162	286
Space system control facilities	5	10
Subtotal	492	916
Hardened targets		
ICBM-hardened	125	138
ICBM-fully hardened	200	396
Submarine bases	30	38
Offensive controls	10	13
Subtotal	365	585
Strategic Nuclear Moderate Urgency		
Soft targets		
Bomber capable fields	110	220
Air defense fields	100	100
Missile storage	20	40
Nuclear/CBR production	30	60
SAM sites	350	406
Subtotal	610	826
Hardened targets		
National regional nuclear storage	68	262
Other nuclear storage	115	315
Subtotal	183	577
Urban-Industrial	210	349
TOTAL	1860	3253

Source: Office of the Secretary of Defense, *Memorandum for the President: Recommended FY 1964–FY 1968 Strategic Retaliatory Forces*, 21 November 1962, p. 14.

Note: Prepared 21 November 1962; projected for 30 June 1969.

late 1962 projected a U.S. superiority of between two to one and four to one by the mid-1960s. A counterforce strike by the United States in the early 1960s could perhaps have fully disarmed the Soviet Union.

The overwhelmingly counterforce character of U.S. strategic nuclear target planning as of the end of 1962 is clearly evinced in the Soviet Bloc Target List which was projected for June 1969 as a guide to the development of the SIOP forces through the end of F.Y. 1968 (see table 3.1). Out of the projected total of 1,860 Soviet-bloc targets, only 210 (or 11.3 percent) were urban-industrial, the rest being strategic and theater nuclear delivery systems, SAM sites and interceptor aircraft bases, command and control centers, and nuclear and chemical/biological weapons production and storage facilities. Of the 3,253 SIOP weapons assigned to this target list, only 349, or 10.7 percent, were allocated to urban industrial targets. With respect to megatonnage, 663 Mt out of a projected total of 6,500 Mt, or just over 10 percent, were assigned for delivery against urban-industrial targets.[22]

However, McNamara soon began to retreat publicly from his commitment to the counterforce/no-cities strategy. There were several reasons for this. First, within the United States there was much criticism of the first-strike implications of the counterforce strategy. One former McNamara aide is reported to have said: "there could be no such thing as primary retaliation against military targets after an enemy attack. If you're going to shoot at missiles, you're talking about first strike."[23] This question was unnecessarily complicated because of the administration's ambiguity on whether U.S. policy completely ruled out striking first. President John F. Kennedy had said in March 1962, for example, that "Krushchev must *not* be certain that, where its vital interests are threatened, the United States will never strike first."[24]

A second factor was the Soviet reaction. In their public statements at least, Soviet spokesmen denied the possibility of controlled counterforce warfare. Avowed Soviet strategy was to strike against military targets, governmental and administrative centers, and cities simultaneously and immediately on the outbreak of general hostilities. Whether in fact the Soviet Union would accept the U.S. strategy was an open question. McNamara himself actually believed that any nuclear attack by the Soviet Union on the United States would include an attack on the major U.S. urban areas. In any case, it was argued, while Soviet missiles were few and vulnerable and U.S. forces numerically so superior, the Soviet Union could not afford to play games of controlled "tit for tat" with each other's missiles. And as the Soviet force grew larger and became hardened and dispersed, McNamara believed the destruction of any large number of missiles would be unfeasible.[25]

A third factor was the unfavorable reaction of West European allies. When McNamara first described the no-cities strategy to them in Athens in May 1962, the audience was reportedly incredulous. Following McNamara's Ann Arbor speech, Secretary of State Dean Rusk made a three-day tour of six Western capitals to explain the new U.S. policy to Western Europe's leaders. But he met with frustration; the NATO allies were obviously unwilling to accept the implications of the no-cities strategy, especially for small, independent European nuclear capabilities. Not only did the Ann Arbor strategy deny the Europeans nuclear independence and fail to consider the different targeting priorities of the European governments, it raised the specter of separating European security from that of the United States. And, by removing the threat to Soviet cities, it also raised the specter of removing pari passu the deterrent to a Soviet attack on Europe, and even the possibility of fighting a nuclear war over European territory while leaving the Soviet and U.S. homelands unscathed.

But most important, McNamara decided to withdraw from his Ann Arbor position for bureaucratic reasons. By the time of the development of the FY 1964 defense budget in late 1962, it was clear to McNamara that the services, and particularly the air force, were using his declared policy of No-Cities Counterforce as a basis for force development, requesting both more Minuteman ICBMs and procurement of a force of supersonic reconnaissance strike (RS-70) bombers, which McNamara believed were unnecessary. He thus came to place more stress on assured destruction capabilities (although by defining the assured destruction criteria conservatively he could still procure sufficient forces to allow some damage-limiting capability). Thus in January 1963 he directed William Kaufmann to brief some dozen air force generals to the effect that they were no longer to take the avowed U.S. strategy as a criterion for strategic force proposals. In separating declaratory policy from action policy, McNamara was to a large extent using strategic doctrine as a weapon in the continuous intramural bureaucratic battles over military programs and defense (and service) budgets.

McNamara did not move immediately to wholesale acceptance of Assured Destruction; rather, declaratory policy from 1964 through 1966 included both Assured Destruction and Damage Limitation as basic U.S. strategic objectives.

The development of the concept of Damage Limitation was principally the responsibility of Lt. Col. Glenn A. Kent (USAF), who headed a study group that McNamara had initially established in the summer of 1962 to undertake a comprehensive analysis of various alternative strategic policies available to the United States, and the weapons systems and force levels that each implied. The results of a pilot survey were ready in July 1963, and the full study, *Damage Limitation: A Rationale for the Allocation of Resources by the US and USSR*, was published on 21 January 1964.

In a memorandum dated 12 March 1964, McNamara asked for an amplification of the January study and requested that the "Services conduct studies during the next six months that would focus attention on 'Damage Limitation" and 'Assured Destruction.' " These studies were integrated by the Weapons Systems Evaluation Group (WSEG) in a two-volume study known as WSEG No. 79 and formally titled *Analysis of General Nuclear War Postures for Strategic Offensive and Defensive Forces of the US and USSR*.

[68]

The Kent study and the associated analyses formed the basis of McNamara's discussion of U.S. strategic policy in his FY 1966 defense budget statement. McNamara there stated:

The strategic objectives of our general nuclear war forces are:
(1) to deter a deliberate nuclear attack upon the United States and its allies by maintaining a clear and convincing capability to inflict unacceptable damage on an attacker, even were that attacker to strike first;
(2) in the event such a war should nevertheless occur, to limit damage to our populations and industrial capacities.
The first of these capabilities (required to deter potential aggressors) we call "Assured Destruction," i.e. the capability to destroy the aggressor as a viable society, even after a well-planned and executed surprise attack on our forces. The second capability we call "Damage Limitation," i.e. the capability to reduce the weight of the enemy attack by both offensive and defensive measures, and to provide a degree of protection for the population against the effects of nuclear detonations.[26]

However, in 1965–66 McNamara began to down-play substantially the Damage Limitation aspects of avowed U.S. strategic policy, and by 1967 the rhetoric was all concerned with Assured Destruction.

The first formal definition of Assured Destruction was given to Congress by McNamara in his FY 1966 budget statement of 18 February 1965:

A vital first objective, to be met in full by our strategic nuclear forces, is the capability for Assured Destruction. What kinds and amounts of destruction we would have to be able inflict in order to provide this capability cannot be answered precisely. But, it seems reasonable to assume the destruction of, say, one-quarter to one-third of its population and about two-thirds of its industrial capacity . . . would certainly represent intolerable punishment to any industrialized nation and thus should serve as an effective deterrent.[27]

The required levels of destruction were later reduced somewhat. McNamara's FY 1968 budget statement, presented to Congress on 23 January 1967, stated: "It seems reasonable to assume that in the case of the Soviet Union, the destruction of, say one-fifth to one-fourth of its population and one-half to two-thirds of its industrial capacity would mean its elimination as a major power for many years. Such a level of destruction . . . should serve as an effective deterrent."[28]

This reduction in the destruction levels did not represent any philosophical reconsideration of the requirements of viable deterrence; rather, it represented a more accurate reflection of American capabilities against the urban-industrial target structure of the Soviet Union.

[69]

It is important to emphasize that these changes in U.S. strategic policy related only to the declaratory and force posture aspects of that policy. McNamara never abandoned his belief in the necessity for flexibility and options, and no substantive changes were made to the 1962 SIOP. Even when Assured Destruction was being stressed most strongly in the rhetoric, it weathered possible substantive change. The last Joint Strategic Operations Plan (JSOP) drawn up under Secretary McNamara, the *JSOP 1969–77* of February 1967, stressed such notions as options, control, flexibility, and sequential attacks.[29]

An assistant secretary of defense in the last years of the Johnson administration wrote in 1971:

> The SIOP remains essentially unchanged since then [McNamara's Ann Arbor speech of 15 June 1962]. There have been two developments, however: 1) it has become more difficult to execute the pure-counterforce option, and its value is considered to be diminishing and, 2) all public officials have learned to talk in public only about deterrence and city attacks. No warfighting, no city-sparing. Too many critics can make too much trouble (no-cities talk weakens deterrence, the argument goes), so public officials have run for cover. That included me when I was one of them. But the targeting philosophy, the options and the order of choice remain unchanged from the McNamara speech.[30]

A two-star air force planner was quite emphatic during an interview in February 1973 that the SIOP was "never reworked under [President] Johnson. It is still basically the same as 1962."[31]

A study of Henry Kissinger published in 1972 actually castigated the national security adviser for failing to "energize the bureaucracy to update the Joint Chiefs' war plan (SIOP), a plan that has remained essentially unchanged since 1962."[32] In fact Kissinger formally moved in 1969 to begin the first major change in American strategic nuclear war plans since 1961–62.

FROM SIOP-63 TO SIOP-5

Current U.S. targeting policy has a direct historical lineage to the beginning of the Nixon administration, when the first substantive moves were made to review the 1962 SIOP. The past decade and a half has been a period of continuous official effort to increase the range of strategic nuclear targeting options available to the president, including an extensive array of counterforce options, and to enhance the possibility that these options could be exercised in such a way that escalation could be controlled.

[70]

On 21 January 1969, the day after the inauguration, the new president's national security adviser, Henry Kissinger, issued National Security Study Memorandum (NSSM) 3, titled *Military Posture*, which directed a review of the U.S. military posture and asked for the development of criteria against which U.S. strategic needs could be measured. The resultant study was primarily the responsibility of Ivan Selin, then the acting assistant secretary of defense for systems analysis, who had previously visited the JSTPS in Omaha and evinced concern that even the most limited options in SIOP-63 involved too many weapons and would produce too many fatalities and hence were unlikely to engender any reciprocal restraint from the Soviet Union.[33] NSSM-3 has been described as follows:

> Among the deeds of NSSM-3 was to kill assured destruction. "Up to now," it read, "the main criterion for evaluating U.S. strategic forces has been their ability to deter the Soviet Union from all-out, aggressive attacks on the United States." However, a nuclear war may not take form as a series of "spasm reactions." It "may develop as a series of steps in an escalating crisis in which both sides want to avoid attacking cities, neither side can afford unilaterally to stop the exchange, and the situation is dominated by uncertainty." If during a future Berlin crisis, for example, the Soviets thought that the U.S. was about to start a nuclear war, the U.S.S.R., rather than being struck first, "might consider using a portion of its strategic forces to strike U.S. forces in order to improve its relative military position. . . ." NSSM-3 conceded that these sorts of attacks "have no precedent in Soviet military doctrine or tradition," making it "highly unlikely that such a situation would develop." Even so, an American capacity for early "war termination, avoiding attacks on cities, and selective response capabilities might provide ways of limiting damage if deterrence fails."[34]

In June 1969, Kissinger pointed out to the president "the dilemma he would face if there was a limited Soviet nuclear attack" and urged him to request the Pentagon to devise strategies to meet contingencies other than all-out nuclear challenge.[35] The president reportedly agreed, and orders to that effect were issued. Criteria of "strategic sufficiency" were then developed that related U.S. strategic planning to the destruction not only of civilians but of military targets as well.[36] The first public hint that efforts were proceeding in this direction was given by the rhetorical questions asked by President Richard Nixon in his foreign policy message to Congress of 17 February 1970: "Should a President, in the event of a nuclear attack, be left with the single option of ordering the mass destruction of enemy civilians, in the face of the certainty that it would be followed by the mass slaughter of Americans? Should the concept of

[71]

assured destruction be narrowly defined and should it be the only measure of our ability to deter the variety of threats we may face?"[37]

In April 1970, it was reported that the development of alternatives to
the policy of Assured Destruction was regarded as a top priority within
the NSC and that a coordinated governmental review of the subject was
currently under way.[38] The thrust of this review was again suggested
in sections of President Nixon's next foreign policy message to Congress,
that of 25 February 1971:

> I must not be—and my successors must not be—limited to the indiscriminate
> mass destruction of civilians as the sole possible response to challenges. . . .
>   We must insure that we have the forces and procedures that provide us
> with alternatives appropriate to the nature and level of the provocation.
> This means having the plans and command and control capabilities nec-
> essary to enable us to select and carry out the appropriate response without
> necessarily having to resort to massive destruction.[39]

There was initially much suspicion and some resistance from the Pentagon to what was perceived as intrusion by the White House into the
formulation of strategic doctrine.[40] By the summer of 1971, however, a
number of officials in the Office of Systems Analysis in the Department
of Defense (DOD) had also become concerned with the need to provide
a more flexible structure for the SIOP's preplanned responses. This group
produced a number of studies that argued that, in the event of a failure
of deterrence, the existence of a range of Limited Nuclear Options (LNO),
which avoided indiscriminate destruction, might provide the means of
avoiding high levels of destruction of urban-industrial centers.[41]

In mid-1972, without public announcement, President Nixon directed
Kissinger to head a top-level interdepartmental group tasked with the
development of additional strategic nuclear war options, including some
involving selective attacks on certain military targets, so that the president might have more flexibility in the event of a strategic nuclear
exchange.[42] At the same time a DOD-wide ad hoc task force was established within the Pentagon, chaired by John Foster (director of defense
research and engineering) and with Brig. Gen. Jasper Welch (assigned
to the Office of Secretary of Defense) as staff director, to further develop
the earlier DOD studies. This group was augmented in due course with
representatives from the CIA, the State Department, and the NSC. Numerous papers were produced, which were reviewed in detail formally
by the JCS as a corporate body. The work of these groups led directly
to National Security Study Memorandum (NSSM) 169, approved by
President Nixon in late 1973.[43]

NSSM-169 led directly to the promulgation of National Security Decision Memorandum (NSDM) 242, signed by President Nixon on 17 January 1974, which began as follows:

> I have reached the following decisions on United States policy regarding planning for nuclear weapons employment. These decisions do not constitute a major new departure in US nuclear strategy; rather, they are an elaboration of existing policy. The decisions reflect both existing political and military realities and my desire for a more flexible nuclear posture.
> ... The fundamental mission of US nuclear forces is to deter nuclear war and plans for the employment of US nuclear forces should support this mission.[44]

The memorandum directed that further plans "for limited employment options which enable the United States to conduct selected nuclear operations" be developed and formally incorporated into the SIOP. Much of the public debate of NSDM-242 was concerned with the reemphasis in these plans on the targeting of a wide range of Soviet military forces and installations, from hardened command and control facilities and ICBM silos to airfields and army camps.[45] This reemphasis, however, was much more declaratory than substantive since, as described above, the SIOP had, at least since 1962 and including the period when Assured Destruction was avowed policy, contained most of these counterforce targets. A more novel aspect of the memorandum was the notion of targeting those Soviet assets that would be critical to Soviet postwar recovery and power. NSDM-242 directed that an objective of U.S. targeting doctrine should be the "destruction of the political, economic and military resources critical to the enemy's post-war power, influence and ability to recover ... as a major power."[46]

The concept of Escalation Control was central to the policy outlined. It was essential that the NCA be provided with the ability to execute their options in a deliberate and controlled fashion throughout the progress of a strategic nuclear exchange. The memorandum directed that the United States must have the potential to "hold some vital enemy targets hostage to subsequent destruction" and to control "the timing and pace of attack execution, in order to provide the enemy opportunities to consider his actions," so that "the best possible outcome" might be obtained for the United States and its allies. NSDM-242 introduced the notion of "withholds" or "nontargets," that is, things that would be preserved from destruction. Some of these, such as "population *per se*," have now been exempted absolutely from targeting; others, such as the centers of political leadership and control, are exempted only for the purpose of intrawar deterrence and intrawar bargaining, and strategic reserve forces (SRF) are to be maintained to allow their eventual destruction if necessary.[47]

[73]

Finally, NSDM-242 authorized the secretary of defense to promulgate the *Policy Guidance for the Employment of Nuclear Weapons* and the associated *Nuclear Weapons Employment Policy* (NUWEP), signed by Secretary James Schlesinger on 4 April 1974 and subsequently known as NUWEP-1.[48] The NUWEP was developed through close military and civilian cooperation, and set out the planning assumptions, attack options, targeting objectives, and damage levels needed to satisfy the political guidance.[49] These concepts and objectives set out in NSDM-242 and NUWEP-1 provided the framework within which the JCS provided the military guidance to the JSTPS in Omaha, Nebraska, for the development of the new strategic nuclear war plans. This military guidance was provided in 1974 by a detailed memorandum to the commanders of the unified and specified commands and the director of strategic target planning (DSTP) in Omaha, and was subsequently incorporated in Annex C (Nuclear) to the Joint Strategic Capabilities Plan (JSCP) which is updated at least annually.[50] The first SIOP prepared under the new guidance was SIOP-5, which was formally approved in December 1975 and took effect on 1 January 1976.[51]

Among the various quantitative objectives set out in NUWEP-1, the one that generated the most activity during the development of SIOP-5 was the requirement that the SIOP forces be able to destroy 70 percent of the Soviet industry that would be needed to achieve economic recovery in the event of a large-scale strategic nuclear exchange.[52] The SIOP had always included a wide range of economic and industrial targets, and indeed, the requirement to destroy 70 percent of the Soviet economic and industrial base had been in the guidance since at least the 1962 SIOP.[53] However, the techniques used to define and identify "targets of economic recovery" and to assess the USSR's postattack powers of recuperation had been analytically very weak.[54] Hence, the emphasis in NUWEP-1 on targets of economic recovery prompted much analytic work within the American defense community on the development of Cobb-Douglas models and input-output tables of the Soviet economy, designed to elucidate critical interdependencies and vulnerabilities for targeting purposes. The JSTPS at Omaha itself developed an econometric model of the Soviet economy for direct application to targeting considerations.[55] The LINK Project was undertaken at the Rand Corporation to refine another econometric model of the Soviet economy, and research institutes such as Rand and Hudson were engaged in the development of models of economic recovery together with the strategic analysis of economic-recovery targeting policies.[56] The JCS also initiated a series of studies, carried out by the Joint Chiefs' Studies Analysis and Gaming Agency (SAGA), which analyzed the relative recovery capabilities of the United States and the Soviet Union following a hypothetical massive

[74]

nuclear exchange. Known as the Comparative Postwar Recovery Analysis (COPRA), the studies were directly related to changes in the SIOP.[57]

THROUGH SIOP-5 TO SIOP-6

Despite some initial expectation that the administration of President Jimmy Carter and Secretary of Defense Harold Brown would move to change U.S. policy back toward something more like Assured Destruction, the concepts and doctrines embodied in NSDM-242 and NUWEP-1 have been essentially retained, and indeed further refined, through to the present day. President-elect Carter and his key national security advisers received their first briefings on then-current U.S. strategic nuclear war plans and capabilities during the interregnum; the most important of these briefings took place in Blair House, in Washington, D.C., on 12 January 1977.[58] The documentary reappraisal of NSDM-242 began with the preparation of Presidential Review Memorandum (PRM) 10, *Comprehensive Net Assessment and Military Force Posture Review*, which was signed by President Carter on 18 February 1977, just four weeks after he assumed office.[59] This five-month interagency study, supervised by Samuel P. Huntington for the president's national security adviser, was a comprehensive assessment of the Soviet-American global power relationship. This assessment included a study titled *Military Strategy and Force Posture Review* (prepared largely by the Office of the Assistant Secretary of Defense for International Security Affairs), which considered details of the military balance and alternative military strategies—including strategies for possible nuclear war with the USSR.[60]

PRM-10 was completed in late June 1977 and, together with its attendant reports, was considered by a cabinet-level group, chaired by Zbigniew Brzezinski, the national security adviser, on 7 July. The PRM-10 conclusions were more sanguine and optimistic than most observers had expected. The study assumed the deployment of Trident SLBMs, the Mark 12A warhead on the Minuteman III ICBMs, the development of cruise missiles, and the continued development of the MX ICBM. Assessing the impact of a major nuclear war between the two superpowers, the study found that, at a minimum, the United States would suffer 140 million fatalities and the USSR 113 million and that almost three-quarters of their respective economies would be destroyed. In such a conflict, the report concluded, "neither side could conceivably be described as a winner." The report stated that neither side would have an advantage in launching a limited nuclear attack against the other's land-based ICBM forces—and, in fact, that "whichever side initiates a limited nuclear attack against the ICBM forces of the other side will find itself

[75]

significantly worse off" in terms of surviving numbers of missiles and missile warheads. The study also found that U.S. antisubmarine warfare (ASW) capability was significantly better than that of the USSR; it also found that even after a Soviet missile attack against U.S. air bases, the surviving U.S. bomber force would be larger than that now possessed by the USSR. Finally, it noted that "Mr. Carter has decided that U.S. missiles and bombers must be able to destroy about 70 per cent of the Soviet Union's so-called recovery resources, meaning the economic, political and military facilities critical to the functioning of society."[61]

On 24 August 1977, following further intensive review of PRM-10 and the attendant *Military Strategy and Force Posture Review* by NSC officials and the departments of Defense and State, and extended debate in the Special Coordination Committee (dominated by Zbigniew Brzezinski, Secretary of State Cyrus Vance, and Secretary of Defense Brown), President Carter issued Presidential Decision (PD) 18, *U.S. National Strategy*. PD-18 both codified certain aspects of existing U.S. strategic policy and called for further study of other aspects. Most important from the viewpoint of targeting policy, PD-18 reaffirmed the continued use of NSDM-242 and NUWEP-1 in "the absence of further guidance for structuring the US strategic posture."[62] It insisted that the United States maintain the capability to inflict "unacceptable damage" on the USSR even if that nation struck first with nuclear weapons. It instructed the Pentagon to develop options for limited nuclear responses by the United States. It directed that a "reserve" of strategic forces be maintained, safe from attack, for use if nuclear war became relatively extended. And it stated that U.S. forces should be strong enough to ensure that any possible nuclear war would end on the most favorable terms possible to the United States.[63] Finally, it directed that three further major studies be undertaken: a Nuclear Targeting Policy Review (NTPR), a modernization of the ICBM force study, and a strategic reserve force study.[64]

The NTPR was an interagency study headed by Leon Sloss in the Pentagon. Undertaken in two principal phases, the first was completed and forwarded to the secretary of defense in December 1978, and the second remained uncompleted when the study group was disbanded in the spring of 1979. Numerous supporting studies were commissioned during 1978, on such topics as the history of U.S. targeting plans, Soviet and Chinese views on nuclear war and nuclear weapons employment policies, the possibility of targeting the Soviet population, targeting economic and political recovery assets, regionalization of the Soviet Union, the C^3 constraints on escalation control, and the question of war termination.

The NTPR reached several important conclusions. The primary systems acquisition requirement identified was that the C^3I system that controlled the SIOP forces should have greater endurance than the present system. It also suggested that more options should be added to the SIOP to give the strategic forces "greater flexibility in targeting than they presently have."[65] More specifically, it suggested that relatively less emphasis be accorded to the destruction of the Soviet economic and industrial base and that greater attention "be directed toward improving the effectiveness of our attacks against military targets."[66] It also suggested that there be some modification of the SIOP to reflect better the political aspects of nuclear targeting. As one White House official stated at the time:

> In the past nuclear targeting has been done by military planners who have basically emphasized the efficient destruction of targets. But targeting should not be done in a political vacuum.
> Some targets are of greater psychological importance to Moscow than others, and we should begin thinking of how to use our strategic forces to play on these concerns.[67]

To exploit potential Soviet fears, some changes were made in the targeting guidance, such as threatening the Soviet food supply and making a target of Soviet troops and military facilities in the Far East so that the USSR would be more vulnerable to attack from China. And some consideration was given to the adaptation of targeting to the dismemberment and regionalization of the USSR, enhancing the prospects for regional insurrection during and after a nuclear exchange. The NTPR also led to the development of a highly complex matrix of targeting "packages" or "building block" options that could be flexibly combined or tailored to suit particular situations.[68] Several targeting issues that required further study were also identified, such as the targeting of the Soviet leadership and political control system.[69] And finally, as a result of the NTPR, the continuing review of United States targeting policy has been institutionalized by incorporation of that function in the charter of the under secretary of defense for policy (USD(P)).[70]

The NTPR formed the basis of a new Presidential Directive drafted in early 1979. Although the NSC staff pressed for the formal acceptance of this draft, there was opposition from the State Department and from some elements within the Pentagon; thus, it was shelved for more than fifteen months—until it was retrieved just prior to the 1980 Democratic Convention, revised and up-dated and formally signed by the president on 25 July as PD-59.[71] As Secretary Brown emphasized, "PD-59 is not a new strategic doctrine; it is not a radical departure from US strategic policy over the past decade or so. It is, in fact, a refinement, a codification of previous statements of our strategic policy. PD-59 takes the same

[77]

essential strategic doctrine, and restates it more clearly, more cogently, in the light of current conditions and current capabilities."[72]

Although PD-59 represented no major changes to the targeting guidance as previously set out in NSDM-242 and NUWEP-1, there were at least three noteworthy features of the Carter directive. First, within the area of economic targeting, the directive deemphasized the concept of targeting to impede Soviet economic recovery in favor of greater emphasis on targeting the Soviet economic war-supporting infrastructure. As Leon Sloss has written:

> After a good deal of study between 1975 and 1978, it was clear that it is extremely difficult to determine how the process of recovery might start and subsequently function after a large-scale nuclear attack, and thus how recovery might be impeded. Furthermore, it was clear that massive and perhaps continuing attacks would be necessary to impede recovery. Such attacks would require expending forces that might be more effectively held in reserve. Instead, greater attention was focused on the targeting of logistics and industries that immediately supported the war effort.[73]

Second, PD-59 emphasized that the preplanned target packages in the SIOP should be supplemented by the ability to find new targets and destroy them during the course of a nuclear exchange. While Soviet strategic nuclear installations and economic and industrial facilities would remain essentially fixed during wartime, there would be much movement of Soviet conventional military forces (including second-echelon formations) and much of the Soviet political and military leadership would presumably be relocated. PD-59 required the development of new reconnaissance satellites and signals intelligence (SIGINT) systems to provide the real-time intelligence capabilities that would be necessary to effect this rapid retargeting.[74]

Third, PD-59 recognized that the current U.S. C^3 system was inadequate to support any policy of extended nuclear war fighting. It stated that the strategy embodied in the directive "imposes requirements in the strategic command, control and communications system, and . . . improvements in our forces must be accompanied by improvements to that system. The needed improvements lie in the areas of increased flexibility and higher assurance of command-and-control survivability and long-term endurance."[75]

In this respect, PD-59 should be considered together with PD-53 and PD-58 and a wide range of other measures undertaken by the Carter administration in 1979–80 which were intended to improve the survivability and the endurance of the U.S. C^3 system. PD-53, titled *National Security Telecommunications Policy* and signed by President Carter on 15 November 1979, proclaimed that "it is essential to the security of the

US to have telecommunications facilities adequate to satisfy the needs of the nation during and after any national emergency . . . to provide continuity of essential functions of government, and to reconstitute the political, economic and social structure of the nation." Its principal goal was to ensure "connectivity between the National Command Authority and strategic and other appropriate forces to support flexible execution of retaliatory strikes during and after an enemy nuclear attack."[76] PD-58, signed by President Carter on 30 June 1980, was concerned with the maintenance of "continuity of government." It directed the DOD and other agencies to improve the capacity of selected parts of the government, from the president downward, to withstand a nuclear attack. The measures under consideration included plans for evacuating military and civilian leaders from Washington in time of crisis; the construction of new hardened shelters for key personnel, data processing equipment, and communication systems; and the improvement of early warning systems.[77]

PD-59 also authorized Secretary of Defense Harold Brown to issue a new *Nuclear Weapons Employment Policy*, variously referred to as NUWEP-2 or NUWEP-80, and issued by Secretary Brown in October 1980.[78] An especially noteworthy feature of NUWEP-2 was the downgrading of the requirement set out in NUWEP-1 for the destruction of "70 per cent of the Soviet industry that would be needed to achieve economic recovery after a war."[79] According to official testimony, this requirement was the "most specific task" outlined in NUWEP-1. It had to be satisfied "under all conditions. . . . We must do that even if we do not do anything else."[80] Under the NUWEP-1 guidance, weapons were then allocated to the other categories of targets "to the extent we can," but neither the relative magnitudes nor the priorities that guided this allocation are matters of public record. NUWEP-2 gave priority to targeting Soviet military capabilities, including both nuclear and conventional forces, and to targeting Soviet military and political leadership and, within the category of economic targets, to targeting war-supporting industry rather than Soviet economic recovery capabilities.

A new review of targeting policy was begun by the Reagan administration in the spring of 1981, under the general direction of Fred Iklé, the USD(P). In a conscious effort to improve the integration of Nuclear Weapons Employment Policy with other elements of U.S. strategic nuclear policy, the Reagan administration produced a *Nuclear Weapons Employment and Acquisition Master Plan.*[81] This was closely followed, in October 1981, by National Security Decision Directive (NSDD) 13, prepared as a successor to PD-59. Finally, in July 1982, Secretary of Defense Caspar Weinberger issued a new NUWEP, designated NUWEP-82. The guidance contained in these documents was then used to develop a new

SIOP, in which increased attention was accorded the requirements of nuclear weapons employment in a situation of prolonged or protracted nuclear conflict.[82] This new SIOP, formally designated SIOP-6, took effect on 1 October 1983.

As a result of these developments, the U.S. target plans for strategic nuclear war are now extremely comprehensive. The current version of SIOP-6 includes some fifty thousand potential target installations, as compared to about twenty-five thousand in 1974 when NUWEP-1 was promulgated and the development of SIOP-5 initiated.[83] These targets are divided into four principal groups, each of which in turn contains a wide range of target types. The four principal groups are Soviet nuclear forces, general purposes forces, Soviet military and political leadership centers, and Soviet economic and industrial base.[84]

Examples of targets within each category were given by the Defense Department to the Senate Armed Services Committee in March 1980:[85]

i) Soviet nuclear forces:
    ICBMs and IRBMs, together with their launch facilities (LFs) and launch command centers (LCCs);
    nuclear weapons storage sites;
    airfields supporting nuclear-capable aircraft;
    nuclear ballistic missile submarine (SSBN) bases.
ii) Conventional military forces:
    barracks;
    supply depots;
    marshalling points;
    conventional airfields;
    ammunition storage facilities;
    tank and vehicle storage yards.
iii) Military and political leadership:
    command posts;
    key communications facilities.
iv) Economic and industrial targets:
    (a) war-supporting industry:
       ammunition factories;
       tank and armored personnel carrier factories;
       petroleum refineries;
       railway yards and repair facilities.
    (b) industry that contributes to economic recovery:
       coal;
       basic steel;
       basic aluminum;
       cement;
       electric power.

[80]

Of course, since the United States has only some ten thousand warheads in its strategic nuclear arsenal, no more than about 20 percent of the fifty thousand potential targets could be hit in any nuclear exchange. The actual number of warheads that would be available for employment depends on the assumptions made regarding alert levels—whether the forces are in a normal "day-to-day" posture or whether they are "fully generated." The day-to-day posture is a worst case situation and for planning purposes assumes that the United States has been struck first. The fully generated posture, on the other hand, is the best case situation where the U.S. forces have been "generated without damage and [the SIOP] executed before a Soviet attack comes down."[86]

The different employment possibilities which pertain in these two situations are reflected in a basic division of the SIOP into an Alert Response Plan and a Generated Operations Plan.

According to one official study, in a generated situation, where the Generated Operations Plan would pertain, U.S. target planners could count on 7,160 weapons arriving on target, in which case the United States could hit more than 8,000 targets, made up as follows:

Nuclear	2,018
OMT	1,603
Leadership	736
E/I (Economic-Industrial)	4,400 (3,572 aim points)
Total	8,757

In a non-generated situation, on the other hand, where the Alert Response Plan would pertain, US target planners could count on some 3,840 weapons arriving on target, in which case the United States would only be able to hit some 5,400 targets, made up as follows:[87]

Nuclear	1,761
OMT	935
Leadership	423
E/I	2,300 (1,793 aim points)
Total	5,419

The SIOP is further divided into four general categories of options available for the employment of nuclear weapons: Major Attack Options (MAO), Selective Attack Options (SAO), Limited Nuclear Options (LNO), which are "designed to permit the selective destruction of fixed enemy military or industrial targets," and Regional Nuclear Options (RNO) which are "intended, for example, to destroy the leading elements of an attacking force."[88] As an example of the use of RNO and LNO, Gen. R. H. Ellis, then commander of the SAC, testified before the Senate Armed Services Committee in March 1980 that "combat missions could be launched from Andersen [Air Force Base in Guam] to the Middle

East" in response to Soviet conventional military activity in that region.[89] As an example of an SAO, plans for nuclear strikes against Soviet military facilities near Iran, including military bases and airfields inside the Soviet Union, have been prepared so as to "significantly degrade Soviet capabilities to project military power in the Middle East–Persian Gulf region for a period of at least 30 days."[90] Within each of these classes of options are a wide range of further options, including so-called withholds,[91] four general categories of which have been publicly identified: population centers, national command and control centers, particular countries targeted in the SIOP, and "allied and neutral territory."[92] Special categories of targets have also been delineated for preemptive attacks against the Soviet Union and for launch-on-warning (LOW) or launch-under-attack (LUA) scenarios in the event of unequivocal warning of a Soviet attack.[93]

The requirement to withhold attacks from population centers derives from a policy decision taken in the early 1970s that population per se was no longer to be targeted. The decision is rationalized strategically in terms of the notion of escalation control—defined by the under secretary of defense for defense research and engineering as the maintenance, inter alia, of "our capability to effectively withhold attacks from additional hostage targets highly valued/vital to enemy leaders, thus limiting the level and scope of violence by threatening subsequent destruction."[94] The second "withhold" involves "avoidance of [the] enemy's national command/control,"[95] the primary purpose of which is also to enhance escalation control, both by preserving the USSR's capability to conduct discriminate and controlled nuclear strikes as well as allowing the possibility of negotiating war termination between the U.S. and Soviet national command authorities. The third "withhold" is that regarding particular countries. According to Henry Rowen, the countries targeted in the SIOP have included the "USSR, the People's Republic of China, and allies of these two powers in Eastern Europe and elsewhere."[96] When the SIOP was first created in 1960 there was no provision for an attack on the USSR that did not also involve attacks on China and the satellite countries, but these were separated for targeting purposes during the 1961–62 revision of the plan. The current guidance also prescribes, however, that the United States hold a secure nuclear force in reserve for application against these withholds should that prove necessary.

The general categories and particular types of targets included in the U.S. war plans have remained remarkably resilient from the late 1950s through to the most recent version of the SIOP. They have consisted of the Soviet strategic forces, the Soviet conventional forces, the urban-industrial structure, and the Soviet military and political leadership centers. Two developments have occurred however. One is that the number of potential target installations in the war plans has increased enormously, from a National Strategic Target Data Base (NSTDB) of 4,100 in 1960, of which the JSTPS selected out 2,600 for attack in the first SIOP, to some 50,000 in the NSTDB that supports SIOP-6 today. Second, these targets have been increasingly divided into a large array of "packages" of varying sizes and characteristics, providing the National Command Authorities (NCA) with "customized" options for an extremely wide range of possible contingencies. Regardless of any future changes in declaratory policy, it would be reasonable to expect that these developments would continue to pertain.

[4]

Soviet Nuclear Targeting Strategy

William T. Lee

Introduction

Both the United States and the Soviet Union reject initiation of nuclear war by a surprise attack "out of the blue" as an instrument of national policy. Both expect nuclear war to arise out of a crisis. At the same time, each superpower suspects the other of harboring dark designs for a surprise attack should the circumstances appear propitious or if some desperate and reckless leader should come to power. In all cases, the bottom line is how each superpower proposes to employ or lay down its weapons: What targets are to be attacked? What degree of damage is to be inflicted? What are the politico-military objectives, if any, of strategic nuclear strikes once deterrence has failed for whatever reason?

Public discussions of such matters in the United States are dominated by two images of how the Soviets would use their nuclear weapons. The first, and probably most prevalent, image is that the Soviets would use their weapons in a "mirror image" of the (now outdated) U.S. concept of Assured Destruction—that is, the Soviets would attack U.S. cities with their large weapons in order to inflict as many millions of casualties as possible (countervalue targeting). The second, less prevalent public image stresses the danger of a Soviet attack on U.S. strategic nuclear delivery systems—ICBMs, heavy bombers, and SLBMs in port (counterforce targeting). According to the second image, the Soviets would withhold strikes on U.S. cities to see if the United States would capitulate or negotiate after losing most of its land-based strategic nuclear forces to the Soviet counterforce strike; thus, the fate of U.S. cities would depend upon whether the United States chose to retaliate for the Soviet counterforce strike. However, in both images the Soviets are assumed to target the general U.S. population.

[84]

Both images have persisted even though the United States has long abandoned both its declaratory policy of attacking population and its targeting of the general Soviet industrial establishment.

One of the U.S. objectives in the Strategic Arms Limitation Treaty (SALT) talks has been to constrain or reduce Soviet forces to limit their effectiveness against hard targets. For this reason, the United States has sought to limit the number of "heavy" Soviet missiles threatening its land-based missiles, while granting the Soviets numerical advantages in missiles that are effective only against soft targets. Meanwhile, the United States would have the advantage in the number of small MIRVed warheads which also are effective against "soft" targets.[1]

These U.S. attempts to limit Soviet counterforce capabilities embodied in Soviet heavy ICBMs have failed at every point. Of the nearly 7,000 warheads in the Soviet ready, on-launcher ICBM inventory, excluding refires, over 3,000, or 45 percent of the inventory, are mounted on the Soviet SS-18 ICBM, the only one presently designated officially as a heavy ICBM. Nearly 2,200 more warheads are deployed on the SS-19, officially a "light" ICBM even though its throw weight is about 3.5 times the throw weight of the "light" SS-11 ICBM it has replaced.

In sum, about 80 percent of the Soviet ready, on-launcher ICBM inventory of nearly 7,000 warheads, not counting refires, is deployed on the SS-18 and SS-19 missiles which were designed to destroy the ICBM leg of the U.S. triad. This is not the result of accident, bureaucratic inertia, the parochialism of the Soviet "military-industrial complex," or Kremlin power politics or whims but of sober military planning and clever negotiating tactics at the SALT talks.

This chapter has three basic theses. First, Soviet targeting strategy differs from popular U.S. perceptions, and more so from the purely countervalue perception than from the mixed counterforce-countervalue version. Second, Soviet strategic targeting strategy applies to both Eurasia and the United States. While U.S. strategic planners equate *strategic* with *intercontinental*, the Soviets do so only in the context of SALT, where acceptance of the U.S. definition of *strategic* is in Soviet interests. To the Soviets, Europe and adjacent areas in Asia are strategic dimensions of equal, if not greater, importance than the "transoceanic" dimension. Third, Soviet strategic ballistic missile systems have been designed to meet the requirements of Soviet targeting strategy, and the deployed Soviet forces have been sized and configured accordingly.

SOVIET TARGETING OBJECTIVES

Since World War II the Soviets have consistently argued that the defeat of the adversary's armed forces is the first and primary objective of military operations in a nuclear war. Two typical Soviet statements from the transition period between the death of Stalin, and of his "permanently operating factors," and the Soviet Union's entry into the nuclear missile age are:

> The defeat of the enemy will be achieved above all by means of an annihilation of his armed forces.[2]

> Wars are won only when the enemy's will to resist is broken and that can only be broken, as the experience of history shows, when the armed forces of the enemy are destroyed.

> Therefore, the objective of combat operations must be the destruction of the armed forces and not strategic bombing of targets in the rear.[3]

The first statement was made in 1955 and the second in 1957.

In 1962 the first edition of *Military Strategy*, edited by Marshal V. D. Sokolovsky, specified nuclear targets and priorities as follows:

> These troops (Strategic Rocket Troops) can, if necessary, be used to solve the main problems of war—destruction of the enemy's means of nuclear attack (the basis of his military might), the main formations of his armed forces, and his primary and vitally important objectives.[4]

> The main means of waging war will be massive nuclear-rocket strikes for the purpose of destroying the aggressor's nuclear weapons, for the simultaneous mass destruction of the vitally important objectives constituting the enemy's military, political, and economic potential, for crushing his will to resist, and for winning victory in the shortest possible time.[5]

One of the most authoritative public statements of Soviet strategic strategy was made by the commander of the Strategic Rocket Forces (SRF), Marshal N. Krylov, in September 1967.[6] (Krylov was commander in chief of the SRF from 1963 until his death in 1972.) Consistent with the view that even a nuclear war would be conducted for positive ends, Marshal Krylov stated that the objective of such a war would be "victory" for the USSR. According to Krylov, the principal targets of the SRF would be the enemy's delivery systems, weapons storage, and fabrication sites; military installations; military industries; and centers of politico-military administration, command, and control.

As is readily apparent, this listing of targets, presumably in approximate order of priority, reflects a plan to fight a war rather than to retaliate against cities. It has nothing in common with "maximum fatality" targeting and is not consistent with any simple Assured Destruction objective.[7] The list is, however, consistent with the damage-limiting missions of Soviet forces and with the "victory" objective interpreted as national-entity survival.

Another typical example of Soviet views on the political nature of nuclear war, Soviet nuclear targeting principles, and the ultimate objective sought is the following:

> Thus if the imperialist forces succeed in unleashing a war against the Soviet Union and other socialist countries then it will be a world war, a supreme armed conflict in which both sides will pursue extremely decisive objectives. In its socio-political essence it will be a war of two powerful coalitions of states.
>
> The appearance and development of nuclear missile weapons determined the emergence of a completely new type of war—the nuclear war, which has as its mean method of conduct the inflicting of nuclear strikes against the means of nuclear attack, enemy troop groupings and naval forces, his military objectives, and the centers of governmental and military control simultaneously over the entire territory of the probable enemy, including the transoceanic enemy as well.[8]

"Let everyone know," stated L. I. Brezhnev in his speech on the fiftieth anniversary of Soviet rule, "that in combat against any aggressor the Soviet country will gain a victory deserving of our great nation; worthy of the homeland of October."[9] In his twenty-sixth Party Congress speech (23 February 1981) Brezhnev said there would be no victors in a nuclear war,[10] but this propaganda ploy was corrected for internal audiences in 1981 by an authoritative book, *Party Leadership in Military Matters*.

SOVIET DEFINITIONS OF THEATERS OF MILITARY OPERATIONS

These general principles of Soviet nuclear targeting strategy must be applied to specific geographic areas of strategic military operations. The targets located in each geographic area are not uniform, and Soviet politico-military objectives are not identical in all political areas of conflict. Each area must be analyzed for differences in the targets located therein, as well as for the most vulnerable points of each target, in order to maximize the military effectiveness of the attack with the least collateral damage that is commensurate with Soviet politico-military objectives in that area.

Whereas the prevalent U.S. concept of strategic nuclear operations is limited to intercontinental exchanges, the Soviet concept of strategic operations begins at the USSR's borders. While this geographic definition of *strategic* may be a very natural result of Soviet history, geography, and physical juxtaposition of states that the Soviets regard as their "probable enemies" in the event of nuclear war, it has far-reaching consequences for the size and characteristics of Soviet strategic nuclear forces.

In the Soviet view, "the theater of military operations (TVD) is defined as the land or sea area within the limits of which armed forces during war execute a single strategic mission. The boundaries of probable theaters of war, along the front and in depth, are established in consideration of their political-economic and military-geographic conditions, and also the possibilities of deploying the forces and material on one or more fronts (fleets)."[11] Geographic theaters of military operations (TVDs) may be land or sea areas, or mixtures of the two. Politically, a TVD may include the territory of Soviet-Warsaw Pact countries and "that of the enemy as well," and "its boundaries may change in the course of the war."[12]

To the Soviets, NATO probably represents at least three, and probably four, TVDs (one or two in central Europe and one on each of the north and south flanks) for the conduct of strategic nuclear operations. China, Japan, Korea, and Okinawa probably constitute another TVD (or two). Finally, there is the "transoceanic" TVD, the United States and its military bases in the Atlantic and Pacific basins. Each of these TVDs is equally "strategic," although the central European TVDs may be first among equals in Soviet strategic force and resource planning. The Soviets have deployed, and continue to deploy, four basic types of strategic weapons systems for strategic nuclear operations in all of the prospective TVDs: intermediate and medium range ballistic missiles (IR/MRBMs), submarine launched ballistic missiles (SLBMs), medium and heavy bombers, and ICBMs. In the Soviet scheme of things, all these strategic weapons systems are equally strategic. Moreover, Soviet ICBMs and SLBMs are employed against targets in all TVDs, not just in the transoceanic theater.

APPLICATION OF SOVIET NUCLEAR TARGETING STRATEGY IN THE TVDS

Certain general factors affecting the conduct of strategic nuclear operations in the TVDs are stated in Soviet literature. Although these factors apply to all TVDs, variations probably exist because (1) the Soviets recognize the differences in the target arrays found in each TVD, and (2) Soviet politico-military objectives vary somewhat among the prospective TVDs. The principal factors governing the application of targeting strategy to each TVD appear to be (1) the political objectives set by the Soviet political leaders; (2) the nature and objectives of planned Soviet military operations in each theater; (3) the requirement to limit collateral damage to population, industry, and urban infrastructure commensurate with achieving military objectives; and (4) the choice of the most vulnerable component(s) of the targets to be attacked.

Although these factors have been either explicitly stated or inferred from Soviet unclassified military and political literature for nearly two decades, they have not been widely accepted in the West. Several statements from *Military Thought*, the journal of the Soviet General Staff, deserve to be quoted at length:

> Political factors and the fact that both warring sides have nuclear weapons exert the main influence on the course of the war as a whole and also on the conduct of its basic operations. This is explained, first of all, by the fact that a modern world war, if the imperialists unleash one, will be a struggle between two opposed social systems in which the belligerents will pursue their own decisive political ends. [13]

> Theses of Soviet military strategy primarily reflect the political strategy of the Communist Party of the Soviet Union. It is in the interests of political strategy that military strategy makes use of the achievements of scientific-technical progress which materializes in weapons of varying power. Some of these weapons are capable of doing considerable damage to a continent. Others only to individual states. This would retard the social progress of their peoples for a long time. Finally, still others lead to defeat of the enemy's armed forces without doing essential injury to the economy or populace of states whose aggressive rulers unleashed the war. Only political leadership can determine the scale and consistency of bringing to bear the most powerful means of destruction, in accordance with the interests of all mankind as a whole, the interests of the world communist movement and the national interests of Soviet citizens. . . .

> Of all factors which affect military strategy, the most important are political factors, which determine the nature of armed forces. This influence is due essentially to the role played by the military doctrine of the state, which officially consolidates specific principles, methods and forms of preparing for and waging war in case of an attack by imperialist aggressors. [14]

Another good example of Soviet concern for limiting collateral damage is contained in the following statement:

> The most important task is to correctly determine economic objectives and targets and vulnerable points, and to deliver strikes to those targets where it will lead to disorganization of the enemy economy. The objective is not to turn the large economic and industrial regions into a heap of ruins (although great destruction, apparently, is unavoidable), but to deliver strikes

[89]

which will destroy strategic combat means, paralyze enemy military production, making it incapable of satisfying the priority needs of the front
and rear areas and sharply reduce the enemy capability to conduct strikes.[15]

This general principle of destroying only what is necessary to achieve
Soviet political and military objectives is further expressed in discussions
of what are the most vulnerable (i.e, vital) components of any given
target array. Some of this discussion is related to contemporary economies; some of it appears in Soviet critiques of Allied strategic bombing
operations in World War II.

In planning attacks on industrial target arrays, Col. M. Shirokov stresses
analysis of the regional distribution of industry and interindustry rela-
tionships; the destruction of plants and facilities engaged in the production of missiles, nuclear weapons, and other modern weapons; and
determination of the "quantity of forces and means required for the
destruction of the target and the capabilities of the enemy to rebuild."[16]
He goes on to say that destruction of one or two key branches of transportation may be sufficient to sap or "significantly weaken" a country's
military potential.[17] Similarly, it may not be necessary to attack all the
plants and facilities engaged in missile production, since it is "sufficient
to destroy a few enterprises producing transistors in order to extremely
restrict the production of missiles for all branches of the armed forces."[18]

In general, Shirokov considers the following economic activities to be
the most lucrative targets in terms of prohibiting the enemy from re-
placing the nuclear delivery systems, nuclear weapons, and other military assets to be destroyed as first-priority targets: transportation, power
stations, facilities producing liquid fuels, chemical industries, and selected bottleneck facilities in other industries.[19] Targeting these activities
also limits enemy capabilities to employ surviving military forces
effectively.

As many other Soviet writers have done from time to time, Shirokov
does not consider general attacks on all types of industrial targets to be
either necessary or militarily effective, and he is particularly critical of
the political and military futility of attacking population and cities.

Most of the latter arguments appear in Soviet critiques of Allied strategic air operations in World War II, for which the Soviets display considerable practical and moral disdain. Their analyses of the military effect
of Allied bombing of German and Japanese industry and cities are not
much different from the findings of the U.S. Strategic Bombing Survey,
or from the observations of Albert Speer.[20] The Soviets also note that
until almost the very end of World War II when the Allies systematically
concentrated on German facilities producing liquid fuel and on selected
components of the rail and barge transport systems, German war pro-

duction showed steady growth. (At the same time, the Soviets give the Allied strategic bombing campaign no credit for tying down large German military assets for air defense. If all those fighter aircraft and 88-mm guns had been deployed on the eastern front, Soviet ground campaigns would have suffered greatly.)[21]

As is generally agreed, bombing German cities did not break German civilian morale. Indeed, the bombing may have increased popular support for the German war effort. Shirokov comments at length about U.S. incendiary-bomb attacks on Japanese cities, concluding: "However, these barbarous bombings did not seriously affect enemy morale."[22] He then notes that Hiroshima and Nagasaki "were pointlessly destroyed and burned" and goes on to charge that the bombing of Japanese cities was designed to intimidate the Soviet Union rather than to break Japanese morale.[23] Other Soviet writers have made the same charge about the militarily pointless destruction of Dresden at the close of World War II in Europe.

Finally, Shirokov charges that the United States deliberately refrained from destroying Tokyo because it would have "impeded the U.S. negotiations with the Japanese reactionaries, with whom they proposed to find a common language."[24]

In these discussions on how to conduct nuclear war and target nuclear weapons, the Soviets conspicuously do not consider population and cities valid targets on political, military, and moral grounds. Rather, they consider such targeting concepts as Mutual Assured Destruction to be yet another manifestation of the evils of imperialism. After all, the Soviets want to promote "social progress," not inhibit it, as long as such progress meets their political and social criteria. On the other hand, this does not mean that the Soviets would not target some population groups, such as business and government elites—the "ruling groups" who are the "class enemy"—and possibly selected concentrations of "scientific-technical personnel" as well.[25] But any targeting of selected population groups evidently would meet specific political and military-industrial criteria and would not be extended to the general population, whom the Soviets prefer to preserve if possible.

POSSIBLE VARIATIONS IN TARGETING STRATEGY BY TVD

Just as individual TVDs present different target arrays, Soviet politico-military objectives are not uniform for every TVD. In the European TVDs, Soviet objectives are clear: to defeat and disarm NATO forces and occupy Western Europe in as intact a form as possible. The Soviets want to limit collateral damage to Western Europe for several reasons.

Politically, they wish to bring their version of social progress to Western Europe in the wake of the next war, just as Eastern Europe was "liberated" after World War II.[26] The Soviets continue to express their belief that the next war will be the grave of capitalistic democracies everywhere and will usher in the era of world "socialism." However, they also believe that they can achieve the same objective without nuclear war and would much prefer to do so. As one of their leading military commissars put it recently:

> Peaceful coexistence between nations with a difference in social systems is an essential, mandatory condition for the upward movement of society, to secure progress and its main content—transition from a capitalist to a socialist socio-economic system. . . . The military might of the USSR constitutes a guarantee to peace, for our social system does not contain sources of war. On the other hand, there are constantly operating in the imperialist camp forces capable of disrupting the peace. Sources of war are to be found in the socio-economic system, in the very nature of "Imperialism."[27]

Whether they are to achieve their political objectives by "peaceful coexistence" or as the outcome of war, the Soviets need strategic nuclear forces commensurate with those objectives. This means the acquisition of forces that will accomplish the necessary military objectives but that will not destroy the human, social, and economic basis for the socio-economic system that is to replace "imperialism."[28] They are not likely to negotiate away the right to acquire such forces in strategic arms reduction talks.

There are two other very practical considerations guiding Soviet nuclear targeting in the European TVDs. First, the prevailing winds are westerly, so it is very much in the Soviet interest to target selectively, avoiding "overkill" with large weapons in order to limit fallout, not only on Eastern Europe and the Soviet Union but also on the Soviet–Warsaw Pact occupation forces. Second, the Soviets could make good use of Europe's economic resources during the course of military operations, thereby helping to rebuild their own resources in the aftermath of a nuclear war:

> The destructive nature of modern warfare, the difficulty of transporting material means from the depth of a country and the great vulnerability of rear area organs make it necessary to devote serious attention to a study of the possibilities for acquiring local resources in theaters of military operations. For this purpose, it is very important to determine which targets and enemy economic regions should be left intact or rapidly reconstructed and used in the interests of strengthening the economic potential of our own country and for supplying the troops. It is also important to determine

which, what, where and in what quantity the local resources can be stored and used in the interest of the troops.[29]

In the Far East, Soviet objectives probably would be more complex. They might wish to occupy sparsely populated regions outside the Great Wall, and possibly Manchuria, but they probably consider it quite infeasible to occupy China proper, where the population density would support a "people's war." In the latter area, the Soviets probably would use strategic nuclear force to disarm the country and to destroy sufficient industrial and transportation facilities to insure that China would not become a threat—nuclear or otherwise—to the Soviet Union for some time. Against Japan, on the other hand, Soviet targeting might be much more selective because Japan, like Europe, could contribute to Soviet postattack recovery.

Finally, there is the question of the "transoceanic" TVD. All the known evidence explicitly or implicitly indicates that Soviet nuclear targeting strategy for the United States is the same as for other TVDs. On the other hand, since the Soviets have no ambition to occupy the United States, they must seek not only to destroy its existing military forces at the beginning of the war but also to prevent it from reconstituting those forces. Hence, Soviet targeting of industry might be more extensive in the United States than in Europe. In all TVDs, however, Soviet literature indicates that Soviet nuclear targeting would be selective with regard both to the targets attacked and to the degree of damage inflicted.[30]

ORIGINS OF SOVIET TARGETING STRATEGY AND DEVELOPMENT OF STRATEGIC NUCLEAR DELIVERY SYSTEMS

Despite his public statements denigrating nuclear weapons and the internal restrictions that he imposed on discussions of their military significance, Stalin probably understood their political and military potential quite well. He spared no effort to develop nuclear weapons as rapidly as possible and gave equal priority to the acquisition of strategic nuclear delivery systems. Soviet nuclear targeting strategy evidently was formulated in the late 1940s or early 1950s by Long Range Aviation in anticipation of having nuclear weapons.[31]

It is often forgotten that soon after World War II, the Soviets produced a large force of strategic bombers copied after the U.S. B-29 aircraft that came to earth in the Soviet Far East during U.S. bombing attacks on Japan. The medium and heavy jet bombers that shocked the United States when they appeared in the mid-1950s, and which precipitated the "bomber gap," were the result of programs initiated under Stalin.

[93]

General V. Tolubko, commander of Soviet Strategic Rocket Troops since 1972, has thrown fresh light on Stalin's appreciation of both nuclear weapons and strategic missile delivery systems, and on the participation of L. I. Brezhnev in associated developmental programs.[32] The first operational unit for future ballistic missile delivery systems was formed in 1946 on the basis of a tactical rocket regiment.[33] Research organizations and design bureaus for ballistic missiles were formed around a scientific-engineering cadre of people—S. P. Korolev, M. K. Iangel, V. P. Glushko, G. N. Babakin, and others—who became the chief designers of many contemporary Soviet strategic missile and space systems.[34] Shortly after World War II, a supraministerial organization charged with missile development was attached directly to the USSR Council of Ministers.[35] Among those who served on that board of missile czars were such prominent marshals of the Soviet Union as G. K. Zhukov and R. Ia. Malinovskiy, as well as Chief Marshals of Artillery N. N. Voronov and M. I. Nedelin.[36] Two nominal civilians who served as missile czars were L. I. Brezhnev, general secretary of the Communist party from 1964 and marshal of the Soviet Union from 1976 until his death in 1982, and D. F. Ustinov, Central Committee member of the Military Industrial Commission (VPK) for more than a decade and marshal of the Soviet Union and minister of defense since 1976.[37]

As a result of the organizational efforts begun under Stalin, the Soviets were able to arm some of their missile units with nuclear weapons in the mid-1950s.[38] These units apparently included not only tactical missiles but also the first Soviet strategic missile, the MRBM designated the SS-3 by the United States and NATO. Operationally, all the strategic missiles— the early SS-3 and later SS-4 MRBMs—may have been under Long Range Aviation before the Strategic Rocket Troops were formed as a new branch of service in 1960. Alternatively, the early strategic missile units may have been directly controlled by the Council of Defense.[39] In any case, from the beginning, the missile units evidently shared Long Range Aviation's (LRA) nuclear targeting strategy and carried it over to the Strategic Rocket Forces (SRF). This is the targeting strategy as stated in the 1960s by Marshals Sokolovsky and Krylov; it has remained essentially unchanged to this day.

It is essential to understand that when formed in 1960, the SRF consisted entirely of MRBM units, with the exception of a handful of SS-6 ICBMs, and that until 1968–69 the SRF had more IR/MRBMs than ICBMs. Thus, early Soviet missile targeting focused on the European and Asian TVDs. The transoceanic TVD came later for two reasons. First, the Soviets consistently have given first priority to targeting the more proximate threat in the Eurasian TVDs. Second, the latter contained few hard targets whereas the transoceanic TVD contained some twelve hundred

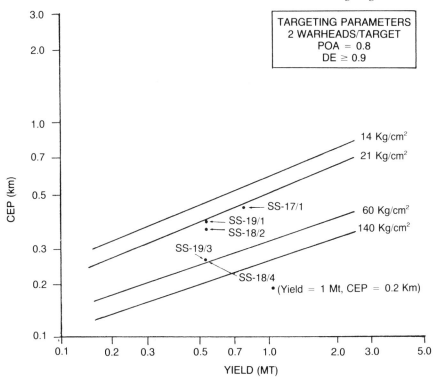

Figure 4.1. CEP versus yield to achieve DE ≥ 0.9

hard targets by the early 1960s. Consequently the Soviets were able to satisfy their strategic nuclear targeting requirements in the Eurasian TVDs by the mid-1960s with the deployment of more than seven hundred IR/MRBMs with single warheads and refire missiles. But it has taken the Soviets nearly three decades, and accurate MIRV technologies, to satisfy their strategic targeting requirements in the transoceanic TVD.

DESIGNING MISSILES TO TARGETING REQUIREMENTS

According to a treatise on the design and testing of ballistic missiles published in 1970, Soviet missiles are designed to destroy typical targets. Deployed ballistic missiles are employed in accordance with targeting strategy and tactics "in accordance with the accepted military doctrine."[40]

This claim to consistency between theory and practice is substantiated by the historical record of Soviet ICBM MIRV development. Figure 4.1

has been developed by G. Binninger and J. Powers of Science Application, Inc., to show the relationship between yield and accuracy (CEP) for damage expectancy of more than 0.9 for two weapons per target when total weapons systems reliability (probability of arrival or POA) is equal to 0.8 and target hardness varies from 14 kg/cm² (200 psi) to 140 kg/cm² (2,000 psi).[41] Plotted on figure 4.1 are the points corresponding to the yield/CEP values reported by John Collins for the Soviet SS-17, SS-18, and SS-19 MIRVed ICBMs.[42] It should be noted that the Soviet first-generation MIRVs deployed in 1974–76 fall on the 14 kg/cm² (300 psi) vulnerability line while the second-generation MIRVs (SS-18 Mod 4 and SS-19 Mod 3) fall on the 60 kg/cm² (850 psi) line. Moreover, if figure 4.1 were replotted for a three-weapons-per-target attack, the SS-18 Mod 4 and SS-19 Mod 3 (.25 km CEP, 0.5 Mt) would fall on the 140 kg/cm² (2,000 psi) line.

Binninger and Powers have traced the Soviet perception of the advertised hardness of U.S. ICBM silos in Soviet literature. In the 1960s the Soviets credited Minuteman silos with their advertised vulnerability—21 kg/cm² (300 psi). All three Soviet first-generation MIRVs began development in 1965–66 after the technology had been demonstrated by two space shots in 1964. In the early 1970s the United States upgraded Minuteman silos to about 2,000 psi. Not surprisingly, the Soviets matched the upgrade, primarily by improving the accuracy of the SS-18 and SS-19, for two- or three-weapons-per-target attacks on each Minuteman silo.

Such correspondence between the capabilities of successful Soviet ICBM models and the changing vulnerability of U.S. Minuteman silos is not likely coincidental. But is has taken the Soviets a long time to develop such missiles and to deploy enough of them to meet Soviet damage objectives against the large numbers of hard targets located in the transoceanic TVD.

SOVIET STRATEGIC MISSILE AND WARHEAD INVENTORIES

Consider the size and composition between Soviet strategic missile forces in 1970 when the SALT process had just begun and Soviet forces in 1983–85 after fifteen years of "arms control" and within the limits of the SALT II Treaty. The launcher and ready warhead inventories are shown in table 4.1. The IR/MRBM upper limit for warheads includes one refire missile because such soft launchers can be reused very quickly. ICBM and SLBM inventories in table 4.1 do not include refire missiles, although extra missiles are stocked, because a few days probably would be required to ready the launchers for the second round. Thus, the total

Soviet strategic missile warhead inventory is much larger, perhaps by as much as a factor of two or more, than the ready inventory shown in table 4.1.

As has been noted, Soviet MIRVed missiles have been designed and developed to destroy hard targets—specifically, U.S. ICBMs, French IRBMs, and strategic missiles of the People's Republic of China similarly protected. Around 1960 the SS-9 was also designed to destroy hard targets, specifically the one hundred Launch Control Centers that, until the mid-1960s, were the "Achilles heel" of the U.S. Minuteman force. But as deployment of the SS-9 began in 1966, the United States removed the Achilles heel by deploying airborne launch control systems (ALCS) that could launch Minuteman missiles directly from the silos. This frustrated Soviet targeting strategy for nearly two decades but did nothing to persuade the Soviets to change their counterforce, warfighting strategy.

These inventories can be matched to the probable Soviet perception of the target arrays to demonstrate that the Soviets have sized the deployments of their strategic missile forces to the requirements of their targeting strategy. But to make that connection it is necessary first to consider the operational principles and damage objectives of Soviet strategic nuclear missiles for attacks on hard and soft targets.

OPERATIONAL PRINCIPLES AND DAMAGE OBJECTIVE

As described in Soviet literature, the Soviets apply their nuclear targeting stratecy according to the following operational principles:

Destroy most threatening enemy forces, that is, those enemy forces most capable of denying Soviet objectives.

Select main "links" and nodes in target sets, for example, enemy national command authority.

Do not destroy large areas or create radioactive deserts.

Use minimum yields ("explosive power") depending on target and delivery system characteristics; that is, the nuclear warhead delivered to a target should not drastically "overkill" the target.

Targeting of population and all industry is unnecessarily destructive and not effective.

Strike simultaneously in several TVDs.

Prepare to strike "most important" targets twice.

Political leaders determine relative weight of strikes in the various TVDs.

Thus, the principles of nuclear force application are consistent with, and follow from, the general tenets of doctrine and strategy. The enemy

Table 4.1. Soviet Strategic Missiles, Warheads Inventories

System	1970		1984–1985	
	Launcher	Warheads	Launcher	Warheads
IR/MRBM				
SS-4/5	650	650–1,300[a]	50–100	50–200[a]
SS-20	—	—	400–450	1,200–2,700[a]
Subtotal	650	650–1,300[a]	450–550	1,250–2,900
ICBMs				
SS-7/8	209	209	—	—
SS-11/13	990	990	580	580–800
SS-17	—	—	150	600
SS-9	228	228	—	—
SS-18	—	—	308	3,080
SS-19	—	—	360	2,160
Subtotal	1,427	1,427	1,398	6,420–6,640
SLBMs				
SS-N-5	102	102	48	48
SS-N-6/8	208	208	634–670	900–950
SS-N-18	—	—	240–256	1,360–1,472
SS-N-20	—	—	40–60	400–600
Subtotal	310	310	998	2,708–3,070
TOTAL ICBM & SLBM	1,740	1,740	2,400	9,130–9,710
GRAND TOTAL	2,390	2,390–3,040	2,840–2,940	10,380–12,610

[a]As has been reported by many sources, including the second edition of *Soviet Military Power* (p. 21), most, if not all, Soviet strategic missiles have refire rounds. Refurbishing silo launchers for a second launch, however, is a matter of a few days. Soft IR/MRBM launchers, on the other hand, can be refurbished for a second launch in a few hours, if not minutes. Consequently, it is reasonable to include one IR/MRBM round in the on-line strategic missile warhead inventory because of the initial strategic nuclear exchange.

Sources: The data for 1970 are from John M. Collins, *U.S.–Soviet Military Balance: Concepts and Capabilities, 1960–1980* (McGraw-Hill, New York, 1980), pp. 443, 448–449, 461; U.S. Department of Defense, *Soviet Military Power*, 2d ed. (Washington, D.C., 1983), pp. 14, 19, 21–23. The 1984–85 data are author's projecions based on Collins and Patrick M. Cronin, *U.S./Soviet Military Balance: Statistical Trends, 1970–1983 (As of January 1, 1984)* (Congressional Research Service, Washington, D.C., 1984), p. 37.

Notes: Sources report a three-warhead MRV payload for the SS-11 and the SS-N-6 as well as three and seven MIRV payloads for the SS-N-18. The Department of Defense (see Sources) indicates that the SS-N-20 MIRV delivers ten RVS (p. 21). However, neither DOD nor John Collins (see Sources) reports the proportion of SS-11 and SS-N-6 launcher inventories equipped with the MRV payloads, or the proportion of SS-N-18s that are equipped with the single RV or the three and seven RV MIRV payloads. The ranges shown here are the author's estimates, which attempt to bound these uncertainties.

is to be defeated by destroying his military forces and by preventing force reconstitution. But the enemy's society is not to be destroyed by attacking the general population and by indiscriminate attacks on urban areas and industrial plants because to do so would vitiate Soviet nuclear war objectives discussed earlier. One cannot make the world safe for "socialism" by destroying it.

Soviet damage criteria and objectives for hard and soft targets may be summarized as follows:[43]

Probability of kill applies to hard targets and to most other elements of enemy nuclear forces. This may be translated into damage expectancy (DE) by taking into account weapon system reliability.

The Soviets evidently seek high levels of damage expectancy (0.9 or better), as shown and as is evident from examples given in Soviet literature.[44]

For most soft targets damage objectives are defined as the percentage of the target area covered to the requisite degree of overpressure (psi). At least two options are specified: "neutralization" at 10 to 30 percent coverage and "annihilation" at 50 to 70 percent coverage of the target area to the requisite overpressure level.

Three damage definitions are specified for soft targets: light, moderate, and severe. Light damage requires minor repair. Moderate damage requires major (capital) repair; severe damage requires replacement. Typical urban-industrial structures and equipment suffer moderate damage at overpressures of 4.5 to 10 psi, which the Soviets evidentally consider adequate for strategic targeting purposes.

The area coverage objectives—neutralization and annihilation—are presented as options. Soviet literature indicates that the Supreme High Command (VGK), composed of the top political and military leaders, would decide on the damage objective options to be applied to various types of soft targets in each TVD. The literature further suggests that the VGK's choice options would be scenario dependent but offers no other clues as to the situations in which Soviet damage objectives would be neutralization or annihilation of soft targets. As will be demonstrated, there are significant differences in yield requirements for these alternative damage objectives. Most important, however, the yields required to achieve these Soviet damage objectives against soft targets usually are much lower than the yields ascribed to Soviet missiles by Western sources.

ESTIMATE OF THE TARGET ARRAYS IN
THE EURASIAN AND TRANSOCEANIC TVDs

By 1965–66 the Soviets had deployed more than seven hundred SS-4/5 missile launchers, about six hundred of which were in the western USSR. When SS-11 ICBMs were deployed in the IR/MRBM fields in the late 1960s, about one hundred SS-4/5s were retired, obviously because the SS-11s had taken over targeting assignments from these IR/MRBMs. Subsequently, deployment has been fairly stable at around six hundred launchers as the SS-20s were phased in, although the number deployed in the western USSR declined to about five hundred in the early 1980s, about half of which are SS-20s.[45]

Deployment of the SS-11s in the SS-4/5 fields in the late 1960s probably was the Soviet response to French deployment of IRBM missiles in silos and to actual or anticipated initial PRC deployment of strategic missiles. The French action raised the number of hard targets in NATO from a few to about twenty, and the SS-4s and SS-5s were too inaccurate to be effective against silos. By the end of the 1970s the PRC had 90 to 120 strategic missiles deployed, presumably also in hardened installations.[46]

These deployment patterns have an obvious inference: the Soviets counted about 750 targets in the Eurasian TVDs according to their targeting strategy as previously described. About 600 of these targets were in NATO. The deployments matched the target arrays. Each launcher with one refire round could put two warheads on each target, thus providing high confidence that the target would be destroyed. Additional refire rounds would hedge against attrition of SS-4/5 launchers if the Soviets did not succeed in preempting.

Except for hardened French IR/MRBMs and PRC strategic missiles, the target arrays in the Eurasian TVDs have changed little in two decades. The changes that have occurred have been accommodated by assigning ICBMs to these targets and by deployment of the SS-20. With the CEP of 360 meters at full range, the SS-20 is a fairly accurate system.[47] However, most of the hard targets in the Eurasian TVDs are located at less than full range from SS-20 bases, and hence the CEP of the system at actual range to target could be as low as 200 to 250 meters, making the SS-20 an effective hard target system in many cases. (The accuracy of inertially guided systems varies directly with range to target, given generic errors in target location and dispersion of warheads by atmospheric effects from reentry to impact.)

In sum, around 1970 there probably were about 750 targets for Soviet strategic missiles in the Eurasian TVDs, about 600 of which were in NATO. Only a handfull of these targets were hardened. As of mid-1983 there has been little or no change in the target arrays in the NATO TVDs. However, the PRC arrays probably have changed significantly. Assuming the Chinese have hardened their strategic missile launchers, the number of hard targets in the Eurasian TVDs probably has grown from about 20 in 1970 to about 130 to 150 by mid-1983.[48] The number of soft targets in the PRC and elsewhere in the Far Eastern TVD is more difficult to estimate. It is reasonable to assume 200 to 300 in mid-1983 as compared to about 150 in the 1960s. In round numbers, this gives 900 to 1,100 strategic targets in the Eurasian TVDs in 1983, about 15 percent of which are hardened.

It may also be possible to determine reasonable approximation of the Soviet view of the strategic target arrays in the transoceanic TVD by following the principles of Soviet targeting strategy and using data readily available from various sources. The approximate number of hard targets in the transoceanic TVD is well known. The United States has some 1,150 ICBM silos and 100 Minuteman Launch Control Centers. There are another 50 hardened command, control, and communications facilities and nuclear weapons storage facilities, making the total number of hard targets in the United States about 1,200.

The U.S. army, navy, and air force have about 475 camps, airfields, naval bases, ports and terminals, depots, and other military installations. About 150 industrial facilities have contracts with the U.S. Department of Defense to provide $1 million or more of military hardware end items each year. Most military R&D is co-located with these military end item suppliers. The U.S. Department of Energy lists some 1,700 electric power generating plants in the United States and nearly 200 petroleum refineries. But about 325 of the power plants generate about 70 percent of the electricity, and 70 to 80 percent of the refineries produce about the same percentage of U.S. refined petroleum products, thus making a fuel and energy package of about 400 installations. This leaves only chemical plants, and some transport, communications, and command centers not already counted as military installations, on the Soviet targeting list. The U.S. chemical plant list is long but not many of these facilities are vital to U.S. military production, and many of the other facilities the Soviets are likely to target with their strategic missiles already have been counted as military ports, depots, and terminals. Moreover, many of these soft targets are co-located so that one weapon (aim point) will account for two or more of them. In sum, the military and economic soft target arrays required to neutralize the United States as a military power probably amount to 1,000 to 1,200 targets.

Given these estimates of the target arrays in the various TVDs, following the precepts of Soviet targeting strategy and principles of force application we can match the inventory in table 4.1 with target arrays

Table 4.2. Critical Characteristics of Soviet Strategic Missile Systems

	Accuracy (CEP in meters)	Nominal Yield (Mt)	No. of RVs[a]
Hard target systems			
SS-17 Mod 1	440	0.75	4
SS-18 Mod 2,4	420,260	1.9,0.5	8,10
SS-19 Mod 1,3	380,260	0.55,0.5	6
SS-20 Mod 1,3	360	0.15	3
Soft target systems			
SS-4	2,270	1.0	1
SS-5	1,270	1.0	1
SS-11 Mod 1,3	1,380,1,090	0.5–1.0	1,3
SS-13	1,820	0.6	1
SS-N-5	2,730	1.0,2.0	1
SS-N-6 Mod 1,3	1,270	0.5–1.0	1,3
SS-N-8	1,450	0.5–1.0	1
SS-N-18 Mod 1,3	1,360	1.0–?	3,7
SS-N-20		?	10

[a]MIRVed versions; the SS-11 and the SS-N-6 have a three-RV multiple reentry vehicle version.

Sources: Collins, *U.S.-Soviet Military Balance*, pp. 446, 453, 461; U.S. Department of Defense, *Soviet Military Power*, pp. 19–21.

and calculate the required laydown in the implicit reserves. Table 4.2 presents the characteristics of the systems that comprise the inventory.

As has been noted, according to the precepts of Soviet targeting strategy there probably are about 800 to 900 soft targets for Soviet strategic missile forces in the Eurasian TVDs at the present time. One warhead arriving on these targets will achieve Soviet damage criteria. Allocating two warheads to each target provides, for any weapon system, reliability greater than or equal to 0.8, more than 90 percent assurance that one weapon will arrive on each target. Thus, the required laydown on the soft target arrays in the Eurasian TVDs is about 1,600 to 1,800 warheads. The two-round SS-4, SS-5, and SS-20 inventory from table 4.2 is 2,500 warheads, or 700 to 900 more than required for very high confidence attacks on the soft target arrays in the Eurasian TVDs, not counting additional refire missiles or any assistance from Soviet ICBM and SLBM forces.

In other words, Soviet IR/MRBM forces alone are quite adequate to meet with high assurance Soviet targeting requirements against the soft target arrays in the Eurasian TVDs, while providing an excess of 700 to 900 warheads, allowing for one refire round. However, this still leaves some 120 to 150 hard targets in the Eurasian TVDs.

In the case of these hard targets, warhead allocations are sensitive to target vulnerability as well as to the degree of assurance desired. As previously noted, the SS-20 is a fair hard target killer at the full range CEP of 360 meters but is more effective if the range to target is less than the SS-20s full range of about 5,000 km. If the hard targets in the Eurasian TVDs typically are 2,000 psi, as in the United States, then the high-assurance allocation is three (or more) warheads per target (depending upon the range to target). On the other hand, if the hard targets in the Eurasian TVDs typically are about 1,000 psi, then two SS-20 warheads per target might well be effective, that is, provide a high assurance of destroying the target in the case of those targets located at less than full SS-20 range. Most hard targets in the Eurasian TVDs probably are at about one-half range.

In the case of some 120 to 150 hard targets in the Eurasian TVDs, at least 140 to 450 SS-20 warheads would be required. With 700 to 950 ready warheads remaining when soft target requirements are met, this is a thin reserve margin, particularly when (*a*) all of the warheads allocated to the hard targets must be SS-20s (since the SS-4 and SS-5 MR/IRBMs are not effective against hard targets); (*b*) some Eurasian targets may be hardened to more than 2,000 psi; and (*c*) some large-area soft targets may require more than two SS-20 warheads for high-confidence attacks, particularly if the Soviets follow their minimum yield principle.

On balance, it seems that Soviet IR/MRBMs alone can satisfy Soviet strategic target objectives in Eurasia, allowing two rounds per launcher, but would not provide a sufficient reserve or insurance against attrition by U.S.-NATO counterforce strikes. Some help from Soviet ICBMs and SLBMs is required and doubtless would be forthcoming. The SS-19s may well target most, if not all, hard targets in the Eurasian TVDs. Soviet SLBMs, particularly the SS-N-5 and SS-N-6, also would supplement the IR/MRBMs in targeting some of the soft targets in the Eurasian TVDs. When these factors are taken into account, Soviet strategic missile forces in the Eurasian TVDs are quite adequate for high-confidence attacks—two-on-one for soft targets and three-on-one for hard targets—on all of the strategic target arrays in these TVDs while providing an IR/MRBM reserve of several hundred warheads, not counting additional refire missiles which may well provide another 2,500 warheads.

In the transoceanic TVD most of the 1,200 hard targets are Minuteman silos rated at about 2,000 psi. As we have seen, the SS-18 Mod 4 and the SS-19 Mod 3 can destroy these targets, with high assurance, by allocating three warheads to each target. Under the SALT II limitations on SS-18 launchers and MIRVed ICBMs, the Soviets have some 5,200 warheads on these missiles, not counting refires. Assuming a three-on-one laydown on all 1,200 hard targets in the transoceanic TVD, the requirement is 3,600 warheads, which leaves a reserve of 1,600. As previously noted, however, SS-19s probably will be used against at least part of the hard target arrays in the Eurasian TVDs. If it is assumed that 250 to 450 warheads are allocated to these latter targets, the SS-18/19 hard target reserve, for all TVDs, probably is about 1,150 to 1,350 warheads.

High-confidence attacks on the estimated 1,000 to 1,200 soft targets in the Eurasian TVDs requires 2,000 to 2,400 weapons. The Soviet soft target ICBM inventory, not counting refires, consists of 1,500 to 1,700 SS-11, SS-13, and SS-17 ICBM warheads (see table 4.1). This is insufficient for high-confidence targeting of the 1,000 to 1,200 soft targets in the transoceanic TVDs. On the other hand, by 1984–85 the Soviets may have some 2,700 to 3,000 warheads in their SLBM forces, more than enough to (*a*) bring the total laydown on the soft targets in the transoceanic TVD up from 1,500 to 1,700 warheads to 2,000 to 2,400; (*b*) allow for SLBMs in repair and overhaul; (*c*) compensate for some SLBM warheads allocated to the target arrays in the Eurasian TVDs; and (*d*) provide a large secure reserve with which to conduct military operations after the initial exchange and to dominate the postwar world.

For high confidence with respect to the hard target arrays in both the Eurasian and transoceanic TVDs, the Soviets need all the warhead yield they can get. If the Soviets could pack more megatonnage into their hard target systems than the Western estimates stated in table 4.2, they probably would. Effectiveness against hard targets is more sensitive to accuracy than to yield by approximately a ratio of 5:1. Nevertheless, packing the most yield into the warhead technology is one way of hedging against unexpected accuracy degradation.

Effective attacks on soft target arrays, on the other hand, require much lower yields, by Soviet soft target damage criteria, than the yields commonly ascribed to Soviet soft target capable IR/MRBMs, SLBMs, and ICBMs. Moreover, effectiveness against soft targets is not very sensitive to large CEP degradations once CEP is reduced to about 400 to 500 meters. As has been noted, the most stringent Soviet damage criteria against soft targets is 50 to 70 percent coverage of the target area. And Soviet damage objectives against most soft targets are satisfied by overpressures of 4 to 10 psi. Moreover, most soft targets do not exceed 100 square kilometers in area. Thus, it is possible to compare the effectiveness against soft targets at reported yields-to-accuracy (CEPs) and with yields required to achieve Soviet targeting objectives for area coverage of soft targets.

Consider first the expected value coverage of soft area targets with reported yields and CEPs as shown in table 4.3 for the low end of the spectrum of soft target vulnerability—4.5 psi. It should be noted that target area coverage at this overpressure is unity (100 percent) or nearly

Table 4.3. Expected Value of Target Area Coverage at 4.5 PSI

	Systems CEP Meters	Yield Mt	Reported Yields		
			5	10	20
First-generation system					
SS-4	2,000	1.0	0.99	0.98	0.96
SS-5	750	1.0	1.0	1.0	1.0
SS-7	2,000	5.0	1.0	1.0	1.0
Second- and third-generation system					
SS-11	1,300	1.5	1.0	1.0	1.0
SS-N-6	1,300	0.6	1.0	1.0	1.0
SS-17	550	0.6	1.0	1.0	1.0
SS-N-8	1,500	1.5	1.0	1.0	1.0
SS-N-18 MIRV	900	0.15	1.0	1.0	1.0
SS-20	450	0.15	1.0	1.0	0.96

Note: Target area is km^2. The yields and CEPs shown here constitute a representative range of those reported from various Western sources, such as the International Institute of Strategic Studies, in addition to Collins as cited in table 4.2. The analysis is not sensitive, for all practical purposes, to those yields in this table and in table 4.4 that differ from the yields in table 4.2.

so, in all cases, whereas Soviet annihilation requires 50 to 70 percent coverage and neutralization requires 10 to 30 percent coverage.

The effectiveness of Soviet strategic missile systems against the typical upper limit for soft target vulnerability, 10 psi, is presented in table 4.4. It is again apparent that Soviet systems equal or exceed Soviet annihilation objectives, even for the most inaccurate systems, against targets

Table 4.4. Expected Value of Target Coverage Range at 10 PSI

	System CEP Meters	Yield Mt	Reported Yields		
			5	10	20
First-generation system					
SS-4	2,000	1.0	0.69	0.65	0.57
SS-5	750	1.0	1.0	0.98	0.88
SS-7	2,000	5.0	0.97	0.96	0.93
Second- and third-generation system					
SS-11	1,300	1.5	0.96	0.92	0.84
SS-N-6	1,300	0.6	0.82	0.74	0.61
SS-17	550	0.6	1.0	0.97	0.78
SS-N-8	1,500	1.5	0.92	0.88	0.79
SS-N-18 MIRV	900	0.15	0.67	0.52	0.33
SS-20	450	0.15	0.89	0.65	0.35

Note: See table 4.3 notes.

Table 4.5. Expected Value of Area Coverage

CEP Meters	Yield Mt	Reported Yields		
		5	10	20
4.5 psi				
2,000	0.05	0.43	0.39	0.33
1,000	0.05	0.81	0.71	0.57
500	0.05	0.98	0.88	0.58
2,000	0.15	0.70	0.65	0.55
1,000	0.15	0.98	0.94	0.82
500	0.15	1.0	1.0	1.0
10 psi				
2,000	0.15	0.28	0.28	0.21
1,000	0.18	0.62	0.49	0.32
500	0.15	0.86	0.63	0.35
2,000	0.5	0.52	0.48	0.41
1,000	0.5	0.89	0.80	0.62
500	0.15	1.0	0.96	0.73

Note: Target area is km².

having an area of 5 to 10 km², and even 20 km² in many cases. Very few area targets fall into the latter category.

Consider now the yields required to achieve Soviet damage objectives against soft area targets with three CEP values—2,000, 1,000, and 500 meters as shown in table 4.5. As is evident from these calculations, when CEP drops to 400 meters or less, Soviet annihilation damage objectives are achieved by warheads having yields of 50 to 150 kt for most area targets. Soviet neutralization objectives can be achieved by even smaller yields. Even at a CEP of 1,000 meters, few targets require yields greater than 500 kt.

It is likely, therefore, that Soviet strategic missile systems designed (or assigned) to attack soft targets have carried much smaller yields than normally are reported. The latter probably represent estimates of the highest yield that could be packed into a given reentry vehicle (RV). Certainly the reported yields are not based on what is required to achieve Soviet damage objectives against soft targets. Hard targets, of course, are another story. As has been noted, when shooting at hard targets a prudent planner is well advised to pack as much yield into the RVs as technology and the supply of nuclear materials permit.

There are many reasons why the Soviets might observe their minimum yield principles when attacking soft targets. First, the Soviets believe a nuclear war with the U.S.-NATO coalition will have a positive military and political outcome. The Soviets and their allies will win; 'capitalism' will be destroyed and 'socialism' will become the universal political system. Second, even air bursts create considerable amounts of fission residue. And in the Northern Hemisphere the winds blow from west to east. Third, the Soviets need West European economic assets to help them recover. For example, a high confidence, two-on-one attack on 600 NATO targets with SS-4 and SS-5 strategic missiles using required instead of reported yields reduces the laydown from some 1,200 to 300–600 Mt. Using only the 250 SS-20 launchers deployed against NATO, the laydown using required yields drops to 100 to 200 Mt, which is one reason the Soviets are reluctant to give up their SS-20s.

Multiple warheads and greater accuracy reduce the required laydown against both hard and soft targets, for the same or greater effectiveness in all TVDs. This explains the Soviet affinity for a relatively large number of MIRVed missiles and, given the number of hard targets around, the Soviet requirements for very effective, high-confidence attacks and the large aggregate throw weight of the Soviet strategic missile inventory.

CONCLUSIONS

Soviet strategic missiles have been designed to achieve Soviet target objectives against hard and soft targets in all TVDs. The design criteria have been derived from Soviet nuclear targeting strategy.

Soviet nuclear targeting strategy is consistent with the Soviet objective to fight and "win" a nuclear war. This strategy rejects all the premises of U.S. Assured Destruction targeting and most of the premises of U.S. "countervalue" targeting strategies.

Soviet nuclear targeting strategy has changed little, if at all, since it was formulated around 1950. The strategy applies to all TVDs although there may be some variations in its execution, in particular TVDs depending upon the scenario and the decisions of the top Soviet political leadership.

Soviet strategic missile forces have been sized to the requirements of the targeting strategy with due allowance for scenario uncertainties and the requirement for a large secure reserve. The forces necessary to achieve Soviet targeting objectives in the Eurasian TVDs were deployed by the mid-1960s; but because of the large number of hard targets in the continental United States, the Soviets were not able to field the necessary forces for the transoceanic TVD until the mid-1980s.

The Soviets negotiated the SALT I and SALT II ceilings on their strategic missile forces to accommodate their targeting requirements. Any reductions in these force levels which the Soviets are likely to agree to will depend on the availability of technology that will reduce Soviet force requirements for high-confidence achievement of their targeting objectives, or changes in targeting requirements due to reductions in the size

[107]

of the target arrays, or the degree of protection provided by hardening, or some combination of these factors.

The Soviets are not likely to agree to any force level for their strategic missile forces in START that will endanger their capabilities to achieve their targeting objectives in all TVDs while also maintaining a large secure reserve force except, perhaps, in return for a total ban on deployment of ballistic missile defenses developed under President Reagan's Strategic Defense Initiative. The Soviet negotiating positions concerning so-called strategic forces in START and so-called theater nuclear forces in TNF are inextricably linked whatever the formalities of the negotiating forums may be.

[5]

British Nuclear Targeting

Lawrence Freedman

The priorities for British nuclear targeting are perfectly clear although the details are shrouded in secrecy. Recent debates on the future of the British nuclear force have revealed an official preoccupation with the quality rather than the quantity of targets threatened. Thus there has been some embarrassment at the prospect of large numbers of independently targetable warheads—a feature of the proposed Trident force—while there has been a notable stress on the ability to attack Moscow. The actual mechanisms of British targeting, by contrast, have been discussed hardly at all, such that an extremely thorough book on Britain's nuclear force published in 1970 could only presume that British targeting plans were separate from those formulated by the Joint Strategic Target Planning Staff in Omaha, Nebraska.[1]

Moreover, even in the area of likely targets, where much can be inferred from past pronouncements and programs, it has not been policy to confirm the inferences. As one senior official has explained: "I think it has been the preference of Governments to allow them [the Soviet Union] to draw their own conclusions rather than to describe precisely what our plans and capability would be in terms of targeting policy."[2]

This chapter explains the development of British targeting policy over the postwar period and provides such information as is available on the targeting process. Such a historical approach should demonstrate the deep roots of the essentially countercity philosophy adopted by Britain and the tension this seems to have generated with the requirements imposed by the assignment of forces to NATO.

During World War II the choice of appropriate targets for the bomber offensive was an extremely controversial topic. The argument was won by those in RAF Bomber Command who claimed that the most decisive contribution that air power could make to the war was to attack directly the German civilian population. The consequent damage to enemy morale would undermine the readiness to continue the war. Alternative strategies were dismissed as "panaceas." The limited achievement of this strategy became the subject of a vigorous postwar debate,[3] but those RAF officers responsible, many of whom later took on responsibility for Britain's nuclear capability, displayed few second thoughts as to the wisdom of the wartime offensive. Even if they had been burdened by doubts, the arrival of the atomic bomb changed all that. The moment for strategic air power to move center stage had arrived. Michael Howard recalled how the old arguments suddenly seemed irrelevant: "All the old targets which had competed for attention—oil, transportation, heavy industry, civilian morale—could be shattered in a single attack."[4]

So it was that from the first tentative and ill-informed studies in 1946 on Britain's own nuclear requirements, the easy assumption was that the targets would have something to do with enemy "industry and population." The contest was not one of planning to use an existing capability but one of working out future requirements, in the first instance for the production of fissile material. The studies were hampered by the fact that until 1948 there was no official permission to consider the Soviet Union as an "enemy," although there was little doubt as to whose territory was under consideration, and also by the lack of information from the United States on nuclear effects in general and its own plans in particular. This information had been cut off following the passage by the U.S. Congress of the McMahon Act in 1946.

The first consideration of possible British requirements produced by the chiefs of staff on New Year's Day 1946 suggested that a "stock in the hundreds rather than the scores" of bombs would be needed to attack an enemy of "widely dispersed industry and population." That summer, the chiefs' Joint Technical Warfare Committee, again with city bombing most in mind, concurred with the view that "several hundred bombs" might be required to bring about the "collapse" of Russia. A year later (July 1947) a Defence Research Policy Committee put the requirement up to 1,000 bombs, but this turned out to have been based on a superficial calculation. Having been informed that the Home Defence Committee believed that twenty-five atom bombs would be needed to knock out Britain, the Research Policy Committee observed that the geographical area "we have in mind" (the USSR was still not officially designated as a potential enemy) was forty times that of the United Kingdom. Thus $25 \times 40 = 1,000$.[5]

By 1947 the chiefs had already stated their assumption that the "knowledge that we possessed weapons of mass destruction and were prepared to use them would be the most effective deterrent to war itself." In 1948, with the cold war coming to dominate official minds, a serious effort was begun to sort out the consequences for military planning of the priority attached to air power and weapons of mass destruction. However, the calculations still did not move beyond back-of-the-envelope estimates based on simple assumptions and round numbers. In the 1948 review of atomic energy requirements, a minimum number of two hundred bombs by 1957 was designated the U.K. requirement. This figure was based on a belief that six hundred bombs would be needed by that date as a total strategic requirement, and that it could be expected that two-thirds or four hundred would be met from the American stockpile.[6]

It should also be recognized that the basic drive behind the British program was the need to have some sort of capability rather than a specific military concept. John Simpson quotes one senior official describing the process of arriving at "the output figure for weapons as being akin to a 'Dutch Auction.' . . . The requirement has never been keyed in any definite way to any plan of strategy or tactics."[7]

To the extent that there was a plan, it was already clear to the British that their prospective nuclear capability was best understood as an adjunct to that of the United States rather than as a basis for standing alone against a Soviet aggressor. They therefore did not have to plan to attack all relevant Soviet targets—just those the Americans could not manage. But this presumption was being made on the basis of a complete lack of knowledge of future American stockpiles and plans. Although a considerable amount of joint Anglo-American military planning was already under way, the question of the strategic employment of nuclear weapons was absolutely excluded.

Aware of this obvious gap in their knowledge, the British chiefs of staff, from early 1949 on, made repeated requests to the Americans for discussions on the subject; but the British were consistently refused. The question was made even more urgent by the fact that since July 1948 a substantial element of U.S. strategic air power had been based in Britain. This placement had been agreed at the height of the Berlin crisis. And though initially the aircraft were not fitted to take atomic weapons, the potential was clearly there for the near future. In fact, by mid-1950 all the B-29s based in England were modified to take nuclear weapons. The initial agreement to accept U.S. aircraft on British soil had been taken with dispatch, but now many in British political and military circles found it intolerable that Britain could serve as a launching pad for an American nuclear strike against the Soviet Union without having a clear idea as to the form the strike was likely to take or indeed without having any veto over its implementation.

It was not until January 1952 that Winston Churchill, recently returned as prime minister, was given a personal briefing on the U.S. air force and told as much about the Strategic Air Plan as had been told to Secretary of State Dean Acheson. By the end of that year the chiefs had received their own briefing on a "highly personal basis," and although they were thereafter well informed, they were unable to communicate any of this to British commanders in chief for planning purposes.[8]

The main discovery was probably the impressive growth of the U.S. stockpile. The prime minister and the chiefs would also have learned of the American planning assumptions. By this time U.S. planners were already considering the importance of targets affecting the Soviet ability "to deliver atomic bombs" as well as those that could help retard Soviet advances in Western Europe. However, the actual target list concentrated on the Soviet liquid fuel, electric power, and atomic energy facilities—the intention being to destroy all these in one massive strike. Although the target list implied discrimination in attack, there were grave doubts about whether or not this could be achieved, given the existing state of intelligence on the Soviet Union and the capacity of the U.S. bomber offensive. At any rate, under the influence of Gen. Curtis LeMay at the head of Strategic Air Command the stress was soon put on less-well-defined urban-industrial targets.[9]

During 1952 the British were still struggling to sort out their ideas on nuclear planning in this context of a complete absence of high-quality information from the United States. It is clear, even with better access to American plans, that great uncertainties would have remained simply because these plans were themselves still in flux. Where there may have been informal contact, such as between RAF Bomber Command and USAF Strategic Air Command, this was likely to have reinforced each other's predilections toward "city busting."

Nevertheless, even in these conditions there was at least awareness that nuclear targeting might have to go beyond preparations for "burning and blasting cities" and that certainly a variety of types of bombs could be developed including some that might serve tactical purposes. Furthermore, if it could be assumed that the United States was building toward a stockpile sufficient to destroy most of the key Soviet targets, then the actual role to be played by British forces in any attack had to be addressed. In the famous Global Strategy Document of the summer of 1952, the chiefs of staff were moving toward a rational for the British nuclear force, which served for much of the 1950s. There was little choice but to rely on the United States for the major deterrent, but there was still a need to maintain an ability to attack targets not of direct strategic interest to the United States. Above all, they argued, for the British to have no part in "the main deterrent in the cold war and the only Allied offensive in a world war would seriously weaken British influence on

United States policy and planning in the cold war and in war would mean that the United Kingdom would have no claim to any share in the policy or planning of the offensive."[10]

These twin themes of political influence and the concentration on targets of particular interest to the United Kingdom came up throughout the 1950s. Our concern is only with the second of these, as expressed for example by Winston Churchill in 1955:

> Unless we can make a contribution of our own . . . we cannot be sure that in any emergency the resources of other powers would be planned exactly as we would wish, or that the targets which would threaten us most would be given what we consider the necessary priority in the first few hours. These targets might be of such cardinal importance that it could really be a matter of life and death for us.[11]

This concern was enhanced when the first TU-16 Badger medium-range bomber became operational in 1954,[12] since this event signaled the development of a direct Soviet threat to Britain. According to one source, Soviet submarine bases were also a particular concern.[13] However, the rapid expansion of Soviet medium-range forces must have soon thrown doubt on Britain's ability to deal with this particular source of threat by itself.

This line of argument also raised questions about the expectations of cooperation with the United States in the design and execution of nuclear attacks as well as the general assumption that the business of a nuclear strike force would be to pose the possibility of and, if necessary, to execute a highly destructive attack.

It must be remembered that Britain could not pose a serious nuclear threat to Soviet territory until the end of 1956 when the first Vulcan bomber squadrons were formed.[14] As a result, much of the discussion was still hypothetical and hampered by a lack of knowledge of American plans (although the signing of a bilateral agreement in June 1955 following the more relaxed U.S. Atomic Energy Act of 1954 did make possible some Anglo-American defense planning in atomic energy matters).[15] In addition, the growing awareness of the power of the new hydrogen bomb, moving the contemplated blasts up from the kiloton to the megaton range, made it difficult to think of matters in terms other than those of mass destruction. The first British thermonuclear weapon was tested in May 1957.

Certainly, the arrival of a substantial British nuclear capability in 1958 led to an assumption that the threat now posed to Soviet cities was the basis of the deterrent and that this regained for the country a freedom of maneuver. For example, Randolph Churchill, M.P., speaking in November 1958, told the American Chamber of Commerce in London that "Britain can knock down twelve cities in the region of Stalingrad and Moscow from bases in Britain and another dozen in the Crimea from bases in Cyprus. We did not have that power at the time of Suez. We are a major power again.[16] Whether Churchill was just making inferences from the number of Vulcan and Victor bombers available and what was known about their range, or whether he was speaking with genuine "inside" knowledge, is unclear. At the time the U.K. inventory probably numbered some sixty bombs.[17] At any rate his statement reflects the belief that the bombers would be targeted against Soviet cities.

It is hard to see how this force operating by itself would offer a serious threat to the Soviet Union unless the force concentrated on cities. The 1958 Defence White Paper, after acknowledging the much greater size of the American nuclear force, still insisted that "when fully equipped with megaton weapons the British bomber force will in itself constitute a formidable deterrent."

But if Britain was now developing a formidable countercity force, what were the implications for the other aspects of the official rationale—the contribution to NATO's overall deterrent that would provide a source of both peacetime and wartime influence over the Americans? The same white paper spoke of NATO strategy being "based on the frank recognition that a full-scale Soviet attack could not be repelled without resort to a massive nuclear bombardment of the sources of power in Russia."[18] The phrase "sources of power" suggested a more discriminating range of targets than just cities. If Britain were to take part in a joint attack with the United States, would the country be assigned different sorts of targets than those that would make sense if Britain were acting alone?

Here we find emerging the familiar tension in British nuclear policy. Was the force to be a contribution to NATO's overall deterrent, in which case it had to fit in with the larger schemes of the United States, or could it serve by itself as a "formidable deterrent"? This tension was one that had to be sorted out in 1958 as the V-bomber force expanded and plans were required should it be necessary to execute a nuclear strike.

Until the late 1950s Britain was unable to do anything other than work out its own target list because it lacked sufficient information on American plans. However, from the late 1950s on, having proved itself in the nuclear area without American help, Britain was able to establish the close working relationship with the United States that had been an objective since 1945. Matters had begun to improve in 1954, when Congress passed the Atomic Energy Act, which enabled the sharing of data with allies on the external characteristics of nuclear weapons. There was still then the possibility of American weapons being carried in British bomb-bays in the event of war. According to Harold Macmillan, in November 1954, "no arrangements had yet been made to specify which enemy targets, especially those most important to the United Kingdom, would be dealt with immediately by American bombers."[19]

In June 1955 two bilateral agreements were signed with the United States which provided for the exchange of information on the military aspects of atomic energy, including defense planning and training in operational use of nuclear weapons. As a result Bomber Command sent out a number of high-level teams to the United States to pick the brain of the Strategic Air Command. According to Andrew Brookes, "this close liaison led to the first combined targeting plan between the two air forces since the combined bomber offensive of 1949."[20] It took some time, however, before these plans were put together. The Bermuda summit of March 1957 between President Eisenhower and Prime Minister Macmillan, which included an agreement to base U.S. Thor IRBM in Britain on a "dual-key" basis, generally improved relations after the post-Suez tension. The two air forces had been engaged in discussions in late 1956, prior to the formal agreements, on the advisability of bringing Thor in Britain.[21]

Through 1957 the two commands began to move closer in terms of joint training, communications, visits, and discussions on matters of mutual interest. In November 1957 members of SAC visited the headquarters of Bomber Command at High Wycombe "to discuss joint operational planning, targeting and other problems of common interest, with the object of co-ordinating nuclear strike plans to their mutual advantage," as air vice-marshal Stewart Menaul later described it.[22]

The strategic nuclear targets at the time were "decided solely by the British Chiefs of Staff on the basis of a recommendation of a special committee in the Ministry of Defence." Nevertheless they were coordinated with SAC in order that "each made the maximum use of the other's knowledge and obtained the maximum coverage of, and concentration on, priority targets."[23]

Menaul, who is the only source on targeting for this period, does not discuss the nature of the targets themselves. At one point his description of how the Bomber Command crews were "capable of destroying most of the major cities in the Soviet Union," suggests that this was still deemed the most likely sort of attack. But how does that fit in with the coordination of plans with SAC for the "purpose of ensuring that the best possible advantage was obtained from the respective striking forces"?[24]

By this time SAC was well past needing any help in destroying most centers of Soviet population. By then the so-called retardation targets, that is, those directly related to halting a Soviet conventional attack on

Western Europe, had been taken over by the U.S. tactical air forces;[25] so presumably they were not part of SAC-Bomber Command exchanges. In the Net Evaluation Sub Committee (NESC) 2009 study conducted for the National Security Council, which was completed in February 1960 and formed the basis of the first U.S. Single Integrated Operations Plan (SIOP) in December 1960, of the 2,021 targets they identified, 121 were ICBM sites, 140 air defense bases, 200 bomber bases, 218 military and governmental control centers, and 124 other military targets, with most of the remaining target installations located within 131 urban centers in the Soviet Union and China. The mix of targets reflected a growing interest in counterforce as a targeting philosophy. The study also indicated priorities of U.S. strikes, and delineated a series of "sequential options," consisting of such target sets as "central strategic systems, other strategic systems, theater threats, and counter-value targets."[26]

Studies such as this gave some credence to the concern expressed earlier in the decade that U.S. priorities would not be the same as those of Britain. For Britain, Soviet theater systems would be a higher priority. If SAC was planning a strike with a substantial counterforce element at that time, then it would have made sense for Bomber Command to concentrate on Soviet medium-range aircraft and missile bases.

If, however, Britain was expecting to act alone, then a counterforce attack would have been inappropriate as, acting on its own, Britain could barely have made a dent in Soviet nuclear capabilities. Urban-industrial centers were also a lower U.S. priority, so again British concentration on these targets would not have contradicted American plans.

If a joint attack was made on the USSR, it was claimed that Bomber Command would get in first. In a parliamentary debate on 26 February 1959, Secretary of Defence Duncan Sandys quoted Gen. Thomas Powers, commander of SAC, to the effect that "having regard to Britain's closer proximity we rely on her V-bombers to provide an important part of the first wave of the allied retaliatory force."[27] The V-bombers were some five hours closer to the Soviet Union than the aircraft of U.S. Strategic Air Command. Again, if the V-bombers were going to get in first, then it would have made sense to go for those counterforce targets of most concern to Britain, namely the submarine bases and medium-range bomber and missile sites. However, if it was preparing the way for SAC, then the most logical set of targets would have been Soviet air defenses. As attacks on some radar, anti-aircraft gun, SAM, and fighter installations would have been required to prosecute even an attack on medium-range bases, it seems likely that some compromise on this matter could have been resolved in RAF-SAC discussions. The basic plan appears to have been for an initial strike on the variety of military targets, with a substantial reserve force able to attack the centers of Soviet population.

In the early 1960s this approach may have seemed perfectly feasible. However, this concept was soon undermined by a series of developments. At its peak in 1963, the V-bomber force consisted of 180 Victor, Vulcan, and Valiant bombers operated from bases in Britain and Cyprus. Free-fall thermonuclear bombs became available in 1961.[28] These each had a one-megaton yield.[29]

This was not actually the peak of Bomber Command's total capability. During 1963, the 60 liquid-fueled Thor missiles, provided under a dual-key arrangement with the United States and operated by Bomber Command, were removed. These also had a one-megaton warhead. According to Menaul, at the time of the October 1962 Cuban Missile Crisis, the nuclear weapons in Bomber Command totaled 230 megatons, which could have been used against 230 targets, and most "would have reached their assigned targets."[30] This figure must have been based on 170 V-bombers and 60 Thor missiles. However, Brookes gives a lower figure of 140 Main Force bombs.[31] By this time sufficient warheads for this total force had certainly been produced.[32]

Britain never again had this number of operational warheads. Thor was removed in 1963, and the next year the Valiant bombers were grounded because of metal fatigue. The loss of the Valiants was serious, not only because of the removal of what was by then a small component of Bomber Command but also because of the need to find replacements for Valiants in other missions. It was decided not to seek replacement for the 24 Valiants assigned in a tactical role to SACEUR, but the others—probably around 50 to 60—assigned to photo reconnaissance and tanker roles had to be replaced. It was reported in early 1965 that the Victors would take over the photo reconnaissance role in 1965 and the tanker role by 1966 and that the total force was to be reduced to 80.[33] By 1967 this level had been reached.[34] The remaining 80 were made up of 25 mark II Victors and 56 Mark II Vulcans, of which half carried Blue Steel missiles. In 1968 the Victors were withdrawn, and the next year the Vulcans were transferred to a tactical role, where they remained until 1982. By this time Polaris had taken over from Bomber Command.[35] One reason for the quick rundown of the force was the need to recycle nuclear materials from aircraft bombs to missile warheads.

The swift decline of Bomber Command was unexpected. In the 1950s it had been presumed that the force would become obsolete by the mid-1960s. However, the RAF maintained some credibility by such means as preparation to disperse the bombers to a large number of airfields in periods of crisis and practice scrambles that allowed the aircraft to escape the runway within a four-minute warning period. The problem of penetrating Soviet air defenses was if anything more serious, and the main expedient here was to practice low-altitude flying to avoid enemy radar.

In the 1960s, with the cancellation of the Blue Streak missile, it was decided to extend the lifetime of the force by the purchase of the U.S. Skybolt air-launched missile. Initially Britain hoped to equip both the Vulcans and the Victors with Skybolts, but the Victors soon proved to be unsuitable (thereby leading to a cut in the order for the Mark II version).[36] The idea was to buy one hundred missiles[37] with two to be carried by each aircraft.[38] This idea was perforce abandoned when the United States canceled the Skybolt program in November 1962, with the result that the British government decided to rely on Polaris for the future. A further blow to Bomber Command came in the cancellation of the TSR-2,which had a planned nuclear strike capability, in April 1965. The American F-111 was then adopted as a replacement, but it was also abandoned in 1967.

The move to Polaris provided an important bonus in both survivability and penetrability but an inevitable drop in target coverage. It is doubtful that at its peak in 1963–64 Bomber Command's V-bombers could have reached all their assigned targets, but they certainly could have found a significant proportion. Moreover, most bombers would have been available at any given time. One insider estimate suggested that some 50 percent of the bombs would have got through to their targets in daytime attacks during the 1960s and up to 40 percent at night.[39]

With Polaris, the overall numbers fell by about two-thirds; further, not all boats could be expected to be on patrol at any given time. The original plan was to purchase five SSBNs, which would have meant two or three on patrol. In 1965 the program was cut to four boats, with the result that only one or two would be patrolling. Last, it had originally been decided to purchase the Polaris A-2 warhead of one megaton, but in 1964 it was decided to go for the A-3 with three (not independently targeted) two-hundred-kiloton warheads. For a net gain in penetration against antiballistic missiles there was a net loss in megatonnage.

Menaul argues that to produce a submarine force equivalent to Bomber Command in 1962 (i.e., 170 V-bombers and 60 Thors) would have required "at least twenty submarines."[40] This was not exactly the alternative. In 1962, the Thors were already scheduled to leave and the real comparison was with 100 Skybolts. Nevertheless, as can be seen in table 5.1, and taking into account the problems of the Polaris patrols, there was clearly a marked decline in the number of deliverable warheads and therefore target coverage during the 1960s.

It was now necessary to consider being able to attack only sixteen rather than around two hundred targets; also it would be very difficult to keep any missiles in reserve. The launch of a missile from a submarine would give away its position and it could then face severe problems

Table 5.1. British strategic nuclear warheads, 1962–1970

Year	Total	V-Bomber	Thor	Polaris
1962	230	170	60	
1963	180	180		
1964	180	180		
1965	120	120		
1966	80	80		
1967	80	80		
1968	72	56		16
1969	48			48
1970	64			64

from enemy antisubmarine warfare. British planners therefore had to think harder than ever before about priorities.

It might have appeared that the question of priorities had been resolved, along with the long-term future of the British deterrent, with the signing of the Anglo-American Nassau Agreement of December 1962. A key part of the agreement was that "allocations . . . from United Kingdom Bomber Command . . . would be assigned as part of a NATO nuclear force and targeted in accordance with NATO plans" (Article VI). This assignment was to occur along with that of some U.S. strategic and tactical nuclear forces. The new Polaris was to be targeted in the same way.

In 1963 the commander-in-chief's directive to Bomber Command on outbreak of war changed from "destroy those targets allocated to it by the British Chiefs of Staff" to destroy "those targets assigned to it by SACEUR in accordance with his nuclear strike plan." The terms of this assignment were ratified on 23 May 1963. Menaul points out that Bomber Command thereafter worked with SHAPE on "targeting, war planning, coordination of strikes and periodic exercises." Direct target coordination with SAC was discontinued but there were still "frequent exchange visits."[41]

Since then targets for first the V-bombers and then the Polaris flotilla have been allocated by the Joint Strategic Target Planning Staff (JSTPS) at U.S. Strategic Air Command in Omaha, Nebraska. A European team, including some British officers (normally around three), participates in the planning. Operational plans are formulated by the Nuclear Activities Branch at SHAPE. The basic targeting plan is the Nuclear Operation Plan (NOP; formerly called the General Strike Plan), which is developed by SACEUR "for the execution of nuclear strikes with the nuclear weapons under his command." This would involve British nuclear-capable aircraft, such as Buccaneers, Jaguars, and Tornados, as well as Polaris.[42]

According to Desmond Ball, NATO planning provides for both selec-

[119]

tive use and general nuclear response, for which the U.K. strategic forces would be most useful. The objectives of general nuclear response would be "to conduct, in concert with external forces, operations to neutralize enemy nuclear capability, destroying his ability and will to wage war, disrupt his command and control, and destroy his land, naval and air forces, including logistic support elements." These targets are divided into a Priority Strike Program and a Tactical Strike Program. The full execution of the NOP would probably occur only in conjunction with the execution of the U.S. SIOP. Most of the targets mentioned are military related, what once would have been described as "retardation" in nature.[43]

These targets are not of a sort that are normally mentioned in the context of a British nuclear force. They are of a sort that would be suitable for the nuclear-capable aircraft and would have been manageable for the V-bombers, but they seem an unlikely collection for Polaris. As Jonathan Alford has noted: "The *Polaris* system is by no means ideal for theatre strikes: it is rather inflexible and unresponsive (communication with submerged submarines remains difficult), and too inaccurate for most military targeting." The only military targets Alford considers possibly suitable are of the larger variety, such as dockyards or airfields.[44] At best Polaris, along with the U.S. Poseidon SLBMs also allocated to SACEUR, would appear as a reserve force for NATO.[45]

With the loss of the warheads and the flexibility involved in the move from the V-bombers to the Polaris system, the idea that the British force was suitable largely for countervalue retaliation, and so to be held in reserve during the early stages of nuclear escalation, gained ground. The question then became "For whom is the British nuclear force held in reserve?" Although assigned to NATO the forces were always under national control, and the Nassau Agreement itself made it clear that national considerations would be overriding.[46] Furthermore, there has been a distinct trend in official descriptions of the nuclear force toward emphasis on its national rather than NATO role: for example, the often-used phrase "ultimate guarantor of national security" or the stress on its "last resort" function in contradistinction to the apparently more penultimate function of attacking theater nuclear forces.[47]

There are separate U.K. plans worked out in Whitehall. These were the responsibility of the Navy Department working with Defence Intelligence Staff. In the reorganization of the Ministry of Defence at the start of 1985, nuclear targeting was made the responsibility of the Nuclear Policy Directorate, headed by a civilian under the Deputy Under Secretary (Policy). This exercise, though separate from that of NATO, presumably draws upon information made available through the NATO exercises and indeed through other U.S.-U.K. links such as that covering intelligence.[48] Until recently this exercise received little input from the civilian policy side. However, while the details of the plans may have been left to the military, there have been clear indications of the sort of broad policy decisions that have been made concerning the targets deemed most important to threaten.

Before examining this policy, it is worth considering the range of targeting options open to Britain. While the public literature on this topic is hardly extensive, two unofficial studies throw some light on the problem. The first is two Adelphi Papers by Geoffrey Kemp, produced in 1974, which look in great detail at the targeting requirements for medium-range nuclear powers. Kemp notes that preparations for attacks on specific military targets require high-quality intelligence information (which presumably is available to Britain), and also a large number of warheads, if the attack is going to have a serious impact. In his analysis Kemp concentrates on countervalue targeting, stating that the "primary requirements for the various strategies will be the ability to threaten or inflict severe damage upon selected Soviet population centers, industrial facilities, resources and institutions, and selected military targets whose location and configuration are likely to be known." He notes certain choices. If the goal is to destroy the highest proportion of the Soviet population, then Moscow would not necessarily be chosen as a target because of the need to penetrate the ABM defenses surrounding Moscow. Kemp also notes, however, that the size and density of Moscow's population, combined with the city's circular pattern and physical location, the diverse concentrations of industry, the other large cities close by, and the key role played by Moscow as the nation's administrative, political, educational, and cultural capital would accentuate the effects of those weapons that did get through. Another choice would be between concentrating on industrial facilities or focusing on population centers.[49]

Kemp identifies four damage levels: the top ten Soviet cities, excluding those protected by the Moscow ABM system;[50] the top ten cities, including Moscow and Gorki; the top fifty cities; and the top two hundred cities. Of these, the first two levels turn out to be the most realistic. Targeting them would put at risk some 15 million people and 15 percent of industrial capacity, and 21 million people and 25 percent of capacity, respectively.[51] Kemp's calculations then become exceedingly complex, particularly as he does not actually compute probabilities for the Polaris A-3 missile with its 3×200 kt MRV, the calculations instead being done for a one-megaton single-warhead Polaris.

Kemp's figures can be taken to suggest that the contents of two Polaris SSBNs would need to penetrate to their targets to have a chance of destroying ten cities. This calculation is made before problems of anti-submarine warfare and ABMs are taken into account. In turn, this scenario suggests that if, as is often the case, only one British boat is on patrol at a given time, then not many warheads would be left over after an attack on Moscow and there would be doubts as to the extent of Moscow's vulnerability. With boats on patrol, at best three or four cities would be at risk, although obviously the sixteen missiles could in principle attack sixteen different targets if the chaos was to be spread.

A later study by Ian Smart looked specifically at the British force. Smart reaches a conclusion similar to Kemp's, by a simpler method. Smart describes the contents of the Polaris SSBNs as equivalent to twenty-three to thirty-three megaton equivalents, which using American data he suggests must threaten 15 to 20 million people and up to 25 percent of industrial capacity. Smart then goes on to observe that "it is not axiomatic that a small deterrent force . . . can usefully threaten only civilian population and industry. Not only civilian targets are "soft" but also airfields, ports and barracks. Then there are also semi-hard targets, including some specialised civilian facilities as well as large fixed radar installations, submarine pens and vaulted aircraft shelters. There are also hardened military targets against which Polaris warheads would be ineffectual." Smart argues that there is a range of choice on targeting which includes "such very sensitive targets as ABM or air defense early warning and control radars, hydro-electric or thermal generating stations, heavy industrial complexes, military airfields and naval ports.[52]

It is reasonably clear that the British government has placed a high premium on being able to attack Moscow. The issue was brought to the fore in the late 1960s with the development of the Galosh defenses around Moscow. At first the issue looked like one of maintaining a substantial threat in the face of nationwide ABMs. By 1968 it seemed likely that only the Moscow area was to be defended. This meant a choice had to be made as to whether Moscow was essential as a target. Having decided that it was, the extent of the defenses around the city meant that a whole boatload of missiles would have to be committed to be sure of destroying the target. Only if two boats were on station could there be any diversity in targets. The situation became easier in 1979–80 when the Galosh system was reduced from sixty-four to thirty-two launchers, but the Moscow criterion would still limit the flexibility of British targeting.

By this time the development of the new front end for Polaris was near completion. Known as Chevaline, it involved two maneuvering clusters of real warheads and decoys, capable of penetrating the Moscow defenses. The decision to develop this warhead had been made by the Conservative government in 1972 when, with the signing of the ABM Treaty, the limits of the Soviet system had been confirmed. In 1974 the Labour government confirmed this decision, though as costs rose there was some skepticism in the small group of ministers considering this matter as to whether the "Moscow criterion" was worth the expense.[53] Michael Quinlan, as deputy under secretary of state in the Ministry of Defence confirmed the Moscow criterion in parliamentary evidence: "There is a concept which Chevaline makes clear, that Governments did not want to have a situation where the adversary could have a sanctuary for his capital and a large area around it."[54] In the future the Moscow criterion would be most threatened by a Soviet move to an endoatmospheric ABM system, which might be better able to discriminate between real warheads and decoys.

The introduction of Chevaline, which began operational service in the summer of 1982,[55] does not commit Britain to an attack on the Moscow area as the only targeting option. However, it may commit Britain to an attack on a few and possibly no more than one large target. Whereas with the A-3 warhead all missiles would have had to be committed without complete confidence of success, with Chevaline a similar number of missiles would be committed but with a much greater chance of success. The Chevaline concept is to rain a series of warheads and decoys simultaneously over the target area so as to swamp it. The effect does not come from the contents of a single missile but from the combined contents of a number of missiles—probably the complement of one SSBN. It is now difficult to disentangle the systems to take on a number of targets at once. For the next decade Britain will have little flexibility in targeting.

The main consolation is that with the arrival of the MIRVed Trident missiles as replacements for Polaris in the 1990s, targeting flexibility will return. With Trident, Britain should have no trouble with any Soviet defenses, based on the state of the art in the 1980s and 1990s, and will also have a sudden surge of extra warheads.

It is clear from the history of the Trident decision that it was not at all driven by any notion of targeting requirements, although the acquisition has been criticized for its "first-strike" implications. Rather the two main factors were the concern over survivability, which led to the choice once again of a submarine-based system, and cost-effectiveness, which encouraged the choice of the latest U.S. SLBM in order to enjoy the benefits of "commonality."

Initially the Trident C-4 was to have been purchased, with eight warheads per missile, but British planners have since followed the United States in moving to the D-5 with its fourteen warheads per missile. However, so embarrassed was the government by the excess of warheads implied that it was stated that the move would "not involve any significant change in the planned total number of warheads associated with our strategic deterrent force in comparison with the original intentions for a force based on the C-4 missile system."[56] It is likely that two and sometimes three Trident boats will be on station at any given time

[123]

(because of the extended periods between long refits), which with this restriction would lead to up to 384 warheads available. Remove the restriction and the number goes up to 672. This is a dramatic increase from the 61 to 32 available with Polaris.

This increase in itself created a requirement to begin rethinking targeting policy. There also seems to have been a view in the civilian secretariats of the Ministry of Defence that insufficient thought had gone into the choice of targets in the past. At any rate a review of targeting policies seems to have been instituted in the early 1980s. Part of the impulse appears to have been the view that it was neither necessary nor wholly proper to concentrate on Soviet cities. This view was associated with Michael Quinlan, the leading civil servant on nuclear issues at Whitehall.

In the 1980 memorandum on the Polaris successor there was a discussion of targeting requirements. One approach suggested was to consider the "type and scale of damage Soviet leaders might think likely to leave them critically handicapped afterwards in continuing confrontation with a relatively unscathed United States."[57] It went on to express doubt that the Soviet leadership would be deterred by "a capability which offered only a low likelihood of striking home to key targets; or which posed the prospect of only a very small number of strikes; or which Soviet leaders could expect to ward off successfully from large areas of key importance to them." After a reminder that British governments do not make public targeting plans, there was the following statement: "The Government however thinks it right now to make clear that their concept of deterrence is concerned essentially with posing a potential threat to key aspects of Soviet state power. There might, with changing conditions, be more than one way of doing this, and some flexibility in contingency planning is appropriate."[58]

The meaning of the phrase "aspects of state power" is unclear. In evidence to Parliament, Michael Quinlan suggested that "Soviet state power" may "embrace a range of targets lying between hitting a large city and hitting a silo."[59] Another clue to Quinlan's thinking comes in a discussion to which he contributed in a Catholic magazine on the morality of deterrence. He observed then that there "is no inherent reason to suppose that [unacceptable disadvantage to an aggressor] can only take the form of massive attack aimed at populations as a retributive execution of 'hostages.' There is assorted public evidence that some but not all western target planning has been of this kind, but that is far from demonstrating that no other kind is available or possible." He goes on to note that "there is no doubt that any extensive strategic nuclear attack will kill great numbers of non-combatants even if this is not its direct intent."[60]

[124]

Another factor encouraging a review of targeting requirements was the notion that at some point Britain might have to agree to a ceiling on warheads as part of an arms control package. It has already been noted that in the move to the Trident D-5, the government unilaterally agreed to hold warhead numbers down to C-4 levels. It is not inconceivable that as a means of heading off pressure on the British force the government might agree to an even lower ceiling.[61]

The existence of these reviews has never been publicly acknowledged, and there is little public information about their conclusions. Rather tentatively, it is possible to identify some of the key issues involved.

One conclusion appears to be that apart from some hydroelectric plants, it is impossible to prevent massive damage to urban population sites in ostensibly discriminating attacks. The main military-related targets considered were command and control centers. Concentration on these centers includes many cities, and certainly Moscow, and so could not significantly reduce the human consequences. Destroying such targets, however, could have a major impact on Soviet military strength. Another possibility, which appears to have been unappealing because of the lack of direct damage to Soviet state power, would have been to attack Soviet ABM and air defense radars, rendering the USSR more vulnerable to a U.S. strike. This, as an attack on command and control, would be in the category of attacks designed to handicap the Soviet Union in a continuing confrontation with the United States. A final question considered was the extent to which it would be sensible or possible with Trident to withhold warheads as a reserve force. This could involve a return to the old idea that the V-bomber force equipped with some missiles would attack targets as required by SACEUR, while others would be held in reserve for use against Soviet cities. The old problem that a submarine could give away its position with a limited volley would still remain.

All this leads, inevitably, to the vexed question of the relationship between national nuclear plans and NATO plans, and whether or not Britain is presumed to be "standing alone" or acting in concert with the United States. The conclusion within government is not known except that it was in the category of "it's very difficult." A NATO attack would not be initially directed at the sources of Soviet state power. SACEUR's objectives would be less ultimate. It is possible to see how Britain's nuclear forces other than its SSBNs would fit in with SACEUR's plans, but the implications for Britain of a commitment at this level of escalation do not appear to have been thought through. At any rate, despite the assignation of Britain's nuclear forces to NATO, the assumptions and dominant plans surrounding their targeting do not naturally fit in with any NATO plans.

The trend in British public pronouncements suggests that the "standing alone" hypothesis is the underlying rationale for the nuclear force. It this is the presumption then the requirements for the deterrent may not be too great. The objective would be to dissuade the Soviet Union from launching an attack on Britain. It is difficult to see what combination of objectives would lead to such an attack outside of a general war in Europe. In the event of a general war, if the Soviet Union had achieved its Continental objectives without triggering a nuclear war, then it would be unlikely to put this achievement at risk by launching an attack on the dubious prize of Britain. By the time such a decision had to be taken, the issue would have been put to the test with France. At any rate, the USSR might calculate that with hegemony over the rest of Europe, Britain would soon come under its influence. For Britain, therefore, a truly "last resort" deterrent might be no more than that required to threaten some real, but not necessarily overwhelming, hurt to the Soviet Union.

It seems unlikely that Britain, by itself, would instigate nuclear war on behalf of West Germany except as part of a combined alliance effort. Britain's land-based battlefield nuclear weapons are all under dual-key control, so they could not be used without American agreement. The aircraft should be able to avoid nuclear commitment if necessary, while the strategic missiles would be kept in reserve for national purposes. The American connection, as has already been noted, would allow Britain a greater flexibility in attacks. However, it is hard to see that making the USSR vulnerable to an American "kill" would commend itself to Britain's leaders when national forces could all but "kill" the USSR on their own. If Britain wished to join the United States in an all-out nuclear attack, it is hard to see exactly how Britain's role could be central in making the attack a success (if anything of this sort could be judged in such terms).

The main benefit of the U.K. nuclear force for NATO might be, therefore, not so much in attacking certain targets for the alliance but in preserving the national territory as a sanctuary, in serving as the major American base close to the battle. Such a role of course would make Britain a target of great importance and therefore would require much more of the national force than simply a desire to warn the USSR off from a country anxious to stay neutral.

These questions are not yet fully resolved. Until the 1980s the trend had been clear. Despite the assignment of forces to NATO in 1962, Britain had been forced, because of the reduction of available warheads, to concentrate on maintaining a threat to Moscow, the major source of Soviet power. In the future, more widespread, flexible, and selective targeting will be possible. This extra flexibility and scope, however, were not sought and seem to have been acquired without any clear sense of how they should be employed.

[6]

French Nuclear Targeting

DAVID S. YOST

To provide the reader with an introduction to French strategic nuclear targeting and closely related topics, the first half of this chapter describes sources on French policy, the basic concept of "proportional deterrence," current targeting doctrine, and existing and projected French strategic nuclear capabilities. The latter half reviews the French debate on the possible merits of flexibility in strategic targeting, the implications of France's refusal to coordinate targeting plans with her allies, and operational employment scenarios. Owing to the strategic nuclear focus of this book, tactical nuclear matters are given less attention.

This omission poses no obstacle to understanding the essential elements of French strategic nuclear planning. The fundamental concept remains one of "proportional deterrence," though current doctrine has introduced economic and administrative targets within the original "anticities" framework. France's strategic capabilities are barely sufficient to carry out declaratory doctrine today, and planned improvements cannot obscure the fact that the technical credibility of France's deterrent largely depends on a benign strategic environment—notably, minimal Soviet ballistic missile defenses. Strategic targeting flexibility has been ruled out largely because of force deficiencies. The practical implications of the French refusal to accept consultation or coordination obligations, even in relation to close allies, should be put in perspective by comparing British and U.S. practice. Scenarios of nuclear operations described by French sources imply a lower threshold than Britain and the United States posit for use of tactical nuclear weapons, but strategic employment policy is probably comparable to that of Britain, the only other nuclear power in a roughly similar strategic situation. The French emphasis on the primacy of deterrence is a logical imperative, given the catastrophic risks that would be involved in trying to sustain France's "sanctuarization" through proportional deterrence in a general East-West war.

The most important primary sources on French nuclear targeting are speeches, articles, and interviews by the president of the republic, the prime minister, the defense minister, and the chief of staff of the armed forces. In France, such statements usually derive from a bureaucratic process conducted with some care, with coordination between the Elysée Palace, the Hôtel Matignon (the office of the prime minister), the Rue St. Dominique (the Defense Ministry), and the Quai d'Orsay (the Foreign Ministry). When the president or prime minister makes a formal speech at, for example, the Institut des Hautes Etudes de Défense Nationale, the text has been prepared with the counsel of key government experts and authoritatively represents official policy. Additional primary sources that are sometimes even more detailed and informative than such high-level declarations (but which inevitably carry somewhat less authority) are occasional articles published by Defense Ministry officials in the quasi-official monthly journal *Défense Nationale*. Such exceptional articles are sometimes signed with pseudonyms but include introductory notes if their official character is to be underlined. Particularly important articles of this type are those prepared by officers in the Defense Ministry's planning department, the Centre de Prospective et d'Evaluations, which in February 1982 was renamed the Groupe de Planification et d'Etudes Stratégiques. Other officers, such as commanders of the First Army or the SSBN fleet, have also made official remarks of note, as have officials such as the director of military applications of the Commissariat à l'Energie Atomique. Statements by the foreign minister and his subordinates, such as the head of the Foreign Ministry's planning department, the Centre d'Analyse et de Prévision, represent official policy as well but are usually less detailed.

Secondary sources include a number of academic studies, unofficial strategic analyses, and legislative documents. While very few academic studies have looked closely at operational and targeting considerations, several provide useful background on the history of France's nuclear weapons programs.[1] Of the unofficial strategic analyses, few are more important than those written by Gen. Lucien Poirier, the leading theorist of the Centre de Prospective et d'Evaluations during the late 1960s and the drafter of the documents that furnished the basis for the still-valid 1972 white paper.[2] While France's Senate and National Assembly have very minimal roles in the formulation of defense policy,[3] and essentially no role at all in nuclear targeting, some rapporteurs of parliamentary committees have prepared valuable studies. The most useful of these remains the so-called Tourrain Report, prepared in 1980 by Gaullist politician Raymond Tourrain on the basis of numerous interviews and apparently with access to classified information. Aside from Tourrain's personal recommendations for future weapons acquisitions and related financial calculations, the 341-page report is generally accurate and authoritative, although unofficial.[4] Finally, journalists—particularly Jacques Isnard of *Le Monde*—have often reported useful information from reliable sources.

PROPORTIONAL DETERRENCE AND ITS IMPLEMENTATION

Because France's current strategic nuclear forces were all planned during Gen. Charles de Gaulle's presidency (1958–69), his strategic concepts naturally influenced decisively France's choice of targeting objectives. No less decisive, of course, were the technical constraints imposed by the operational limitations of France's first strategic nuclear means. From 1964 to 1971, France's sole means of delivering nuclear weapons to the USSR consisted of Mirage IV bombers. Each carried (and still carries) only a single sixty-kiloton bomb, and can only strike targets in the USSR with in-flight refueling on the way to and from missions. Since only sixty-two Mirage IVs were delivered between 1964 and 1968, General de Gaulle had little choice but to aim at Soviet population centers as a deterrent.

When the first Mirage IV bombers became operational in 1964, General de Gaulle announced a doctrine that has since been refined but not changed in its essence.

> In 1966, we will have enough Mirage IVs and tanker aircraft to be able to strike at once, at a distance of several thousand kilometers, with weapons whose total yield will surpass that of 150 Hiroshima bombs. . . . The path of deterrence is henceforth open to us, for the act of attacking France would be equivalent for any aggressor to undergoing frightful destruction himself. Of course, the megatons that we could launch would not equal in number those that Americans and Russians are able to unleash. But, once reaching a certain nuclear capability and as far as one's own direct defense is concerned, the *proportion* of respective means has no absolute value. In fact, since a man and a country can die but once, deterrence exists as soon as one can mortally wound the potential aggressor and is fully resolved to do so, and he is well convinced of it.[5]

Most of the Gaullist verities are implicit in this statement. Proportional deterrence theory, or the "deterrence by the weak of the strong" (*la dissuasion du faible au fort*), holds that France's threat of nuclear retaliation can deter the Soviet Union because the damage France could cause by targeting Soviet cities exceeds what the USSR would stand to gain in conquering or destroying France. This capability must be obtained and maintained if France is to avoid status as a U.S. protectorate. Dependence on the U.S. guarantee would be strategically unwise as well as politically humiliating since the United States is judged unlikely to honor its guarantee, if put to the test. Just as the United States would probably use its strategic nuclear forces only to protect its national "sanctuary," the French say, France's strategic nuclear forces are most credible as means to "sanctuarize" the national territory.

The Centre de Prospective et d'Evaluations of the Defense Ministry in the late 1960s prepared an elaborate theoretical defense of the "proportional deterrence" concept. General Poirier, for example, has written that the probability of successful proportional deterrence depends on a concept he calls "politico-strategic hope," which means the degree to which vital interests are at stake for both France and the USSR. The vital interests of France's independence and institutions should give France's retaliatory threats enough credibility to dissuade the Soviets from attacking France since the conquest or destruction of France is but a marginal interest for the USSR in view of the possibility of French retaliation against Soviet cities. In Poirier's words,

> Deterrence presumes the asymmetry of the respective interests of the weak and the strong: vital for the first (national sanctuarized space), marginal for the second. . . . In a possible conflict between France and the USSR, the latter will always be *the first player*, the party having the initiative and being obliged to decide to pass beyond the prohibition made against his attacking our country . . . A singularly uncomfortable position for its decision makers, knowing what it would cost to wager on nonretaliation and to lose. . . . The safeguarding of our integrity and our identity is for us a vital stake, justifying our going all the way and taking extraordinary risks; this confers a nonzero probability, even an elevated one, on the execution of our threat of nuclear retaliation on the opposing sanctuary.[6]

Proportional deterrence has thus been the fundamental concept of French strategic nuclear planning since the beginning. Officially propounded theories of proportional deterrence stress the disproportions between (*a*) French vital interests and Soviet marginal interests and (*b*) the advantages the USSR might gain in conquering or destroying France and the losses it might suffer from the French retaliation against Soviet cities. Although Raymond Aron and other critics of the proportional deterrence doctrine have, in contrast, emphasized the disproportion between the damage France could cause in the USSR and the residual

[130]

Soviet capability to retaliate against France,[7] countless official statements defend the concept. In the words of President Valéry Giscard d'Estaing, France's strategic nuclear forces have created "an almost unprecedented disparity between what an aggressor stands to gain and what he risks losing as a result of his aggression."[8]

Most official statements of proportional deterrence theory have been as vague and imprecise as this Giscardian assertion. Prime Minister Pierre Mauroy's declaration that France's anticities strategy aims "to be able to inflict on the aggressor . . . damage judged superior to the stake that the vital interests of the country represent for him" nonetheless contains a basic indication of France's sufficiency criteria.[9] Similar phrases have been repeated by such authoritative commentators as Col. Guy Lewin of the Defense Ministry's planning department and Gen. Jeannou Lacaze, chief of staff of the armed forces.[10] Lacaze has even been careful to use Mauroy's exact words, noting that the adversary would suffer "damage 'judged superior' to the demographic and economic potential that we represent."[11]

The anticities orientation of proportional deterrence was apparently long focused on causing a certain number of Soviet fatalities. In 1970, it was officially estimated that France's anticities targeting could cause 14 to 18 million Soviet deaths even if only half of the weapons were delivered,[12] with attrition presumably owing to reliability, survivability, and penetrability uncertainties. More recently, in the spirit of the above statements by Mauroy and Lacaze, commentators have referred to a sufficiency criterion of being able to cause with high confidence a number of Soviet fatalities roughly equivalent to the population of France (i.e., approximately 50 million),[13] though a more realistic estimate of current French capabilities might be 20 million.[14]

CURRENT STRATEGIC TARGETING DOCTRINE

Declaratory French strategic targeting policy underwent a significant refinement in 1980. Previous declaratory policy stressed that *anticities* meant targeting population centers, while the new policy places greater emphasis on threatening to destroy the infrastructure of the Soviet economy and administration as a deterrent. The published evidence for this change suggests a partial explanation. As early as March 1977, Gen. Guy Méry, who was then chief of staff of the armed forces, suggested that Soviet civil defense programs could weaken France's anticities deterrent power.

> But the organization of modern societies is such that human and industrial potential are often concentrated in the same zones, and that certain eco-

nomic zones are enormously important even if they are not highly populated. The question therefore is one of choosing targets and seeking accuracy, which is not an insurmountable problem; certain studies are now directed to this end, and I think they will be successful in a few years, and without putting the general framework of our strategy into question.[15]

This observation was seconded the following year by a high official in the Defense Ministry's planning department, who referred favorably to the possibility of targeting economic assets in view of the uncertainties created by Soviet civil defense.[16] The decision to adopt a new declaratory policy was probably made in 1979.

In January 1980, Colonel Lewin announced that, although Soviet civil defense programs could not be fully effective in providing the populace protection against French nuclear strikes, in the future France would threaten damage in addition to high numbers of fatalities in an anticities strike.

> The neutralization of the adversary [state's] administrative, economic, and social structures, the destruction of the framework of life and activity of millions of persons constitute damage that would be difficult to accept, even if a part of the population concerned by these destructions escapes immediate death. Let us imagine, for example, the situation of the USSR with 100 or 150 of its largest cities destroyed, some tens of millions of people killed, and as many persons displaced who must be taken in charge by a state emptied of its substance. Would this situation be tolerable for the leaders of a great power that wants to continue to play a preponderant role in the world? Obviously not . . . [17]

In a later article in 1980, Lewin introduced a term that has since appeared in a number of official and semiofficial commentaries on French nuclear targeting—*oeuvres vives*. The *oeuvres vives* of a ship constitute all that is contained by the hull below the water line, the ship's "vital works" of propulsion and supply. The term also implies that the ship could well sink if struck below the water line. In introducing the term, Lewin suggested that French adoption of this targeting concept reflected the opportunity offered by prospective deployment of the multiple warhead M-4 SLBM in addition to responding to Soviet civil defense programs:

> The response is undoubtedly to be sought in the multiplication of targets and selectivity, the aim being to reduce to nothing the structures and the "vital works" [*oeuvres vives*] of the adversary state, even if part of the population of the objectives targeted escapes destruction. Thus one differentiates between an "anticities" strategy and a strictly "antidemographic" strategy. This strategy will without doubt lead to obtaining an important

[132]

number of medium-yield warheads, preferred over megaton yields. In this respect the M-4 program constitutes a remarkable increase in the value of our nuclear armament.[18]

This decision to respond to Soviet civil defense programs by targeting the infrastructure of Soviet administrative control as well as industrial and economic assets has also been referred to as "an enlarged anticities strategy."[19] The new targeting policy is described as "a concept of the same strategic nature but more complete and, therefore, more operational and credible."[20] Another discussion referred to exploiting greater accuracy in order to select as targets "centers of political power and control. The threat of antidemographic nuclear strikes could then be preceded and completed by that of a disorganization of the adversary's political framework."[21] The presumption (similar to that of a number of U.S. theorists) is that Soviet leaders fear loss of administrative and economic power even more than high numbers of fatalities. Some French interview sources have conceded that this interest in targeting the Soviet control structure might logically stress the Russian over the non-Russian portions of the USSR, but no published sources seem to articulate this aspect of French targeting. In late 1980, Prime Minister Raymond Barre referred to France's ability to cause an aggressor "the assured destruction of *a notable part of his cities and of his economy.*"[22]

This refinement of declaratory French policy has been continued under President François Mitterrand. Defense Minister Charles Hernu has stated that Mitterrand's strategic-force modernization decisions (all of which had been planned under Giscard d'Estaing) do "not imply any change in our anticities strategy, corollary of deterrence of the strong by the weak."[23] French interview sources indicate that General Lacaze's statement that deterrence is "a matter of persuading him that such an action would present unacceptable risks because of the losses in *human lives* that he could suffer"[24] does not signify any return to the original anti-population concepts.

It should be noted, moreover, that French strategic nuclear doctrine does not encompass certain concepts that have erroneously been attributed to it. Two examples are *tous azimuts* and the notion of catalytic or "trigger" employment. *Tous azimuts*, meaning "all the points of the compass," was a concept discussed in 1967–68 by Gen. Charles Ailleret, then chief of staff of the armed forces. Ailleret advocated the development of an ICBM force that could protect France from threats potentially coming from "all directions" (*tous azimuts*). Ailleret's willingness to sacrifice tactical nuclear weapons, if necessary, to finance ICBM development was consistent with his doctrine, which amounted to immediate strategic nuclear retaliation, once major units clashed. While Ailleret personally favored what amounted to a posture of armed neutrality, with France targeting various states in addition to the USSR, his notions were never made the basis of operational planning or force development (France has no ICBMs); nor did General de Gaulle seriously consider the renunciation of the North Atlantic Treaty, which would have been inevitable with such a posture.[25]

A second major myth is that France sees its deterrent potential as resting on an ability to "trigger" U.S. honoring of the strategic nuclear guarantee to Western Europe. This possibility was discussed in France on various occasions in very oblique terms (i.e., not allowing France to become a conventional weapons battlefield of the superpowers) during the 1960s by General de Gaulle himself and, somewhat more explicitly, by theorists such as Claude Delmas and Gen. André Beaufre; but there is no evidence of its having ever been adopted as operational doctrine. In fact, in 1972 Defense Minister Michel Debré went out of his way to deny that any such concept was part of France's planning, or could be credible.[26] This denial was consistent with the Gaullist doctrine that no government will wage nuclear war in defense of another country.

A distinct but related notion, however, was expressed officially in 1977. General Méry declared that the "damage that we could cause to either superpower would immediately place it in such a situation of imbalance regarding the other superpower that it is doubtful that either could afford to tolerate suffering that damage at any time."[27] Prime Minister Barre also referred to the "decisive disequilibrium" that France could bring about in the Soviet-American strategic nuclear balance as a deterrent.[28] The logic of the contention apparently went beyond the damage France could cause the USSR to the strategic capability the USSR might expend in retaliating against France. Both the damage and the expenditure of strategic forces would place the USSR at a disadvantage vis-à-vis the United States. But this notion was apparently dropped from France's declaratory policy in that it did not recur until 1984.

The concept reemerged in General Lacaze's May 1984 speech at the Institut des Hautes Etudes de Défense Nationale:

In the hypothesis whereby he would judge that he would run only the risk of our strategic strike, the aggressor should still consider the situation in which he would find himself after having suffered the destruction of a non-negligible part of his cities, of his industrial and administrative means, and of his communications, when the other great nuclear powers would retain their economic and military potential intact. This argument seems fundamental to me and shows you how, in the assessment of our strategy of [deterrence by] the weak of the strong, it is advisable to situate this well within the world geopolitical context.[29]

[134]

This formulation's allusions to the "other great nuclear powers" and the "world geopolitical context" differed from the 1977 statements in that the latter emphasized the USSR being put in an unfavorable position with respect to the United States. Resurrecting the concept in this form obscures the degree to which France's security depends on the United States while furnishing an additional argument for the credibility of the "enlarged anticities" threat French strategy poses for the Soviet Union.

STRATEGIC CAPABILITIES

Whether France can physically carry out her deterrent threats must depend on such factors as the survivability, penetrability, reliability, and accuracy of her weapons and delivery systems, plus her ability to command and control them in adverse circumstances. The survivability criterion is especially important, as some official French statements have frankly acknowledged that a Soviet first strike could well destroy the Mirage IV bombers, the IRBMs, and the SSBNs in port, leaving France dependent on its SSBNs at sea.[30]

In contrast to the past emphasis on achieving certain levels of fatalities, the new *oeuvres vives* or enlarged anticities doctrine seems to depend on a sufficiency criterion of numbers of cities. The principle seems to be that France's surviving SLBM warheads alone—after a Soviet first strike—should be able to strike a number of major Soviet cities at least equal to the number of major French cities. Lewin's reference to striking 100 or 150 of the USSR's largest cities has been echoed by other sources, with comparable numbers. Pierre Riou, for example, suggests 100 to 200 "vital centers."[31]

The term *vital center* is not defined precisely, nor is it clear whether this level truly constitutes an official sufficiency criterion. The idea of 100 vital centers may simply represent a vague figure suitable for release to the public. It may, however, be used for heuristic analytical purposes if we assume that *100 vital centers* simply means an ability to strike 100 key urban, industrial, and administrative targets within the framework of the anticities strategy.

France's physical ability to achieve these targeting aims is minimal today. The systems—34 single-bomb Mirage IVs, 18 single-warhead 1-Mt (megaton) S-3 IRBMs, and 80 single-warhead 1-Mt M-20 SLBMs, and 16 six-warhead M-4 SLBMs (making the unrealistic assumption of the operational availability of all 6 SSBNs)—add up to 228 warheads, 98 of which have yields of one megaton. All six SSBNs could theoretically be available in a French first strike since SSBNs in port could obviously fire SLBMs capable of reaching the USSR.[32] If two submarines in overhaul or refitting are subtracted, France's total of deliverable strategic warheads declines to either 196 or 116. (The sole M-4 equipped SSBN, the *Inflexible*, became operational in May 1985, and accounts for 96 warheads.) If a Soviet first strike destroyed most of the bombers and IRBMs and SSBNs in port and the SSBN communications systems, France's retaliatory potential would be reduced below apparent doctrinal requirements. This judgment assumes that at least one warhead would be required per vital center, however. It is possible that French planners envisage a one-megaton warhead as destroying two or more such centers.

The definitional obscurity as to what a vital center specifically represents helps conceal the precise meaning of the targeting information France has made public. If Moscow were the target, at least six 1-Mt warheads would be required to cause a minimum of 5 psi overpressure over the whole city.[33] French sources at the Commissariat à l'Energie Atomique estimate that the six 150-kt (kiloton) warheads of the M-4 SLBM (first deployed in May 1985) could cover an urban target as effectively as a single 2-Mt warhead.[34] Indeed, assuming that eighteen 150-kt warheads could effectively destroy Moscow, only three M-4-equipped SLBMs would be required in contrast to the six single-warhead 1-Mt-yield M-20 SLBMs currently required for roughly equivalent target coverage. A vital center may then simply represent some specific portion of the top Soviet industrial-administrative centers.

During the 1980s and 1990s, the technical credibility of France's deterrent should improve as command, control, and communications (C^3) systems are hardened, the ASMP air-to-ground missile is deployed, the M-4 SLBM is introduced, and the SX mobile IRBM development is completed. The key facts regarding these projected systems may be summarized as follows.

Protecting C^3

The main command post for France's strategic nuclear forces, Taverny outside Paris, is buried under concrete sixty meters below the surface and equipped with several redundant communication links with the Elysée Palace, the Ministry of Defense, and the command posts for the strategic aircraft, IRBMs, and SSBNs. Moreover, there is a duplicate national command center for the strategic forces at Lyon-Mont-Verdun. It has been reported that France's SSBN force can receive messages, including orders to fire, in an optimal fashion only if the two key transmitters at Rosnay and Kerlouan can function. While capabilities exist to use several other transmitters, possibly including ones attached to balloons, if these two centers are destroyed or incapacitated, Rosnay and

Kerlouan obviously represent attractive targets. Destroying, or simply degrading, such key strategic C^3 centers could be functionally equivalent to destroying the nuclear weapons themselves since no French nuclear weapon could be used without redundant confirmation of launch authority from the chief of state.[35]

On the other hand, compared to those of the United States and the USSR, French C^3 requirements are relatively simple because France has no limited strike policy and relatively small numbers to manage. Nor could the USSR be certain of having destroyed all the C^3 links, a fact the French raise when C^3 vulnerabilities are noted. In addition, France in 1982 initiated the Astarte program, which will consist of Transall aircraft equipped for SSBN and other strategic nuclear C^3. France is investing the approximate cost of another SSBN in the Astarte program and its land-based network called Ramses,[36] which are to become operational in 1988.[37] Finally, the doctrine calls for immediate strategic nuclear retaliation for any attack against France's vital interests and declares that no "nibbles" against the C^3 of her strategic forces will be tolerated. But could such retaliation be carried out if strategic C^3 were disabled?

Defense Minister Hernu has repeatedly stressed the need for France to develop greater C^3 redundancy and to harden its C^3 networks, particularly against electromagnetic pulse (EMP).[38] Hernu's reasoning may be that a high-altitude nuclear explosion producing EMP would be an especially attractive means for the Soviets to disrupt French strategic C^3 since it would not require any direct strikes on French soil.

ASMP

Eighteen of the more advanced Mirage IVs are scheduled to remain in service until approximately 1992–94, all to be equipped with the ASMP medium-range air-to-ground missile (*air-sol moyenne portée*) by 1987. The ASMP standoff missile, with a speed approximating Mach 2.5, will carry a 100- to 300-kt warhead. ASMP range has been reported as 100 to 300 km,[39] and 50 to 100 km.[40] The reduction in numbers of Mirage IVs in service as strategic launch vehicles has been subtly deemphasized in formulations that stress the higher yield of the ASMP warhead over the bombs currently carried. This explains General Lacaze's statement that the yield of France's air-delivered strategic force will be doubled.[41] A key purpose of the ASMP is to improve prospects of penetrating enemy air defenses while reducing aircraft vulnerability. The Mirage 2000N (for both strategic and tactical missions) and the Super Etendard carrier aircraft will also be equipped with the ASMP.

[137]

M-4 SLBMs

Since January 1983, three SSBNs have been on patrol at all times. (Prior to that date, a third SSBN was available only 150 to 200 days a year.) A sixth SSBN, the *Inflexible*, equipped with the new M-4 SLBM, came into service in 1985. Four of the earlier SSBNs (all except the first, the *Redoutable*) are to be retrofitted with M-4 SLBMs as well between 1985 and 1990. In July 1981, Mitterrand announced that a seventh SSBN would be constructed during the 1985–90 period, and that it would not be "necessary to go so fast" regarding a decision on an eighth submarine, given that a "sufficient capacity" for deterrence had been established.[42] In September 1981, General Lacaze announced the decision, later confirmed in the October 1981 Conseil de Défense, to defer delivery of the seventh SSBN to 1994. Lacaze added that it would not be reasonable, in view of France's "sufficiency needs for deterrence," to have more than seven SSBNs by the end of the century; more than seven or eight SSBNs would lead France away from the "sufficiency" principle.[43] The seventh SSBN will receive an advanced SLBM, the successor generation of the M-4 that entered service in 1985.

The multiple warhead capability of the M-4 SLBM—6 warheads of approximately 150-kt yield—significantly increases the number of survivable warheads France can threaten to launch. By 1991, when M-4 retrofitting is to be completed, the five SSBNs equipped with M-4s will theoretically be capable of threatening 480 targets (5 SSBNs × 16 SLBMs each × 6 warheads per SLBM).[44] In practice, only three M-4-equipped SSBNs will always be at sea, giving a total of 288 M-4 SLBM warheads available at all times. To this will be added the M-20-equipped *Redoutable* part of the time. In a crisis, a fourth M-4-equipped SSBN might be returned to sea in as little as seventy-two hours. This would raise the number of M-4 RVs to 384. Other significant features of the M-4 SLBM include its range (in excess of 4,000 km), its accuracy (with published estimates as high as 220 to 450 meters CEP),[45] and its warhead separation system.

The M-4 warhead separation system has sometimes been described as MRV (multiple reentry vehicles) rather than MIRV (multiple independently targeted reentry vehicles). Confusion seems to have arisen because French sources disagree as to the quality and purpose of the warhead separation system. Some describe the M-4 as an MRV but with separation effects comparable to those of a MIRV in so far as frustrating enemy defenses is concerned. The director of military applications at the Commissariat à l'Energie Atomique notes that RV separation will be such that, in conjunction with hardening, no enemy interceptor will be able to destroy more than one RV.[46] Similarly, the elliptical "footprint" of arriving RVs is projected to be comparable to that of a MIRV. On the other hand, despite the impressive accuracy figures offered by some observers, other French authorities have stated that the accuracy of the M-4's RVs is not comparable to that of U.S. and Soviet MIRVs because individual RV guidance has not yet been perfected to such levels. Moreover, they add, such high accuracy would be needed only for counterforce operations and is unnecessary for France's enlarged anticities strategy. The point is overcoming Soviet ballistic missile defenses, not attacking hardened targets.

More recently, however, technical authorities such as Pierre Usunier, director of the ballistic and space systems division of Aerospatiale (principal contractor for the M-4), have stated emphatically that the M-4's six warheads can be directed with "independent guidance to six distinct targets or arrive spaced on a single target."[47] On balance, it appears more accurate to describe the M-4 as a MIRV system. With the M-4, the rate of SLBM firing is to be increased (with the time required reportedly cut in half),[48] in order to make less likely the possibility of Soviet backtracking to destroy the SSBN before all its missiles could be launched.

SX Mobile IRBMs

The urgency of developing a solution to France's IRBM vulnerability through mobile launchers has been minimized. One official source wrote in 1980 that the IRBMs would be survivable and credible for at least ten more years,[49] while the director of military applications at the Commissariat à l'Energie Atomique wrote in the same year that they would remain in service until the year 2000.[50]

It appears that solutions in the form of variations of launch on warning (including launch through attack, launch on attack assessment, etc.) were long ago ruled out as (*a*) technologically too costly, if not too challenging, and (*b*) strategic nonsense, owing to the risk of catastrophic accidental launches and the loss of political control implicit in an automatic launch system. On the other hand, the solid-fuel IRBMs are ready for prompt release and may be sufficiently hardened for successful launch through attack, even though such a solution does not form part of France's officially declared policy. Several official and quasi-official analyses during 1977–80 discussed the question of a land-based missile successor to the S-3 primarily in terms of mobile IRBMs (called the SX) and secondarily in terms of ground- and air-launched cruise missiles. During his last year in office, Giscard d'Estaing made the basic decision to support construction of a land-based missile.[51]

While it was increasingly presumed that the SX would be a ballistic missile, not until October 1981 did a Conseil de Défense presided over by Mitterrand finally determine that the new land-based missile would be ballistic rather than cruise and that it would come into service as the Mirage IVs were withdrawn in 1992–94.[52] This date was extended to 1996 in the 1984–88 *loi de programmation* approved in July 1983.[53] Basing modes for the SX have yet to be determined, however. Permanent mobility raises difficult questions of security, logistics, and communications, while mobility limited to certain periods would raise the problems of adequate warning time for dispersal (and the political will to use it).

Technical Credibility Prospects

The M-4 SLBM, by greatly increasing numbers of survivable warheads and permitting more efficient target coverage, will obviously constitute the most vital medium-term addition to the technical credibility of the aspirations of the enlarged anticities strategy. In the meantime, however, the military environment could significantly change. While Soviet submarine detection means may not improve appreciably, Soviet ballistic missile defense (BMD) could prove France's essential reliance on ballistic missiles unfortunate. The decision to rely primarily on ballistic missiles is understandable, given the magnitude of Soviet air defenses and France's inability to build cruise missiles of sufficient sophistication in large numbers (owing in part to a lack of suitable satellites to provide mapping information for guidance systems); but significant Soviet BMD would severely threaten the technical credibility of France's deterrent posture.[54] In short, France's technical ability to wreak all the damage required by the enlarged anticities strategy does not yet appear to be fully developed and remains ultimately dependent on a favorable strategic environment.

France today could nonetheless probably do significant damage to a large number of Soviet vital centers. Even if only three SSBNs armed with M-20 SLBMs survived a Soviet first strike, these three SSBNs could theoretically deliver forty-eight one-megaton strikes against Soviet cities of economic and administrative importance. (This assumes that French C^3 systems could operate, that all the SLBMs and warheads would be sufficiently reliable, that Soviet defenses would not intercept any warheads, and so forth.)

For years some analysts have assumed that this number of anticity strikes, or even a quarter of that number, "would suffice to deter the Soviet Union from unacceptable behavior."[55] Col. Jonathan Alford, deputy director of the International Institute for Strategic Studies, has argued, for example, that "there was no real need . . . to increase the capability, as defined in terms of the number of targets in the Soviet Union, that the United Kingdom should hold at risk—and we felt that the requirement to hold some 12 major Soviet conurbations hostage to the British nuclear forces would remain adequate."[56] Other British experts have also argued that a medium power like Britain (or France) requires no more than "a deterrent capability equivalent to the present Polaris deterrent capability—25 to 30 MTEs [megaton equivalents]."[57] While France's SSBN force alone exceeds these criteria for technical sufficiency, potential specific situations must also be considered in assessing political and strategic credibility.

STRATEGIC TARGETING FLEXIBILITY?

When the United States first displayed interest in counterforce options and city-avoidance targeting in early 1960s (most visibly in Secretary of Defense Robert McNamara's Ann Arbor phase), France was striving to build a plausible anticities retaliatory threat based on its Mirage IV bombers. France was thus hardly capable of imitating the American example, even if she had been disposed to do so. In contrast, the continuing U.S. articulation of limited strategic nuclear options since January 1974 (especially in the Schlesinger doctrine and its successor, PD-59) has coincided with the expansion of French strategic nuclear forces, including improvements in accuracy and the initiation of the multiple warhead M-4 SLBM program. In these changed material circumstances a number of French observers, including Michel Tatu and François de Rose, have suggested that strategic targeting flexibility might be a sensible policy for France.[58]

General Pierre Hautefeuille in 1980 presented perhaps the most thoroughly argued case for nuclear targeting flexibility. Hautefeuille included, more or less explicitly, all the arguments made by other flexible targeting proponents: (*a*) greater deterrent credibility because of reduced likelihood of self-deterrence before the initial use decision; (*b*) retention of an anticities reserve for intrawar deterrence and war termination negotiations; and (*c*) a potential ability to deter Soviet limited strikes by being prepared to respond in kind.

Hautefeuille kept his analyses within the framework of orthodoxy by proposing that France's initial strategic nuclear strikes against the Soviet Union constitute in effect an extension of the tactical nuclear "warning shots." The same purpose as with the tactical nuclear weapons in the national deterrent maneuver would apply. That is, the Soviets would only have committed aggression because they doubted France's will to use nuclear weapons. France's limited strategic nuclear strikes would supply the Soviets with palpable proof of their error in evaluation, and they would then abandon their aggressive course: "For the medium power this is a victory. . . . The "all or nothing" formula would unavoidably lead the medium power to total defeat. An initial measured strike, by enabling it to hold in reserve the bulk of its means, would in contrast prompt the great power to renounce its aggression and its goals."[59]

Hautefeuille conceded that Soviet reactions to France's limited strikes might be irrational and emotional, owing to vengeance motives and prestige considerations. In that case, Soviet retaliation against France might well be disproportionate. "But many other cases are conceivable where the margin of the medium power's capability would be fairly sizable and the 'vengeance' and 'prestige' reactions weak enough for the great power to be impelled to renounce its aggression. . . . Consideration of emotional factors reduces in short the 'rational' chances of success of a 'measured' nuclear initiative of the medium power." In other words, Hautefeuille could not offer any guarantees that a French policy of limited initial strikes would prove uniformly successful. His position was that such a policy "would not always succeed. But it alone could succeed."[60]

Serious government discussion of the merits for France of targeting flexibility apparently took place in the late 1970s. In 1980, however, numerous government spokesmen rejected the concept, giving several interrelated reasons. The first and most important reason was that France lacks the means—not only current numbers of warheads and delivery vehicles, but also the financial resources—to aspire to a credible capacity for limited options, including counterforce. It would be too costly for France to build up to credible levels of strategic nuclear power, if targeting flexibility was required.

A second reason was an extension of the first: the "equalizing power of the atom no longer applies in counterforce actions."[61] Soviet counterforce superiority would place France in a position of helpless inferiority. As Defense Minister Yvon Bourges said, "faced with countries like the superpowers, it is totally unrealistic to imagine that you can say: 'Well, if I were subjected to an attack limited to one or two regions, one or two towns in the territory, my response would be limited' because in this game I know perfectly well who would be the loser."[62] General Méry likewise condemned as "totally stupid" the suggestions of limited, initial counterforce strikes against the USSR by France: "even if we had sufficiently accurate weapons, we would destroy only a truly minor part of his entire order of battle, and we would then be assured of his immediate retaliation."[63]

The argument that the French threat of anticities retaliation could only be a credible deterrent to a Soviet strike against French cities had been well put by Alexandre Sanguinetti: "we will not respond to the demolition of the base at Cambrai by crushing the city of Kharkov."[64] This proposition was singled out by a government spokesman as representative of widespread misunderstandings supportive of the retaliation-in-kind argument for limited strategic options. The argument, the government held, unrealistically attributed highly limited collateral damage to highly improbably isolated Soviet strikes. The Soviets would not be interested in such limited strikes but would in all probability attack all French nuclear weapons systems, strategic and tactical, and would therefore explode at least a hundred warheads on the order of three hundred kilotons each on French soil, with attendant damage to French cities. "Would this not amount to a sufficiently defined aggression to justify, as much in the eyes of the French as to the aggressor, our strategic nuclear retaliation on the cities of the enemy?"[65]

Moreover, government spokesmen added, in a restatement of the original argument, only an anticities strategy conformed to France's means.

> We aim at the adversary's cities because these targets are easy to reach, without great accuracy in the missiles required, and especially because one can thus cause important damage with a limited number of weapons.... It is only in the framework of an anticities strategy that the desirable level of damage can be guaranteed with the means that remain in proportion to the scientific, industrial, and economic possibilities of France. Any other strategy would necessitate much more important means, without doubt beyond our reach, and could not but weaken deterrence.[66]

Prime Minister Raymond Barre likewise stressed that "For our country, the problem of choosing between an antiforces strategy and an anticities strategy does not arise."[67]

The final justification for rejecting proposals of targeting flexibility was doctrinally the most satisfying—that is, that an anticities posture would maximize the probability of successful deterrence. A declared strategy of initially limited strikes would inform the Soviets that they could count on manageable French retaliation. Implying that France would not respond as massively as possible could undermine the deterrent and invite Soviet aggression. As General Poirier had long argued, the medium power's "threat can only have deterrent value if the threatened party knows that he would experience the effects of one blow, without his losses being spaced out over time."[68]

The government would not have rejected the concept of flexible targeting so emphatically if it had not been determined to forestall the development of greater interest in the idea. That such interest may persist is implied in the Mitterrand government's having underlined its rejection of the concept for the same reasons given under Giscard d'Estaing. In reviewing several of these reasons, General Lacaze added that "This idea implies in itself a doubt in the presidential determination to have recourse to strategic reprisals and, consequently, would lead to weakening the credibility of our deterrence by the weak of the strong."[69] French interview sources have added that a superpower can afford to develop limited strategic options in order to avoid fundamental choices, while France's deterrent posture may derive added credibility from having made the simple logic of her decision for an anticities posture clear.

No further reasons for rejecting the ideas of limited initial strike options and targeting flexibility have been given by French government spokesmen, but technical factors may have also led to the French decision. Targeting flexibility would require rapid attack analysis and decision-making capabilities, including retargeting and force coordination challenges, that may well be beyond the immediate reach of French command, control, and communications equipment, especially for an extended period of time. Another technical constraint might be uncertainty about the advisability of launching only a portion of the missiles carried by an SSBN, owing to the possibility of Soviet back-tracking to the point of launch. Although the SSBN could move in an attempt to evade Soviet detection and destruction, a "split launch" could well jeopardize the survivability of the remaining SLBMs. The chances of detection by Soviet intelligence means would at any rate be increased by some unmeasurable amount, depending in part on the degree of Soviet proficiency in the difficult task of back-tracking.

Other than isolated assertions by Gen. Pierre Gallois that France targets "at least some Soviet soft military targets in the Kola peninsula,"[70] there is little evidence to support a judgment that the French may have secretly prepared some limited initial strike options. The French government might deem it wise to prepare such options in case they would prove useful in some crisis management and negotiating situations. But publicly announcing the policy would contravene the established anticities doctrine, even in its enlarged anticities form. Without improved French capabilities, only some type of anticities policy is technically credible, even if the political and strategic credibility of the anticities policy remains associated with significant uncertainties. Moreover, too much domestic political capital has been invested in the anticities policy—in political circles, in the bureaucracy, and in the military—for it to be altered very readily.

No Coordination or Consultation with Allies

France has apparently never accepted any formal consultation obligations regarding use of her nuclear weapons, either with NATO or with specific allies such as West Germany and the United States. Nor, it appears, has France ever agreed to any explicit understanding as to allocation of strategic or tactical nuclear targeting responsibilities, although French officers did participate in the deliberations of other allied officers at the Joint Strategic Target Planning Staff at Offutt Air Force Base, near Omaha, Nebraska, during the period 1963–66.[71] Given the long history of U.S. obstructionism with respect to French nuclear weapons programs and the French tendency to define national independence in terms of freedom from superpower constraints, it is unlikely that any explicit secret agreement on consultation or targeting obligations exists between France and the United States.

At the time of withdrawal from NATO, in the March 1966 memorandum addressed to her allies, the French government declared that the "very nature" of nuclear forces precluded France's remaining a part of NATO's integrated institutions.[72] More recently, when Gen. Jeannou Lacaze, chief of staff of the armed forces, summed up France's cooperation policy in September 1981, he noted that "cooperation only involves conventional forces, and therefore excludes all nuclear force employment planning."[73]

The French view is that an agreement on a division of labor in targeting objectives would deprive France of her independent strategy. French officials have implied that the United States has vainly sought such agreements by declaring that France must maintain the "total" independence of her nuclear forces, despite superpower pressure "seeking plans for coordinated strikes through which we would lose part of our autonomy."[74] Similarly, despite erroneous reports to the contrary,[75] and genuine West German interest in such consultations,[76] Mitterrand's statement of October 1982 remains France's official policy regarding nuclear weapons consultations with West Germany: "There is no question of associating the FRG with France's nuclear strategy."[77] Lothar Ruehl has added, from a West German point of view, that "the persistent refusal of France to allocate French nuclear weapons designed for battlefield support or use in the extended theater of war in Europe to the planning, direction, and procedures of NATO, much less to make them directly available to NATO, has not permitted either an effective harmony in defense planning or a coordinated deterrence."[78]

Despite the absence of formal consultation or coordination obligations, Giscard d'Estaing acknowledged the value of exchanging some information concerning nuclear employment planning:

> the essential decisions on employment of our means of deterrence are national decisions . . . we have never spoken with our alliance partners of the conditions in which we would take such decisions; on the other hand, it may be interesting to know what are each other's ideas, what their reflections are, what are their possible time-tables, but without there possibly being any agreement to act together, that is, more or less joint decisions.[79]

This statement implies that France and NATO may have exchanged information concerning basic employment concepts, perhaps including request and release procedures. Some exchanges of information may be almost unavoidable, owing to France's dependence on her allies for early warning of attack and other intelligence that could be related to target acquisition. Even excluding formal consultation or strike coordination, such contacts could be valuable both tactically and strategically. Particularly on the tactical level, they could help avoid dual targeting of the same enemy assets, strikes hindering each other's plans, and potential harm to allied forces and civilians.

On the strategic level, exchanges of information might theoretically be desirable to provide adequate target coverage and avoid gratuitous overkill. Tacit understandings might also help resolve the potential problem of "fratricide," which could be construed in an unusually broad sense. For example, besides the risk of Allied missile warheads or gravity bombs exploding at roughly the same time in close proximity, one could imagine the explosion of a U.S. Minuteman ICBM warhead inadvertently destroying a Mirage IV flying over Soviet territory.

Although such intraalliance fratricide might hypothetically arise, it seems most improbable for three reasons. First, France might well not launch its strategic nuclear forces in the course of a Soviet-American intercontinental war, unless attacked by the USSR. It might be in France's interests to await the war's outcome and retain her forces for war termination bargaining. Second, the French government would presumably realize how uncertain the prospects for aircraft penetration would be at such a juncture, even if missiles could penetrate. Third, even if France did employ her strategic nuclear forces during a Soviet-American nuclear war, the anticities orientation of French targeting could minimize overlap with that of the United States, which has a counterforce emphasis. Because of this basic difference in targeting orientation, the potential benefits relating to target coverage and overkill avoidance seem more theoretical at the strategic level than at the tactical level.

At the tactical level, it is only just to put French behavior in perspective by comparing it with that of the United States and Britain. The French refusal to accept formal consultation agreements contrasts with U.S. and British behavior in the NATO Nuclear Planning Group and Nuclear Defense Affairs Committee; in the planning exercises of these entities, thorough political consultation precedes all decisions to employ nuclear weapons. On the other hand, as various European observers have noted, the Athens guidelines only oblige the United States and Britain to consult "time and circumstances permitting." This formula is obviously necessary for deterrent credibility, but some Europeans find it a cynical "escape clause" that puts the United States and Britain on the same level as France.

In practice, lack of time could mean that neither Britain, France, nor the United States could engage in much effective consultation with each other, to say nothing of other allies. The preplanned NATO guidelines on nuclear use need not necessarily inhibit Britain or the United States any more than France. Moreover, as some European observers have noted, depending on the circumstances, French use of tactical nuclear weapons could be less likely than use by the United States, and could be less destructive than U.S. use as well, owing to the small size of the French tactical nuclear stockpile.

Other potential disadvantages for the alliance also reside in France's capability for independent nuclear options. Some of France's allies (notably the United States) have repeatedly raised the possibility that an uncoordinated and precipitate French use of tactical nuclear weapons could lead to SACEUR losing whatever control over escalation he might have retained until that point. From a Soviet viewpoint, it could be hard to distinguish between British, French, and U.S. warheads. French restrictions on nuclear targeting to protect allied troops and civilians could prove unrealistic. The result could thus be the premature triggering of a wider and more destructive war. The Soviets could well retaliate against both France and NATO, and NATO could find itself militarily defeated, when greater caution and deliberation might have led to successful management of the crisis. In Senator Sam Nunn's words,

> France by its policies reduces the possibility of a conventional defense, and significantly lowers the nuclear threshold. . . . French tactical nuclear weapons, if used in the midst of a conventional engagement between NATO . . . and Warsaw Pact forces, could force the U.S. into a nuclear war. The Alliance has been able to tolerate this bad situation during the period of U.S. nuclear superiority, but strategic parity makes the French position totally at odds with the best interest of NATO and stability in Central Europe.[80]

The French rejoinder might well be that such risks constitute part of the price of maintaining an alliance that includes independent nuclear powers; that if the United States initiates use of nuclear weapons in Europe, the Soviets could well retaliate against France as well, even if France had not yet entered the war; and that NATO's own restrictions on nuclear targeting could also prove unrealistic, doing harm to French as well as Allied interests. The French government's judgment has been that, quite apart from France's own national deterrent purposes, its independent nuclear weapons policies make a contribution to Allied deterrence that outweighs any irritation and anxiety they may cause some allies. In the words of Jacques Andréani,

> It is obvious that a country that would be risking its very existence would not do so lightly and nothing proves that France's crossing the nuclear threshold would ignite a total holocaust in circumstances where that would not be likely to happen anyway. If the French force adds a supplementary element to the nuclear risk, that is what a potential aggressor would have to reckon with, complicating his calculations and thereby increasing, not insecurity, but—on the contrary—protection.[81]

In the long term, in contrast to the inflexible anticities strategic targeting policy that has recently been reconfirmed, the French may be drawn to consider more flexible targeting plans in response to improving Soviet capacities for long-range conventional and nuclear discriminate strike options against France, for example, coordinated counterforce strikes with accurate, low-yield nuclear weapons or conventional explosives. Soviet preemptive destruction of part of France's nuclear arsenal in this fashion would highlight the "all or nothing" dilemmas of an anticities strategy.[82] While French officials have to this point generally rejected this threat as implausible and unlikely, in the future they may well concede that France would retain a stake in survival and escalation control in such circumstances, and that a capability for limited retaliation in kind might be necessary. Anticities threats could then appear obviously incredible and self-deterring in comparison to more proportionate and usable options. If the French do pursue this path, they may recognize that cooperation and coordination with their allies in nuclear targeting would be desirable for deterrence as well as for operational employment and would not necessarily deprive them of decision-making autonomy in any ultimate sense. Coordination agreements would have to be devised with care, for any arrangement raising doubts about the genuineness of French autonomy could diminish the deterrence benefits for the alliance as a whole which derive from France as an independent center of nuclear decisions.

OPERATIONAL EMPLOYMENT SCENARIOS

To some extent, the operational meaning of French targeting doctrine is kept deliberately ambiguous. Giscard d'Estaing pointed out repeatedly that the adversary "must not be able to calculate what would be the reaction to this or that initiative that he might take."[83] Giscard d'Estaing's prime minister, Raymond Barre, also stressed that "it is not possible nor especially desirable" to define employment scenarios,[84] adding that "Employment policy is not fixed and remains sufficiently supple to respond in a rational fashion to all the requirements of our security and to the diversity of marginal situations."[85] A basic principle is that French nuclear employment planning (like NATO's) is "more oriented toward the political management of crises than toward military effectiveness."[86] Some French officials even maintain that operational issues such as targeting are a narrow and secondary concern compared to what is the central issue for them—France's strategic independence in relation to its allies and the superpowers.

Release procedures are similar to those presumed to prevail in all nuclear weapons states, with authorization dependent on the highest political leaders. In November 1980, President Giscard d'Estaing described release procedures in some detail:

> These decisions are naturally prepared with all the chain of command and responsibility, notably the chief of staff of the armed forces, who plays an essential role in managing these means. But the decision and the execution depend on the president of the republic alone . . . who gives a formula transmitted by relays to the means of execution. . . . There are no modifications or changes in all the chain of command . . . for example, the commander of the submarine does not know on what target his missile will strike.[87]

The crews of the Mirage IV bombers constitute an obvious exception to this secrecy about targeting choices: the Mirage IV crews are advised of their objectives on takeoff. But, as is the case in the IRBM command posts and in the command centers of the SSBNs, two officers on each bomber must separately receive coded orders to fire and then act simultaneously for the nuclear weapons to be armed and launched.[88] Detailed descriptions of the various command posts and their interrelationships have been published in, for example, the Tourrain Report.

The specific agencies responsible for preparing strike plans have changed over the years. While the Defense Ministry's planning department, the Centre de Prospective et d'Evaluations, furnished a detailed rationale for proportional deterrence and sanctuarization after its establishment in February 1964,[89] a decree in January 1964 had already stipulated that the commander of the strategic air forces (the Mirage IVs) would report directly to the minister of defense regarding operational strike plans. In September 1968, given the imminent deployment of IRBMs and SLBMs, the leading responsibility for the preparation of targeting plans was transferred to the chief of staff of the armed forces.[90] The procedure since that date for selecting targets has been summarized as follows:

The security and release arrangements are independent of the lists of objectives—selections of possible targets—which are assigned to the delivery vehicles (planes, missiles, and submarines) and which are enumerated and regularly updated by the command posts at Taverny and Lyon-Mont-Verdun. It is the chief of state, assisted by his Conseil de Défense, who designates these targets from a catalogue submitted to him.[91]

The Centre de Prospective et d'Evaluations (reporting directly to the defense minister) apparently played a role in the change to the *oeuvres vives* concept in 1979–80, but the chief of staff of the armed forces and his subordinates (e.g., commanders of the specific strike forces) no doubt also contributed to the proposed change. It seems clear that the change could not have been implemented or announced without the approval of the president and the leading officials concerned with national security who compose the Conseil de Défense.[92]

The strike plans might function differently in various scenarios. The most explicit and emphatic statements of when France's strategic nuclear forces might be used concern direct nuclear attack on France. This is the circumstance in which French nuclear retaliation against the USSR would be most probable:

> As concerns the use of nuclear weapons, there are all sorts of situations and possible hypotheses. We are not here in order to enumerate them. But there is a central point in our planning, that any nuclear attack on France's soil would automatically provoke strategic nuclear retaliation.[93]

> Any nuclear action on French soil would have strategic significance because of the small area and high population density; it would automatically bring about anticities nuclear retaliation.[94]

Both of these statements refer to nuclear attack on France, but other statements are broad enough to include any direct attack, nuclear or conventional, on France. Colonel Lewin of the Defense Ministry's planning department has, for example, written that "an aggression against the national territory, whether it aims at our cities, our industries, or our defense means, always puts our vital interests in question and brings about the use of our strategic nuclear forces."[95] Similarly, raising the question of France's IRBM vulnerability always elicits an official statement that France's SLBMs and surviving bombers would retaliate against the aggressor.[96] General Lacaze qualified the range of contingencies that might provoke strategic nuclear retaliation by referring to "*major* military action against our country."[97]

Retaining the bomber capability is significant for operational employment planning. It is logical to use the most vulnerable forces first, and bombers offer controllability advantages. Both Prime Minister Mauroy and Defense Minister Hernu have noted that, since bombers are "slow to take offense," they could help in managing crises by demonstrating French resolve without taking irrevocable employment decisions.[98] If the IRBMs and SLBMs were launched, all the missiles would be fired in close succession, with all eighteen IRBMs reportedly capable of being fired within seven minutes. Adm. Jacques Bonnemaison, commander of the Force Océanique Stratégique (the SSBN fleet), has stated, "We wouldn't operate in sausage slices. We give them the entire sausage."[99]

Scenarios in which tactical use would precede strategic employment form the basis of the tactical targeting doctrine, but they are qualified by the nonbelligerency and sanctuarization options as well as by a desire to declare solidarity with key allies. As far as the latter desire is concerned, at the beginning of his presidential term in 1974, Giscard d'Estaing offered a restrictive definition of the efficacy of France's nuclear deterrent, confining it to "a nuclear threat against our soil by a nuclear power, or to a threat of invasion of our soil."[100] Prime Minister Jacques Chirac's 1975 declaration that "we cannot be content to 'sanctuarize' our own territory, and we must look beyond our frontiers" was followed by the *sanctuarisation élargie* controversy in 1976.[101] Since that controversy, high French officials have repeatedly suggested that the vital interests protected by France's nuclear deterrent may include allies, or at least portions of Allied territory. Barre's allusions to the "approaches" to France, "neighboring and Allied territories,"[102] and to "immediate neighbors,"[103] have been echoed in Mauroy's remark about "the impossibility of our taking no interest in our immediate neighbors."[104] In his 1981 and 1982 speeches to the Institut des Hautes Etudes de Défense Nationale, Mauroy deliberately repeated that "Aggression against France does not begin when an enemy penetrates the national territory."[105]

On the other hand, the same officials have been careful not to exclude the option of nonbelligerency, nor to offer any more precise criteria for commitment to war or nuclear weapons employment. Intrinsic deterrent credibility problems could well restrain France from offering an explicit guarantee to the Federal Republic of Germany or other allies, even if domestic political factors did not also exclude such guarantees. Although French officials can scarcely contend that France's cultivation of a nonbelligerency option contributes to the robustness of the overall deterrent of the Atlantic Alliance, they have tended to argue that the very vagueness of French commitments and employment criteria promotes effective deterrence.

Giscard d'Estaing declared, for example:

In our reflection about the employment of this [tactical nuclear] weapon, we will take account of the following given: France is directly concerned with the security of neighboring European states. . . . This affirmation is interesting so long as it remains stated in this fashion . . . there are in defense policy, and in particular on the employment of certain means, indications which must be given in a form that allows a possible listener to ask himself a certain number of questions.[106]

Hernu has added a similar explanation of why France will not define her "vital interests": "Are they tied to geographic, economic, and political criteria? I will respond that we are the judges of that, and not the adversary, who will have to make an inventory of all that we might place in that category. It is up to him to make hypotheses, knowing that an error of analysis could turn out to be immediately mortal."[107]

Some French political parties (for example, the Socialists and the Union pour la Démocratie Française) indicated in mid-1985 an unusually high degree of willingness to extend France's nuclear deterrent protection to the Federal Republic of Germany.[108] An opinion poll suggested that the same sentiment was shared by 40 percent of the French public.[109] Defense Minister Hernu's June 1985 speech at Münsingen nonetheless said simply that West Germany is "the closest of our allies, from all viewpoints, and we maintain with her the most intense relations in the domain of defense and security. France and Federal Germany share security interests in common." Jacques Isnard pointed out that "security interests" are not "vital interests" and that France had not in fact extended a guarantee more constraining than in the past, despite the new tone of solidarity.[110] The French doctrinal insistence on promoting uncertainty for deterrence, the need to maintain the credibility of France's autonomy of decision making, and a concern not to look presumptuous will probably continue to constrain France from offering an unambiguous nuclear guarantee to West Germany.

Just as incalculability and ambiguity may be helpful for deterrence, explicit employment criteria could be harmful. Giscard d'Estaing's view that "There is no deterrent if the adversary knows in advance in which conditions it will be used" has been seconded by Hernu and others.[111] On the other hand, despite France's having cultivated a nonbelligerency option and deliberate ambiguity as to her intentions, French officials have not hesitated to suggest at times that France's deterrent commitment could well be more reliable for Western Europe than that of the United States: "because of her geographical position, France would feel herself rather directly aimed at in any attack in Europe, which would obviously not be the case of the United States."[112]

One of the most explicit statements of when France might use tactical nuclear weapons independently was provided in 1980 by Gen. Claude Vanbremeersch, then commander of the First Army:

Either we fight alongside the alliance forces in the second line during a counterattack which has failed at a point on the front within range of French territory, and we will have to try to right a compromised situation. Or the whole Allied defense system will have been quickly defeated and we have to make this final stopping blow in front of our borders to signify to the adversary that he will not enter our country without a fight and that if we fail we are prepared to rise to the strategic level.... For me the choice is very clear.... If the First Army fights alongside the allies and, the forces' cohesion being broken, the Americans use their nuclear weapons in time, the commitment of our Plutons will have no essential significance. They will at least have had the merit of placing our forces on the same "nuclear" footing as the others with full freedom in the use of tactical weapons.

On the other hand, if the Allied forces do not use nuclear weapons when the front is broken, the French government will be able to decide to use its nuclear weapons when it considers the country to be directly threatened. It is up to me to insure that our weapons have the greatest possible effect by using their strike power in order to provide an obstacle that will be highly significant and very clearly marked. After doing that the First Army will have accomplished its mission.[113]

Vanbremeersch's uncertainty concerning whether the Americans will "use their nuclear weapons in time" highlights an implicit difference between France and NATO in timing the initial use of nuclear weapons (assuming, of course, that the Soviets do not precede all Western countries in their use). Since the early 1960s, when the United States first introduced the Flexible Response concept, France has contended that the United States sets the threshold for using nuclear weapons higher than would be most effective for deterrence. The refusal to "tolerate a conventional conflict of long duration in Europe"[114] is joined to a determination to be ready to use tactical nuclear weapons promptly and far forward. Gen. Arnaud de Foïard has, for example, suggested that

a warning shot, made when Western Europe was three-fourths invaded, its armies smashed and the military success of the opposing forces established, would not have in its timidity but an effect destined to insignificance. ...What aggressor could think an opponent hesitant to employ tactical weapons would have the audacity to use strategic means?... Currently the forces of the Atlantic alliance, of which we are a part, do not have the conventional means to stop for more than some *tens of hours* the invasion of Western Europe by a massive offensive by Warsaw Pact conventional forces.[115]

French authorities have suggested repeatedly since the mid-1960s that their policy of threatening what might be called "early nuclearization" of a conventional war in Europe contributes to effective deterrence and thus to the security of their allies. The policy is usually stated vaguely, as simply obliging potential aggressors to take the risk of nuclear war.[116]

CONCLUSION

While the French refer to their strategic targeting doctrine much more frequently than the British, its operational content is probably comparable. Both governments have moved beyond the anticities targeting of the 1960s to notions of attacking, in the British phrase, "key aspects of Soviet state power"[117]—that is, administrative and economic control assets. This move in both cases seems to have been encouraged by developments in Soviet defenses (active and passive), by the prospect of new capabilities (especially improved accuracy and increased numbers of warheads), and perhaps by attention to increased targeting sophistication in the capabilities and declaratory policies of the United States and the USSR. Moreover, Britain and France serve similar functional deterrent roles in the Atlantic alliance in that each adds to the Western arsenal facing the USSR, and each provides an additional center of decision making for Soviet leaders to take into account. The practical significance of France's contribution to the Atlantic alliance's overall deterrent posture cannot be gauged readily, given the lack of targeting and release coordination between the French and the U.S., British, and NATO nuclear decision-making entities—to say nothing of the scarcity of publicly available Soviet assessments of France's deterrent credibility.

A third similar functional role is one the French discuss more candidly than the British—the options their strategic nuclear forces may offer in an uncertain future.[118] Increased U.S. unreliability, the end of the Atlantic alliance, its restructuring, or other events (e.g., fundamental political changes in Germany) may give the independent strategic nuclear forces more credible missions in changed international contexts.[119] While official French statements place particular emphasis on guaranteeing France's security without U.S. assistance, unofficial arguments, even among Gaullists and partisans of proportional deterrence, stress the role French nuclear forces may someday play as the nucleus of an autonomous and united European deterrent force. For example, Raymond Tourrain argues that "we must develop our nuclear forces to render *technically possible* the defense of Western Europe when it will be *politically* feasible."[120] Prime Minister Mauroy has added that Europeans should reflect on "the perspective of [Western Europe] as a political whole maintaining an autonomous defense," in view of U.S. unreliability.[121]

Indeed, while the British frequently affirm their confidence in U.S. reliability, the French almost as regularly deny that the United States can be trusted to honor its guarantee to Western Europe. This is a prime justification for France's independent deterrent. French officials frequently assert that, in the words of the director of the Foreign Ministry's planning department, France's nuclear deterrent "guarantees the security of our territory, and the safekeeping of our political sovereignty . . . [and] assures her diplomatic independence in security matters, with respect to the United States as much as the Soviet Union, which is something fundamental."[122] Such rhetoric is readily exaggerated into an extreme view that claims for France a "politico-strategic insularity," allowing her to assure her security "without anyone's help."[123] In practice, however, French behavior suggests full awareness that France's security depends mainly on the state of East-West military balances and political relations, inside as well as outside Europe. France's continued membership in the Atlantic alliance and her security diplomacy regarding the maintenance of the U.S. presence in Western Europe and in West Germany in particular illustrate France's prudence and realism.

This prudence and realism are appropriate in view of the probability that any attempt to sustain sanctuarization through tactical nuclear employment and the threat of strategic strikes in an East-West war would fail, and given that the benefits of any successful sanctuarization would be meager and transient. Proportional deterrence theory would probably become irrelevant the moment the USSR came to see the destruction (or, more likely) the conquest of France as a vital war aim. Actually executing the anticities or *oeuvres vives* threat by striking the USSR could guarantee France's more total defeat through Soviet nuclear retaliation, a harsher Soviet occupation regime, or both. Gen. Guy Méry, chief of staff of the armed forces during 1975–80, implicitly acknowledged in 1976 the limited deterrent effectiveness of French nuclear forces in such circumstances by expressing doubt that "in an extreme case when everything in Europe had collapsed about us, the national will would remain to have recourse to the threat of *massive destruction*, even to assure our survival."[124] Méry's doubt was most pertinent in that recourse to actual "massive destruction," as opposed to the threat of doing so, would clearly not ensure France's survival or independence.

The same principle could also apply to the hypothetical option of more flexible targeting, depending on Soviet aims and risk assessments. French inferiority in nuclear war-waging capabilities could rapidly become as obvious with threats of selective and limited strikes as with threats of causing massive destruction in the USSR. The French would in effect be engaging the Soviets in a trial of mutual resolve in which each side's ability to carry out and sustain nuclear strikes would be tested. The French posture based on a theory of the "equalizing power of the atom" could be overwhelmed by a Soviet posture built to implement concepts of controlling escalation, enemy behavior, and the process of war-termination through a superior array of force employment options and defensive capabilities.

In short, France's nuclear deterrent threats are most likely to be efficacious in the least challenging strategic contingencies. As France's most subtle expositors of proportional deterrence have conceded, the anticities threat is most likely to deter the USSR from doing what it has only marginal or zero interest in doing—for example, striking French cities with nuclear weapons with no provocation. The more the scenarios resemble the grave situations that might well arise in an actual East-West war, the less likely the successful functioning of proportional deterrence.[125] As French strategists have argued, France might be able to exert some "crisis management" leverage in a limited conflict within Europe, depending on the restraint of the USSR and other governments. Proportional deterrence would nonetheless be least likely to guarantee France's security and independence in the circumstances where that security and independence would be most severely threatened—in a more general and intense East-West war, in which the USSR might well find it a vital aim to destroy certain targets in France or to conquer France. The French emphasis on the primacy of deterrence and war prevention understandably parallels that of the Atlantic alliance as a whole.[126]

PART III

ISSUES IN STRATEGIC NUCLEAR TARGETING

[7]

The Dilemmas of
Counterpower Targeting

Jeffrey Richelson

The last decade has seen a resurgence in the discussion of alternative nuclear strategies that the United States might adopt. This resurgence has stemmed from a feeling shared by many analysts both inside and outside of the government that the traditional emphasis on all-out countervalue retaliation in response to any Soviet attack was too inflexible and incredible.

This uneasiness led to two prominent strategy shifts during the Nixon-Ford administrations. The first shift involved the adoption of the concept of Limited Nuclear Options (LNOs).[1] Under this concept, the United States was to be prepared to respond to various-sized Soviet nuclear attacks with U.S. attacks appropriate to the circumstances. The size of the appropriate attack might vary from just a few weapons to a few hundred to the entire U.S. arsenal. Supporters of the change argued that it would offer a more credible deterrent to less-than-all-out attacks than would the threat of a massive response and would also increase the prospects for early war termination and damage limitation should deterrence fail.

The second shift involved an emphasis on the SIOP-level (Single Integrated Operational Plan) attack, should the conflict reach that stage. Primary attention was shifted from targeting war-supporting industry to targeting a broader set of industrial and related targets. The objective of such an attack would be to delay for as long as possible the Soviet Union's recovery to the status of a major military and economic power. This strategy, as detailed in NSDM-242 implementing documents, specified the destruction of 70 percent of the Soviet economic recovery base.[2]

Shortly after taking office, the Carter administration initiated a review of targeting policy. As a result of this review, President Carter signed Presidential Directive 59, "Nuclear Weapons Employment Policy." As a result emphasis was switched from targeting the Soviet recovery base to targeting Soviet political and military assets.[3] This emphasis was confirmed by President Reagan's signing of National Security Decision Directive-13, also titled "Nuclear Weapons Employment Policy." Such plans incorporate elements of a strategy that, proposed by several strategic analysts in the 1970s, are referred to as countercombatant or counterpower targeting.[4]

Counterpower targeting also may include attacks on certain economic resources and war-supporting industry (e.g., oil refining). This paper focuses on the targeting of political and military assets. Specifically, I am concerned with the feasibility of such targeting as well as its possible effects on prewar deterrence, intrawar deterrence, and the prospects for early war termination.

A DIGRESSION ON STRATEGY

Before proceeding with the discussion, several points are worth making concerning the treatment of strategy choices. First, discussions of alternative strategies often give the impression that the choice of strategies consists of choosing between mutually exclusive strategies or target sets. Thus, the choices may be depicted as between a countervalue or an antirecovery or a counterforce strategy. More realistically, U.S. war plans have traditionally included attacks on all types of targets—military, recovery, urban-industrial, and political.[5] Indeed far more potential targets (25,000) than weapons are available.[6] What has shifted from time to time are the emphasis and priorities assigned to various types of targets. Thus, it could be safely assumed that under the antirecovery strategy the United States also targeted certain military facilities and political assets but that these targets were assigned a lower priority than targets considered crucial to Soviet recovery capability. Hence, sufficient weapons would be assigned first to those targets making up the Soviet economic recovery base to ensure destruction of that recovery base, and only then to military and political targets.

Second, there is a difference between weapons allocation priorities and execution priorities. Thus, while economic recovery targets may be the first targets to be assigned weapons, military targets might be assigned execution priority—that is, weapons assigned to military targets would be fired before those targeted against economic facilities. Such a tactic could be expected because many of the Soviet military targets, especially aircraft and missiles that might be used in a second wave, would be considered time urgent while economic facilities would not be. Additionally, the land-based weapons assigned to attack Soviet military targets are more vulnerable than the sea-based weapons assigned to economic targets.

Finally, there is another consideration that might influence timing. It may be imprudent to attack first those assets the Soviets value most highly, especially if such attacks produce irreversible results. Thus, if the initial attacks are part of a set of limited attacks, it is important to keep alive the prospects of intrawar deterrence and early war termination. Attacking the Soviets' most highly valued assets first would not contribute to these prospects. Additionally, it has been argued that should war even reach the "general war" stage, deterrence can continue and discrimination in target selection is still desirable.[7] In this view, attacks on certain highly valuable targets might be made *only* if the Soviets were to attack those targets the United States values most. Of course, the type of targets the Soviets value most highly need not be of the same type as those the United States values most highly.

COUNTERPOWER TARGETING: POLITICAL TARGETS

As noted above, a counterpower strategy includes attacks on both political and military assets. Political targets are of three basic types. First, there is the political leadership itself. This leadership consists of more than the members of the Politburo and Defense Council. It includes those individuals plus key officials throughout the Soviet Communist party, government, and armed forces. Specifically, key officials in the Administration of Affairs, Administrative Organs Department, Organizational Party Work Department, and Propaganda Department of the Party would be part of that leadership, as would key officials of the Council of Ministers, State Planning Commission (GOSPLAN), Military-Industrial Commission, and the ministries of Defense, Foreign Affairs, Internal Affairs, and Defense Industry.[8] Taken together, it was estimated in 1978 that the Soviet leadership consists of 110,000 individuals.[9] It is believed that there is protection available for the entire group at the many dispersed shelters that would serve as alternative government control centers.[10] Attempts to kill a significant portion of these individuals would involve attacks on these hardened and buried shelters.

A second type of target is the lines of communication between the leadership and those charged with carrying out their orders. Interruption of such communications would involve blocking airborne transmissions as well as destroying buried cables designed for wartime communications. Even should the former objective be attainable, the second might prove to be much less so.

A third set of targets would be the facilities and individuals through which the leadership maintains political control. Such targets would include: (1) the headquarters of organizations such as the Ministry of Defense, KGB (Committee for State Security), MVD (Ministry of Internal Affairs), GOSPLAN, and Administrative Organs Department; (2) KGB and MVD facilities and troops throughout the Soviet Union and Eastern Europe; (3) border troop outposts near the Chinese border; and (4) army troops stationed in Eastern Europe and the Soviet Union. In case (4), substantial overlap might occur between political and military effects since such troops could be used for either maintenance of political control or conventional military action.

The intent of such targeting is to destroy the ability of the Soviet leadership to continue to exercise political control over its domestic and "colonial" territory—either by killing the leadership itself, making it impossible for the leadership to communicate with its subordinates, or by destroying the means (people and facilities) by which the leadership's orders are carried out.

Attacks on border troop outposts on the Chinese border would threaten the Soviets with the loss of territories in Soviet Asia that have been repeatedly claimed by the Chinese. Attacks on the KGB, MVD (Ministry of Internal Affairs), and military troop barracks in the USSR and Eastern Europe, it has been argued, would create the prospect of Hungarian-type revolts against Russian domination both in Eastern Europe and within areas of the USSR such as the Ukraine, Georgia, Armenia, and Byelorussia, where separatist sentiment is strong.[11]

Whatever specific political targets are chosen, it has been argued that incorporation of such targets into U.S. nuclear war plans would have several desirable results. To the extent that this plan threatens the Soviet regime in a way that killing civilians or destroying industry does not, it creates a more severe threat than other strategies. As one analyst has argued, "Any Soviet government rational enough to be deterred by the threat of a city-busting attack is likely to be deterred by the threat of a countercombatant second strike that would subject the nation to great calamities and leave it at the mercy of historically unfriendly peoples both within and adjacent to its border."[12] At the same time, it is argued, such a strategy would be far more credible than reliance on threats of countercity retaliation, which if carried out would result in Soviet counterstrikes against U.S. cities.

Second, to the extent political targets might be substituted for urban-industrial targets, at least in the initial stage of conflict, this plan would replace a strategy involving the mass slaughter of innocent civilians—a strategy that is questioned on both moral and practical grounds. The moral argument is obvious and is strengthened by the obvious lack of control Soviet citizens have over their government. Additionally, it is argued that the Soviet population serves as both a hostage and a problem to the Soviet regime—to support, maintain, and control.

Finally, a strategy whose objective was the destruction of the Soviet state would, according to Colin Gray, "provide an unambiguous and politically meaningful war aim."[13]

COUNTERPOWER TARGETING: OTHER MILITARY TARGETS

Traditionally, the military targets in the Soviet Union that have received the bulk of attention in discussion of military targeting have been those associated with Soviet strategic nuclear forces—ICBM sites, SSBN ports, strategic bomber aircraft and airfields, and related C³I facilities. This focus on Soviet strategic forces, particularly Soviet ICBMs, has been so great that the terms *counterforce* and *countersilo* have been used virtually interchangeably by many analysts.

A counterpower strategy would sharply increase the numbers of weapons and the priority assigned to other military targets (OMT).[14] These targets include both conventional and theater nuclear forces that the Soviet Union would need for successful "power projection," that is, forces that would be used in wartime to expand the direct area of Soviet control into Western Europe, the Middle East, or Asia. Types of targets would include troops, means of transportation, command and control facilities, and weapons systems.

Specific targets would include: IRBM and MRBM sites; bomber, fighter, tanker, and transport aircraft, and airfields; nuclear weapons storage and production facilities; naval bases and shipyards; major troop concentrations; air defense sites; maintenance and repair depots; ammunition depots; military district and fleet headquarters; and production facilities for aircraft and tanks. Attacks on such targets, it is believed, could be feasible under SALT II limitations.

Targeting such forces would have three objectives. The first would be to deny the Soviet Union control over areas presently not under its control by disrupting command and control and destroying the means by which such control would be achieved—troops, transportation, and weapons. A second objective would be to make such control, if initially achieved, impossible to maintain by the destruction of stocks of matériel, maintenance, and repair facilities as well as aircraft and tank production facilities. Third, such attacks would impose a severe cost on the Soviet military by destroying valuable equipment and facilities.

As was the case with counterpolitical targeting, one suggested advantage would be the avoidance of attacks on innocent Soviet civilians. Certainly, given the Soviet penchant for secrecy, one might expect a large number of the type of installations mentioned above to be isolated from the public.

Targeting such forces, it could be argued, would more effectively deter Soviet action than targeting Soviet cities since the former would represent a strategy of deterrence by denial rather than deterrence by punishment. By threatening to deny the Soviet Union the very gains it is seeking via a conflict, we can be more certain that Soviet decision makers will refrain from such aggression than we can by threatening losses on another, unrelated, dimension of value—civilian population.

In addition to being a more effective deterrent, it can be argued that such a strategy would also be more credible than threats of countercity retaliation. The line of reasoning here would be the same as that with respect to attacks on political targets. U.S. attacks on Soviet cities ensure Soviet attacks on U.S. cities, attacks the United States would certainly want to avoid. Furthermore, such attacks would be a logical response to Soviet attacks on Europe, the Middle East, and other areas. Finally, since deterrence by denial is the essence of Soviet doctrine, a strategy based on such a concept is more likely to be believed by Soviet decision makers.[15]

DILEMMAS OF COUNTERPOLITICAL TARGETING

In evaluating the feasibility and desirability of targeting either military or political assets, several issues of importance must be considered: adequacy of intelligence in locating the targets; mobility and hardness of the targets; possibility of attaining the immediate objectives of the attack; as well as likely effects on prewar deterrence, intrawar deterrence, and prospects for early war termination.

Two possible components of counterpolitical targeting mentioned above involved direct attacks on the leadership and its lines of communications. One might question both the feasibility and desirability of such attacks. One problem is the difficulty of locating the targets to be destroyed and the difficulty of destroying such targets if located. In times of severe crisis, or once a decision to attack the United States has been made, Soviet leaders will certainly be evacuated to the alternative government control centers. A first requirement, then, would be to locate these centers. Some alternative government control centers have been identified, and all such known shelters are subject to attack. However, whether such shelters could be effectively attacked is open to question. One report that deals with Soviet leadership shelters describes shelters buried 65 to 130 feet below ground capable of withstanding a one-megaton airburst directly overhead.[16] Shelters could be buried even deeper, further reducing vulnerability. Also, it is believed that many other facilities exist that have not been located and identified, which could assure the survival of a large percentage of this leadership.[17] Amrom Katz's dictum that the United States has never found anything the Soviets have successfully hidden is especially pertinent here.[18]

Even if the destruction of the leadership and its lines of communication were feasible, it might not be desirable. Effective targeting of the political leadership might only turn command of the war over to the Soviet military. Whether or not this would be a good thing is not clear. Hitler's military was certainly more reasonable than he was. On the other hand, the German military in World War I was less reasonable than the political leadership. Whether the Soviet military would be more reasonable than the political leadership is not known at this time.

Furthermore, effective attacks on the leadership and its lines of communication may interfere with the objectives of intrawar deterrence and early war termination. A major question that must be answered is whether the lines of communication between the Soviet leadership and its agents can be destroyed without also destroying its lines of communication with the United States. And if so, will they be of any value? A leadership that can come to terms with the United States but cannot communicate those terms to its agents does the United States little good.

The alternative, of course is to concentrate the counterpolitical attack on those who enforce the leadership's edicts and protect Soviet borders from its traditional enemies. As mentioned earlier, this would involve attacks on the KGB border troops stationed near the Chinese border, KGB and MVD facilities throughout the Soviet Union and especially in those republics where anti-Russian sentiment is strong, and KGB and army facilities in Eastern Europe. Such attacks, it is argued, could be accomplished without direct massive attacks on cities by concentrating attacks on targets located away from cities, such as troop barracks in Eastern Europe, and by use of high-accuracy, low-yield weapons systems such as cruise missiles and (eventually) precision guided maneuvering re-entry vehicles (PGMRVs).

One might question that the respective populations would respond as predicated. Some Soviet dissidents, for example, believe that the outbreak of a major war would lead to violent uprisings.[19] On the other hand, in a situation of war or imminent war, Soviet leaders would portray all cities as being under the threat of imminent nuclear attack. Furthermore, the Soviet leadership would have control of food, shelters, transportation to the shelters, medical supplies, and communications to the outside world.[20] Under such circumstances revolt might not be the reaction of the population, regardless of past hostility. Such a revolt might occur well after the dust had settled, but such postwar revolts

[165]

would have had no value in bringing about the end of the war or limiting damage. Nor might the "threat" of such postwar revolts contribute much to deterrence—their dependence on so many varied factors, psychological as well as physical, might make their occurrence appear highly unlikely, at least to the Soviet leadership.

Another consideration with respect to the likelihood of such revolts is the extent to which prewar covert activity is required. Foster has written that "it is possible that the national spirit of the non-Russian Soviet Republics *can be ignited during peacetime* so that during wartime some leadership could become available that would lead to a national independence movement of some of the Republics, for example, the Baltic states of Estonia, Latvia, Lithuania and the southern Soviet republic of Georgia."[21] But what does "ignited during peacetime" mean? The only reasonable interpretation seems to be covert operations. Certainly, one does not expect the Soviet leadership to agree to an American-sponsored series of lectures titled "Byelorussia as a National Entity in the Postwar World." On the other hand, the notion of covert operations may be no less ludicrous.[22] Even if there were no restrictions (formal or informal) on such CIA activity, one could certainly expect the KGB to detect and neutralize such activity, with consequent damage to U.S.-Soviet relations.

One might also question that such attacks could really be effective without becoming countercity attacks. Certainly, any attack on the leadership and key administrative organizations would require an attack on Moscow.

Avoiding other populated areas could also be quite difficult. Bruce Russett notes that troops in Eastern Europe are bivouacked away from civilian areas in order to prevent fraternization and "contamination." Likewise, Foster suggests cities and population of potential areas of revolt be spared while Soviet military forces in those areas should be targeted. However, once a crisis begins, one would expect that those troops would be moved into city areas to "provide aid and assistance," protect against saboteurs, and exert direct control over the population. Thus targeting such troops would require targeting the cities in which the potential rebels live.

Likewise, targeting KGB and MVD complexes also presents serious problems. Such facilities must obviously be located primarily in urban areas, near the population to be controlled and spied upon. Destroying these facilities without destroying large parts of the respective cities might be accomplished by use of low-yield or even nonnuclear warheads delivered by cruise missiles and PGMRVs. However, leaving the majority of each of these cities intact would invite the KGB and MVD to create redundant headquarters or be prepared to adopt makeshift headquarters once attack became imminent. Regular police stations, for example, could certainly be used to house KGB contingents.

Attacks on isolated border troop outposts near China might be accomplished with minimum collateral damage while effectively laying areas of Soviet Asia open to Chinese invasion. Of course, the Chinese might not be so eager to seize this territory unless the Soviet state was virtually totally destroyed. Certainly the Soviets could be expected to reserve part of their strategic arsenal for deterrence of just such land grabs. While the Chinese might seek to seize such territory once they were already involved in a Soviet-Chinese war, they might not consider it worthwhile to risk war over this territory.

Even assuming that the United States could selectively target Soviet political control forces and border troops to produce the desired effects while avoiding heavy civilian casualties, we might ask if such attacks would be rational once a war had begun. That is, would such attacks, if effective, contribute to intrawar deterrence and early war termination? It is not obvious that they would. If such attacks produced the desired revolts, what would the United States have to offer the Soviet leadership as an incentive to end the war on terms favorable to the United States? It seems overly optimistic to believe that the United States could fine-tune its attacks to cause only the beginnings of revolt and then cease these attacks if an agreement is reached. On the other hand, faced with the dissolution of their control, the Soviet leadership would have little incentive to refrain from "doomsday" attacks against the United States. Thus such attacks might be threatened as retaliation for Soviet attacks against U.S. cities, not as an initial response to the outbreak of war.

One might even question the deterrent value of the threat of such attacks. Certainly, if the Soviet leadership believed such effective attacks could and would be launched by the United States, the threat of such attacks would serve as the ultimate deterrent. However, as noted above, whether such attacks would be effective depends on many more uncertainties and intangible factors than attacks on more conventional targets. Hence, there is much greater room for subjective interpretations of the likely results of such targeting. Thus the Soviet leadership might not share the perceptions of U.S. strategic planners as to its vulnerabilities. Rather, Soviet leaders may believe—owing either to ideological blindness or to their control of resources and the efforts they have made to ensure "national entity survival"—that the Soviet system is sufficiently resilient to withstand such attacks. In this case U.S. strategy might present a minimal threat: Soviet leaders would expect minimal damage to population and industry while retaining political control.

OMT TARGETING: DILEMMAS AND POSSIBILITIES

Other dilemmas present themselves with regard to targeting the class of targets referred to as other military targets (OMT). An important subcategory of this set of targets is the power projection forces mentioned earlier. The very name and purpose of such forces suggest they will be used in areas outside the Soviet Union and Eastern Europe, and thus may be on the move before any U.S. weapons targeted on either their bases or points of departure from the Soviet Union arrive.

This possibility raises the question of whether such forces—be they naval, airborne, or ground forces—can be monitored and attacked while they are on the move. One might certainly question U.S. capabilities in this regard, especially when one considers that such capabilities are certain to be prime targets for Soviet forces in the event of such a conflict. Movements via air could be especially difficult to monitor—the speed and number of aircraft involved may make estimating destination an impossible task.

Even if it were possible to monitor the movement of power projection forces, it might not be possible to effectively target them, at least not without a great deal of collateral damage. The mobility of such forces means they will not be a fixed-site target; the purpose of such forces suggests, as already noted, their being dispatched to nations who are allies or potential allies of the United States. Effectively targeting such forces might require blanket attacks on the general area around which they have been located. Such attacks could result in severe collateral damage to the very areas we intend to protect. Certainly, a strategy designed to avoid the indiscriminate slaughter of the civilians of the aggressor country should also seek to avoid the indiscriminate slaughter of the civilians of a country being attacked.[23]

In addition to the problems involved in monitoring and targeting Soviet power projection forces, there are obvious difficulties associated with targeting Soviet intermediate- and medium-range missiles. The newest Soviet IRBM, the SS-20, is a mobile system. In any case, the SS-20 and other IRBM/MRBMs might have long left their launchers by the time any attacking weapons arrive.

On the other hand, the list of OMTs given above contains a large number of fixed-site targets within the USSR whose potential destruction the Soviet leadership, civilian and military, could hardly be indifferent to—nuclear weapons storage and production facilities, airfields and ports, naval bases and shipyards, and aircraft and tank production facilities, among others. Certainly in the long run, destruction of such targets would seriously impair Soviet ability to effectively occupy and control areas outside those presently controlled. Troops need to be resupplied and reinforced and new weapons produced and distributed. Such tasks cannot be carried out with destroyed production facilities, depots, airfields, and ports. Even areas presently under Soviet control, such as Eastern Europe, could become much more difficult to control after such attacks.

Such a strategy could increase the chances for intrawar deterrence and early war termination. Initial attacks on other military targets could be limited to levels considerably below the SIOP level and still have an impact. For example, ammunition and other stores of matériel might be attacked first and the Soviets put on notice that unless a settlement is reached, or Soviet troops withdrawn in a certain period of time, another set of targets, possibly production facilities, would be attacked next. In other words, the variety and number of targets allow for a finely tuned plan of attack that can be used to deter further Soviet action and bring the conflict to a halt below the SIOP level. As discussed above, such fine tuning might be considerably more difficult when it involves political targets.

CONCLUSIONS

My analysis has been extremely skeptical of the feasibility and desirability of counterpolitical targeting. The uncertainties involved make it a questionable means of increasing deterrence. Nor is it clear that attacks on political targets would contribute to intrawar deterrence and early war termination.

On the other hand, attacks on other military targets seem more promising. While there are also dilemmas involved in such targeting, they seem to be less severe than in the case of counterpolitical targeting. The uncertainties involved in OMT targeting appear to be fewer—the destruction of a certain percentage of such targets (the fixed-site ones) can be expected to have more calculable effects than the destruction of political targets. Of course the most predictable effects are those involved with the destruction of cities, if not population. But, for the reasons discussed above, there would seem to be good reasons, both moral and practical, for accepting this additional uncertainty.

It is impossible at the unclassified level to reach definitive conclusions about the feasibility and desirability of either counterpolitical or OMT targeting. However, it would certainly seem worthwhile seriously to consider making OMT targeting the main element of our strategic doctrine. At the same time further research into counterpolitical targeting might be pursued. If such research produces positive answers concerning the feasibility of such attacks, they might be threatened as a response to Soviet attacks on U.S. cities, with the United States disavowing any intention of attacking Soviet cities under any circumstances. If U.S. cities, which we would consider our greatest assets, were placed under attack, it would be by the decision of the Soviet leadership, not the Soviet population. The proper response to such attacks would be to destroy those who initiated them. Because we will have nothing or very little to lose, the issues of intrawar deterrence and early war termination would no longer have much meaning. Punishing the Soviet leadership would.

[8]

Targeting Problems for Central War

Colin S. Gray

STRATEGY IN CENTRAL WAR?

The designing of targeting schema is a strategic task—that is to say it is an exercise in applied strategic thinking. Strategy is supposed to relate military assets to political purposes. In principle, at least, there can be no argument but that strategic judgment should guide sub-SIOP, SIOP, and post-SIOP targeting plans. In practice, there is considerable ground for philosophical dispute. One commentator expressed the following, fairly popular view: "the sheer destructiveness of nuclear war has invalidated any distinction between winning and losing. Thus, it has rendered meaningless the very idea of military strategy as the efficient employment of force to achieve a state's objectives."[1]

For politically more authoritative expressions of opinion along not-dissimilar lines, one need look no further than to President Jimmy Carter's State of the Union address for 1979, wherein he extolled the deterrent merits of a single Poseidon-carrying SSBN,[2] or—with somewhat greater ambiguity—to Secretary of Defense Harold Brown's *Department of Defense Annual Report Fiscal Year 1979*, where the following opinion is signaled: "I am not persuaded that the right way to deal with a major Soviet damage-limiting program would be by imitating it. Our efforts would almost certainly be self-defeating, as would theirs. We can make certain that we have enough warheads—including those held in reserve—targeted in such a way that the Soviets could have no expectation of escaping unacceptable damage."[3]

As a matter of principle, as implied above, few if any people would endorse the idea that military force should ever be employed for other than clear political purposes. But, at the level of practice, many people—not excluding some senior officials—have difficulty seeing how a central nuclear war really would merit description as *war*. The scale of destruction certain to be imposed even by strategic forces targeted with a view to minimizing undesired collateral damage is widely anticipated to be such that no political purpose could be served. This chapter will adopt an agnostic stance on that issue. After all, how are we to calculate, or judge, what level of damage a political system or a society (very different concepts in the Soviet case) would find "acceptable" in political circumstances that cannot be predicted with confidence? Appropriate preliminary judgment is to the effect that if the United States would find civilian casualties in excess of, say 1 or 5 million intolerable (in the context of what political issues at stake?), whereas the Soviet state took a more brutally instrumental view of the expendability of, say, 10 or 20 (or more) million of its "citizens"—then the "Western world," really, would be out of business. The bedrock of U.S. security guarantees vis-à-vis NATO-Europe and friends and allies in the Middle East—a central nuclear threat to the Soviet homeland—would crumble at the first serious test. U.S. (nuclear) strategy would be a bluff: the United States could be "outbid" in its willingness to accept domestic damage at a rather modest level of nuclear violence.

On both ethical and practical grounds, a policy of nuclear bluff, as indicated above, is defensible. Soviet leaders could not be certain that it was a bluff, and it may be that Soviet readiness to accept domestic damage is far less impressive than many American commentators believe. The apparent views of President Carter and Harold Brown may be valid if one can assume that the USSR will assuredly lead a process of competitive escalation. In other words, the threat to impose "unacceptable damage" (ignoring for the moment just what that damage would be) may suffice to deter a Soviet Union that is compelled by defeat, or frustration, to face the choice between escalation or accommodation. But, how does the "unacceptable damage" thesis fare if it is the United States that is seeking an improved political outcome at successively higher levels of violence? If, following Brown's advice, the United States eschews (or cannot achieve, regardless of effort) acquisition of "a major . . . damage-limiting program,"[4] why would not an American president be deterred from inflicting "unacceptable damage" by the certain knowledge of the unacceptable character of the anticipated Soviet retaliation? Deterrence through the promise of societal punishment is appropriate as a strategic concept only to a country that has clear superiority in general purpose forces. For a country like the United States, with the geopolitics of its alliance structure virtually ensuring local Soviet military superiority in regions of major importance (NATO-Europe, the Persian Gulf), deterrence-through-punishment ideas lack integrity.

The United States cannot hope to sustain a favorable international order by means of an "ultimate" threat to punish the Soviet Union, unless it is willing to accept a very high level of punishment itself. In theory, one might attempt to argue that a targeting strategy intended to inflict punishment—in other words, a bluff—should suffice for all anticipated foreign policy needs. If the moment of decision vis-à-vis SIOP option execution ever arrived, one could always choose to accommodate. Moreover, to revert to a previous theme, one might argue that since a central nuclear war would prove to be intolerably destructive, regardless of attempts at sophisticated fine tuning of targeting plans, the danger of war—and war expansion—is reduced if the "war as general holocaust" truth is made quite explicit.

Final judgment cannot be passed on the merits of the above thesis, but several grounds should incline the U.S. targeting community to be skeptical (though not totally dismissive).

—1. Even if it is judged probable that a central nuclear war would entail mutual receipt of unacceptable levels of damage, it is not certain. Societal-punishment targeting schemes guarantee that the worst case will occur should the pace of military operations outrun diplomacy (a condition that would hardly be surprising in the context of a central war).

—2. A perceived inability to fight a war in a militarily sensible fashion could easily have a debilitating impact upon the quality of pre- and intrawar deterrence. It appears that the Soviets believe an efficient war-fighting capability to be critical for the quality of deterrent effect. (As Soviet defense analysts are fond of saying, "what is deterrence without war fighting?")

—3. While the United States must be careful not to design a force posture and doctrine that, in and of themselves, might function as a proximate cause of war (analogous to pre-1914 mobilization schedules), there can be no guarantees that prewar deterrence will "work" forever—as Fred Iklé reminded the defense community forcefully in his January 1973 article in *Foreign Affairs*: "Can Nuclear Deterrence Last Out the Century?"[5] Furthermore, a U.S. president might find himself in a situation where intrawar deterrent considerations, at least in the early stages of a conflict, appeared to be as irrelevant in Soviet calculations as had been putative prewar deterrent calculations. In short, a U.S. president might well find himself in a situation where he was desperately interested in strategic employment options that made military and political sense, both in and of themselves and with respect to the Soviet ability, or willingness, to strike back.

WAR AIMS

To argue that there should be strategy in, and beyond, the SIOP is not to assert that central wars are "winnable." Rather it is to claim that one should not threaten, let alone execute, particular strategic employment options simply because one has exhausted the menu of politically intelligent options. For example, to refer to a topic addressed in more detail below, is the United States really interested in wreaking great damage upon the Soviet recovery economy (as opposed merely to threatening such damage)? How would such an exercise help the United States in its conduct of the war? How would it promote favorable conditions for war termination? And what character of a Soviet response should be anticipated?

It is most useful to begin Nuclear Weapons Employment Policy (NUWEP) analysis by identifying some possible, alternative, war outcomes and then proceed to track back from the outcomes to see if paths to their attainment can be plotted. There cannot be a "standard or dominant scenario" for the outbreak of a central war. Also, it would be prudent for the U.S. defense community to assume, for SIOP design purposes, that once a conflict takes on a central war character, that conflict cannot be subsumed within a single framework of political assumptions. These caveats are not offered with great confidence because there are reasons to believe that a Soviet political leadership might just delegate control of the dynamics of a military conflict to its military professionals (who might believe that "central war is central war"— regardless of why and how that war began).

In ascending order of ambition, the United States could seek to (1) deny the USSR victory (on its own terms), (2) defeat the USSR (on its own terms), and (3) win.

To deny the Soviets victory might be, in some circumstances, the equivalent of imposing defeat. If victory denial were achieved over an issue of very great political importance, and at considerable military cost, the domestic consequences within the USSR might be traumatic, if not revolutionary. The defeat of the Soviet Union is not, of course, the same as victory for the United States. Both superpowers might be reduced to radioactive anarchy. For the United States to win a central war, the Soviet Union would have to surrender—or be in such poor political-military condition that the issue of an instrument of surrender would be an irrelevance—*and* the United States would have to be intact as a political entity, able to recover on fairly short order from the damage suffered (courtesy of voluntary, and some no-doubt coerced, assistance from undamaged economies abroad), able to continue or resume military operations, and generally be in a position to organize, and enforce, the terms of the new postwar international order.

DAMAGE LIMITATIONS

Strange to say, perhaps, these three goals—victory denial, defeating the enemy, and winning—although distinguishable in principle, in practice carry a common, major, yet vastly underappreciated implication for U.S. defense policy. Specifically, they all require a serious U.S. effort to achieve a worthwhile measure of damage limitation. While I am not dismissive of the now-traditional objections to damage-limiting programs, I am fully cognizant of the charges that they would be (1) very expensive; (2) self-defeating and futile, in that they would simply spur the arms competitor to offset them; and (3) dangerous, in that they might mislead a president into believing that a central war was survivable and perhaps winnable.

Damage limitation may be judged expensive, but what is "expensive" for a country with a $3 trillion GNP when the issue is survival? Naturally enough, the Soviet Union would be interested in offsetting any American strategic program that carried a major promise of enhancing U.S. war-waging efficiency (including the ability of U.S. society to survive and recover). In and of itself that observation is close to being axiomatic; it hardly warrants description as a devastating argument against U.S. damage-limitation programs. Why must it be assumed that the damage-limiting path would prove to be self-defeating? With respect to the dangers that might flow from damage-limitation programs directed toward the goal of assured survival, it is exceedingly unlikely that a president, indeed any president likely to be elected, would be confident that American societal damage could be kept very low. (By the standards of potential damage in a nuclear war, *very low* would be very high in the context, say, of casualties suffered in World War II.) The somewhat implausible danger that might attend trusting the U.S. government with a major damage-limitation capability needs to be set against the much greater dangers that would attend a U.S. government entering acute crisis interactions bereft of virtually any ability to limit damage to the society whose well-being was its charge.

The case for offensive and defensive (active and passive) programs designed physically to constrain the amount of damage that an enemy could otherwise impose, may be summarized as follows:

—The geopolitical asymmetries that distinguish the Soviet empire from the American-led alliance,[6] render it very likely indeed that it would be the United States that would need to lead the escalation process into, and perhaps up through different stages of, central war. Given the extant, and predictable, balance of projectile military power vis-à-vis the Eurasian "rimlands," it is difficult to write plausible scenarios wherein Soviet forces in, say, Europe or the Persian Gulf region would face local defeat—thereby leading the Soviet government to seek "central use compensation" for impending regional disaster.

—If the Soviet Union should choose to counterescalate to, and within, central war in only a very measured way (which is far from certain)—

responding to U.S. countermilitary attack options and, eventually, to selective countereconomic recovery options, in kind and with roughly the same weight of attack—the United States soon would find its employment options paralyzed through the functioning of self-deterrence. No matter how flexible U.S. strategic employment planning may be, if it is not matched by some significant actual ability to defend North America, it would amount, in practice, to suicide on the installment plan. Flexibility, per se, carries few advantages. Indeed, the flexibility is substantial, and if the enemy agrees tacitly to a fairly slow pace of competitive escalation, it provides noteworthy time for the self-deterrence process to operate.

—Damage-limitation programs may have no bearing whatsoever upon the occurrence of central war or Soviet operational method as reflected in their conduct of a central war. Damage limitation, simply, might have meaning in the context of the character of war termination and the condition of the United States after the war.

—No matter how intelligent a U.S. strategic targeting doctrine may be, in terms of its speaking to real Soviet fears and vulnerabilities it would lose much, if not most (or even all), of its deterrent influence if Soviet leaders believed that a U.S. president would be deterred from putting it into effect by the prospect of intolerable Soviet retaliation. There can be no argument in favor of a politically unintelligent targeting doctrine, but it is sensible to recognize that some considerable physical ability to defend American society would act as a "deterrence multiplier."

A realistic damage-limiting posture can offer only modest performance and comes without any guarantees. Civil defense, ballistic missile defense (BMD), air defense, antisubmarine warfare (ASW) and an impressive scale of prompt countermilitary (including hard target) capability could well mean the difference between day and night with respect to U.S. war recovery potential. But, preclusive damage limitation is not even remotely feasible. A U.S. damage-limiting posture would do well if it kept American prompt casualties below the 20 to 30 million range. Those are horrific numbers in ethical terms and in light of U.S. historical experience. However, those numbers are only modestly in excess of Soviet losses between 1941 and 1945 and are almost certainly within range of serious Soviet anticipation vis-à-vis a central war with the United States. If the United States is prepared, in extremis, to wage a central war—which certainly is current policy—then it has to be prepared to accept millions of prompt casualties, if the damage-limitation mission is approached responsibly. If damage-limitation, as a very deliberate planning objective, is eschewed—as at present—then the United States is prepared, so it says, to wage, in extremis, a war in which in excess of 100 million prompt casualties should be anticipated. It should be noted that President Reagan's Strategic Defense Initiative is intended only to explore the feasilibility of defense against ballistic missiles; it is not a contemporary commitment to damage limitation.

Unfortunately for freedom of doctrinal and postural choice, damage limitation is not simply a war fighter's dream. It should be anticipated that even the most modest of the three central war aims of interest to the United States—the denial of victory to the Soviet Union—is likely to be defined in Moscow as the functional equivalent of a resounding defeat. It is unlikely that the Soviet Union of the late 1980s or 1990s would acquiesce either in a local stalemate or clear local defeat without being tempted to take the conflict to a higher level. So traumatic might the political implications of such a stalemate or defeat be for Soviet authority in Eastern Europe and at home that Soviet leaders may believe that the best of a short range of bad alternatives is to initiate a central war. Logically, at least, the United States cannot expect so to manage a conflict process that damage-limitation (or war-fighting) capability would be an irrelevance: whatever permutation of local strength/weakness and central systems strength/weakness one plays, the case for competence in damage limitation retains its integrity.

—If the Western alliance is relatively weak in locally deployed (or assigned) forces, then it should be the party with the strongest incentive to lead the process of escalation to a higher level of violence. Needless to say, the United States could not hope to prevail through intrawar (central war) deterrence, let alone fight the war through to a favorable military conclusion (which might be required if the United States declines to surrender, and the Soviet Union declines, or is unable, to negotiate), if damage to the American homeland could not be limited to a large degree.

—If the Western alliance is relatively strong in local forces, and were to impose some fair facsimile of a resounding local defeat upon Soviet arms, the Soviet incentive to initiate central nuclear employment should be influenced by perception of likely American damage-limiting prowess. To repeat, no guarantee of deterrent success can be offered. The Soviet Union might feel so desperate that, counting on the well-advertised U.S. proclivity toward targeting restraint and flexibility, and hoping for a failure of U.S. presidential nerve and will, it would attempt to force an improved political outcome through competitive strategic escalation. Or, defining the political context as the "Day of Judgment," Soviet leaders might decide that, regardless of the adverse state of the strategic balance, they are compelled to see the conflict through to the bitter end.

[177]

It should be apparent by now to the reader that strategic targeting, or, more broadly, nuclear weapons employment policy, is not a subject that has integrity in and of itself. Strategic targeting has to be considered in the context of U.S. defense policy as a whole. At the same time that the U.S. defense community reviews its strategic targeting philosophy, it would also consider the ways in which Soviet targeting initiatives and responses can be deterred or, if need be, physically thwarted. To repeat a critically important refrain, a supremely intelligent targeting doctrine for the United States would be of little avail if, in real historical circumstances, a U.S. president lacked adequate material means to implement it, and/or was (self-) deterred by the prospect of the likely Soviet reply. These cautionary words are not intended to detract from the importance of reviewing and improving U.S. targeting doctrine, only to remind readers that conflict is (at least) a two-person game.

A basic truth concerning strategic targeting design is that the credibility, effectiveness, and real-time attractiveness of lower level (of damage) strike options has to be a function of the credibility and assessed probable effectiveness of the entire strategic targeting design. In other words, every stage of strategic force application (or every "building block," if that terminology is preferred), as threat or in execution, can have utility only if the entire design of U.S. defense policy is sound. For example, it could be extremely dangerous were the United States to plan a set of selective targeting building blocks for prospective rounds one, two, and three of strategic force application, while rounds four and five entailed truly massive countereconomic strikes, the actual implementation of which could never be in the U.S. interest (because of the character of the anticipated Soviet retaliation). In short, the United States needs a targeting design that has integrity from first to last. To a substantial degree that integrity can only come from a robust domestic war-survival and recovery program. The principal weakness in the strategic flexibility thesis that James Schlesinger advertised so forcefully was that it neglected (at least, in public exposition) to explain how the United States thought it could deter Soviet responses.[7]

Strategic flexibility, with its emphasis upon selectivity and restraint, is really the targeting doctrine appropriate to a country that is strategically very superior—a country that has a plausible theory of how it can limit damage to itself in the possible event that the enemy is not sufficiently impressed by very limited American central strategic employment. When designing nuclear weapons employment policy vis-à-vis a country like the Soviet Union, which has displayed no known interest in the idea of intrawar deterrence, and whose military science seems totally dedicated to improving the efficiency of force application, it is only prudent to assume that one might not be permitted to wage a central war of limited liability. Indeed, a great deal of Anglo-American theory on the subject of limited central war (with its associated concepts of flexibility, thresholds, bargaining, and negotiated—formally or tacitly—war termination) may reflect nothing more substantial than an enduring "insular" tradition in strategic thinking.[8] Whether or not the Soviet Union should cooperate in conducting a central war as an intrawar deterrent bargaining process is beside the point: such an approach might be alien to Soviet strategic culture and may find no place in Soviet strategic planning. James Schlesinger said that "doctrines control the minds of men only in periods of non-emergency. They do not necessarily control the minds of men during periods of emergency. In the moment of truth, when the possibility of major devastation occurs, one is likely to discover sudden changes in doctrine."[9]

This much-quoted thought has provided some comfort for those who wish to believe that the U.S. defense community should not take at face value what it reads in the Soviet defense and political-military literature concerning the likely character of Soviet behavior in a central war. For political reasons, so the argument goes, the Soviet Union is unable or unwilling to admit that it might use nuclear weapons in a deliberate and constrained manner as an act of policy. One cannot help but speculate, however, that it is not self-evident that Soviet leadership in a moment of central war crisis would be expected to be imaginative and to reverse its heretofore authoritative doctrinal principles for the guidance of force application.

The moral of this brief excursion for the U.S. defense community is that it would be unwise for it to assume any likelihood of a real-time Soviet proclivity to wage a central war according to American-favored rules. Such tacit Soviet cooperation as might occur, to arrest the slide to total war, may well have to be coerced. It is not unreasonable to speculate that in the event of the outbreak of a central war, a U.S. president would be almost as interested in securing prompt war termination as he would be in denying victory to the Soviet Union.[10] Unfortunately, it would be consistent with the evidence at hand to claim that a Soviet leadership would be more interested in securing an outcome that it could call victory than it would be in achieving a prompt termination of hostilities. This is not a prediction, but it does point to a distressing potential mismatch of objectives which the U.S. defense community is obliged to take seriously. Wishful thinking has no place in war planning.

ESCALATION CONTROL AND INTRAWAR FIREBREAKS

Whether or not the United States purchases substantial passive and active defenses for the goal of domestic damage limitation, there is everything to be said for designing the U.S. strategic posture and for advertising appropriately in a general way its probable operational utility, with a view to maximizing the prospect that the Soviet Union would lack attractive strategic counterescalation options. No one can guarantee that intrawar deterrence will function to the U.S. advantage, but intelligent postural design—married to a well-orchestrated declaratory policy—should stack the deck as favorably as psychological, political, and military conditions permit.

It seems probable, though it is far from certain, that a major duty laid upon the Soviet strategic force posture is strategic counterdeterrence: in short, to deny the United States the initiative, or freedom of employment action, with its strategic forces.[11] If, as seems safe to predict, the United States will be unable for the foreseeable future to be confident that it could effect a (total) surprise preclusive disarming attack against Soviet strategic forces, design of a U.S. strategic force posture that can deter attack upon itself has to take logical priority over targeting doctrine. To stand a modest though worthwhile chance of controlling the escalation process, the United States needs an "intrawar firebreak" that would deny the Soviet Union the ability to wage a largely counterforce and counter-C^3I war. In practice this advice means that the United States should deploy an ICBM force that the Soviet Union could not attack with profit;[12] a manned bomber and cruise missile carrier (CMC) force that could not be attrited catastrophically by Soviet SLBMs fired on depressed trajectories; and a C^3I system (including the National Command Authorities [NCA]) that looks remarkably unattractive as a target set. Such a U.S. posture would not freeze the Soviet Union out of the escalation competition, but it would counteract, markedly and usefully, Soviet strike options. Above all else, Soviet defense planners would be placed in what for them would almost certainly be a nightmare condition—they would be expected to prosecute a central war in a militarily intelligent fashion while the United States would retain essentially an inviolate strategic posture.

Counterforce incompetence (vis-à-vis strategic force assets) should be expected to have a far more discouraging impact in Moscow than in Washington. In effect, such a condition would checkmate what is known concerning Soviet doctrine and operational method.[13] The concept of deterrence through societal punishment, although probably reflected imperfectly in actual U.S. targeting plans, has nonetheless been the dominant strain in Western deterrent philosophy for more than twenty years. Soviet political and military leaders might believe that they could win a process of competitive escalation wherein societal and nonstrategic military assets would dominate the targeting lists of both sides, but it would not be unreasonable to argue that a largely nontargetable U.S. ICBM, SSBN, bomber, and CMC force structure would promote healthy traumas for the Soviet general staff, and would vastly increase the prospects of an intrawar deterrence mechanism functioning fairly promptly to Western advantage. However, to repeat, there are no guarantees. Firebreaks, so called, may cease to work as intended. The United States cannot eschew active and passive defenses on the grounds that a nontargetable ICBM (et al.) force should enforce escalation discipline. What if it does not?

SOVIET FEARS—U.S. INTERESTS

U.S. strategic deterrence and targeting problems defy simple characterization. Nonetheless, two questions above all others serve to focus discussion. These are: What does the Soviet Union fear most? What targeting strategy would be in the U.S. interest to implement? It is not implied here that identification of the worst Soviet fears need necessarily point to an optimum U.S. strike doctrine. In some circumstances, the United States need not brandish the most fearsome threat, and some Soviet fears may not actually be exploitable by U.S. strategic action (though advertisement of such a U.S. threat may have considerable deterrent merit). At this juncture it is appropriate to comment that a general East-West war would embrace every kind of military instrument, and it could be a great mistake to approach the general war problem as though it were almost entirely a central war waged between so-called strategic forces. Indeed some of the more promising ideas for denying victory to, or defeating, the Soviet Union require imaginative offensive actions by Western general purpose forces, not the clever placement of strategic nuclear warheads.

The leitmotiv for U.S. targeting design should be the known Soviet obsession with political control. In answer to the question, What does the Soviet Union fear most? one can reply, loss of political control. In extremis, loss of political control at home means the demise of the Soviet state. Since the early postwar years, the territorial integrity of the Soviet imperium has been nonnegotiable (save in one very special case—the

[181]

Soviet occupation zone in Austria). The essential, defensive reason for this Soviet stance appears to be the Soviet fear (whether well founded or not) that it could not contain the consequences of what its subjects would view as a process of retreat.

Ideally, *the* Western deterrent against Soviet misbehavior would be a credible threat to unravel the Soviet empire in Eastern Europe. If the United States could field a strategic force posture married to domestic war-survival programs such that a Soviet leadership would be unable to discern any "theory of victory" at the level of central war, any Western military success in central Europe would have truly traumatic implications for the stability of Soviet holdings. There is an instability potential in Eastern Europe (meaning that even a modest shock to the status quo could have quite immodest consequences), which is the West's greatest potential deterrent asset. Some defense analysts would proceed much further and suggest that the Soviet empire at home is none too solid a structure.

It is moderately obvious that the Western enemy is the Soviet state and its instruments of domestic and external corecion, while a potentially decisive, important ally is certainly the vast majority of the population of Eastern Europe and, much less certainly, the large sections of the Soviet population itself. Identification of the Soviet state as the enemy is the essential first step in the design of an intelligent targeting strategy. If the United States and its allies (and potential allies in Eastern Europe) are able to wage war against the Soviet state, there is every good reason for desisting from imposing damage upon the Soviet citizenry and its means of livelihood.[14] Indeed, if the Soviet state can be brought down (a task far more likely to be effected 1917-style—i.e., by disaffected soldiers, workers, and peasants—than by a flock of U.S. MIRVs) through precisely targeted action and reverses suffered by Soviet projection forces abroad, any successor regime would stand an improved prospect of political success if its economy had not fallen victim to the U.S. SIOP.

Countereconomic targeting, even in the refined form of countereconomic recovery targeting, is fundamentally flawed both as a deterrent and as an operational concept. This is not to deny that the prospect of suffering a major degree of economic damage has some probable merit as a deterrent. No Soviet leader would lightly place at risk the physical accomplishments of nearly seventy years of socialism. In addition, there could be circumstances wherein a U.S. government might wish to damage the Soviet economy, with a view to influencing the postwar balance of power. Unfortunately, no one has yet been able to explain why a Soviet leadership would be likely to believe that an almost entirely unprotected (by passive and active defenses) United States would actually implement the threat of large countereconomic strikes, or why a moderately prudent U.S. president would ever believe that actual execution of large-scale countereconomic strikes would promote U.S. interests. Given the failure of the countereconomic and countereconomic recovery strike concepts to pass the tests of credibility or of U.S. interest in execution, they should be seen to be of little, if any, relevance to U.S. war planners. As a final word on this issue, it is not sound even to think of a large countereconomic strike as comprising the SIOP threat or option "of last resort." The U.S. "last resort" threat should target the Soviet political control structure. If the war had to be fought through to the very end, our ultima ratio should consist of a large strike against such identifiable targets as the essential bureaucratic and coercive organs of the Soviet state. Such a strike would, at least, be related directly to the most expansive of U.S. war aims—the demise of the Soviet state—and should contribute constructively to the transition to non-Soviet regimes in what previously had been Soviet territory. By way of sharp contrast, a massive strike against Soviet economic targets would be purposeless and almost certainly suicidal. (Although damage to the Soviet control structure just might impair the ability of the remaining Soviet forces to continue the war, it is more likely that it would trigger a spasm response.)

POLITICAL CONTROL IN THE SOVIET UNION

In practice, the Soviet state almost certainly cannot be targeted directly by the United States with anything even approaching high confidence. Prominent among the weaknesses in the concept of counter-political-control targeting are the following:
—The potential target set is very large.
—The location of some of the targets is not known precisely.
—The most important targets are of a superhard area kind that are impervious to all U.S. weapons.
—It will be difficult, if not impossible, to know exactly who will disperse to which facility.
—The communication equipment in many of the facilities must remain a matter for speculation.
—The effect of countercontrol strikes upon Soviet ability to conduct military operations and organize a postwar recovery effort cannot be predicted with confidence.
—Once executed, a very large strike against the Soviet political and administrative leadership would mean that the U.S. had "done its worst." If the Soviet government, in the sense of an NCA, were still able to function, it would probably judge that it had little if anything left to fear.

—If very successful, a large (or small but superefficient) counterpolitical strike would probably impair fatally the ability of the USSR to negotiate war termination, or even to accept some face-saving offer that amounted to surrender.

Just how seriously the U.S. government should regard the above objections depends in good part upon the role(s) assigned counterpolitical targeting. Aside from the most obvious and urgent necessity—a need to know just how feasible it would be to impose particular kinds of damage upon the Soviet control system—two alternatives dominate consideration of this question. First, countercontrol targeting could be approached as a major war-fighting task in the hope or expectation that Soviet ability to conduct the war would be impaired very substantially, and to the U.S. advantage. Ideally, in this view, a prompt large strike against the central Soviet leadership cadre would (should?) paralyze the Soviet war machine. If they could be deprived of direction (meaning highly centralized direction), Soviet forces may not need to be attrited. Second, the counter-political-control option might, as suggested above, serve as the "ultimate U.S. threat." In this second approach, the countercontrol threat would comprise the major safeguard intended to deter a massive Soviet strike on U.S. cities. In part (though only in part), a persuasive-appearing countercontrol threat might perform as the functional equivalent of a major U.S. damage-limitation capability.

In practice, many difficulties would appear—in addition to those already cited.

—The countercontrol option as the defender of U.S. cities (in deterrent prospect) could only work as outlined here if the Soviet Union was the deteree and the United States was the deterrer. In real life, it could well be the case that the Soviet Union had secured major net advantages through the countermilitary war—meaning that the next move would be up to the U.S. president (who would know or suspect that the execution of the countercontrol option would result in Soviet countervalue retaliation).

—Neat central war sequences of move and countermove (or decisions not to move) may amount to little more than academic fantasy: the pace of competitive SIOP execution(s), amidst the devastation of C^3I assets, could translate into no clear "rounds," with each side halting as at a whistle prior to the next "play."

—The Soviet fear of the large countercontrol strike probably would need to be enhanced through some small precursor strikes intended to demonstrate the vulnerability of the Soviet control system.

—There could be a strong military case for striking early in a war at some of those Soviet C^3I assets in the USSR, which bear upon Soviet ability to control projection forces. Such a strike might be too successful in that it would speak to the believed Soviet anxiety over loss of political control and might provoke a rapid Soviet panic escalation of the war.

—Many Soviet political control targets are in or fairly close to major cities. U.S. strikes on almost any scale against the political control structure could well be indistinguishable, in Soviet eyes, from a countercity attack. This may or may not be an important point: it depends on the timing of such a strike (early in the war as a warning or late in the war as either a warning or the U.S. ultima ratio).

Because of the known and enduring Soviet obsession with central political control of their imperium, the case for threatening to impair the quality and quantity of that control is overwhelming. Less overwhelming is the case for actually striking at what is identified as the most important nodes in the Soviet control system. Should the United States ever execute such a strike, a maximally punishing Soviet response (probably launched on warning of the U.S. countercontrol strike) should be anticipated. However, as noted above, for reasons to do with a theater war, or for the purpose of illustrating vividly just how vulnerable the Soviet political control could be, the U.S. targeting community should look closely at small and very selective countercontrol strikes (intended to have both a military effect and, in some cases, a definite political effect).

There is some small danger that the option of targeting the Soviet political leadership, and the organs for centralized control of its military, police, and economic activities, might attain the status of fashionable. Countercontrol as threat and in execution is, rightly, of enormous interest to the United States, but it is not a panacea—necessarily able to function as a "great equalizer," compensating for deficiencies in U.S. military (and civilian) programs. In addition, the very importance of the political-control target set should lead the U.S. defense community to approach it with great caution and with all the sophistication that can be mustered.

Countercontrol targeting also raises the question of the nature of a tolerable postwar world. "Regionalization" of the USSR (dismemberment or Balkanization, if preferred) has been much studied of recent years, and perhaps with good reason. However, it would be refreshing to read a persuasive analysis of just why such regionalization would constitute a preferred condition, in U.S. perspective. The deterrent merit of such a threat in Soviet eyes can scarcely be doubted. Nonetheless, the question remains, why would the United States, in practice, favor a regionalization of what is now the USSR? While recognizing that regionalization might occur as a consequence of the chaos attendant upon a nuclear war, regardless of the political vision informing U.S. targeting design, it still behooves us to consider the following points: a regionalized former USSR (1) would be prey to still-powerful neighbors or near neighbors (China, Germany?); (2) would almost certainly be condemned to interregional war for a long period, probably followed by imperial reorganization in the interest of the strongest successor state or states; (3) would probably require (largely) U.S. "ordering" and policing on a truly major scale (a foreign entanglement of unprecedented magnitude and complexity); and (4) would constitute a series of scarcely, or non-, viable military and economic entities, governed dictatorially (of necessity), and racked by civil and international conflicts.

For all its deficiencies and imperfections, the cause of international order (and peace) was not well served by the demise of the Austro-Hungarian empire. Regionalization of the USSR should be approached as a temporary (though possibly highly useful, for the West) embarrassment for Moscow, as a permanent condition (with what implications for the future balance of power in Eurasia?), as a threat, and as a succession of execution options. There is always the danger that a flurry of "how to do it" (regionalization) studies may obscure the logically prior question—should it be attempted?

SOVIET MILITARY POWER AND U.S. TARGETING

Inherently the Soviet military posture constitutes the most interesting target sets for U.S. defense planners. Soviet military power of all kinds, almost certainly directed with great determination against Western military assets, would be *the* Soviet policy instrument that needs to be blunted and defeated in short order. If Soviet military power cannot be denied its military goals, and—moreover—crippled in the process, none of the other possible U.S. war-waging schemes (countereconomic and political control targeting, for leading examples) are likely to have an intolerable and enduring effect. In short, to misquote Gen. Douglas MacArthur, "there is no substitute for victory denial." If the Soviet military is able to win theaterwide campaigns in Europe and the Persian Gulf, and perform very well in central-war counterforce missions in aid of homeland defense), the undoubtedly catastrophic damage the United States could impose upon Soviet industrial structures, the degree of regionalization that might be imposed, and even the disruption possibly enforceable against the political control system would constitute only temporary inconvenience (albeit of a very painful kind). A militarily victorious Soviet Union could (and should be expected to) use the rest of the world, as it chose, for a recovery base, and could restore domestic authority at its leisure.[15]

Countermilitary targeting capability (of all kinds) has the manifold merit of (*a*) minimizing, if not eliminating, the problem of self-deterrence, (*b*) being inherently sensible (which assists credibility), and (*c*) enjoying immense respect in Soviet eyes. From the perspective of escalation control, the better the U.S. counterforce capability, the less pressure there should be on a U.S. president to initiate those kinds of countereconomic and political control strikes that would invite a large Soviet countervalue response. In addition, of course, the more successful the strategic counterforce strikes, the more manageable the problems become for civil defense, air defense, and—one hopes (for the future)—area ballistic missile defense.

If one is serious about the need for a war-waging capability on both (pre- and intrawar) deterrent and prudential defense grounds, then there has to be a judicious balance between offense and defense. For example, in practice it is entirely possible that most of the Soviet strategic force payload will be immune to U.S. offensive attention: most of the SSBN fleet would be at sea; most of the strike assets of Longe Range Aviation would be in the air; and Soviet ICBMs may not wait for the arrival of U.S. reentry vehicles. Bearing that strong possibility in mind, it is necessary that much of the U.S. strategic forces' posture essentially be untargetable and that proper U.S. defensive provision be made for thwarting the purpose of Soviet offensive force missions. The United States should, with high confidence, be able to enforce at least a stalemate upon the Soviet Union in any countermilitary phase of a theater or central war. The stress laid in this chapter upon the need for damage limitation through homeland defense rests upon the anxiety that what the Soviet Union cannot accomplish through force-on-force engagements, it might gain as a consequence of the very unequal provision made by the two states for domestic survival and recovery. Also, of course, if the United States should fare badly in a counterforce exchange, following a disaster in Europe, it would be the United States that would have to contemplate very seriously the risks of escalating to the level of counterpolitical strikes (with all of the self-deterrent problems thereto connected).

It should not be forgotten that damage wrought against the Soviet military machine translates, in Soviet perspective, into threats to the political integrity of the Soviet Union. This is one of the healthy asymmetries in the Soviet-American competition, and its importance should not be undervalued. Military defeat would be a national tragedy for the United States (and for hundreds of thousands of American homes), but the defeat would have to be on a monumental scale before one would expect the very stability of the U.S. political system to be shaken. Even a clear military defeat in (and confined to) Europe probably would not result in a military coup in Washington, or any similarly dramatic discontinuity in U.S. constitutional forms. Can one imagine what the effect of defeat in Europe would be upon the domestic political stability of the Soviet empire? Stable democracies like the United States and Great Britain can lose campaigns, even in humiliating style (recall the spring of 1940 and Dunkirk), but the troops (even if they are conscripted, or "duration-only," civilian soldiers) do not come home breathing revolution. At worst, scapegoats are located and fired, and the political-military ledership is shuffled. In terms of deterrent effect in Soviet official minds, the prospect of suffering enormous military losses in campaigns that are not obviously succeeding has to be far more dissuasive an anticipation than would be the prospect of very large civilian population or industrial damage.

The practical problems that must attend any U.S. endeavor to target Soviet projection forces are formidable. To mention but a few:

—By the time the deep-strike nuclear systems of the Supreme Allied Commander (not to mention U.S. SIOP-assigned forces) would be released, the Warsaw Pact forces that really mattered, in the context of a minimum warning (four days of mobilization) attack, would probably be deep into Western Europe, or clustered in central Europe. There are thousands of non-strategic-force fixed military targets inside the USSR, but striking at these, say, ten to fifteen days into a war in Europe would not save NATO-Europe.

—Very early nuclear employment, against fixed targets on the reinforcement routes the Soviet third echelon must transit en route from the three westernmost military districts of the USSR to central Europe, could have a useful delaying effect. However, militarily intelligent target plans and politically intelligent nuclear release practice might be very different indeed. Moreover, the warhead yields on the ICBM and strategic bomber forces probably render them overly muscular for strikes into central Europe, while the SLBM force has communication, on-station, and force-loading inflexibility constraints. It is far from obvious that SACEURs in-theater, deep-strike, nuclear-capable assets would be survivable in adequate quantity through to the time of desired mission execution.

—The targeting of projection force assets within the USSR subsumes the superpower homeland threshold, or sanctuary, problem. For example, if a large American expeditionary force in the Gulf region (say, in Saudi Arabia and Kuwait) were being defeated, in part as a consequence of Soviet air missions flown out of Soviet homeland-located air bases, it is not at all obvious that a U.S. president would choose to strike at those bases. At the very least such a strike would license Soviet attacks upon U.S. carrier task forces (and the U.S. navy would argue that it could not afford to lose a carrier in a "sideshow") which theretofore probably would have enjoyed sanctuary status (as off Korea and Vietnam).

—It is a fact that there are no agreed "rules of engagement" vis-à-vis strikes at projection-force target sets in Soviet territory. This fact and some of its less pleasant possible implications underlie much of the West European uneasiness over the deployment by NATO on European soil of systems capable of striking the Soviet Union.

CONCLUSIONS AND IMPLICATIONS

The U.S. defense community, with respect to its strategic targeting problems, should recognize frankly the domain of uncertainty. It is hoping to deter, and—if need be—conduct military operations, in a situation for which there is no close precedent. No one honestly can affirm confidently that careful postural and SIOP design will have any marked effect upon the quality of pre- and intrawar deterrence, or even upon the outcome of a general war. There can be no peacetime "road tests" of the adequacy of the U.S. strategic posture and its preferred targeting schemes. If an acute political crisis has a nonviolent resolution, it is unlikely that strategic historians will agree on why the crisis did not explode into war.[16]

Nonetheless, the indeterminacy of peacetime planning problems, for which there are probably no demonstrably correct solutions, does not absolve the planners and their policy-making masters from behaving responsibly. With respect to strategic targeting issues, it is responsible to attempt to understand the "Soviet way," or Soviet strategic culture, style, and probable operational methods. A continuing weakness in U.S. defense thinking is the relative neglect of likely Soviet objectives and methods.[17] It would not be prudent to advance recommendations for U.S. NUWEP or NUWEP implementation, resting upon even a sophisticated appreciation of Soviet vulnerabilities, in the absence of a balancing assessment of U.S. vulnerabilities.

Also, it is responsible to attempt to design nuclear employment plans and capabilities that would coerce the enemy into waging the war in ways most advantageous (or least disadvantageous) to the United States. In practice one might not succeed, but there could be no excuse for a failure to attempt this. The United States needs a theory of victory (or victory denial) to which each building block in the nuclear (et al.) employment design ultimately relates.

Finally, it is responsible not to assume that preferred outcomes are very probable. For example: it is prudent to take the problem of war waging seriously because there can be no guarantees that prewar deterrence will "work" forever; it is prudent to design U.S. employment building blocks so as to optimize the prospects that intrawar deterrent effect will lead to early, and not unfavorable, war termination; but, it is also prudent to make damage-limiting provision for the eventuality that intrawar deterrence falls victim to the "fog of battle" or to Soviet hostility to the prospect of anything other than a clear military verdict in the contest.

This chapter reflects analysis in progress, so the following "conclusions" should be viewed as both tentative and contingent upon a great deal of additional supportive detail.

1. Regardless of the SIOP design preferred, there is an absolute need for the United States to be able to limit damage to itself. Indeed, a good deal of the potential value of a well-designed nuclear employment policy will be negated, or undermined (courtesy of the self-deterrent effect), if American society is totally in a hostage status.[18]

2. A targeting review exercise has to be married to a campaign analysis that is understanding of Soviet strategic style and method. Our design of building blocks, thresholds, and the like might be brought to nought by a very un-American style of strategic employment on the part of the Soviet Union.

3. Following (2), the United States defense community should think carefully about ways in which the USSR might be coerced, or induced, into waging a central war along U.S.-preferred lines, for a U.S.-preferred outcome. In other words, it would be inappropriate to be unduly skeptical of the prospect for agreeing tacitly upon some "rules of engagement": through appropriate postural design, and perhaps in part through negotiated arms control agreements, Soviet employment options should be capable of being constrained.

4. When designing building blocks, the U.S. targeting community should, wherever possible, identify high-leverage "threat multiplier" strikes. In other words, a limited strike today should open the door to a far more damaging strike tomorrow. Near-ideal-type illustrations of this tactic would be corridor-blowing strikes against Soviet air defenses and against the Moscow ABM radar: such strikes would inflict only very modest damage on the Soviet homeland, but should guarantee U.S. (et al.) penetrating aircraft and cruise missiles a free ride in the (near) future. One can conceive of limited strikes against some Soviet C^3I and general-purpose-force elements that, similarly, should function as threat/vulnerability multipliers.[19]

5. The design of the war plans should have political integrity, considered as a whole. In extremis, ideally, they should reflect a progressive unfolding theory of U.S. victory. Even if such an outcome is implausible, for reason (among others) of the vulnerability of U.S. society to

Soviet retaliation, identification of a clear, ultimate (though not exclusive) war aim—the demise of the Soviet state—should enable the U.S. defense community to track back in search of strike options that ought to promote that end. This particular, definitive, war aim has several obvious merits. First, by definition, its accomplishment would deny success to Soviet leaders. Second, in and of itself, it would have operational appeal to a U.S. president. Third, practical difficulties aside, Soviet appreciation of this American war aim should have an enormous deterrent effect (this is one threat that Soviet leaders would be most unlikely to undervalue).

6. In the absence of a very capable civil defense program, and survivable air and missile defenses, a large U.S. strike against what can be identified of the essential Soviet political control structure could not prudently be executed as an initiative. The threat to the rule of the Communist Party of the Soviet Union should be thought of as the United States's "Sunday punch," intended to deter the Soviet Union from striking at U.S. cities.

7. Careful attention needs to be paid to which side would be the deterrer, and which the deterree—a question that requires campaign predictions embracing the war outbreak scenario. The large countercontrol threat could function as a war terminator, but only if the onus of further escalation lay with the Soviet Union.

8. Following (7), the efficacy, indeed relevance, of the counter-political-control threat depends almost entirely upon U.S. (and U.S.-allied) military prowess in the war to date. Soviet knowledge (or belief—whether well or ill founded) that the United States could degrade Soviet political control, perhaps fatally, should discourage strikes against the U.S. homeland of such a character that the U.S. leadership might reason that it had nothing left worth preserving (i.e., freed from obedience to any ethic of consequences, the U.S. leadership could "do its worst"). Many, if not most, of the credibility problems that attend different SIOP designs stem from the prospective fact that the United States has to assume that *it* will need to take the initiative at all stages of a conflict—in other words, the burden of decision to escalate will be on American, not Soviet, shoulders. In practice, this logic might not apply. Soviet military literature is unequivocal on the virtues of seizure of the initiative: this reflects not poor escalation reasoning (which it is—in U.S. terms), but rather an apparently different approach to the conduct of war.

9. Some aspects of the counter-political-control strike option require careful political consideration from the perspective of U.S. interests in a postwar world. The issue was raised above of whether "regionalization" of the current USSR necessarily would serve the end of a

viable and defensible international order. A further question pertains to long-term U.S. relations with the People's Republic of China (PRC). It would certainly be feasible for the United States to inflict great damage upon the Soviet projection forces (52 divisions at present) deployed along the Sino-Soviet frontier, and thereby perhaps "kick the door in" for Chinese acquisition of a lot of territory. However, it is not obviously in the U.S. interest that the PRC should profit greatly from an East-West war. Because the United States could open the gate for the Chinese People's Liberation Army (PLA) does not mean that it should—notwithstanding any functional U.S.-PRC alliance. Nonetheless, if one had to choose, the United States should prefer a strong PRC to a strong Soviet Union.

10. It is debatable whether a substantial fraction of U.S. strategic nuclear assets should be allocated for strike options against Soviet economic targets. The United States has great interest in ensuring that the USSR does not win a war but somewhat less interest in impeding Soviet economic recovery from war.[20] Given the absence of a U.S. domestic war-survival and recovery program, a large threat to the Soviet recovery economy would be (*a*) incredible, (*b*) suicidal if implemented, and (*c*) quite possibly less than very deterring—even if Soviet leaders believed the threat to be a real one. A case can be made for targeting Soviet war-supporting industry, resting upon the reasoning that it is prudent not to assume a very short war and that the Soviet Union probably places such targets in the analytical and operational category of "military" rather than "urban/industrial." It has become almost popular to argue for "endurance" in the strategic force posture and in its related C³I, and to be skeptical of very short war assumptions. However, the assertions that endurance is important and worth paying for, and that a general war may last months rather than weeks, days, or hours, require careful exmination. While I am friendly to the idea of purchasing much greater "endurance," I wish to record the caveat that the long-war thesis (with its associated implications regarding the importance of the Soviet and American mobilization bases) is in dire need of politico-strategic analysis. There is some danger that the United States might slip from one set of apolitical and mindless assumptions concerning war duration (which become a self-fulfilling prophecy—because a posture was evolved that lacked endurance) into another such set.

11. Unlike past bureaucratic practice, it would be desirable if U.S. (and NATO) research and development, procurement, targeting, and arms control planning could move more roughly in step, each with the others. Although it is desirable to build flexibility into the force posture, there is no denying that substantial changes in strategic asset

allocation between very different target systems carry with them some very different postural requirements. Similarly, START policy planning should not be innocent of targeting considerations. For example, really deep cuts in strategic force levels could have dramatic implications regarding target coverage (for the USSR as well as for the United States), and those implications need not be benign for stability.

12. Strategic nuclear targeting reviews naturally, and quite properly, encourage imagination and ingenuity in designing force application options. On the negative side, they carry the risks of discouraging reflection both upon what cannot be accomplished, or can be accomplished only very imperfectly, with strategic nuclear weapons, and upon the quantitative underpinning of U.S. strategy. General war, and particularly a protracted general war (to reflect the recognition of the need for endurance in the strategic force posture and its C^3I), should be approached, after Soviet practice, as a "combined arms" problem. Strategic nuclear application may well help in the unraveling of the Soviet empire, but the "liberation" potential of an Mk 12A warhead is limited and probably of a terminal character. The U.S. defense community can usefully be chided for its apparently enduring neglect of strategy in favor of managerial competence. However, some targeting problems reflect not so much intellectual deficiencies as they do muscular inadequacy.

[9]

On Keeping Them Down; or, Why Do Recovery Models Recover So Fast?

MICHAEL KENNEDY AND KEVIN N. LEWIS

INTRODUCTION

Current U.S. targeting guidance specifies that an all-out U.S. strike should prevent the USSR from recovering from the effects of nuclear war faster than the United States would recover. This general war targeting objective, known as Assured Retaliation, was first articulated in 1973–74 in the Nixon administration's decision document NSDM-242. NSDM-242 issued something like the following guidance (articulated by then secretary of defense Donald Rumsfeld in his *Department of Defense Annual Report for Fiscal Year 1978*: a severe U.S. strike against the USSR should "retard significantly the ability of the USSR to recover from a nuclear exchange and regain the status of a 20th century military and industrial power more rapidly than the U.S."[1]

Since about 1977, the strategic debate has seen a rise in concern with the sufficiency of U.S. retaliatory forces. This debate has been connected with SALT II's meanderings, with the need to decide on the shape of the U.S. strategic program for the 1980s, with the rediscovery of expanded Soviet civil and active defense efforts, and with certain adverse trends in the strategic balance. In connection especially with worries about Soviet civil defense, many technical reports appeared that contended the United States cannot satisfy the technical requirements of Assured Retaliation.

So that we should not find ourselves on the wrong side of an economic recovery gap, strategic planners have sought to assess the recovery potential of the Soviet economy by means of careful inspection of its constituent capabilities. Once this planning task is joined, however, a significant gap divides impression and analysis. While the popular view holds that one hundred or one thousand or three thousand warheads is enough to finish off the USSR for good, economic analysis frequently suggests that Soviet industrial might can bounce back to prewar levels within a very few years of the most punishing U.S. attacks.

Much of this debate has been conducted on an official or classified level, but some prominent assessments in the open literature have alleged that the USSR can recover from even an all-out U.S. strike in the short interval of four years at the least, and on up to fifteen years at the outside, depending on the severity of the U.S. attack and the performance of Soviet active and civil defenses.[2] Typical results suggest full recovery to prewar GNP within about five years if a U.S. attack destroys, say, less than half of Soviet capital and relatively little labor; seven to ten years with population-only civil defense; and perhaps fifteen years in any event. The U.S. force committed to the attack in such models often runs to several thousand warheads.

Such findings must be taken seriously because, to the extent that anybody attributes significance to them, they cast doubt on the effectiveness of U.S. deterrent forces. In turn, requirements for extra forces may be generated and American credibility may be undermined. For this reason, review of these models is not simply a question of professional validation and review of theoretical soundness; important policy issues may lie in the balance as well. If, on the other hand, these models do not reflect realistic characteristics of the postattack environment, then we should not, as a result of our misgivings, risk endorsing the view that the USSR's wartime prospects are better than suspected.

In this chapter, we will explain the peculiar result of the very rapid recovery that has caused such anxiety in our targeting deliberations. To accomplish this task, we will detail, by means of a simple illustrative model, how simple assumptions made in most recovery analyses give rise to apparently speedy Soviet recovery from all-out war. Subsequently, we shall touch on a few implications of these results for our own nuclear planning.

EXPLAINING VERY RAPID ECONOMIC RECOVERY FROM NUCLEAR ATTACK

The conclusion of many analyses is that, even in the face of full SIOP-level urban-industrial attacks, the attacked economy can quickly regenerate economic output, measured specifically in terms of arms stocks, industrial output, and so forth. This result seems excessively optimistic: with more than, say, half the preattack capital stock, arms inventories, and labor force destroyed, how can an economy rebuild these capabilities to preattack levels in only a few years?

In the next few pages we will explain this fundamental and pervasive characteristic of economic recovery modeling by presenting a simple example of this type of model and analyzing its behavior. The example we present is kept simple so that both the basic economic relations in it and the way that these relations lead to the kinds of results described above will be transparent. This simple model will illustrate the internal workings of the more complex models actually used in recovery analysis and show the reasons why these models get the results they do.

A danger of using a simple model, of course, is that the additional detail of the larger models may add basic new content to the analysis, to the extent that our smaller model is not an accurate analogue. We believe this caveat does not apply to the class of models used in recovery analysis and that the simple model we have chosen reflects faithfully those basic economic relations that drive the larger models. Thus, we maintain that our conclusions about why recovery models recover so fast can be applied intact to the larger models. After a presentation of our simple model, we will discuss the kinds of additional structure that more complex models have and the effect the additional structure would have on analytic results.

We now proceed to a description of our model. The economy we are considering produces three kinds of output: consumer goods, investment goods, and military output. This output is produced by two factors of production: labor and capital. Capital is simply the stock of physical assets that are used to produce output: factories, machinery, office buildings, warehouses, commercial vehicles, and so forth. It is, of course, exactly these physical assets, located in a finite number of installations, that are targeted in an economic attack.

Military output, for example, consists of production of weapons and the maintenance of military strength. Weapons are produced by capital (weapons factories) and labor (workers in those factories). Military strength is likewise produced by capital (bases, airfields, depots, command and communication facilities, etc.) and labor (military personnel). Both of these kinds of military capital are prime target candidates; the goal of their destruction is the reduction of the amount of military output that can be produced after an attack.

Before we continue, a special word about investment goods output is in order because it plays a large role in analysis of the recovery process. Investment goods output is simply the production of new capital goods— that is, the production of new factories, warehouses, military bases (an output of the construction industry), and the production of new machinery and equipment that is in turn used to produce other goods (the

[196]

output of the machinery sector). New output is used to augment the productive capacity of the economy by adding to the capital stock, that is, by increasing the number of factories (and the equipment inside them) so that more of all kinds of goods can be produced. The output of this sector is vital in rebuilding and recovering after a countereconomic attack because the goods produced by this sector are used to replace destroyed structures and machinery. These investment goods are themselves produced by capital and labor, of course, by factories that make machinery and building materials (capital) and by machinists and construction workers (labor).

Our model is summarized in figure 9.1. The boxes in the first row represent the capital stock of the economy. There is a separate box for the capital used in producing each kind of output; this represents our assumption that capital goods, once built, can produce only the kind of output they were designed for. This assumption is called *nonshiftability* of capital in technical terms, and means, for example, that factories built to produce consumer goods cannot be used to produce military goods. (The implications of relaxing this assumption will be discussed below.) Thus, our model will not recover quickly because we are not allowing surviving physical productive assets to be modified to produce exactly the goods that are needed for recovery.

The next row of figure 9.1 shows a single box for labor, and the arrows indicate that it can be allocated to produce any of the three kinds of output. This *shiftability* assumption is the opposite of our capital assumption, and implies that workers originally employed in consumer goods plants can be reassigned to (say) military equipment plants (provided they exist) and produce military goods in them. Again, we will discuss below the consequences of modifying this assumption.

Finally, figure 9.1 indicates that labor is used with the three specific types of capital stock to produce the three kinds of output. The dashed arrow shows that the investment goods output is used to add to the capital stock so that production of the three kinds of output can be increased in the future. The sum of consumer goods, investment goods, and military output is the gross national product (GNP) of the economy.

We will use this simple economic structure to illustrate the effects of an attack on the economy. It is convenient to begin the analysis with a picture of the base, or preattack, economic situation. This is given in table 9.1, which shows the level of the capital stock, labor force, and production of each of the three kinds of output. We note a few aspects of this economy: investment goods constitute 20 percent of GNP, the capital output ratio is 2.5, and military output is 10 percent. These numbers are characteristic of those national economies in which recovery modelers are generally interested. The "per capita consumption index"

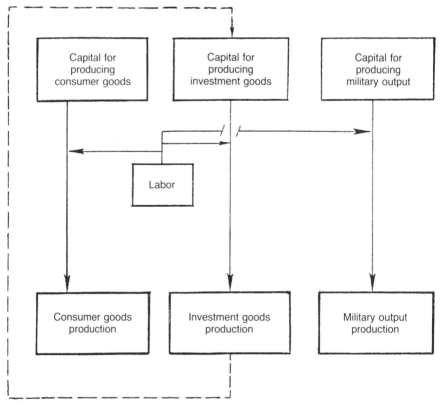

Figure 9.1. Diagram of a recovery model

is simply an index of the ratio of consumer goods output to the labor force.

We now impose a fairly severe attack on the economy that destroys half the capital stock in each sector and half the labor force. (This again is roughly characteristic of the kinds of numbers used in recovery analyses.) What effect does this have on the economy? Our model provides the desired results if we make two assumptions:

A.1. The 'survival' or 'reorganization' phases of the post attack period are assumed to have passed. Postnuclear attack analysis traditionally has divided the aftermath of an attack into two phases: During the first (which itself has been characterized as, or subdivided into, the 'survival' or 'reorganization' phases), the surviving political leadership of the attacked nation regains effective police control, provides and distributes sufficient food and medical supplies to stabilize the size

Table 9.1. Preattack economy

Economic Sector	Capital Stock	Labor Force	Output (GNP)
Consumer goods	175	70	70
New capital goods			
(investment goods)	50	20	20
Military output	25	10	10
TOTAL	250	100	100

Note: Per capita consumption index = 1.00.

and composition of the population, and achieves sufficient control over available economic administrative mechanisms so that its allocation and production orders are carried out. In addition, it is assumed that communication and transportation networks are restored to the point where national production can be effectively coordinated. This phase is considered to be over when the preattack technical laws of the economy again hold. This means that a given amount of labor in a given capital facility (i.e., plant with its equipment) will produce the same amount of output as it did before the attack.

Economic recovery models are generally silent on the issue of the length of this initial postattack phase. Once it has been completed, the "recovery" phase begins, and economic models predict the course of the economy from that point.

A.2. Our second assumption is that of constant returns to scale (CRS). All economic recovery models embody at least a close approximation to this assumption. The assumption says that if the capital and labor used for producing a certain kind of output are reduced by a given, equal percentage, the amount of output of that kind actually produced will fall by the same amount. It has intuitive appeal if one thinks in terms of a certain percent of the facilities being completely lost, along with their workers. The surviving factories could produce exactly what they had produced before, and the proportionate reduction in total output would be simply the proportion of factories lost.

The combination of these two assumptions enables prediction of a post attack economy, beginning just at the moment the recovery process is about to commence, as shown in Table 9.2.

The first two columns show our assumptions about the results of the attack; the capital stock available for producing each kind of output has been reduced by half, and the total labor force has also been halved. Assuming that workers are allocated to capital facilities in the same proportions as before the attack (an assumption that will be explained below), the resulting output will be as shown in the last column. Not surprisingly, due to A.2, this output is exactly half that produced before

Table 9.2. Postattack Economy: economic activity when recovery begins

Economic Sector	Capital Stock	Labor Force	Output
Consumer goods	87.5	35	35
Investment goods	25	10	10
Military output	12.5	5	5
TOTAL	125	50	50

Note: Per capita consumption index = 1.00.

the attack. Thus, GNP is 50, half the preattack GNP, and the per capita consumption index is the same as before the attack, since the labor force has fallen the same amount as consumption goods output. Our simple model (and all more complex models) thus predicts that once the economy has been reorganized so that surviving assets are employed with the same effectiveness as they were before the attack, and attack that destroys one half the assets will result in an economy that produces at one half the pre-attack level, and at the same per capita level.

The result is not, of course, the surprising "rapid" recovery that most models show. This simply gives us a starting point for recovery analysis. Indeed, it is a starting point with output at one-half the prewar level, a considerable drop in historic terms. The interesting question then is how quickly these output levels can be restored to preattack levels or beyond, and how this restoration is possible. To analyze this question, we now consider the progress of the economy, from the starting point shown in table 9.2, through time. In performing this analysis, we make three additional assumptions:

A.3. We assume a condition of shiftability of investment. This crucial assumption says that investment goods output can be used to rebuild any kind of capital. A certain amount of new capital goods will be produced each year by the investment goods sector (for example, 10 units in table 9.2), and we assume that these new capital facilities can be built so as to produce any kind of output. Put another way, the structures and machinery newly produced by the investment goods sector in any year can be used to add to (or rebuild) any of the three kinds of capital stock. For example, the surviving military capital stock in table 9.2 is 12.5 units; assumption A.3 says that if all new investment goods (10 units) were used to rebuild military capacity, this capital stock could be increased 80% the first year.

A.4. Our second new assumption is that of prioritization. That is, the leadership of the postattack economy can designate some sectors as priority ones and rebuild their capacity first while letting the output of other sectors stagnate.

[200]

Table 9.3. Postattack economic evolution

	Capital stock in I-producing sector	Capital stock in M-producing sector	GNP
Year 1	25.0	12.5	35.0 C 10.0 I 5.0 M
New investment after year 1	(6.7)	(3.3)	
Year 2	31.7	15.8	31.0 C 12.7 I 6.3 M
New investment after year 2	(8.5)	(4.2)	
Year 3	40.2	20.0	25.9 C 16.1 I 8.0 M
New investment after year 3	(10.7)	(5.4)	
Year 4	50.9	25.4	19.5 C 20.4 I 10.1 M

Note: We assume that all new capital goods are divided according to ratio 2:1 between rebuilding I-sector and M-sector.

A.5. We temporarily introduce a last assumption of no capital-labor substitution. This says that in order to produce output, labor and capital must be used in exactly the preattack proportions. In other words, a given capital facility, such as a factory, can produce only as much output as it did before the attack, no matter how much additional labor is employed in it. Equivalently, any reduction in labor used in the factory will cause a proportionate reduction in output. (This assumption justifies our allocation of labor across sectors in table 9.2, since any other allocation would have reduced output in one sector without increasing it in others.) This assumption will be relaxed later in the paper, and the alternte assumption that output from a plant can be increased by using labor in excess of preattack amounts will be substituted.

Given these assumptions, let us examine the path of the economy through time. We will assume in this example that the priorities of the economic leadership in the recovery period are such that they only rebuild the investment goods and military output sectors (i.e., that all new capital is used to rebuild the facilities that produce these kinds of goods). We assume that they rebuild these two capital stocks in the prewar proportions of two units of capital for producing capital goods to one unit for producing military goods.

Table 9.3 traces the economic path of this economy through a few years. The first two columns show the level of capital (and thus of output)

[201]

in the military and investment sectors. These levels (and, in parentheses, the per year increments to them due to production and installation of new capital goods) are traced through time down the columns. Thus, we see in the first period the following surviving capital stock in each of the sectors: 25 in investment and 12.5 in military, as in table 9.2. The last column shows GNP (or the output of each of three kinds of goods) in each period. Output of I and M goods are simply proportional to the amount of capital stock available for producing them. (How output of C, consumption goods, is determined will be explained momentarily.) Therefore, the last column shows output of 10 in the I-sector and 5 in the M, again corresponding to the figures in table 9.2.

We will now inspect the continued evolution of the system through time. The first-period output of new capital goods, 10, is available to be added to existing capital stocks (i.e., available to rebuild part of the attacked economy). Using the allocation (or prioritization) assumptions made above, we use none of this to rebuild capacity for producing consumer goods and divide the total between investment and military sectors in the proportion 2:1. This means that 6.7 is added to the capital stock used for producing I goods, boosting the level of that stock to 31.7, and 3.3 is available for rebuilding the capacity of the M sector, increasing that capital stock to 15.8. These new investment activities are shown in the second row, and the resulting capital stocks available for year 2 in the next row. Then, using our no-capital-labor-substitution assumption, we can derive that output of I goods will be 31.7/2.5, or 12.7, in the second year, and output of M goods will be 6.3. Then again, this investment good output, or new production of plants and machinery, is used to further augment production capacity in the economy, and so on. The bottom line is perhaps the most startling: in the fourth period, output of the M- and I-sectors is *restored* to the pre-attack level. This example illustrates the essential results from the actions of the two mechanisms, shiftability of investment and prioritization, that led to rapid recovery of key economic capabilities in post-attack models. The reader may want to work out the alternate case in which investemnt is split in exactly the pre-attack proportions (7:2:1) among all three capital stocks.

We have one loose end to tie up here: what happened to labor? According to our strict 'no substitution' assumption, when the plant, or capital stock, of a sector is increased, workers there must be proportionately increased also. This means that of the surviving labor force of 50, 30.5 must be engaged in production of new investment goods or military output by the fourth period. This leaves only 19.5 in the consumption goods production sector, and again by our strict no-substitution assumption, output of consumption goods must then fall to 19.5. However, across the entire four-year horizon, per capita production of consumer goods is 80 percent of the preattack level. In terms of prioritization, we generally assume the population will be made to do with less after an attack, and this allotment of goods for consumption seems generous.

We now consider a second example of a postattack economic evolution, to illustrate the sensitivity of these kinds of results to changes in assumptions. Here, we replace assumption A.5 with the possibility of capital-labor substitution, that is, that a given plant can increase its level of output if additional labor is used in it. In particular, we will assume that if the number of workers is doubled, output can be increased by one-half. (This is approximately the degree of substitutability implied by a Cobb-Douglas production function with a labor coefficient of 0.6.) Finally, we will assume that only the investment goods sector is rebuilt and that the level of military output is allowed to remain at one-half the prewar level.

The combination of these two assumptions, of course, will greatly increase the ability of the postattack economy to increase its output of new capital goods, and thus to rebuild its civilian capital stock. This capital stock will have a different composition than the prewar stock, though; it will be heavily weighted toward industrial production and away from consumer goods production. This overall situation is roughly analogous to the heavy Soviet industrialization drive of the 1930s.

In a more complex example allowing capital-labor substitution, one must decide how much labor is allocated to each sector. For simplicity, we shall assume that exactly enough workers are assigned to plants in the investment goods producing sector so that the output-capital ratio is increased to 0.6 (i.e., the capital-output ratio falls to 1.67), or that a given investment goods plant does, in fact, increase its output to one-and-a-half times the preattack level.

Table 9.4 traces the path of such an economy over time. It is exactly analogous to table 9.3, except the military capital stock column is omitted. Here, the first-period capital stock available for production of investment goods is 25 as it was in table 9.3 (this 25 is just the amount surviving the attack). However, in this example, by assumption, output of new capital goods, or new plant, can be increased from 10 (the one-year level in table 9.3) to 15 by reassigning workers in other sectors of the economy to work more intensively surviving plant. This first-period output of new capital goods is used solely to rebuild the capital good producing, or investment, sector, again by assumption. Thus, we add the 15 units of new plant to the 25 surviving the attack and get 40 units of plant and equipment available for producing new capital goods in the second period. Again, by adding more workers, we can operate at an output-capital ratio of 0.6, and thus produce 24 units of investment goods in the second period. And so on.

[203]

Table 9.4. Postattack economic evolution

	Capital stock in I-producing sector	GNP
Year 1	25.0	15.0 I
		5.0 M
New investment after year 1	(15.0)	
Year 2	40.0	24.0 I
		5.0 M
New investment after year 2	(24.0)	
Year 3	64.0	38.4 I
		5.0 M
New investment after year 3	(38.4)	
Year 4	102.4	61.4 I
		5.0 M

Note: We assume capital-labor substitutability, and all new capital goods are used to rebuild I-sector.

The end of this process after only four years is startling indeed: output of capital goods is three times the preattack level! In addition, if the surviving capital in the M- and C-sectors (12.5 and 87.5, respectively) is added to fourth-period capital in the I-sector (102.4), we get an economywide capital stock of 202.4, over 80 percent of the preattack level. Thus, if we make these substitution and prioritization assumptions, we see how surviving productive capacity as a share of the entire economy comes close to that of the pre-war situation. (Recall the different structure of the economy.) This reflects the inexorable logic of geometric compounding, a fundamental aspect of all economic growth models.

We will now discuss the aspects of the more complex models actually used in recovery analysis that may cause them to give different sorts of results from the ones presented here. First we will discuss those assumptions that may lead to slower recovery paths than the ones predicted by our simple model.

1. *Non-shiftability of investment.* A crucial assumption of this analysis was that new investment goods could be used to rebuild any sector, thus enabling the rapid recovery of military and/or industrial output at the expense of consumer goods. One might want to modify this assumption so that not all new capital could be used to rebuild priority sectors. The obvious way to implement this would be to disaggregate the investment goods sector into three: one that produces capital goods used for consumer goods production, one that produces capital goods for investment goods production, and one that produces capital goods for

military output production. To our knowledge, however, no recovery model incorporates this disaggregation: all models contain homogeneous "machinery" and "construction" sectors. To slow down predicted recovery rates, some models may put constraints on the rate at which military or industrial capital stocks can be rebuilt, but these constraints reflect the judgement of the analysts and not the structure of the models.

2. *Input-output and intermediate goods.* Most recovery models have a considerably more complex economic structure than the one presented here and include basic industries (such as metallurgy), resource industries (such as agriculture), and intermediate processing industries (such as oil refining), all of whose outputs are intermediate goods eventually being transformed into final consumer, investment, and military products. However, this does not change our results since the use of the outputs of these intermediate industries can be prioritized as easily as investment can, and they can simply be routed to the appropriate final processing plant. The fact that more transportation and communication links are needed in a more complex economy may prolong the "reorganization" period, of course, and will make appropriate economic coordination more difficult during the recovery phase. No formal recovery model, however, incorporates the coordination function, and all models instead simply assume it can be accomplished. The existence of intermediate industries in fact may make recovery easier, since it makes capital shiftable in the sense that a plant that had made steel that eventually wound up in consumer goods before the attack could make steel that goes to military production afterward.

3. *Intermediate industries.* However, the existence of intermediate industries leads to the possibility of bottleneck targeting. If a crucial link in the economy (such as oil refining) could be completely destroyed, recovery might be very difficult. The possibility of prioritization of output, however, counteracts the bottleneck threat; if only a small amount of a key sector's capacity survives, it can be used in crucial production areas, and in particular, in producing goods needed to rebuild that capacity.

4. *Shiftability of labor.* Furthermore, labor may not be freely shiftable across sectors. However, this could be offset by the possibility that some kind of capital may be shiftable. (For example, civilian auto and truck plants may be adaptable to military vehicle production.)

Finally, certain complexities incorporated in larger models will in fact make recovery faster than indicated by our simple model. These include recruitment of more persons into the labor force, double shifting, and optimal allocation of labor and investment resources rather than the rule-of-thumb allocations used in this chapter.

In the previous pages, we have documented the general effect of the three-recovery-model phenomena of (1) *shiftability of investment*—basically a technological issue; (2) *prioritization*—a political, or more specifically, a leadership issue; and (3) *capital labor substitutability*—another technological question. (The postattack society, even after a severe SIOP-level attack, is shown to rapidly restore levels of output in key economic areas, such as military force and industrial output. This is done by consciously directing resources such as labor and new investment goods into rebuilding specifically those sectors.)

What do these results, which reflect certain general properties of, albeit, more complex and bulky models, imply about targeting? A few points come to mind.

Perhaps an effort should be made to attack those plants that produce capital goods specific to rebuilding the sectors we are concerned about. That is, if we can find areas where the shiftability-of-investment assumption is patently contradicted, we can exploit this vulnerability by targeting heavily those plants that produce machines used to produce goods whose output we are interested in seeing suppressed. (For example, if a certain kind of electronic equipment is needed to produce missile guidance systems, and if only a few plants can produce this equipment,[3] then if those plants are knocked out, it will be impossible to restore missile production until both the missile plants themselves and the specific equipment plants are rebuilt.[4]

This notion endorses the generic targeting theory of "bottlenecking" which has been at the heart of U.S. air war planning since the 1930s. This assumption forms the core of a useful strategy because it assists in force sizing and makes possible more confident estimation of the consequences of attack. Moreover, it allows us to selectively expand the data bases we use in recovery analysis, thereby avoiding a pitfall of standard input-output modeling, namely, an unregulated increase in the number of sectors in an economy with a concomitant dramatic growth in the complexity of the problem.

Three difficulties arise with this strategy, however. First, identification of such plants may be very difficult and uncertain at best. In the broadest sense, we have not identified all industrial value, and complete and precise economic intelligence is difficult to accumulate. A second issue, one of prudent efficiency (or risk aversion) in targeting arises here: do we want to expend a large number of weapons on a few plants (at the cost of other targets that we could not then bring under attack) that we think may be crucial for rebuilding key sectors? A collateral problem is

that the adversary can probably identify such crucial capital goods producing sectors as well and may take steps to harden and/or disperse the
plants. Finally, we may not have a suitable appreciation for the ability
of the other side to "jury rig," substitute, draw from stocks and inventories, or obtain (by capture) resources from nations it can subjugate in
the course of fighting. To devise an effective bottleneck strategy therefore
requires resolution or compensation for these possibilities.

A related strategy would be to concentrate targeting on the capital
goods producing industry itself, that is, to try to draw down the capacity
of the industry that itself produces the goods necessary for rebuilding
any sector. The problem with this strategy is that machine building and
construction are typically greatly dispersed in a modern economy and
targeting a high percentage of their capacity with confidence is very
difficult (and can be made much more so by countermeasures such as
stockpiling, camouflage, dispersal, and hardening).

In this context, survival and reorganization become relatively more
important subperiods of the canonical postattack pathway because they
intervene between the attack and the beginning of recovery. Of course,
it is not understood at all how to translate the relative objectives of
massive attacks into the length or difficulty of each period, let alone to
define them in terms of observable phenomena. Note that this particular
question lies at the roots of the theoretical differences encountered in
comparisons of Assured Retaliation with Assured Destruction.

Reconnaissance, retargeting, and continuing attack become very attractive options for "keeping them down." The survivors can concentrate
their resources on rebuilding plants that produce outputs of special
importance to them (and which may pose a special threat to us). By the
same token, we can attempt to frustrate these efforts by identifying and
attacking the rebuilding and rebuilt assets. This factor definitely has
implications for the missions and roles of the strategic reserve forces in
the case of economic targeting.

Although it is only implicit in the preceding examples, the importance
of labor survival for economic progress after an attack is a function of
the degree of capital labor substitutability. A related factor of unpre-
dictable significance is the state's ability to organize surviving labor into
a coordinated productive effort and to maintain confidence in the rebuilding effort, thereby ensuring momentum in recovery. When contemplating force allocations in SIOP planning, it is also essential to keep
in mind those management, geographic, demographic, transportation,
and regional issues that will influence all elements of the recovery economy. There will be questions that cannot be answered with quantitative
finality which ultimately would determine the effectiveness of labor reorganization. These issues include currency reform, devotion of re-

sources to internal security pursuits, and so forth. But in theory as well as in previous experience it has seemed as though surviving (especially skilled) population has been the linchpin of recovery. Therefore the demographic issue is critical; so too, with management, transportation, and other infrastructural features of the problem.

Finally, as one economist studying this problem has noted, the importance of economic models in analyzing the postattack world is that they incorporate the fact that military output is embedded in a larger economy and can, therefore, deal with the economywide resource constraints that limit possibilities for military reconstitution. The sentence is true, but its emphasis seems wrong. Economic models basically allege that since resources (new capital and labor) are flexible and can be directed to many uses, by allowing low-priority economic activities (such as nonsubsistence consumption) to stagnate, the postattack society can rebuild important economic capabilities relatively quickly.

[10]

Exemplary Industrial Targets for Controlled Conflict

Frederic S. Nyland

INTRODUCTION

This chapter presents a cursory examination of the location and distribution of U.S. industrial activity, with a view to determining whether there are some obvious industries for which a limited number of production or distribution sites accounts for a crucial or disproportionately large share of the output. After identifying certain industries that are economically important and geographically concentrated, it examines their vulnerability to various levels of nuclear attack. Finally, it analyzes ways in which nuclear weapons might be used to maximize physical damage while limiting collateral human casualties. The purpose is to select some exemplary sets of economic targets for use in planning preparedness measures, not to predict what targets an enemy planner might select.

The context of this examination is that of a controlled conflict. As defined by the Federal Preparedness Agency (FPA), a controlled conflict is, in part, one in which the contending powers use or threaten to use military force, including nuclear weapons, on a scale restricted enough to avoid precipitating a general war. Implicit in the FPA's definition of controlled conflict is the assumption that an attacker would (1) avoid striking strategic retaliatory systems and their assorted command and control networks and facilities and (2) provide warning of nuclear strikes, including specific aim points and targets. While the probability of the occurrence of a controlled conflict is admittedly low, it is nevertheless not zero.

The data used in this analysis are now somewhat dated, but this work serves as an example of how to approach the targeting of major industries.

Some generic plans for population evacuation in the event of such a contingency have been formulated by the Federal Emergency Management Agency. Detailed planning for each section of the United States is the responsibility of individual state and local governments. Thus in the event of an attack many lives could be saved in those areas where detailed plans existed and were followed.

INDUSTRIAL STRUCTURE

This section examines the industrial structure of the United States in an effort to identify industries that are economically important either to the general public or to other industries that use their products. In addition, it examines industrial concentration in a geographic sense.

Economic Importance

The first step in any identification of high-economic-value industrial facilities is an examination of the relative importance of various industries in the U.S. economy and, at the same time, an attempt at some first-order judgments about geographic concentration. To achieve this purpose, the total sales of major industries has been selected as an indicator of economic importance. Table 10.1 shows the U.S. industries that have an output (in terms of sales) exceeding $20 billion per year. The data are based on an input-output model for 1967.[1]

Many of the industries in table 10.1 can be quickly eliminated from consideration as they are clearly not concentrated enough to meet our general criterion. For example, wholesale and retail trade or transportation and warehousing involve so many discrete locations, each of such small output or throughput as not to be of interest in this examination. There are industries, however, that while similarly dispersed, are critically dependent on products of other industries that are concentrated. For example, motor vehicles and equipment are manufactured at many different locations, but all depend on metal products such as aluminium and steel.

Almost all industries and the general public are dependent on energy. The sharp curtailment of electrical service could present some critical problems. Examination of the system of electric power distribution in the United States indicates both that the number of sites is large and that there is a fair degree of substitutability, should a portion of the network be damaged. The brownout problems of the northeastern section of the country some years ago led the public utility companies to provide switching arrangements within the power distribution grid. Gas,

Table 10.1. Largest industries of the United States in 1967
(output in excess of $20 billion)

Rank	Industry	$ Billion
1	Wholesale and retail trade	163.36
2	Real estate and rental	113.25
3	Food and kindred products	89.45
4	Government industry	81.65
5	New construction	79.89
6	Business services	56.44
7	Transportation and warehousing	52.82
8	Medical, educational, and nonprofit organizations	48.51
9	Finance and insurance	47.71
10	Motor vehicles and equipment	43.74
11	Electric, gas, water, and sanitary services	37.32
12	Primary iron and steel manufacturing	31.72
13	Livestock and livestock products	30.64
14	Other agricultural products	28.54
15	Petroleum refining and related industries	26.98
16	Maintenance and repair construction	23.39
17	Chemicals and selected chemical products	23.28
18	Apparel	22.57
19	Printing and publishing	22.12
20	Primary nonferrous metal manufacturing	20.87
21	Hotels; personal and repair services, except automotive	20.80

water, and sanitary services are grouped with electric service in table
10.1. Natural gas is considered part of the petroleum industry since the
two are so closely related in production and distribution. While the
individual electricity- and water-supply facilities appear to be widely
dispersed from a national viewpoint, they may seem concentrated if
looked at on a regional basis.

Primary iron and steel production is generally thought of as an important element of the U.S. economy. Although it is not the largest
industry shown in table 10.1, its output is widely used (see table 10.2)[2]
both by the iron and steel industry itself and by other industries to
which it sells its products. Motor-vehicle manufacturing is the largest
outside consumer of steel in the table 10.2 categorization. The category
of heating, plumbing, and structural-metal products, combined with that
of new construction, form another significant industrial group dependent on steel. As is obvious from the remaining users of steel shown in
table 10.2, there is virtually no direct sale of steel to the public. Thus,
the steel industry is an example where the loss of output would not
directly affect the public in the short term, but its effects would become
apparent in the longer term since there is no quick way to replace steel
mills, furnaces, coke plants, and other fuel and raw-material production
facilities.

[211]

Table 10.2. Distribution of primary iron and steel output in 1967

Rank	Consumer	$ Billion	Cumulative consumption ($ Billion)
1	Primary iron and steel industry	6.017	6.017
2	Motor vehicles and equipment	3.103	9.120
3	Heating, plumbing, and structural metal products	3.018	12.138
4	Stampings, screw machine products, and bolts	2.208	14.346
5	Other fabricated metal products	2.200	16.546
6	New construction	1.456	18.002
7	Construction, mining and oil-field machinery	0.951	18.953
8	Metal-working machinery and equipment	0.695	19.648
9	Farm machinery and equipment	0.655	20.303
10	Ordnance and accessories	0.523	20.826
11	Special industry and machinery equipment	0.484	21.310
12	Engines and turbines	0.384	21.694

Note: Total = $31.723 billion.

The supply of a form of energy—petroleum products—is known to be critical and growing more so each year. The petroleum-refining industry appears in table 10.1 to be fairly important economically. The loss of petroleum output, however, unlike the loss of steel production, would have a direct and immediate effect on the public. Table 10.3 indicates that the public is the largest user of petroleum products, consuming by value about 40 per cent of the market output.[3] Transportation would be affected severely by the loss of the petroleum industry, as would other industrial users. Some consumers, for example, electric power plants, may have alternative sources of primary energy, such as gas and coal. If a large portion of petroleum output were curtailed, it is generally believed that the public would be the consumer most severely

Table 10.3. Distribution of petroleum and related industry output in 1967

Rank	Consumer	$ Billion	Cumulative consumption ($ Billion)
1	Individual households	10.194	10.194
2	Transportation and warehousing	1.999	12.193
3	Petroleum refining and related industries	1.831	14.024
4	Chemicals and selected chemical products	1.800	15.824
5	New construction	1.400	17.224
6	Wholesale and retail trade	1.375	18.599
7	Federal government	1.078	19.677
8	Other agricultural products	0.905	20.582
9	Real estate and rental	0.720	21.302
10	Maintenance and repair construction	0.624	21.926
11	Electric, gas, water, and sanitary services	0.275	22.201

Note: Total = $26.975 billion.

Table 10.4. Distribution of primary nonferrous-metal manufacturing output in 1967

Rank	Consumer	$ Billion	Cumulative consumption ($ Billion)
1	Primary nonferrous metal manufacturing	6.723	6.723
2	New construction	2.155	8.878
3	Heating, plumbing, and structural metal products	0.874	9.752
4	Engines and turbines	0.872	10.624
5	Primary iron and steel manufacture	0.859	11.483
6	Aircraft and parts	0.732	12.215
7	Motor vehicles and equipment	0.673	12.888
8	Electric industrial equipment and apparatus	0.605	13.493
9	Stampings, screw machine products, and bolts	0.524	14.017
10	Optical, ophthalmic, and photographic equipment	0.371	14.388
11	Chemicals and selected chemical products	0.322	14.710
12	Miscellaneous electrical machinery, equipment, and supplies	0.318	15.028
13	General industrial machinery and equipment	0.308	15.336
14	Ordnance and accessories	0.298	15.634
15	Other transportation equipment	0.291	15.925
16	Electronic components and accessories	0.283	16.208
17	Radio, television, and communication equipment	0.279	16.487
18	Household appliances	0.266	16.753
19	Service industry machines	0.265	17.018
20	Electric lighting and wiring equipment	0.260	17.278
21	Metal-working machinery and equipment	0.231	17.509

Note: Total = $20.87 billion.

affected, and one can only guess at the public reaction toward the government or whoever might be blamed for the loss of output. The slight curtailment of crude oil by the Arab countries during the 1972 Arab-Israeli war hints at what would be the effect of a physical impairment of the petroleum industry. If, simultaneously, gas-production and/or distribution facilities were disrupted, then the effect on the public might be even more dramatic because of the wide use of both oil and gas for heating, especially in the Northeastern region of the United States.

Another large industry—primary nonferrous metal manufacturing—is similar to the steel industry to the extent that its products are used not by the general public, but by other industries, as indicated in Table 10.4.[4] As in the case of steel production, new construction and the manufacture of heating, plumbing, and structural metal products together consume a sizable portion of the primary nonferrous metal industry output—in this instance about 15 percent. The output of this industry, in contrast to that of the steel industry, is used by somewhat higher technology industries, such as the optical, electronic, and electrical equipment manufacturers. In the transportation sector, the aircraft industry consumes slightly more aluminium, but the aircraft currently in commercial and military service do constitute a considerable reserve. For such aluminium consumers as manufacturers of products for the building trades, reserve stocks may be quite limited, but other materials could be substituted in some cases.

On the basis of the foregoing, we will draw our examples of economically important industries for purposes of preparedness planning from those producing metals and energy.

Industrial Concentration

What patterns of concentration are found in the metal and energy industries? To answer this question it is necessary to look carefully at a few specific industries: the petroleum refining and distribution system, the natural gas distribution system, the steel industry, and segments of the nonferrous metals industry. The degree of concentration of each industry has been determined on the basis of an examination of existing reference materials and data bases.[5] The results are shown in figure 10.1, which indicates the capacity in percentages of the production facilities of each industry as a function of the number of separate facilities, ranked in order of capacity.

The petroleum refineries as a set of facilities are the least concentrated of the examples shown. Even so, some thirty plants account for about 50 percent of the industry's capacity. The curtailment of the production of these thirty refineries would be roughly equivalent to denying all sales of finished products to the general public and to the transportation industry. With regard to the distribution system of the petroleum refining industry, there are some interesting regional peculiarities. Two pipelines from Louisiana to the northeastern states carry almost all of the finished products used in this heavily industrialized area. In addition, there are no pipelines between the source of the crude oil and the refineries near New York City and on the Delaware River. All crude oil is delivered to these areas by ship.

The steel industry of the United States is more concentrated than are the refineries. About 80 percent of the steel-making capacity is contained in about forty facilities. In contrast to the curtailment of petroleum products, which would be felt directly by individual persons, the deprivation of steel would be felt by other industries. These industries use the metal to fabricate products, and it is the absence of these manufactured goods that would be felt by the public. The steel industry has a peculiarity in

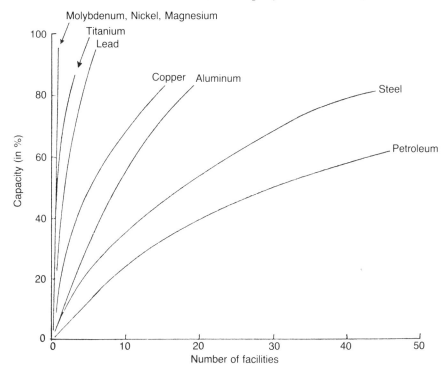

Figure 10.1. Concentration of selected industries

its source of supply: about 80 percent of all iron ore used in this industry passes through the locks at Sault Sainte Marie, Michigan.

The concentration of production is particularly high in the nonferrous metal industries shown in figure 10.1. The loss of the supply of molybdenum or nickel would have serious effects on the making of higher grades of steel. The major part of the magnesium produced in the United States comes from a single Dow Chemical Company plant in Texas, and the bulk of the strategic stockpile of magnesium is stored at this same facility.

INDUSTRIAL VULNERABILITY

The focus of this section is on (1) the potential damage that would be caused by either of two different sizes (1 Mt and 30 kt) of nuclear weapons that the Soviets might use in an attack on industrial targets and on (2) the physical vulnerability of the targets themselves.

Weapon Yield and Accuracy

The selection of typical weapons that the Soviets might use in attacks on the industrial sector of the U.S. economy is based on estimates of weapons in the Soviet strategic forces. The projection of future Soviet weapons is based on educated guesswork and extrapolations of current U.S. technology.

According to public estimates, the Soviets have on the order of one thousand SS-11 and six hundred SLBMs with warhead yields of one to two megatons.[6] The probable delivery error (CEP) of the ICBMs has been reported to be about five hundred to seven hundred meters, but some defense officials have indicated that these reports may be somewhat optimistic.[7] For purposes of this study, a "standard" yield of one megaton and a delivery accuracy of about three thousand feet are assumed representative of the capability of ICBMs, which the Soviets possess in large numbers and which they would be likely to use to conduct limited attacks in a controlled conflict.

A projected yield of thirty kilotons is used here to represent more specialized weapons that the Soviets might procure in the future for operations against industrial targets. It is assumed that the Soviets will have designed these weapons to meet some possible constraints related to reducing collateral casualties. A delivery accuracy of about one thousand feet is assumed as possible within Soviet technological capability at some future date. The estimates of severe damage to typical industrial structures ($VN = 15Q7$) are shown in figure 10.2. These damage probabilities are high, usually better than 90 percent.

One form of restraint in attacks on industrial facilities might be observed by an enemy planner. This restraint, which is incidental to some degree, would be to use airbursts rather than contact bursts. One might argue whether or not this is really a form of restraint. If the attack planner is attempting to maximize damage to various above-ground structures, then the height of burst that is appropriate is far enough above the ground so that the fireball does not touch the ground. Under such circumstances, the amount of fallout is much smaller than from a surface burst and consists mostly of bomb debris. The amount of fallout is usually considered insignificant by U.S. attack planners and analysts. If the reliability of Soviet fusing mechanism is less than unit value, however, one would expect some weapons not to explode until they impact, if contact fusing is used as a backup to fuses intended to detonate the weapon at altitude. In such cases, the weapon miss distance would be

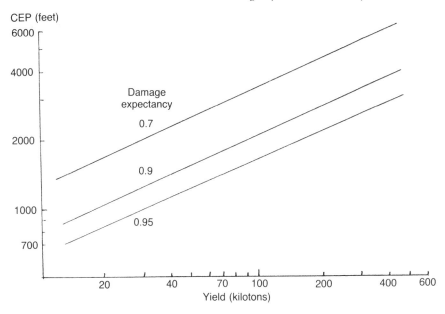

Figure 10.2. Weapon requirements for industrial damage

larger and a considerable amount of radiated dust and debris would be created. In a subsequent section, estimates of casualties will be based on the assumption that all weapons are successfully burst at altitudes high enough so that there will be little fallout.

Industrial Facility Damage Levels

Basically, industrial facilities can be divided into two groups: (1) circular-cross-section, towerlike structures and (2) rectangular buildings. The first category includes smokestacks and fractionation towers used in refining processes. The second category includes almost all types of industrial buildings. Rather than draw on classified sources, this analysis is based on the report of actual blast damage done by the explosion of a twenty-kiloton weapon at Hiroshima,[8] with the weapon radii scaled according to the commonly accepted cube root law. A smokestack has been chosen to represent refineries. In Hiroshima, a smokestack at 1,800 feet from ground zero was severely damaged. Also, severe damage was sustained by a two-story steel-frame building with seven-inch reinforced-concrete wall panels at a distance of about 2,100 feet from ground zero. Above-ground pipelines, however, are somewhat more resistant to blast

Table 10.5. Scaled weapon radii for industrial structures (in feet)

Building Type	30 Kiloton	1 Megaton
Towerlike structures	2,050	6,610
Steel frame with reinforced-concrete wall panels	2,400	7,800
Above-ground pipe (16-inch diameter)	1,390	4,470

damage; there is one example of a sixteen-inch pipe that was severely damaged about 1,200 feet from ground zero at Hiroshima. Table 10.5 shows the corresponding weapon radii for one-megaton and thirty-kiloton devices.

These radii are uncertain because they are taken from single data points. In calculating damage probabilities, a 30 percent uncertainty in weapon radii is included to account for such uncertainties. A special damage-probability computer was used to make the computations.[9] The damage probability for each type of structure and each size weapon is given in Table 10.6 for the CEPs of interest.

Two other types of structures are of interest in the investigation: buried pipelines and underground tanks for storing finished petroleum products. Examination of their vulnerability indicates that a ground burst is needed to inflict severe damage and that several weapons should be aimed at each targeted point to result in a high probability of damage. The use of these tactics would result in large amounts of fallout. It is assumed that if the Soviets were to show restraint, they would attack the more vulnerable above-ground parts of pipelines and refinery complexes.

The Soviets might, under certain circumstances, attack canals and locks. The vulnerability of each target must be determined on a case-by-case basis since size and material used in construction may vary widely. As an example, the vulnerability of the Sault Sainte Marie locks has been studied. Figure 10.3 shows some typical results. It was assumed that the Soviets would employ ground bursts to maximize damage. It is apparent that locks are more damage resistant than typical industrial structures. The ground burst of multiple weapons or single very-large-

Table 10.6. Damage probabilities for industrial structures

Building Type	30 Kiloton	1 Megaton
Towerlike structures	0.85	0.88
Steel frame with reinforced-concrete wall panels	0.90	0.92
Above-ground pipe (16-inch diameter)	0.66	0.70

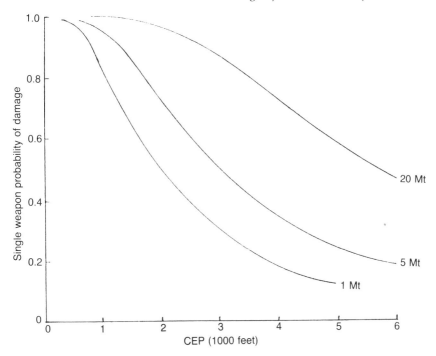

Figure 10.3. Damage probability to locks

yield weapons would cause extensive fallout. Whether or not the Soviets might aim weapons at such targets is not known.

Were the Soviets to aim at an industrial facility without knowing its exact location, the damage probabilities would decrease if the location error were of the same order of magnitude as the CEP or greater. However, the chance-of-location errors would be small for locating facilities in the United State if the Soviets use the readily available charts prepared by the Geological Survey. Large industrial complexes are clearly shown on these charts, and it is estimated that aimpoints could be selected with less than a hundred-foot error. For example, figure 10.4 is a Geological Survey chart showing the steel facility at Sparrows Point, Maryland, in great detail. One can conclude that target location errors can be ignored in calculating damage probability to industrial targets.

EFFECTS OF ATTACKS ON SELECTED INDUSTRIES

It seems fairly obvious from the preceding sections that the probability of destroying any single above-ground structure could be high. How-

[219]

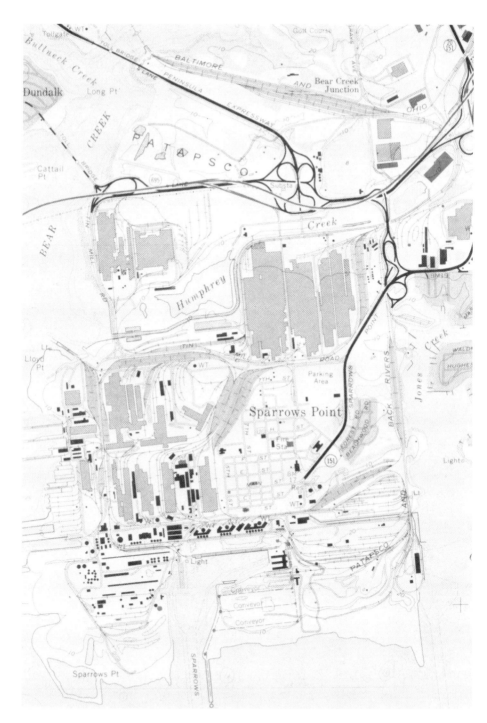

Figure 10.4. Steel plant at Sparrows Point, Maryland

[220]

ever, the collateral effects of limited attacks on a significant portion of any one industry are not so straightforward. In this section, attacks on significant parts of various industries will be examined and the collateral prompt casualties will be estimated. The industries selected here as examples are steel, aluminium, oil, and natural gas. For each industry possible attacks are suggested that would be small and disruptive; larger attacks on the primary industrial facilities are suggested as well.

The reason for examining different kinds of attacks on an industry is to explore the range of possible targeting options available to the Soviets. If the object of an attack were to deny the use of industrial structures, then weapons would be aimed directly at these facilities. As noted, the damage probability would be very high for reliable weapons, but the major collateral damage would result primarily from prompt effects, such as blast and instantaneous radiation. If, on the other hand, the intent of the attack were to deny temporarily (either to other industries or to the general public) the products of such facilities, then the source of basic supply or the distribution of the finished products might come under attack. Some of the peculiarities of the U.S. industrial structure could be considered for disruptive attacks by an attack planner.

Examples of Disruptive Attacks

Some U.S. industries have peculiarities—either of supply or distribution of finished products—that might lead an enemy planner to consider limited interdiction attacks on the economic sector. We will describe a number of these.

In the case of the petroleum industry, it would be possible to cut off the supply of finished petroleum products to the northeastern section of the United States by attacks on pumping stations along pipelines. Two pipelines that run from Louisiana to the northeastern states carry nearly all of the finished products. Two nuclear weapons could, in theory, disrupt these pipelines; prompt casualties would be low since the pipeline routes generally pass through sparsely populated countryside. A surface burst would be required to attack the pipelines themselves, but airbursts would be sufficient for attacks on the pumping stations and the above-ground portions of the pipelines. The detailed routing of these two petroleum pipelines is available through open sources that may be sufficiently detailed for targeting purposes when augmented by unilateral verification.

Another area of vulnerability in the petroleum industry is the distribution of crude oil to northeastern refineries.[10] All crude oil is delivered by ships, and one could imagine the effect on shipping if a few very large tankers were brought under torpedo attack. This kind of attack, coupled with an attack on the pipelines, could have far-reaching impact on the most populous and industrialized part of the United States. Naval forces could, if alerted and deployed in advance, attempt to locate and sink the Soviet attack submarines, but the risks of battle may be perceived as unacceptable to the owners and operators of oil tankers, many of whom may not be U.S. flag carriers.

Somewhat larger attacks on the distribution systems for crude oil, finished petroleum products, and natural gas could have widely disruptive effects. Almost all pipelines of major importance cross the Mississippi River. Detailed location information on every such crossing is available from open sources and is verifiable by unilateral means. The impact on industries using natural gas and petroleum could be profound. Power plants that could switch to coal would be able to remain in service, depending on the extent of their coal reserves. In the Tennessee Valley Authority, the coal reserves were adequate to last through a coal strike; but had the strike not been settled, the reserves would have depleted one week later. Labor strikes are somewhat predictable and permit the stockpiling of supplies. This may not be the case with nuclear strikes.

Some indication of the disruptive effect of various-sized attacks on natural gas, crude oil, and finished products pipelines is implicit in the El Paso Natural Gas Company's 1973 estimate that about 20 percent of the U.S. total daily capacity flows to the East through pipelines connected to their system. Such a flow could be interrupted with eight reliable weaons. It is estimated that twenty to twenty-five weapons could interrupt all major natural gas pipelines (those with diameters of twenty-four inches or greater equivalent cross-section) serving the northeastern United States.[11] Finally, an attack directed at interrupting all major natural gas pipelines and all major crude oil and finished products pipelines (twelve inches in diameter or greater) would require about sixty weapons placed at or near the various points where the pipelines cross the Mississippi River, or at nearby pumping stations.

The vulnerability of the supply of iron ore to the steel industry was noted above, where it was pointed out that 80 percent of the ore used in the United States passes through the locks at Sault Sainte Marie. It was also noted that locks are less susceptible to damage from nuclear weapons than are industrial buildings. A near-surface burst would be needed to maximize damage to these locks and would result in large amounts of fallout, contamination of the waterway, and the death of Sault Sainte Marie residents (about twenty thousand on the U.S. side). The damage probability for various-sized warheads was illustrated earlier; larger Soviet ICBMs could inflict a high degree of damage in a single shot. The steel industry would probably not have to shut down immediately because iron ore is normally stockpiled so that production can continue during winter months when the Great Lakes are closed to shipping. The locks could be bypassed using an existing rail line from Marquette to Escanaba, Michigan. If the attack ocurred when no ships were on Lake Superior, then rail could be used as a substitute method of shipping from the Mesabi Range to Escanabe.

Direct Attacks on Production Facilities

In this section, direct attacks on production facilities and the effect of such attacks on the surrounding population are considered. Warhead yields considered are one megaton and thirty kilotons, both assumed to be detonated at altitudes of four thousand feet and one thousand feet, respectively. For the larger yield, the dominating collateral damage mechanism would be blast. For the lower-yield weapons, such damage mechanisms as radiation become important. The degree to which the population can be shielded or protected from these effects would make an important difference in the estimation of fatalities and total casualties. The measure of collateral damage is taken to be total casualties, based on the assumption that (1) none of the population is warned in advance and (2) no effort is made to evacuate potential target areas. Because of these assumptions, the levels of collateral casualties to be shown here might be considered "almost-worst-case" results. More casualties might be inflicted if an attack came during the process of an evacuation, or if the bulk of the population of a large city was simply not protected. On the other hand, there are special circumstances where the casualties might be considerably lower. These circumstances are very special, however, since they are based on the assumption that the attacker communicates the nature of his contemplated strike in great detail and then waits long enough for evacuation plans to be executed before launching his weapons. If one believes, however, that a large fraction of the population could be evacuated, say 80 to 90 percent, then the number of collateral casualties might be reduced by a factor of five or ten. One might also expect even fewer casualties if the remaining population could be protected by effective shelters. As pointed out earlier, it is felt that this situation would be a special one.

Because it is difficult to estimate casualties under such circumstances, and because they could vary so widely depending on the scenario envisioned, this examination of the collateral casualties is based on the assumption that the population remains "in place" during a controlled conflict. The method of estimating total casualties is to employ TANDEM (Tactical Nuclear Damage Effects Model), developed by Weiner and Wegner at the Rand Corporation, but applying it to the 1970 U.S. census population data base rather than to a foreign data base. This model has been widely used in studies of potential wars by various agencies in the defense community but has also been converted to estimate damage in the United States.

A simpler but more tedious method of estimating casualties is to specify a single target, and then, consulting a detailed population data base, to count manually the number of people within the weapon radius of the target. The weapon radius depends to a great extent on the degree to which the population can be protected, and TANDEM incorporates a sophisticated damage function. The level of protection must be recognized as highly uncertain because it is a function of the hardness and radiation resistance of available shelters (if any), and even more important, whether or not the population uses those shelters. For the purposes of this study, very light protection is assumed and a weapon radius corresponding to a vulnerability number of 4 psi is used in all estimates of casualties.

Several different attack types will be discussed. First, attacks with one-megaton and thirty-kiloton weapons will be considered against 35 large oil refineries, 31 steel plants, and 19 aluminium plants, assuming that the attack tactic is to maximize the capacity destroyed per weapon committed without regard to civil casualties. Figure 10.5 shows the potential casualties as a function of the percentage of the industry's capacity at risk for attacks with one-megaton weapons: the indications are that attacks on the oil refineries and steel plants would involve casualties ranging into the millions when 50 percent to 70 percent of the capacity of each industry is at risk. On the other hand, casualties from an attack on aluminium plants would be below one million, with the potential of destroying more than 80 percent of the industry's capacity. Aluminium plants appear to be located in much less densely populated areas than are refineries and steel plants.

If the Soviets were to develop a low-yield (30 kt) weapon for possible use in attacks on these same industries, the casualties would be lower than shown in figure 10.5. Figure 10.6 shows the possible outcome of such an attack when production facilities are attacked in order of their production capacity. As expected, the level of casualties is lower than that resulting from attacks with one-megaton weapons: for the oil refineries and steel plants, casualties were lower by a factor of about ten, and for the aluminium plants, by a factor of about five. In addition, the population appears to be much more concentrated around steel plants than around oil refineries. An attack on 35 oil refineries would result in about two-thirds the number of casualties that would be produced by an attack on 31 steel plants. In the case of oil refineries, the greatest number of casualties would be incurred from an attack on those located along the Delaware River, in the Philadelphia area. But, because these refineries, as well as those in New Jersey, depend heavily on imported

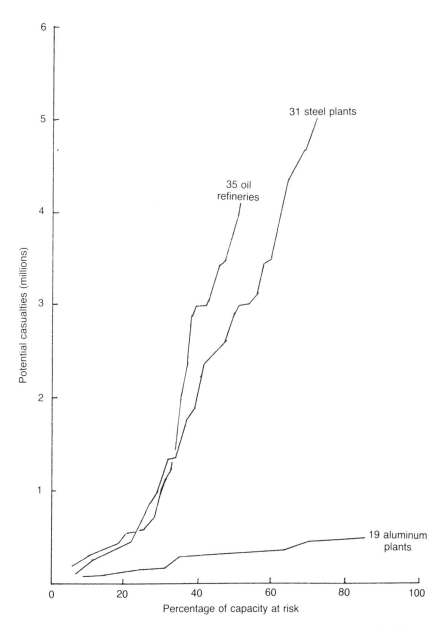

Figure 10.5. Potential collateral casualties as a function of attacks on oil refineries and steel and aluminum plants (in order of capacity) with 1-Mt weapons

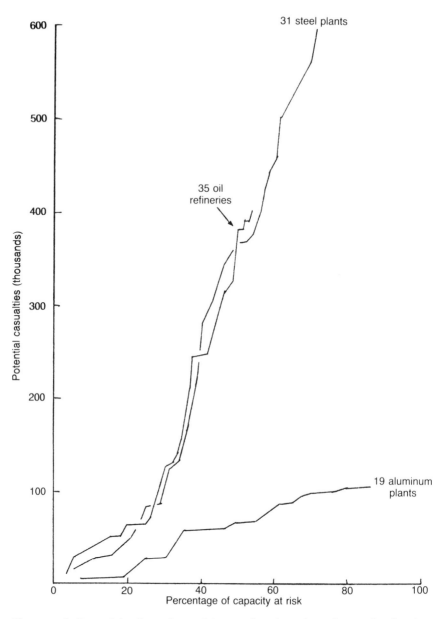

Figure 10.6. Potential collateral casualties as a function of attacks on oil refineries and steel and aluminum plants (in order of capacity) with 30-kt weapons

oil, which might not be available in time of crisis, it is questionable whether an enemy would consider them worth attacking in a limited war.

Another possible attack strategy might be to attack U.S. industrial production in such a way as to minimize the number of casualties per increment of production capacity destroyed. In other words, the attacker might try to minimize the number of people injured per barrel of oil produced each day. This attack order does make a difference in the potential number of people killed or injured when the percent capacity at risk is low. But if the aim is to destroy a large percentage of the capacity, the number of casualties is more a function of the size of the warhead used than of the order of the attack. Figure 10.7 compares the results of (1) one-megaton-weapon attacks on the steel industry, ordered to minimize casualties per unit output at risk, and (2) attacks without regard to casualties. Figure 10.8 makes the same comparison for the petroleum industry. If the aim of the attack is to destroy the same large percentage of capacity, then there is no difference in the estimated number of casualties. But if the attacker should observe some restraint, then a slightly smaller attack might approach the capacity-destruction goal while considerably reducing the number of collateral casualties.

Figure 10.9 exhibits for attacks on refineries with thirty-kiloton weapons a trend similar to that shown in figure 10.8 for one-megaton weapons, but with a factor of about ten fewer casualties. Since most large steel plants and refineries are in densely populated areas, one would expect casualties to be reduced in proportion to the yield raised to the two-thirds power. This rule holds approximately for steel plants and oil refineries [$(1000/30)^{2/3} = 10.36$], but not for aluminium plants, which are located in less populous areas.

Several points emerge from these examples of attacks on industrial targets. With one-megaton weapons, significant numbers of people might be killed or injured, even if the attack were constrained to airbursts so that fallout would be negligible. If smaller weapons (30 kt, for example) were used, again assuming airbursts, the estimated casualties would be reduced by a factor of about ten for the steel and oil-refining industries. A lesser reduction would be expected for industries—the aluminium industry, for example—that are not, for the most part, located in densely populated areas. The same expectation would apply in the case of those steel plants and oil refineries—the Geneva Steel plant in Utah and the Continental Oil Company refinery in Ponca City, Oklahoma, for example—that are in less populated areas.

In addition to the casualty reductions that the Soviets could achieve by using smaller weapons and airbursts, they could obtain even further reductions by attacking industrial sites not in order of their production capacity but on the basis of the ratio of a plant's capacity to the potential

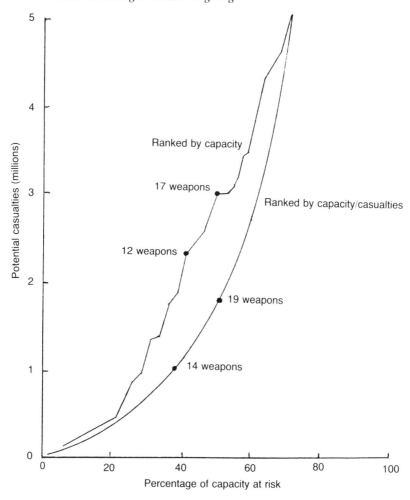

Figure 10.7. Potential collateral casualties as a function of 1-Mt weapon attacks on steel plants ranked by (1) capacity and (2) capacity-to-casualty relationship

casualties. Where the attack size is limited to twenty to forty weapons, such as in the examples presented above, this procedure does not seem to be as effective in reducing casualties as the use of a smaller weapon.

CONCLUDING OBSERVATIONS

The purposes of this study were to examine the economic importance

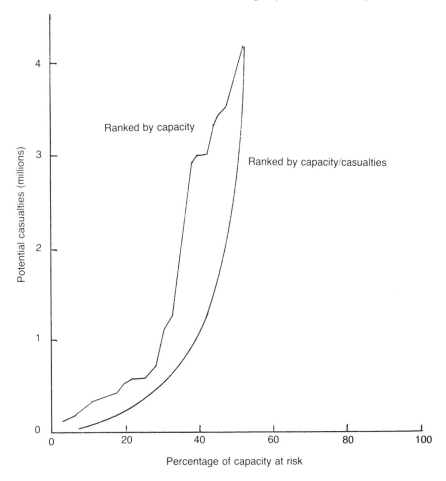

Figure 10.8. Potential collateral casualties as a function of 1-Mt weapon attacks on refineries ranked by (1) capacity and (2) capacity-to-casualty relationship

of various industries and, on the basis of location, their vulnerability to various levels of nuclear attack, and to suggest some ways in which restraint might be exercised by an attacker with the aim of reducing collateral casualties in some exemplary industrial target sets.

The method used for selecting examples of industrywide target sets for preparedness planning involved a number of steps, some of which may overlap or merge. No claim is made to originality for the approach used here, nor is it necessarily the best, although it appears to be practical.

The initial step was an effort to identify economically important in-

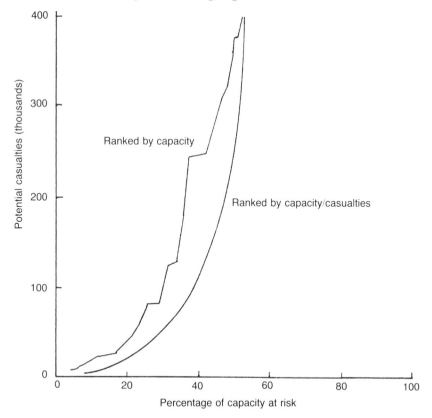

Figure 10.9. Potential collateral casualties as a function of 30-kt-weapon attacks on refineries ranked by (1) capacity and (2) capacity-to-casualty relationship

dustries through the use of an input-output table of the U.S. economy. This approach offers the analyst a rough method of assessing broad categories of industries and, at the same time, permits judgments about which industries are and which are not geographically concentrated. In addition, the distribution of the outputs of various industrial categories provides some insight into industrial interdependence as well as a way to identify industries on which the consuming public is directly dependent.

The second step was to determine which industries are geographically concentrated as well as economically important. Of course, the criteria of concentration and economic importance are matters of judgment. Also, in this analysis, the process could not be exhaustive. The examination of various industries, however, did lead to the identification of two useful examples for planning purposes: energy and metals.

Next, an attempt was made to ascertain whether some elements of selected industries were more susceptible than others to damage when attacked with nuclear weapons. It was found that present-day Soviet weapons (typically, 1 Mt or so) are suitable for attacks on (1) above-ground industrial structures and (2) such underground structures as buried pipelines and storage tanks, which may not sustain as much damage. In the speculation about future weapon developments, it was noted that improvement of delivery accuracy (about 50 percent) would permit large reductions in the weapon yield (1 Mt to 30 kt, for example) needed to inflict severe damage to above-ground industrial structures.

Once the vulnerability of various types of structures has been established, the effect of attacks on selected industries may be examined. The attacks considered may be directed against production facilities, or they may be disruptive attacks, for example, directed against sources of supply or facilities for the transport of finished products. In this study, disruptive attacks usually involved fewer warheads than did attacks directly on production facilities. The time needed to repair the damage of such attacks is judged by the author to be on the order of months, or more, but repair times should be studied further to assess their actual effects. The economic effects of disruptive attacks on the country as a whole have not been explicitly assessed here, but they appear to be substantial for certain sections of the United States, particularly the disruption of oil and gas pipelines which would deprive both industry and the public of energy for manufacturing and heating. Direct attacks resulting in severe damage to production facilities would probably involve much more extensive repair or rebuilding. The extent to which an attack is disruptive or disabling depends on the alternative products or reserves available as substitutes in industrial processes or for use by the public.

An examination of attack effects discloses various possibilities with regard to attack restraint. In the context of controlled conflict, the number of weapons is almost automatically assumed to be constrained. Depending on an attacker's objectives, which may or may not be known to the U.S. government, the attacker may exercise more or less restraint. Restraint includes using air-burst weapon fusing, reducing the weapon yield, and ordering attack weapons to reduce collateral fatalities. This study found that fusing for air-burst weapons increased the damage probability to many types of industrial structures and might be attractive to an attack planner on this ground, rather than as an exercise in restraint. As noted, reduction in weapon yield (if improvement in delivery accuracy is achieved) may result in large reductions in collateral casualties. Not quite so effective in reducing such casualties, but still a form of restraint, would be an attack planned to inflict damage on industrial capacity based on the selection of industrial targets that are not located in densely populated areas. The examples used in this study indicate that casualties may vary widely, depending on whether or not the population has been evacuated from the vicinity of the targets. If an evacuation could be completed before a strike, assuming that the intended targets were known ahead of time, then the casualties might be very low. If the warning time of an attack were short, then the number of casualties might be somewhat larger than the results shown here if the people were outside any shelters or buildings and were thus less protected.

Several important questions have been raised during the conduct of this preliminary investigation. Are there any "choke points" that might be particularly attractive as targets in controlled conflict situations? Do the assumptions about an attacker's behavior (given in the introduction to this chapter) make any difference as far as possible target selection is concerned? In answer to the first question, this analysis indicates that there are no small numbers (one, two, or perhaps three) of potential targets whose loss would cripple the important economic industries examined here. Attacks on particularly vulnerable or important elements of the metals and energy industries would be disruptive, but the effects of such attacks could be somewhat ameliorated either by temporarily substituting other resources, relying on stockpiled reserves, or by taking action to repair or rebuild damaged facilities. For example, an attack on the Sault Sainte Marie locks would halt shipping until they could be rebuilt, but rail transport could be used as an alternative method of transport around the locks. The alternative would be more expensive, but feasible. Disrupting the flow of finished petroleum products through pipelines could cause problems for the public in the northeastern section of the country. Through the use of strict rationing procedures, combined with active measures to repair the pipelines, one could conclude that though the experience would not be pleasant, the public might survive the effects of such an attack until repairs were completed. While this study has not exhaustively examined the economic structure of the United States, the major U.S. industries have been examined and no choke points were found. This finding does not mean that there are no choke points but may indicate that the probability of their existence is low.

With regard to the question of whether the assumptions about controlled conflict—particularly the assumption that an enemy would not attack strategic retaliatory forces or their command and control facilities—would impose any critical limitation of selection of targets within the United States, it does not appear that target selection would be particularly limited by such a constraint. In one or two examples in which the objective of an attack might be to disrupt natural gas or crude oil pipelines that cross the Mississippi River, an enemy attack planner might not wish to select targets in Missouri near Whiteman Air Force Base, but alternative, and equally effective, points for disruption are available elsewhere. The major reason for the lack of the assumption-imposing limitations on target selection is that the U.S. military forces are not generally located near large industrial facilities, nor are they located near particularly large concentrations of population. One exception is that submarine bases supporting the operation of fleet ballistic submarines are located near large population centers.

This study is incomplete with regard to controlled-conflict situations in that only industrywide attacks were addressed. Other examples of controlled-conflict targets should be investigated and should include regional attacks (mixed industrial attacks) and attacks on military targets of a support nature. Large strikes against strategic retaliatory forces are not included in the concept of controlled conflict. Other types of attacks will probably occur to the reader.

[11]

Population Targeting and U.S. Strategic Doctrine

Jeffrey Richelson

Among the alternative targeting options discussed in the Phase I report of the Carter administration's Nuclear Targeting Policy Review Panel was the option to Punish Soviet Society.[1] Specifically, this meant targeting Soviet population and industry, regardless of the role played in Soviet war-making activities.

While the primary results of the targeting review, as manifested in Presidential Directive 59 and reaffirmed by Reagan administration National Security Decision Directive-13, were an increased emphasis on military and political targeting and the requirement of a capability for conducting a prolonged nuclear exchange, urban-industrial targeting remains a possibility—at least as a 'final' option when war has escalated to spasm level. Thus in his Fiscal Year 1979 posture statement Secretary of Defense Harold Brown maintained that the United States needed to retain the capability and option of destroying the two hundred major Soviet cities.[2] And in 1981 two strategic analysts considered the capability of cruise missiles to inflict certain levels of fatalities on the Soviet population.[3]

Aside from the threat of urban-industrial destruction resulting from direct targeting, the threat of the inevitable significant levels of collateral damage resulting from the large-scale use of nuclear weapons—even in a purely counterforce attack—still plays an important role in strategic thinking. The concern exhibited about possible Soviet ability via civil defense programs to sharply curtail fatalities and even industrial destruction highlights the significance of this factor in the strategic calculus. Indeed, it would not be facetious to suggest that present strategic planners would be perturbed if weapons systems could be developed that eliminated collateral damage.

This chapter focuses on the past and present role of population targeting in U.S. strategic planning. As used here the term *population targeting* refers to the targeting of population per se—in which case targeting of population away from urban areas, that is, in evacuation and relocation areas, may occur—as well as to the targeting of urban-industrial areas. In the latter case individual targets may consist of economic installations but be so numerous and widely distributed as to be equivalent to anticity attacks. Prior to the discussion of targeting in the early nuclear era it is appropriate to consider the prenuclear heritage of population targeting.

PRENUCLEAR HERITAGE

Urban-industrial targeting on a mass scale was one of the "innovations" of World War II. Two factors that combined to produce this innovation were the theoretical discussions of the utility of such bombing in the period between the world wars as well as the technical limitations that foreclosed more discriminate targeting options.

The major theoreticians of population or urban-industrial targeting were Italian brigadier Giulio Douhet and British air marshal Trenchard. Douhet argued that urban-industrial bombing was inevitable. Previously a nation could "shield itself behind the stout armor of an army and navy."[4] It was inevitable, however, that

> The air arm . . . will strike against entities less well-organized and disciplined than the army and the navy, less able to resist and helpless to act and counteract. It is fated, therefore, that the moral and material collapse will come about more quickly and easily. A body of troops will stand fast under intensive bombings even after losing half or two-thirds of its men; but the workers in shop, factory, or harbor will melt away after the first losses.[5]

A similar vision was expressed by Trenchard, who felt that the object of war was to defeat the "enemy nation," not merely its army, navy, or air force. Further, according to Trenchard, it was easier to affect the morale of a nation by air attack than the morale of an army in the field. Thus the civilian population constituted the

> points at which the enemy is weakest. The rifleman or the sailor is protected, armed and disciplined, and will stand under fire. The great centres of manufacture, transport and communications cannot be wholly protected. The

personnel again, who man them are not armed and cannot shoot back. They are not disciplined and it cannot be expected of them that they will stick solidly to their lathes and benches under the recurring threat of air bombardment.[6]

Further, he argues that

"The effect on the workers of a nation of an intensive air campaign will again be infinitely greater than if the main part of the air attack was launched at the enemy's airdrome and airplanes which may be many miles from vital points."[7]

Thus, according to Quester, Trenchard would have passed up a "no-cities" targeting policy if it had been offered, "believing that the quick way to disarm the enemy's military forces was not to strike at air bases but at the civilian sector that supported the bases."[8] To Trenchard, destruction of morale and economic capabilities were intimately linked to success.

Despite this intellectual support for urban-industrial targeting, World War II initially involved no such strategy. Thus British expectations of an immediate "knockout blow" attempt by the Luftwaffe in the opening rounds of World War II saw no bombing raids at all on the populated areas of Britain and France. Nor were such attacks directed against Germany.

Thus by 15 May 1940 a program of "precision" night bombings of military and industrial targets in Germany had already begun.[9] Such attempts at precision bombing presented Britain with a delimma, however. The limitations of British technology precluded nighttime precision bombing. At the same time, the effectiveness of German defenses during daylight made daytime attacks too hazardous. Hence night bombing as a means of reducing losses of aircraft and personnel required an acceptance of severely reduced accuracy.

According to the official British history of British intelligence operations in World War II, "it was on account of these [the previously mentioned] difficulties, as much as under the influence of the general arguments for strategic bombing, that Bomber Command, which had abandoned day bombing as early as April 1940, embarked on the transition from precision to area bombing in October 1940, from which date it had concentrated its night bombing against single towns or industrial areas instead of against specific industrial installations."[10]

This early emphasis on area bombing was not shared and sustained to the same degree by the United States. At the end of the war the United States was primarily concerned with precision bombing of communications and oil transport targets.[11] At the same time the United

States was also engaged in area bombing in both the European and Asian theaters. Thus the United States participated with Britain in a joint raid on Dresden on 13–15 February 1945 which killed approximately 135,000 people.[12] In Japan, the United States launched an attack on Tokyo on 9 March 1945 with 334 B-29s, dropping incendiary bombs on the city and killing over 83,000 people while leveling a large portion of the city by fire.[13] Because this raid was rated a success, the area offensive was continued—with the objective of leaving no Japanese city standing.

The morality of such attacks was questioned both during and after the war. Arguments against their morality focused on Catholic principles of just war and proportionality—that the deliberate killing of innocents was forbidden and that their deaths as the "unintended" result of military action were justified only if that action saved more lives that it took. Thus Grenville Clark noted the "great moral issue involved in drifting into a war in which the premeditated plan of campaign calls for (or at least inevitably involves) the destruction of non-combatants on a great scale."[14]

Others argued that such attacks could be justified as long as they "saved" more lives than were lost. Thus the atomic bombings of Hiroshima and Nagasaki have been justified on the grounds that the levels of U.S. (and Japanese) casualties which would have resulted from the "inevitable" U.S. invasion of the mainland far exceeded the numbers killed by the use of the atomic bomb.[15]

POPULATION TARGETING AND U.S. NUCLEAR WAR PLANS, 1946–1982

The same factors that contributed to the emphasis on urban-industrial targeting in World War II continued to be factors in the early nuclear era—the theoretical utility of destroying enemy urban-industrial areas, and the technological limitations.

The technological limitations were of several varieties, including the extremely small atomic weapons stockpile as well as the delivery aircraft range and other limitations.[16] As of 30 June 1946 there were available the nuclear components for only nine implosion weapons. As of 30 June 1947 there were only thirteen.[17] Thus a top-level committee, appointed by the commander of the army air forces in the fall of 1945, later concluded that given the expense and limited availability of the A-bomb it "is primarily an offensive weapon for use against very large urban and industrial targets."[18] This view was reinforced by the development of the "super" or H-bomb; it was felt by strategists that the destructive power of such a weapon eliminated any possibility of its being employed in a discriminating fashion.[19]

Additionally, U.S. intelligence capabilities were in no way adequate, prior to the advent of aircraft (e.g., U-2) or satellite (e.g., SAMOS, Corona) reconnaissance capabilities to determine the location of the full spectrum of Soviet military assets.[20] On the other hand, cities were easy to find and destroy.

The theoretical arguments in favor of population/urban-industrial targeting were also similar to World War II arguments concerning the destruction of enemy war-making capability and morale. Thus the authors of the DROPSHOT requirements study (written in 1949) stated: "It may become advisable to abandon the concept of destruction of the enemy's physical means to wage war in the favor of a concept involving the destruction of his will through selective attack of limited complexes or mass attack of people."[21]

Thus a late 1945 target list specified 20 Soviet cities, including Moscow and Leningrad, that would be bombed in the event of war. A 1946 revision called for hitting 17 of the 20 cities with a total of 98 atomic bombs, with another 98 being held in reserve.[22] The anticipated effects of such attacks were discussed in a 1947 memorandum:

> it seems reasonable to anticipate that the use of this weapon would create a condition of chaos and extreme confusion. Not the least of this effect would be an increased element of hopelessness and shock resulting from the magnitude of destruction; the fear of the unknown; the actual lingering physical after effect of atomic explosions; the psychological effect arising from the necessity to evacuate large densely populated areas; and the attendent psychological state which these factors will create.[23]

The 1948 war plan, FLEETWOOD, called for the use of 133 bombs in a single massive attack against 70 Soviet cities. Eight were to be targeted on Moscow and meant to destroy forty square miles of that city while 7 bombs would be allocated to destroy Leningrad.[24] If the war lasted as long as two years, approximately 200 more atomic bombs would be directed against Russia, obliterating as much as 40 percent of Soviet industry and 7 million people. Thus at the end of 1948 the SAC emergency war plan stated that the "highest priority target system is that system constituted by the major Soviet urban-industrial concentrations."[25]

A subsequent plan, TROJAN, provided for a total of 300 atomic bombs to be dropped on Russia and included the all-out bombing of Soviet cities and industry. The atomic air offensive would kill between 3 and 5 million Russians and leave up to 28 million homeless.[26]

In examining these early war plans, we should keep two important qualifications in mind. First, the concentration of population urban-industrial targeting was partially the result of perceived technological-economic limitations and partially the result of the perception that given these limitations the most effective way of blunting a Soviet attack was the destruction of war-making capacity via the destruction of factories and workers. Second, while there was a significant allocation of bombs to urban-industrial targets, there was also a substantial allocation of bombs to other targets. These other targets included military forces, stockpiles, bases, political and administrative centers and Soviet nuclear forces. Thus the DROPSHOT study, drawn up in 1949 which assumed a war beginning in 1957, included the following target sets: (1) stockpiles of weapons of mass destruction as well as the facilities for their production and means of delivery; (2) key governmental and control centers; (3) lines of communication, military supply lines, troop concentration, and naval targets; and (4) important elements of Soviet and Soviet-satellite industrial economy.

The plan required that about three hundred atomic bombs and twenty thousand tons of high-explosive conventional bombs be dropped on about seven hundred targets located in approximately one hundred urban areas.[27]

DROPSHOT reflected the findings of the Harmon Committee, set up in mid-1949 by Secretary of Defense James Forrestal to evaluate the impact of an atomic air offensive against the Soviet Union. The group estimated that the attack on seventy cities called for in FLEETWOOD would produce a 30 to 40 percent reduction in Soviet industrial capacity and as many as 2.7 million fatalities and 4 million casualties. However, the report also concluded that industrial losses would not be permanent and could be either alleviated by Soviet recuperative action or augmented, depending on the weighted effectiveness of follow-up attacks. More important, the capability of Soviet armed forces to advance rapidly into selected areas of Western Europe and the Middle East and Far East would not necessarily be impaired. The committee also concluded that planned air attacks would not "destroy the roots of Communism or critically weaken the power of the Soviet leadership to dominate the people."[28]

Hence DROPSHOT gave substantial attention to targets other than population and industry—although many of the military and political targets were located in or near urban areas. This, combined with a continuation of population/urban-industrial targeting, produced the large number of weapons targeted on urban areas. This state of affairs continued throughout the Eisenhower administration, when the first integrated war plan, the SIOP (Single Integrated Operational Plan), was drawn up. The first SIOP called for attacks on all major Soviet and other Communist cities in the event of war.[29] In some cases ten bombs were targeted on a city.[30] No alternative options were available, and no forces were to be held in reserve. In the event of war, 360 to 525 million casualties were predicted.[31]

The SIOP was inherited by the Kennedy administration, one of whose early major tasks was the SIOP's revision. As a result of the revision a spectrum of attacks became possible—only one of which included direct attacks on cities—and the concept of population avoidance was introduced into strategic war planning. The spectrum of potential attacks progressed from attacks on Soviet strategic forces, Soviet air defense away from cities, Soviet air defense near cities, and Soviet command and control centers, only finally moving to spasm attacks on cities.[32]

This shift in war planning was first made public in a speech by Defense Secretary Robert McNamara on 17 February 1962. It is his now-famous commencement address at the University of Michigan, however, which best spelled out the logic of the change in strategy. Thus McNamara stated:

> The U.S. has come to the conclusion that to the extent feasible, basic military strategy in a general nuclear war should be approached in much the same way that the more conventional military operations have been regarded in the past. That is to say, principal military objectives, in the event of a nuclear war stemming from a major attack on the Alliance, should be the destruction of the enemy's military force, not of his civilian population.[33]

A variety of factors compelled McNamara to backtrack, quickly and publicly, from his statement. These factors included hostile reactions from both European allies and the Soviet Union and, most important, use of the statement by the air force to justify large increases in funding for strategic forces.

Thus McNamara made U.S. ability to destroy specific percentages of Soviet population and industry in a retaliatory strike (the Assured Destruction capability) the cornerstone of United States *declaratory* policy. Thus, in his 1965 Posture Statement, McNamara spoke of the U.S. need to be able to destroy 25 to 33 percent of Soviet population and 67 percent of Soviet industry to ensure deterrence.[34]

Despite this public emphasis on urban-industrial targeting, U.S. *employment* policy, as evidenced in the SIOP itself, remained the same, with attacks on Soviet cities being considered a last resort. Thus, as a result of various pressures, McNamara in public talked of only the nuclear capability and strategy required for the last phases of an all-out nuclear conflict—"the sufficient reserve striking power to destroy an enemy society if driven to it" that he mentioned in his Ann Arbor address—and eschewed further discussion of counterforce targeting.

This state of affairs remained constant throughout the Kennedy, Johnson, and Nixon administrations. Thus an assistant secretary of defense in the last years of the Johnson administration has written:

> The SIOP remains essentially unchanged since then [McNamara's Ann Arbor speech of 16 June 1962]. There have been two developments, however: (1) it has become more difficult to execute the pure-counterforce option, and its value is considered to be diminishing and, (2) all public officials have learned to talk in public only about deterrence and city attacks, no warfighting; no city-sparing. Too many critics can make too much trouble... so public officials have run for cover.[35]

It was during the Nixon administration, however, that consideration was given to further revisions in the SIOP and in public declaratory policy. Soon after taking office in January 1969, the Nixon administration began a series of studies concerning nuclear targeting options. These studies led, eventually, to National Security Study Memorandum (NSSM) 169, approved by President Richard Nixon in late 1973, and in turn to National Security Decision Memorandum (NSDM) 242, signed by the president in January 1974.[36]

On the basis of NSDM-242 the first significantly limited nuclear options were developed and announced. At the same time NSDM-242 implementing documents specified that in the event of an SIOP-level attack, the primary objective of U.S. strategic forces was to delay for as long as possible the Soviet Union's recovery as a major economic and military power. This was to be accomplished by destruction of 70 percent of the Soviet economic recovery base.[37] Population per se was not to be targeted. This change in targeting policy was first announced by Secretary of Defense Elliot Richardson, who testified in April 1973: "We do not in our strategic planning target civilian population *per se*."[38] Care is now taken in developing the SIOP to select Desired Ground Zeros (DGZs) for SIOP targets so that their planned destruction is optimized in terms of this policy constraint.[39]

It is clear, however, that even if population destruction is not an objective of strategic targeting, even at the SIOP level, given the collocation of population and industry (discussed in more detail below) any attack designed to cripple the Soviet economic recovery base would produce massive civilian casualties. Thus U.S. officials have acknowledged that "strategic nuclear warfare would not be so neat that you would only get the factories" and that "we are not targeting people here but we are indeed causing many, many casualties."[40]

Indeed, the casualties resulting from such attacks may be considered desirable. The desirability may be based on the perception of certain subgroups of the population (e.g., workers) as economic assets to be destroyed as a means of hindering economic recovery. Thus, during the Vietnam war, it was the policy not to bomb the population per se, but workers were regarded as an economic resource and hence exempted from this injunction.[41] This view has been endorsed in the nuclear context: "A number of studies done in the U.S. have examined the factors influencing industrial recovery of a nation following a nuclear attack. Taken collectively, the results indicate that survival of the work force is by far the most important factor in industrial recovery."[42]

Further, the overall threat of population fatalities in enhancing deterrence has been cited by U.S. officials in discussions of U.S. strategic programs. Thus one official, in testifying before the Senate Armed Services Committee, said, "I think you have to understand we have several levels of a requirement to have assured destruction to a population base and then you have the overall general SIOP plan, and I think one of the things we would have at a minimum constraint is that we would always be able to deliver some reasonable number which would be a threat to the population base."[43] And John Walsh, when deputy director of Defense Research and Engineering, was reported by the *Los Angeles Times* as stating that "an important factor in deterrence is the Soviet comprehension of what may be involved. . . . We do target industrial sites which are co-located with population centers"; he went on to explain that civilian casualties were a factor in potential damage assessments.[44] Finally, as mentioned by Desmond Ball, Secretary of Energy James Edwards indicated that the yields required for U.S. nuclear weapons systems were partially a function of Soviet civil defense capabilities.[45]

Upon entering office, the Carter administration launched the National Targeting Policy Review (NTPR) with PD-18, titled *U.S. National Strategy*, and continued NSDM-242 in force until further notification. As a result of the review, PD-59 was issued, which shifted emphasis from economic recovery targeting to political leadership and military assets (both strategic and conventional) targeting.[46] The target set included 700 underground shelters throughout the country for key Soviet officials, 2,000 strategic targets (including 1,400 ICBM silos and 600 C^2 bunkers, nuclear storage sites, and strategic air and naval facilities), 3,000 other military targets (500 airfields, plus military units, supply depots, and critical transportation links), plus 200 to 400 key factories.[47] Again, population per se was not to be targeted in the initial stages of the war. However, the capacity for such targeting in the event of a Soviet attack on U.S. urban-industrial areas was specified. Thus, in the secretary of defense's annual report for Fiscal Year 1979, Harold Brown wrote: "It is essential that we retain the capability at all times to inflict an unacceptable level of damage on the Soviet Union, including destruction of a minimum of 200 major cities."[48]

This continued importance of an urban-industrial destruction capability was evidenced in the following exchange between Gen. Kelley Burke, air force deputy chief of staff for Research, Development, Test, and Evaluation, and Congressman Norman Dicks:

MR. DICKS: You haven't taken away any weapons aimed at the urban industrial base of the Soviet Union, have you, but you've added weapons to the military targets? Is that a fair way of putting it?

GENERAL
BURKE: Yes.[49]

Continued U.S. interest in the capability to destroy a significant portion of the Soviet populace, "if necessary" was evidenced in several recent government or government-funded studies. Thus the Department of Defense's 1977 "Alternative U.S. Civil Defense Programs," ACDA's 1978 "Civil Defense Study," and the 1978 PRM-32 paper, the "Strategic Usefulness of Civil Defense–Attack Related Effectiveness" all considered the effects of civil defense on Soviet population fatalities.

A 1978 study by Scientific Applications, Inc., conducted as part of the Nuclear Targeting Policy Review, indicated continued U.S. interest in the possibility of population targeting. The study, titled *The Feasibility of Population Targeting*, addressed the question of whether—given projected U.S. force characteristics and alternative Soviet civil defense postures—the United States would be able to inflict a specified level of fatalities.[50] The study considered alternative combinations of urban sheltering and evacuation to host areas and allowed for U.S. targeting of host areas to kill relocated population. Thus population fatalities were not only sought in targeting urban areas but also were to be sought by attacking relocation sites.

Hence, although the United States has adopted a policy of not targeting population per se at all and not targeting urban-industrial areas in the initial stages of a nuclear conflict, there is still concern over U.S. capability to inflict civilian casualties indirectly, "if necessary," and U.S. expectation that the projected urban-industrial/population destruction resulting from a large-scale use of nuclear weapons is useful in enhancing deterrence.

RATIONALE FOR POPULATION AVOIDANCE

There are several reasons why a nation may adopt a population-avoidance strategy in one form or another. Population targeting is clearly

[243]

immoral—there is no philosophical justification for deliberate attempts to kill or terrorize noncombatants. If there is any significant debate concerning morality and population targeting it revolves around whether even the threat of such targeting can be morally justified.[51] However, nations have not been notably influenced in the past, especially in wartime, by philosophical considerations of morality. Nor do the populations of countries at war seem to be particularly concerned that their armed forces observe restrictions in attacking enemy nations.

On the other hand, nations, especially in peacetime, want at least to give the appearance of conforming to international law. During the reviews of U.S. targeting policy and plans which took place in the early 1970s, both State Department and other officials pointed out that the targeting of population contravened a number of international laws to which the United States was a signatory. It was decided that the national guidance in 1974 should make explicit mention of the fact that population per se was not targeted.[52]

The U.S. legal obligation was further strengthened by U.S. ratification of the 1977 Protocol I to the 1949 Geneva Convention. Article 85 of the 1977 Protocol I prohibits "making the civilian population or individual civilians the object of attack."[53] Such a prohibited attack would include one that

(*a*) treats as a single military objective a number of clearly separated and distinct military objectives located in a city, town, village or other area containing a similar concentration of civilians or civilian objects;

(*b*) . . . may be expected to cause incidental loss of civilian life, injury to civilians, damage to civilian objects, or a combination thereof, which would be excessive in relation to the concrete and direct military advantage anticipated; and

(*c*) [are] attacks against the civilian population or civilians by way of reprisals.[54]

A practical consideration in decisions to pursue population-avoidance strategies, at least in the initial phase of a war, is credibility. Thus it is argued that a U.S. threat to destroy Soviet cities in response to Soviet attacks away from U.S. cities (on U.S. ICBMs, for example) is not a credible one since such an attack would result in direct Soviet retaliation against U.S. cities. Likewise, U.S. threats to attack Soviet cities in response to a Soviet attack on Western Europe would, according to this logic, be even less credible.

Additionally, and perhaps most important, pursuing a population-avoidance strategy would give the Soviet Union an incentive to refrain from attacks on U.S. cities and create an obvious set of "bargaining chips" in pursuing escalation control/intrawar deterrence and war termination objectives.

FEASIBILITY OF POPULATION AVOIDANCE

That there is a rationale (or rationales) for pursuing a population-avoidance strategy does not necessarily imply that there is a meaningful way to achieve it—even if the objective is to sharply limit casualties rather than simply to appear to conform with international law. A crucial question is technical feasibility. Unless a nation is able to develop a strategy that when carried out produces significantly less population/urban damage than would be incurred as a result of a deliberate attempt to kill population, the nation's strategy will be meaningless, both morally and strategically, whether or not it has formally adopted a policy of not targeting population per se.[55] Certainly, unless the Soviet leadership can distinguish population-avoidance attacks from urban-industrial attacks in terms of effects, their response will include U.S. urban-industrial areas.

Hence it is important to consider whether it is realistically possible to meaningfully reduce fatalities given present strategic policies. Some have argued that urban-industrial targeting and the mutual hostage relationship is inevitable in the nuclear era—that the location of targeting and weapons characteristics and effects are such that massive population losses are inevitable regardless of targeting strategy.[56]

An SIOP-level attack that involved targeting of Soviet military and political assets as well as major manufacturing installations would produce civilian casualties at a level that would make population-avoidance a theoretical footnote. Thus the Office of Technology Assessment has reported that "a U.S. attack that struck the full set of Soviet targets in the SIOP—but avoided population *per se*—would still kill from 50–100 million people and injure perhaps 30 million others, while destroying 70–90% of major Soviet military and political leadership facilities, 20–50% of other military targets, 70–90% of Soviet manufacturing capacity."[57]

Nor is it likely that attacks on even one specific target set would be compatible with a serious reduction in civilian casualties. Thus, if one were to consider a large-scale attack on Soviet industrial installations, it is doubtful, given the collocation of population with industry shown in Table 11.1, that large-scale civilian casualties could be avoided.[58]

Even assuming the use of 40-kt *Poseidon* warheads to attack industrial installations a significant fraction of the 80 million Soviets within 1.5 NM would be expected to be either killed directly from blast or thermal effects or killed by the destruction of buildings and other exposed objects. With the replacement of the 40-kt C-3 *Poseidon* by the 100-kt C-4 *Trident*, the destructive radius will expand further—the 10 psi radius for a 100 kt weapon being approximately 1.0 NM.

[245]

Table 11.1. Collocation of Soviet population with industry

Within (nautical miles)	Urban (millions)	Rural (millions)	Total (millions)
1.0	40	1	41
1.5	78	2	80
2.5	106	6	112
5.0	113	18	131

Source: U.S. Arms Control and Disarmament Agency, *ACDA Civil Defense Study Report Number 1*, 16 November 1977, p. 11.

Obviously, civil defense programs would reduce fatalities to some degree. Shelters at key economic installations could accommodate about 12–24% of the total Soviet work force. In a crisis, non-essential and off-duty workers would be evacuated. If one-half of the work force is dispersed, from 24 to 48 percent of the remainder could be sheltered. A minimum of 10 to 20 percent of the urban population (including essential workers) could be accommodated at present in blast-resistant shelters. By 1985, the percentage of urban population that could be sheltered would rise to 15 to 30 percent, assuming no change in the 1978 rate of shelter construction.[59]

However, short of large-scale evacuation there is apparently little that can be done to sharply reduce Soviet civilian casualties. Thus, the CIA concluded that "the critical decision to be made by the Soviet leaders in terms of sparing the population would be whether or not to evacuate cities. Only by evacuating the bulk of the urban population could they hope to achieve a marked decrease in the number of urban casualties.[60] Of course, this assumes that an evacuation decision could be effectively implemented.

One possible means of achieving significant damage to Soviet industry without massive civilian casualties would be an attack based on the concentration of Soviet industry. Soviet industries produce more than half their products in less than two hundred plants. These facilities produce primary metals, chemicals, petroleum construction equipment, agricultural equipment, railroad equipment, synthetic rubber, and electric power generation. There are only 8 copper refineries, 16 heavy-machinery plants, 34 sizable petroleum refineries, 18 integrated iron and steel mills, and 15 agricultural machine products plants. Nine tractor plants make 80 percent of the Soviet Union's entire tractor output. Chemicals are largely produced in 25 cities. The entire central and Volga regions, with a total population of 60 million, gets their electricity from three hydroelectric plants and nuclear plants located near cities.[61]

However, aside from the problems with the econometric and input-output models used to determine the ripple effect on the Soviet economy of such targeting, it is likely that attacks on the above targets alone would produce massive civilian casualties, given the likely collocation of such targets with population.

Nor could one reasonably expect an attack on strictly military targets to prevent large-scale casualties—given present warhead numbers and capabilities. Such an attack would involve, in addition to SLBMs, the 1-Mt Minuteman IIs, the 335-kt Minuteman IIIs, the 170-kt air-launched cruise missiles and, in the future, the 500-kt MX warheads.

Whether the targets were primarily strategic nuclear targets, especially ICBM silos, or power projection/other military targets would make little difference. Thus Ball has noted that "a U.S. retaliatory strike against Soviet ICBM fields, on the other hand, must cover nearly the entire geographic expanse of the Soviet Union, including the more heavily populated and industrial areas west of the Urals."[62] Such an attack would involve two thousand to three thousand warheads, depending on damage requirements and the specific warheads used.

An attack on other military targets would require in the neighborhood of three thousand warheads. Most of these warheads would be directed against targets in western Russia—both because the preponderance of such targets is located there and because the targets' destruction is necessitated by a strategy designed to halt a Soviet advance into Europe.

If large-scale political targeting is involved, large-scale fatalities can be expected to result, insomuch as attacking the Soviet political control structure would involve attacking the urban areas where it is located. Thus the headquarters of the Communist party, whether at the national or republic level, are located in major urban areas, as are the administrative centers of the forty-seven economic-administrative regions (*Sovnarkhoz*). Likewise, the headquarters of the sixteen Soviet military districts are located in major Soviet cities—including Moscow, Leningrad, Minsk, and Kiev.[63]

Similarly, attacks on the KGB, MVD, or army troops used to maintain order would require attacking the cities either where they are permanently located or where they would move in the event war seemed a serious possibility. Massive casualties could be expected to result.

Even a political targeting policy directed solely at the seven hundred leadership bunkers would be problematical in producing negligible civilian casualties. Such bunkers would probably be located fairly close to the major cities in which the leadership resides. Further, it is likely that the higher-yield weapons in the U.S. arsenal would be employed to attack the bunkers so as to counteract their underground location and hardening. Together, these factors could mean significant collateral damage to the surrounding city areas.

[247]

Hence it seems unlikely that, at present, population avoidance is likely to be meaningful given the location of targets, the number of weapons that can be expected to be employed, and the characteristics of those weapons systems.

CONCLUDING REMARKS

Despite the pessimism expressed above concerning the present feasibility of meaningful population-avoidance strategies, it should not be taken as an endorsement of a Mutual Assured Destruction posture. The pessimism is an indication that statements by U.S. officials to the effect that "we do not in our strategic planning target civilian population *per se*" can be taken only as a statement of targeting mechanics rather than as a meaningful description of the effects (relative or absolute) of such a strategy.

Such a state of affairs implies that present distinctions between alternative targeting policies are of little consequence with regard to the damage to Soviet society. As Bernard Brodie has remarked: "It is useless to talk about strategies being counterforce strategies, as distinct from counter-economy or counter-population strategies, *unless* planners were actually to take deliberate restrictive measures to refrain from injuring cities. . . . Otherwise it can hardly mean much to the population involved whether the destruction of cities is a by-product of the destruction of airfields or vice versa."[64]

And, in fact, Department of Defense Instruction 5500.15, dated 16 October 1974, requires that all Defense Department actions concerning the acquisition and procurement of weapons and their planned use in war be consistent with all U.S. international obligations, including obedience to the laws of war.[65] According to Carl Builder and Morlie Graubard of the Rand Corporation, the instruction further obligates "any reasonable improvements that might enhance the conformance of such weapons to the law of armed conflict"—including avoidance of unnecessary injury to civilians and their property.[66]

Some might argue that there is nothing planners *can* do short of disarmament to avoid massive population/urban-industrial damage. However, the suspicion that such an effort might prove fruitless is no reason not to attempt it—especially since such an effort could be compatible with serious arms reductions. It would seem to be a minimum moral requirement of the possession of nuclear weapons to seek to reduce to as great an extent as possible the loss to civilian lives and property which would result from the use of such weapons.

Such an effort would involve identifying military, political, and war-supporting industrial targets whose destruction with very-low-yield (significantly less than the 40-kt Poseidon warheads) high-accuracy warheads would produce significantly fewer casualties. In such an effort the objective would be to determine a target list whose destruction with appropriate low-yield weapons would severely limit damage to the Soviet population yet severely damage the Soviet military-political position. Obviously, in addition to developing the target list, present U.S. strategic weapons systems would have to be replaced by more appropriate systems.

The feasibility and/or wisdom of such a program might be questioned on several grounds. First, as noted above, it might be argued that such a program is impossible to achieve—that the targets whose prospective destruction are necessary to deter the Soviet leadership cannot be destroyed without significant civilian casualties—due to the targets' location and/or the weapons necessary to destroy those targets. Such a view generally assumes the weapons and their characteristics to be similar to present systems. However, if the weapons systems are variables, as envisaged above, the possibility of limiting damage exists.

Second, it might be argued that such a program will give the impression that a "bloodless" nuclear war can be fought, thus increasing the probability of war. Such an objection implies acceptance of the view that decisions to go to war are largely based on calculations concerning the expected results of a nuclear exchange. A more realistic view would stress the relative (and indeed, absolute) lack of influence of the "state of the strategic balance" on such decisions when compared with the nature of a particular political/strategic conflict. The decision to go to (or seriously risk) war is far more dependent on the threat perceived to a "vital" national interest than to targeting policies or arsenal capabilities.

Finally, it should be noted that such a program may provide impetus for arms control and restraint. Clearly, weapons such as the 500-kt MX or 335-kt version of the Trident D-5 are not appropriate for limiting collateral damage. Hence it can be argued that Department of Defense development and procurement plans for these weapons is in violation of Instruction 5500.15.

Targeting Nuclear Energy

BENNETT RAMBERG

American nuclear weapons planners included Soviet electrical generation plants and associated facilities in their target lists as early as the late 1940s.[1] More recently power plants were included among the economic and industrial targets in the Carter administration's guidance for strategic nuclear planning (PD-59) and the Reagan administration's "Fiscal Year 1984–1988 Defense Guidance."[2] Other nuclear-armed nations may plan likewise. What distinguishes such targets today from those of the immediate postwar period is nuclear generation. As table 12.1 demonstrates, 398 power reactors were in operation in 1985 in twenty-eight nations, with construction under way or planned in ten others.[3]

Because atomic power plants and their support facilities, including fuel fabrication, spent fuel, reprocessing, and waste storage installations, contain large reservoirs of radioactive material, they pose unique wartime hazards that, even in a nuclear conflict, could add significantly to the immediate and long-term effects of the conflagration. This chapter explores why such plants will be attractive nuclear weapons targets, and it examines what the consequences of destruction, the strategic implications, and the difficulty in finding remedies are likely to be.

THE ATTRACTIVENESS OF NUCLEAR FACILITIES TO MILITARY DESTRUCTION

Perhaps the most obvious attraction of nuclear energy to military destruction is energy production. Electricity is vital to sustain a war effort. Without it, machines are unable to produce the material to continue combat. The logic of this argument is obvious, though uncommonly applied, so that conflict is needlessly prolonged.

[250]

Table 12.1. Power reactors in operation, under construction, or planned in 1985

Country	No. of units operating	Total Mwe	No. of units under construction or planned	Total Mwe
Argentina	2	935	1	1,627
Austria[a]	—	—	—	—
Belgium	7	4,456	1	5,475
Brazil	1	626	4	4,916
Bulgaria	4	1,620	6	4,366
Canada	17	10,025	7	15,345
China	0	0	11	5,950
Cuba	0	0	2	816
Czechoslovakia	4	1,570	12	8,392
Egypt	0	0	2	1,800
Finland	4	1,500	0	2,310
France	34	32,938	36	38,903
GDR	5	1,702	10	5,702
FRG	19	16,395	13	31,907
Hungary	3	1,224	5	3,264
India	5	1,034	10	3,024
Iraq	0	0	1	900
Israel	0	0	1	900
Italy	3	1,285	14	12,789
Japan	34	23,370	24	44,799
Korea, South	4	2,685	7	8,994
Libya	0	0	2	816
Mexico	0	0	2	1,308
Netherlands	2	507	0	507
Pakistan	1	125	1	989
Philippines	0	0	1	620
Poland	2	880	2	3,660
Rumania	3	1,887	2	2,924
South Africa	1	922	1	1,844
Spain	8	5,577	10	15,125
Sweden	12	9,465	0	9,465
Switzerland	5	2,882	2	4,947
Taiwan	6	4,884	2	6,684
Turkey	0	0	3	2,800
United Kingdom	37	11,130	7	16,690
United States	78	78,758	33	115,317
USSR	51	26,099	73	100,364
Yugoslavia	1	615	1	1,615

[a]Austria has a 692 Mwe reactor that is completed but has not been approved for operation.
Source: "Country by Country Status," *Nuclear Engineering International* 30 (August Supplement, 1985), 7–15.

During World War II, power plants were only secondary targets in both German and Allied attacks. The Allied policy in Germany is partially explained by the existence of a national grid that could make up for local disruptions, dispersal, inaccuracy of munitions, and high costs of the large number of bombs necessary to destroy these targets. However, it appears that poor planning may have been the principal reason. After the war, the chief electrical engineer for RWE, Germany's largest utility, summed up the German view of the Allied oversight as follows:

> The war would have finished two years sooner if you had concentrated on the bombing of our power plants earlier. The best plants to bomb would have been the steam plants. Our own air force made the same mistake in England. They did not go after English power plants and they did not persist when they accidentally damaged a plant. Your attacks on our power plants came too late. This job should have been done in 1942. Without our public utility power plants we could not have run our factories and produced war materials. You would have won the war and would not have had to destroy our towns. Therefore, we would not be in a much better condition to support ourselves. I know the next time you will do better.[4]

Such opinions were typical, contributing to the conclusion of postwar analysts that "had electric utility plants and large substations and the largest industrial power plants been made primary targets as soon as they could have been brought within range of Allied strategic bombing attacks, all evidence indicates that the destruction of such installations would have had a catastrophic effect on Germany's war production."[5]

More recently, power plants have been prime targets in wartime. In Korea, these attacks came after two years of conflict. The delay was due to an early decision by the United States not to destroy large hydroelectric dams on the Yalu River which served both China and North Korea in order to avoid giving Peking an excuse to intervene. The decision was reversed in June 1952 when negotiations deadlocked and destruction of the plants seemed necessary to hasten the conclusion of the war and to make more difficult the repair work the communists were conducting in small industrial establishments and railway tunnels.[6]

In the Middle East during the 1973 war, Israeli planes destroyed power stations at Homs, Syria, in order to subdue Syrian military activity and to deter other countries from entering the conflict.[7] In Vietnam the United States destroyed some electrical facilities, but these were not primary targets, given their small size and Hanoi's limited industry and reliance on imports from abroad.[8] More recently power plants were targets in the ongoing Iran-Iraq War that began in 1980.

Energy production is only one rationale for targeting nuclear plants. Theodore Taylor speculated almost two decades ago that nations may regard the civil nuclear energy plants of adversaries as guises for nuclear weapons programs and thus try to sabotage them at the outbreak of war.[9] Israel's destruction of Iraq's nuclear research reactor in June 1981 lent credence to Taylor's speculation. Such plants also may be attractive because of their enormous inherent value. With capital costs well over $1 billion, it is difficult to imagine other targets of comparable value that could be rendered permanently useless through military action.[10]

In each of these cases the release of radioactivity may be an incidental by-product of destruction, but it also may be the primary objective. In either event, there is the possibility that extensive territory may be contaminated—well beyond the contamination produced by a nuclear weapon alone and lasting for a longer period. There are many precedents for such massive damage to the environment. Fire, herbicides, and floods have been used as effective weapons of mass destruction throughout recorded history. Samson released several hundred foxes with their tails burning so as to set afire the Philistines' agricultural and horticultural fields. American incendiary bombing of Japan and Germany during World War II is to date the most costly use of fire in terms of human lives lost. The Boers used incendiaries to destroy crops during the 1899–1902 war with England; the British did likewise in their counterinsurgency campaign in Malaya in the 1950s. In Vietnam, the United States used incendiaries as well as herbicides and tractors with large blades, called Rome ploughs, to destroy crops and forest cover.

Flooding caused by destruction of levees, dikes, or dams has at times been even more devasting than fire. In its conflict with Japan during the late 1930s, China destroyed a dike on the Yellow River, drowning several thousand Japanese soldiers and stopping their advance along the front, but it cost the Chinese several million inundated hectares of farmland and thousands of destroyed villages, resulting in the displacement of millions of Chinese. During World War II the Dutch destroyed their dikes to hamper the German invasion. As the war turned against Germany, the Germans flooded large tracts of Dutch land as they withdrew from the country. In the Korean War the United States attacked irrigation dams in the north, causing widespread devastation. It also bombed dams, dikes, and seawalls during the Vietnam War, albeit inadvertently according to official accounts. In addition, it employed weather modification techniques to increase rainfall during the wet season, making military operations for its adversary more difficult.[11] Destruction of nuclear energy facilities will have effects both similar and distinct from these manipulations of the environment.

The Physical Consequences of Nuclear Weapons
Destruction of Nuclear Energy

Given that nuclear installations may be attractive military targets, how vulnerable are they to nuclear weapons destruction and what are the consequences? The vulnerability of such facilities to nuclear weapons has never really been in doubt. The U.S. government provided some insight in studies authored by Conrad Chester and Rowena Chester early in the 1970s.[12] The Chesters argued then that atomic power plants could be destroyed either in a direct hit or in a hit some distance from the plant. However, given the relative inaccuracy of ballistic delivery systems at that time, to do so would be at a cost inordinate to the value of the target.

This conclusion was based on the presumption that the criterion for preferentially targeting a nuclear reactor would be to produce significant additional casualties through the addition of the atomic plant's inventory to that of the nuclear weapon. To do so required that overpressures on the order of between 100 and 200 pound-seconds per square inch be delivered to the heavy steel and reinforced concrete reactor containment structure. A 100-kt weapon detonated within two hundred feet from the reactor or a 10-Mt weapon within two thousand feet will provide such impulse. This achievement would split the reactor vessel and fragment the reactor core and add its contents to the nuclear weapon fireball later falling back to earth as prevailing winds carry the radioactive plume. Basing their research on the accuracies of ballistic missiles for the late 1960s and projections for the 1970s, the Chesters estimated that seventy-eight 100-kt weapons, eighteen 1-Mt or two or three 10-Mt weapons were required to achieve a 50 percent probability of generating 100 to 200 psiseconds impulse to the target. Given the numbers of nuclear munitions required, the authors concluded that the costs of targeting these facilities would be out of proportion to the gains. By 1976, however the Chesters recognized that the accuracies of ballistic missiles were improving at a pace not anticipated earlier in the decade and that the superpowers could now economically destroy the plants.[13]

Great precision, while necessary to entrain an atomic plant's contents in the nuclear fireball, is not required to induce a conventional melt-down. Nuclear detonations of one hundred kilotons up to 6,800 feet from the reactor, or ten megatons up to six miles, would generate an overpressure sufficient to upset the cooling systems of nuclear instal-lations.[14] In the case of a reactor, the release of radioactive products would occur within one-half to two hours. According to Steven Fetter, the combined effects of thermal radiation, air blast, cratering ejecta, and ground shock may extend these distances.[15] In 1976 Demetrios Basdekas, an engineer with the Nuclear Regulatory Commission (NRC), brought to the NRC's attention the possibility that high altitude detonations of nuclear weapons through the release of an electromagnetic pulse (EMP) could disrupt the electrical systems of atomic plants at distances of hundreds of miles from the detonation. The 1962 Pacific nuclear testing program demonstrated the effectiveness of the pulse when in one detonation electric power grids and devices failed on the island of Oahu in Hawaii, eight hundred miles from ground zero. The NRC was reluctant to study the matter until Basdekas took the issue to President Carter. The resulting study declared that EMP would not have acute affects upon nuclear plants. The findings, published in 1983, were subjected to peer review. The most notable reviewer was Conrad Longmire, an acknowledged EMP expert. He disputed the commission's findings on the grounds that they were based on a line of reasoning from which almost any conclusion could be derived. Thus the challenges posed by EMP for nuclear energy may yet remain an open question.[16]

Figure 12.1 and table 12.2 depict the consequences of nuclear reactor and waste storage destruction. Figure 12.1 compares the gamma dose rate in time for a one-megaton fission weapon, a 1,200 megawatt electric (Mwe) reactor core, a ten-year storage at the reactor, a thirty-day high-level storage, and a ten-year high-level storage at a reprocessing plant. The considerably greater long-lived contribution of all elements of the nuclear fuel cycle compared to the nuclear weapons cycle is notable, with the greatest prominence estimated for high-level liquid wastes. In the American context, the Chesters concluded that 850,000 megawatts of nuclear generation coupled to an equivalent of 1,700 reactor cores stored in nuclear fuel reprocessing plants or temporary (ten-year) high-level waste storage, if added to nuclear weapon fallout, increases residual radioactivity after one year by an amount equivalent to thirty thousand megatons of 50 percent fission weapons. This figure could be sixty thousand megatons by the year 2020. They conclude: "Therefore the reactor cores and nuclear waste storage facilities can make a very respectable contribution to the fallout problem, especially if the situation one year or longer after the attack is considered."[17] The fallout can be significant even in the period immediately following an attack. Figure 12.2 compares the consequences from a 2,700 megawatt thermal breeder reactor destroyed by a direct hit. In this case the lethal range of the nuclear fallout is estimated to be 17 percent for a week's exposure and 33 percent for a month's exposure.[18]

Table 12.2 provides yet another way of looking at the problem, comparing the consequences from a one-megaton weapon, a reactor meltdown, a weapon landing on a reactor, and a weapon landing on a waste storage facility. The noteworthy point is the extent to which the reactor magnifies the effect of the weapon: one week after detonation the reactor-weapon combination contaminates more than twice the land (upon which human habitation should be prohibited) than would the weapon alone; after one month there is three times the contamination; and after one year there is almost twenty-five times. This reflects the relatively longer-lived radiation contained by the reactor. Also, after one year a reactor

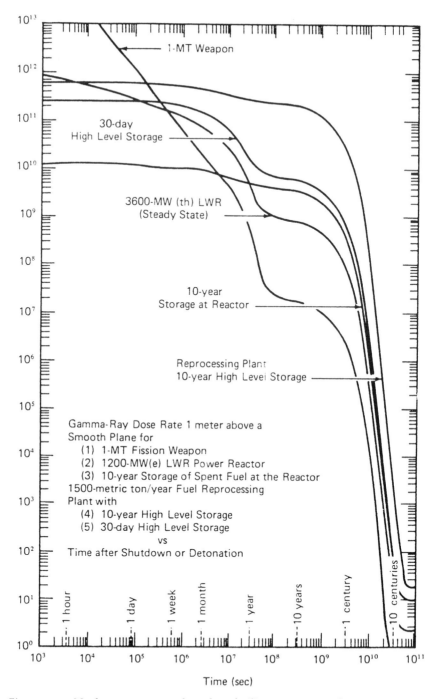

Figure 12.1. Nuclear weapon and nuclear facility gamma-ray dose rate versus time after detonation and shutdown

Source: Conrad V. Chester and Rowena O. Chester, "Civil Defense Implications of the U.S. Nuclear Power Industry during a Large Nuclear War in the Year 2000," *Nuclear Technology* 31 (December 1976), 333. Copyright 1976 by the American Nuclear Society, La Grange Park, Illinois.

Table 12.2. Area in square miles that must remain uninhabited for a given time for different nuclear energy facilities release scenarios

Time uninhabited	1-megaton weapon	Reactor (1000 Mwe) meltdown	Weapon on reactor	Weapon on waste storage facility
1 week	31,000	2,200 (5,300)[a]	79,000	113,000
2 weeks	26,000	2,000	72,000	110,000
1 month	21,000	1,800	64,000	103,000
2 months	17,000	1,600	54,000	100,000
6 months	5,000	1,200	33,000	83,000
1 year	1,200	900	25,000	67,000
2 years	150	680	17,000	49,000
5 years	11	320	10,000	35,000
10 years	2	140 (550–4300)	6,000	30,000
20 years	1	68	3,200	25,000
50 years		50 (240–3300)	1,200	14,000
100 years		20	180	2,400

[a]The figures in parentheses are drawn from Beyea. They "assume that occupation would be restricted if the resident population would otherwise receive more than a 10 REM whole body radiation dose over 30 years. This corresponds to about a three-fold increase over the natural background dose in the same period. A ten REM whole body dose has associated with it a risk of a .05 to .5 per cent chance of cancer death."

Sources: Steve Fetter and Kosta Tsipis, "Catastrophic Nuclear Radiation Releases" (Program in Science and Technology for International Security, Department of Physics, Cambridge, Mass., Report No. 5, September 1980), tables 2, 3, 6, 8. Figures in parentheses are from Jan Beyea, "Some Long-Term Consequences of Hypothetical Major Releases of Radioactivity to the Atmosphere from Three Mile Island" (Princeton University Center for Energy and Environmental Studies, Princeton, N.J., PU/CEES No. 109), p. B-13.

Note: Fetter and Tsipis assume that an area becomes uninhabitable for a given time assuming the maximum allowable dose is 2 REM per year.

meltdown alone will begin to contaminate considerably more land than the weapon itself. However, the worst case pertains to waste storage, which in combination with a nuclear weapon will contaminate many times more land than that damaged by the weapon alone. Any instance involving the addition of nuclear facility radiation can thus significantly complicate the task of postwar recovery.[19]

STRATEGIC IMPLICATIONS

The increasing vulnerability of nuclear installations to nuclear weapons bombardment has important implications for regions and nations where such weapons conceivably could be used, and most particularly for the Soviet Union, Europe, and the United States.

[257]

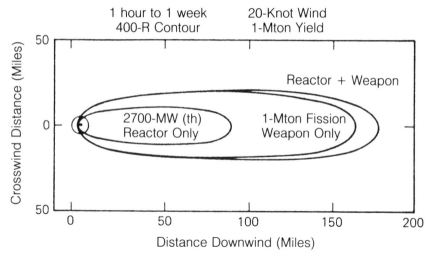

The 400-R isodose contours for one hour to one
week for fallout from a 1000-MW(e) reactor,
1-Mton fission weapon, and combination.

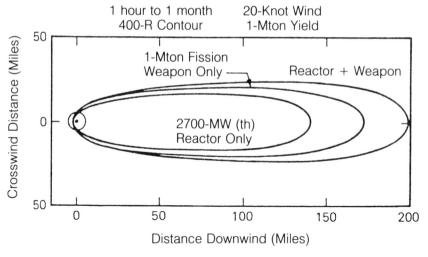

The 400-R isodose contours for one hour to one
month for fallout from a 1000-MW(e) reactor,
1-Mton fission weapon, and combination

Figure 12.2. 1,000-Mwe liquid metal fast breeder reactor and 1-Mt fission weapon
contours

Source: Conrad V. Chester and Rowena O. Chester, "Civil Defense Implications of a LMFBR in a Thermonuclear Target Area," *Nuclear Technology* 21 (March
1974), 191. Copyright 1974 by the American Nuclear Society, La Grange Park,
Illinois.

Soviet Union

The Soviet Union has either in operation or under construction and planned 124 civil reactors producing from 100 Mwe to 1,500 Mwe and an unknown number of military reactors producing nuclear material for its weapons program.[20] Figure 12.3 shows the approximate location of Soviet power reactors while table 12.3, specifies their designation, type, capacity, location, and the land use in the vicinity. Factors unique to Soviet nuclear facilities both enhance and diminish Soviet relative vulnerability and the consequences resulting from destruction. The average population density of ten to fifty per square kilometer near most reactors is considerably less than that of other European countries.[21] For example, in West Germany the figures range from one hundred to three hundred persons per square kilometer.[22] Consequently, the number of people in the Soviet Union who could be irradiated beyond safe thresholds could be proportionately less than in Europe. The Soviet Union further mitigates the threat to its population through a civil defense program that requires every citizen to take a twenty-hour civil defense course and be prepared for relocation in time of war. Urban shelters are also provided.[23]

Each of these advantages is offset by countervailing factors. Although the Soviet Union is less densely populated than most Western European countries, some of its installations are situated very close to major population centers. Soviet power plants are inherently more vulnerable because they often lack many of the redundant emergency systems characteristic of Western reactors.[24] And Soviet evacuation and shelter plans may be only marginally effective in dealing with the hazards posed by nuclear facility radiation. One critique points out that the effectiveness of the Soviet program rests on a number of dubious assumptions: the ability to relocate large populations quickly while relying on limited transportation, the ability to shelter people in poorly stocked facilities, and the ability to provide urban shelter while relying on air filtration powered by external energy sources. Whatever effectiveness the plans may have in reducing prompt lethal exposure, as currently designed they are of little help against long-term ground contamination because the population is expected to return to their houses after the attack and await further instructions.[25]

Given these vulnerabilities, a number of nuclear-armed antagonists might choose to reduce their own susceptibility to Soviet intimidation and overt military actions by targeting the Soviet nuclear energy facilities. Although current American strategic targeting doctrine calls for destruction of energy facilities generally, conceivably some rhetorical emphasis by the U.S. Department of Defense on Soviet nuclear facility vulnerability to nuclear weapons (and conventional weapons) and the

[259]

consequences deriving therefrom—particularly problems for Soviet recovery—could enhance American deterrence. The vulnerability of Soviet nuclear energy facilities could be made part and parcel of a strategy of coercive diplomacy and, if Soviet facilities were situated near military bases, military strategy. Such manipulation of the vulnerability of atomic plants might prove even more attractive to countries with limited nuclear arsenals which are less certain they can inflict unacceptable damage to deter Soviet coercion. For example, Britain and France might enhance the credibility of their nuclear forces if they threatened to ground burst a portion of their nuclear arsenal or air burst a fraction at high altitude and thereby take advantage of the effects of EMP. China could do likewise if it modernized its nuclear forces.

Western Europe

With well over 200 nuclear power plants, and at least 6 reprocessing and mixed oxide (plutonium-based) fuel fabrication plants operating, under construction, ordered, or planned, Western Europe (Belgium, Finland, France, West Germany, Italy, the Netherlands, Spain, Sweden, Switzerland, and the United Kingdom) has the greatest concentration of nuclear energy of any region in the world outside the United States.[26] However, the facilities may be less attractive targets than are Soviet plants since the Soviet nuclear weapons arsenal already has the ability to inflict massive destruction on Western Europe. Thus there appears to be little rationale for the Soviet Union to release radioactivity from Western European nuclear facilities other than to maximize the difficulty of recovery. Moreover, to do this might prove counterproductive, particularly with ground-burst nuclear weapons, because prevailing westerly winds could carry radioactivity across Eastern Europe into the Soviet Union itself.

Destruction of Western European facilities might prove attractive for reasons other than release of radioactivity—notably to stop electrical generation—but this could be achieved through conventional destruction of those portions of the plants devoted to the transmission of electricity. Even such a conventional attack, however, poses dangers since if the electrical systems required for the operation of a plant's cooling system are disrupted, a meltdown will occur.

United States

The United States had approximately 111 reactors built, under construction, or planned, in addition to fuel fabrication facilities, reprocessing plants, and high-level waste storage areas.[27] Should the Soviets

Table 12.3. Soviet Union map key

Nuclear plant no.	Designation of plant	Type[a]	Power Mwe (100 +)[b]	Location and nearest urban populations within forty miles[c]	Land use in vicinity
1	Kola 1	PWR	400	Kola Murmansk 396,000	forest
	Kola 2	PWR	440		
	Kola 3	PWR	440 U/C		
	Kola 4	PWR	440 U/C		
2	Leningrad 1	LGR	1,000	60 miles west of Leningrad	dairy farming
	Leningrad 2	LGR	1,000		
	Leningrad 3	LGR	1,000		
	Leningrad 4	LGR	1,000		
3	Drukshai 1	BWR	1,500 U/C	Vilnus 514,000	dairy farming
	Drukshai 2	BWR	1,500 ?[d]		
	Drukshai 3	BWR	1,500 ?		
	Drukshai 4	BWR	1,500 ?		
4	West Ukraine 1	PWR	440	Rovno 147,000	livestock, grain, other crops, woodland
	West Ukraine 2	PWR	440		
	West Ukraine 3	PWR	1,000 U/C		
5	Smolensk 1	LGR	1,000 U/C	Smolensk 278,000	livestock, grain, other crops, woodland
	Smolensk 2	LGR	1,000 U/C		
6	Kalinin 1	LGR	1,000 U/C	Kalinin 429,000	livestock, grain other crops, woodland
	Kalinin 2	LGR	1,000 U/C		
7	Chernobyl 1	LGR	1,000	Chernobyl Kiev 2,160,000	livestock, grain other crops, woodland
	Chernobyl 2	LGR	1,000		
	Chernobyl 3	PWR	1,000 U/C		
	Chernobyl 4	PWR	1,000 U/C		
8	Kursk 1	LGR	1,000	Kursk 363,000	livestock, grain, other crops
	Kursk 2	LGR	1,000		
	Kursk 3	LGR	1,000		
	Kursk 4	LGR	1,000 U/C		
9	South Ukraine 1	PWR	1,000 U/C	Nikolaev 428,000	livestock, grain, other crops

Table 12.3. Soviet Union map key (continued)

Nuclear plant no.	Designation of plant	Type[a]	Power Mwe (100+)[b]	Location and nearest urban populations within forty miles[c]	Land use in vicinity
10	Novovoronezh 1	PWR	210	Novovoronezh Voronezh 880,000	livestock, grain, other crops
	Novovoronezh 2	PWR	210		
	Novovoronezh 3	PWR	440		
	Novovoronezh 4	PWR	440		
	Novovoronezh 5	PWR	1,000		
11	Armenia 1	PWR	440	Oktemberyan Yerevan 1,055,000	cotton, fruit, vineyards
	Armenia 2	PWR	440 U/C		
12	BN 350	LMFBR	350	Shevchenko	desert
13	Beloyarsk 1	LGR	100	Sverdlovsk 1,200,000	forest
	Beloyarsk 2	LGR	200		
	Beloyarsk 3	LMFBR	600		
14	Siberian 1	LGR	100	Troitsk 76,000	grain, forest
	Siberian 2	LGR	100		
	Siberian 3	LGR	100		
	Siberian 4	LGR	100		
	Siberian 5	LGR	100		
	Siberian 6	LGR	100		

[a]LGR: light water-cooled graphite moderated reactor.

[b]U/C: under construction.

[c]All population data are 1980 estimates except for Troitsk, which is a 1960 estimate.

[d]?: Mwe output uncertain.

Sources: Joseph Lewin, "The Russian Approach to Nuclear Reactor Safety," Nuclear Safety 18 (July–August 1977), 438–450; "World List of Nuclear Power Plants," Nuclear News 25 (February 1982), 101–102; Nuclear Engineering International, "Map of the World's Nuclear Power Plants" (IPC Business Press, London, 1977); Population Division, Department of Economic and Social Affairs, U.N. Secretariat, "Trends and Prospects in the Populations of Urban Agglomerations, 1950–2000, as Assessed in 1973–1975" (United Nations, N.Y., ESA/P/WP.58, 21 November 1975), pp. 57–60; Editors of Life and Rand McNally, Life Pictorial Atlas of the World: Comprehensive Edition (Time Inc., New York, 1961), p. 267; Central Intelligence Agency, USSR Summary Map–Land Use (Central Intelligence Agency, Langley, Va., no. 501614, April 1974); J. G. Bartholomew et. al., Atlas of Meteorology (Denoyer-Geppert, Chicago, 1899), plates 12, 20; Paul E. Lydolph, Climates of the Soviet Union (Elsevier Scientific Publishing Co., Amsterdam, 1977), p. 354.

Notes: Geostrophic winds over European Russia, where most reactors are situated, tend to be southwesterly in winter and northwesterly in summer. Surface winds are variable. Precipitation is greatest from June through August, averaging two to four inches a month along a latitudinal zone 40 degrees by 60 degrees extending into Siberia to 140 degrees longitude. Most regions get less than an inch of precipitation a month during the remainder of the year.

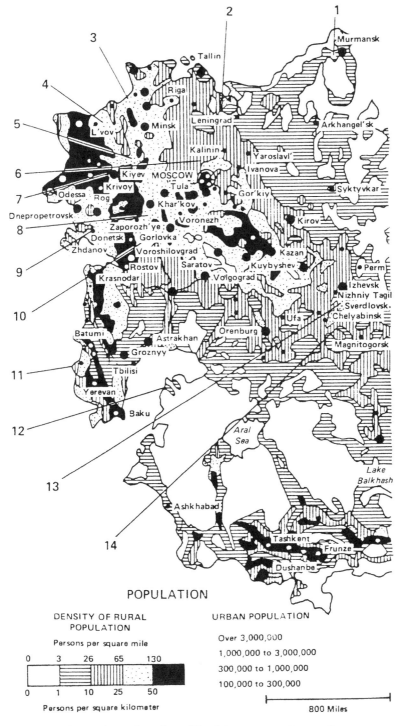

POPULATION

DENSITY OF RURAL
POPULATION

Persons per square mile

| 0 | 3 | 26 | 65 | 130 |

Persons per square kilometer

| 0 | 1 | 10 | 25 | 50 |

URBAN POPULATION

Over 3,000,000
1,000,000 to 3,000,000
300,000 to 1,000,000
100,000 to 300,000

800 Miles

Figure 12.3. Approximate location of Soviet power reactors, 1982
  Source: Central Intelligence Agency, *USSR Summary Map—Population* (CIA, Langley, Va., 501604, April 1974).

use their increasingly accurate ballistic missiles to destroy American nuclear installations, the consequences could be significant, perhaps doubling the cancer rate due to residual radiation in the postattack environment. The Chesters contend that these effects are relatively minor: "A few hundred thousand additional cancer cases per year starting a decade or more after the attack, from targeting nuclear industry would be difficult to detect against the background of a total of 100 to 120 million immediate fatalities and from weapons effects and cancers induced by the large fallout radiation absorbed by survivors."[28]

Even after 100 million deaths, however, hundreds of thousands of additional cancer deaths per year, even ten years after a conflict, is not something to take lightly. Still, it is unlikely that, given the nuclear weapons threat the United States already confronts, the Soviet Union will acquire additional leverage over the United States for purposes of intimidation. It might afford the Soviet Union additional deterrence leverage should it be concerned about a belligerent America. Militarily such a senario would complicate any operations following bombardment. Above all else it would make postwar recovery more difficult.

REMEDIES?

Are there any remedies to eliminate or minimize the hazards posed by atomic power in nuclear war? Unfortunately none of the conceivable remedies—international law, defense, engineering measures, and alternative energy—is practical.

International legal restraint is likely to be the most expeditious way to try to address the problem. The law of war prescribes norms of international conduct: it "attempts to reconcile minimum morality with the practical realities of war" through treaties, customary practice, and perhaps resolutions by the United Nations General Assembly.[29] At the present time only the 1977 "Protocol Additional to the Geneva Conventions of 12 August 1949" addresses the legitimacy of the destruction of nuclear facilities in war. This document is a mixture of ambiguity and contradiction. It prohibits the destruction of power plants if severe losses would result among civilians but leaves uncertain what constitutes severity. More serious, it stipulates that destruction of nuclear power plants is permitted if they provide electric power "in regular, significant and direct support of military operations." This provision competes with another demand that "care" be taken to protect the environment "against widespread, long term and severe damage."[30]

In addition, the Protocol is restricted in application. The document neglects large depositories of radiation at reprocessing plants, spent fuel and waste storage facilities, and fuel fabrication installations recycling plutonium. Finally, it overlooks the fact that threats to destroy plants could be used for political coercion.

Unfortunately, this codification is not compensated by related conventions, such as the 1977 international environmental codification agreement. Efforts are under way at the Conference on Disarmament in Geneva to incorporate a comprehensive ban on nuclear facility targeting,[31] but whether such a prohibition would be meaningful is questionable. The ban might have utility in a conventional war by providing a common standard in an area that would otherwise depend upon prudential judgment. It would introduce a new element into the decision-making process, which might gain partisans inside and outside bureaucracies that would act as pressure groups to assure its observance. This norm might have utility even in a limited nuclear conflict.[32] However, in a spasmodic nuclear attack it would be meaningless.

Both engineering safeguards and defense offer at best very modest means to safeguard facilities and protect populations. From the engineering perspective, facilities could be situated underground. Such construction could prevent the entrainment of the installation's contents in the weapon and at a multiunit site could prevent destruction of more than one plant.[33] Such placement, however, could increase the costs of reactor construction significantly, perhaps by as much as 40 percent.[34] An alternative would be to locate nuclear facilities in remote regions and, most particularly, far from other military targets. This plan might be practical for the Soviet Union but, given their limited territory, is certainly not for the Western European states. In any case such location could increase transmission costs.

Military defense is unlikely to be successful against ballistic missiles. Civil defense, by contrast, can be modestly improved. Governments should educate populations in the vicinity of nuclear plants about the dangers of radiation and about prophylactic measures. Evacuation routes should be planned, populations advised, and exercises practiced. Radiation shelters could be constructed and civil defense authorities should acquaint the public with such expedient protective measures as remaining indoors. In addition, every household should have a supply of potassium iodine tablets which would block the intake of radioiodine. Although such measures may mitigate the effects of short-lived radioactivity, they do not address the consequences of long-lived ground contamination which would be difficult to address save for the prohibition of habitation.[35]

A final alternative is reliance on other forms of electrical generation.

This would certainly be a foolproof remedy, but even in this period of retarded nuclear energy growth it is unlikely that most countries that have adopted the nuclear option will turn back.

In sum, the vulnerability of atomic energy to nuclear weapons destruction adds a significant additional cost to nuclear war. Should nuclear facilities be destroyed, the consequences for postattack recovery could be severe, making the idea of winning a nuclear war that much more remote.

[13]

Ethnic Targeting: Some Bad Ideas

DAVID T. CATTELL AND GEORGE H. QUESTER

The intention of this chapter is to discuss the outlines, and the serious drawbacks, of some new targeting approaches based on ethnicity, approaches that would take note of the languages people spoke as nuclear missiles or even conventional missiles were being fired in some future war. Among the advisers and supporters of Ronald Reagan, and already earlier in the Carter administration, and even in the public literature of the last several years, we have seen discussions of a use of missile accuracy to separate one ethnic group from another or to impose higher casualties on one group than on another. The first approach may, at the very least, be beset with some practical difficulties. And the second is beset with some important moral problems as well.

The United States will surely have the physical capability to discriminate on ethnic grounds. Ballistic missiles such as the MX will offer an accuracy much greater than any the United States possessed in the past. Even better accuracy will be offered by the new cruise missiles that are to be added to the United States arsenal in this decade.

Such extreme accuracies have already long worried arms controllers because the accuracies might threaten the survivability of the opposing side's strategic forces, and thus in some crisis panic the enemy into "a war nobody wanted." Advocates of the new accurate missile systems have accordingly acknowledged this particular risk and have suggested deployment modes and policy pronouncements to avoid it.

Yet one must then ask whether such extreme accuracies could be put to any other use, more beneficially reinforcing U.S. deterrence, while not threatening the USSR with an American first strike. It is in these other suggested uses for such accuracies that we now slide into something more worrisome.

The logical basis for an American ethnic-targeting strategy is not difficult to spell out. The Soviet leaders are assumed to be concerned mainly (or only) with power. They would launch a war if they could thereby enhance their power but would abstain from aggression if it would lead to a rebuff that constricted Kremlin power.

To deter Soviet attack, the United States must thus allegedly aim its forces so that it would take power away from the prospective aggressor, so that the aggressor will choose to abstain from aggression. Threatening to destroy Soviet tanks is one way to do this, and threatening to destroy Soviet factories (or leadership bomb shelters) is another, but what if neither suffices to ensure that aggression would be a net loss in terms of the Kremlin's power lust?

The proposals advanced for targeting new missiles thus shifted into ethnic considerations. The Soviet Union is seen as being in many ways a continuation of the old Russian empire, especially in the way that Great Russians continue to dominate the non-Russian nationalities in the day-to-day exercise of political power. Power and territory is what the Soviet leadership is assumed to crave; ethnic domination is an important tool in the holding of that power, just as it has been in the past.

Why not then convey the message to the Kremlin's Great Russian oligarchy that any future nuclear war would sever the links by which they control the many minorities of the USSR? Or why not warn them that in any future nuclear war the United States would mostly kill ordinary Russians, while tending to spare non-Russians, tipping the ethnic balance and thereby undermining this oligarchy's grip on its domain? Looking ahead to any such war, the Kremlin would encounter an early and stark version of the demographic change that is already in the cards of the basis of birthrates alone—relatively fewer Great Russians, relatively more Uzbeks and Kazaks.

THE SOURCES: MISSILE ACCURACY AND SOVIET DOCTRINE

If one wished to identify the root causes of this line of reasoning, it might be a mistake to direct criticism at any individual strategic analyst reaching logical conclusions here. The sources of our difficulty may rather be in the technology of high missile accuracy and (even more) in the gamesmanship of our Soviet strategy adversary.

It is always necessary to aim at targets about which the Soviet leadership is certain to care, for deterrence otherwise cannot be assumed.

Many Americans might assume that the mere threat of destruction of the cities of the USSR would suffice as a deterrent, but Soviet pronouncements still pretend to be intent on victory in any future war (although always claiming it would be the capitalist countries that would start such a war). Political power would be theirs in the end, as a matter of victory and conquest, and they never admit quite clearly enough that the destruction of Moscow and Leningrad would be too great a price, would make the war a net loss for the Soviets.

Soviet obtuseness thus keeps alive the debate about what is an adequate deterrent for shielding North America and Western Europe. If the Russians will not clearly admit that they regard the normal costs of a nuclear war as outweighing any prospects of military victory and political power, then some analysts naturally will conclude that more deterrent is needed. Most particularly, such American strategists conclude that the deterrent must come in the very same measure and category as the assumable goals of any Soviet aggression.

Thus we can not assume that a minus in category A will outweigh the Soviet prospects of gain in category B. Rather, to be sure of deterring Soviet attack, we must apply our forces to inflict a minus in category B itself. Since it is power and territory that the Communist leaders would be seeking rather than the welfare of the Soviet population, the United States must apply the accuracies of its new missiles so that any Soviet aggression would lead to a *loss* rather than a gain. And here, of course, we have the premise for various forms of ethnic targeting.

BREAKING UP THE USSR

Several defense contractor studies have been devoted to applying the more accurate missiles such as the MX, the Trident II, and the cruise missile and to breaking the Soviet empire into small independent national units.[1] This strategy would confront the Kremlin leadership with the prospect of being politically weakened, as Russia after a war would become a second-rate power.

Yet the feasibility of such an approach must be subjected to some scrutiny. Such studies to date have focused mainly on the technical requirements of such a strategy and on the environmental-geographical conditions that would be relevant to its success. These studies thus focus on the U.S. ability physically to separate various republics from the Russian Soviet Federated Socialist Republic (RSFSR) by the nuclear or conventional destruction of bridges, dams, and rail lines, and on the hindrance of Soviet troops by rainfall and local topography if they attempt to enter the republic. We will focus here instead on the more political requirements of any such strategy intended to break up the Soviet empire.

We have come to believe in the twentieth century, with the development of a strong sense of national identity among ethnic groups throughout the world, that a multinational empire, particularly one ruled from the center and dominated by one national group, is an anachronism. One of the major characteristics of the post–World War II era has been the struggle of the Third World against colonial domination and the continued struggle by ethnic minorities, both in the advanced industrial countries and in the newly independent states, for more autonomy and independence. While some of these national movements resort to peaceful protests, as in the case of the French-speaking Canadians, more often they have resorted to terror and guerrilla warfare, as in the cases of the Kurds of Iraq and Iran, the Eritreans in Ethiopia, and the Biafrans in Nigeria. In this climate of strong nationalism, a multinational empire such as the Soviet Union would seem to be subject to severe centrifugal forces, against which the empire can be maintained only by the extensive use of coercion; any relaxation of this control would make the empire fly apart. Therefore, after the destruction of the center and/ or the isolation of the ethnic groups from their imperial masters, these ethnic groups would seek independence. But can such a simple assumption be made about the situation in the Soviet empire? What are the conditions necesary for breaking up the Soviet empire, and can such a goal be achieved by the limited use of nuclear weapons?

For such a strategic scenario to work against the Soviet Union several minimal conditions would have to be fulfilled: First, either the missile attack would have to cut communications and transportation between central Russia and the republics and keep them inoperative for a sufficient length of time to permit republican forces to organize themselves for overthrowing Russian hegemony, or the missile attack would have to be directed at the top military and civilian leadership, thereby destroying the central government and giving the republics time to set up their own independent authority before the central government reorganized itself. Second, the Soviet forces stationed within the regions must not be sufficiently loyal and/or strong enough to put down the rebellion. If there are native military forces stationed in the republic, it must be certain either that they support independence and will defy the discipline imposed on the nonnative officers or that they are destroyed. Third, the native population must be sufficiently discontented to go along with the rebellion and willing to give enough active support to organize armed resistance. And fourth, either the native leaders must be willing to defect or alternatively the dissident nationalist forces must be large enough and sufficiently organized to remove the Soviet-imposed leadership and be recognized as the legitimate leaders of an independent republic. Unless these minimal conditions are realized it is difficult to see how the Soviet empire would fall apart as a result of a limited and short-term military strategy undertaken by the West.

THE SOVIET REPUBLICS

The Soviet Union is made up of fifteen republics representing major nationality groups. Within these fifteen republics, which theoretically have the right to secede from the union, there are over one hundred different national groups. The Soviet Union has granted those groups that have a large concentrated population administrative identities as autonomous republics, autonomous regions, and national areas. There are a total of fifty-three units based on nationality.

By far the largest republic is the Russian Soviet Federated Socialist Republic (RSFSR). It includes more than half of the population of the USSR and three-quarters of the land mass and is the core of the Soviet empire. Although many of the minor nationalities are located in the RSFSR, primarily in Siberia and the northern Caucasus region, the majority of the population in this republic (more than 80 percent) is Great Russian.

The remote, sparsely populated areas of the eastern half of the RSFSR (i.e., Siberia) contain the largest amount of as-yet-untapped resources in the world; in the western half are located the major industrial centers of the Urals, the central region around Moscow, and the Leningrad area.

The next most important republic closely associated with the RSFSR is the Ukraine. With its important industrial center in the Donets Basin and its valuable agricultural land, the Ukraine, together with the RSFSR, makes up the core of the Soviet economy. For example, these two republics produce more than 90 percent of the steel in the USSR. It would not be easy to separate these two republics in spite of certain nationalistic and separatist feelings among Ukranians. These two republics have long been integrated economically and ethnically, with more than 7 million Russians living in the Ukraine.

The remaining thirteen republics form a frontier area around the inner core, serving in large part as a buffer zone against the outside world. The eight republics in central Asia and the Caucasus are over a thousand miles from Moscow and the center. Together these republics account for less than 13 percent of the energy produced in the USSR and less than 20 percent of the cereals. The Moldavian republic on the border with Rumania is small and of marginal economic importance—more of an appendage to the Ukraine. The Belorussian republic is closely asso-

[271]

ciated with the RSFSR. Its industry is not highly developed and, because of its geographic proximity and the closeness of its population ethnically and linguistically to the Great Russians, this republic is the most assimilated of the republics. The three Baltic republics, although their populations and territories represent only a small portion of the USSR, are valuable for the technical contribution they make to the economy. But because of these republics' proximity and strategic importance, Russians have been moved into them in large numbers. For example, the percentage of Latvians living in Latvia declined from 62 percent in 1959 to 53.7 in 1979; for Estonia the figures are 74.6 percent to 64.7 percent. Thus the regime seems to be making a special effort to integrate these republics into the central core.

FEASIBILITY OF THIS STRATEGY

Physically separating the republics from the core is the condition that seems most likely to be fulfilled during wartime, which probably explains why this strategy appeals to some military strategists. The vast size of the Soviet Union and the great distances between national centers and Moscow makes the strategy plausible. Furthermore, one of the weakest links in the Soviet economy and the defense system is the underdeveloped railroad and road connections throughout the country. As a result it seems to be possible to separate the central Asian and Caucasian republics and some of the more remote peoples of Siberia from Moscow. But how serious would be the loss? For the Soviet Union to lose these areas would not cut into the heart of the USSR's economic strength, which is primarily concentrated in European Russia and the Urals. More serious would be the loss of the Baltic republics and the Ukraine, which are key elements of the Soviet industrial strength. But as discussed earlier, these regions are physically close to the central core and cannot be so easily separated; if they were temporarily cut off they would easily be recaptured by Soviet troops, which are trained to operate under conditions of nuclear war. A strategy that resulted only in the cutting off of the central Asian and Caucasian republics would hardly be worth the effort.

A more difficult condition to fulfill would be to neutralize the Soviet forces normally stationed in the various republics. The Soviet military does not concentrate its troops in the central regions but disperses them throughout the Soviet Union, with the heaviest concentration in peripheral areas. Can their destruction be accomplished without the destruction of the settlements and towns in which they may be located? How precisely can the troops be located at the crucial time of the attack?

In dispersing its troops the Soviet Union does not customarily station forces made up of a large number of non-Russians in their native areas. Even projecting into the future when more and more of the recruits will come from the Moslem population, and when it might be necessary to station Moslem troops in central Asia, the officer corps will undoubtedly be predominantly Russian in order to ensure discipline. The Soviet leaders after their experiences in Eastern Europe are well aware of the possible disloyalty of native troops stationed in their home region and will most likely take steps to avoid such an eventuality. And even if potentially rebel native troops form a part of the military in occupation, how in target planning can they be separated from non-native forces? Thus any independence movement would have to be able to mobilize forces at least equal to the well-armed Soviet troops stationed in the republic. Finally, while Soviet troops may be well trained to fight under the conditions of nuclear attack, the native population under such conditions would have survival as their number one priority. As Bernard Brodie so succinctly pointed out,

> the person preoccupied with dodging enemy missiles does not find much time to think about other matters which might otherwise disturb him. He is unlikely to be brooding on the historic sins and errors of a government to which he can scarcely conceive an alternative. He is politically apathetic, and his apathy may look a good deal better to those whose job it is to control him than did the discouraged restlessness that perhaps preceded it. Besides, if he has been bombed out of house and home, he is grateful for small offerings, and he may acquire a more favorable attitude toward the regime merely from being given coffee at the refugee station.[2]

Proponents of the strategy to break up the Soviet empire assume that nationalism among most non-Russian nationalities has reached the point where they deeply resent Great Russian domination and would be willing to fight for independence. In fact, however, the incidents of open national resistance have been very few. The only widespread and documented political resistance in recent years occurred among the Crimean Tartars and Lithuanians. Although the post-Stalin regime rehabilitated most nationalities that were exiled to Asia by Stalin for alleged disloyalty during World War II, the Crimean Tartars were not allowed to return to their homeland, despite their appeals and protests in the 1960s.[3] In Lithuania from about 1968 to 1974 there occurred a rash of appeals, protests, and even self-immolations, closely associated with the Catholic church, against national dispossession.[4]

Among the more than one hundred other recognized ethnic groups in the Soviet Union the level of nationalism varies considerably. Some groups are moving toward assimilation by the Russians, either because the groups are so small they cannot easily hold out against the predominant Russian language and culture or because their language and culture is close to that of the Russians. The Belorussians are an example of the latter. Others, particularly those with large populations and cultures distinct from the dominating Russian culture, have resisted assimilation, but this does not mean that they are ready to revolt.

Lenin thought of the future Communist society as a community without national distinctions or inequalities and planned that it be accomplished in three stages: First, nationalities would be allowed to "flower" and develop their individual national identities. Second, a "rapprochement" among the various cultures would bring the peoples closer together until, finally, the national groups would "fuse" into one culture with one language. In fact from the beginning the Soviet leaders have pursued the three stages almost simultaneously. While promoting local languages and customs, the regime has made sure that the local customs have had a common socialist content and, as the first step toward fusion, have insisted on Russian as the second language to be taught in all the schools. Stalin had thus hoped in his lifetime to create the universal Soviet man. But even with the widespread use of terror and coercion Stalin could not achieve his goal. His succesors have fared little better and have decided that the widespread use of force will not hasten the process.

In permitting and even aiding the "flowering" of the various national cultures, the Soviet regime raised the economic level of the less-developed peoples and, through education and the use of native languages and customs, promoted a sense of national identity. Even though the Soviet regime controlled the content of the national customs and crushed any native movement that looked to separation from the Communist system, the sense of national identity among almost all the peoples of the USSR has significantly increased since the revolution and is making the stages of rapprochement and assimilation much more difficult. Although the regime has been putting more emphasis on rapprochement and assimilation, it has for the most part not done so with a heavy hand, and the various nationalists have been successful in adjusting themselves or resisting the pressure. For example, the Georgians and Armenians would, given the choice, prefer independence, but have been able to take advantage of the system and play an important role in Soviet society. And when the regime in drafting the new constitution for Georgia seemed to be promoting the Russian language as the first language, the Georgians successfully resisted and Georgian was kept in the constitution as the primary language.[5]

The regime has tried, as it has with all religions, to undermine the Islamic religion. But the regime has refrained from crushing it entirely and has made peace with what remains of the religious hierarchy, as the regime has made peace with other religious hierarchies that have accepted the Soviet system. Even more important, the regime continues to tolerate Moslem culture which has a strong religious core, trusting that modernization will in time win the population over to the secular culture of Communism. Thus the average Moslem, who is not much concerned with the religious organization and hierarchy, is content that he can follow undisturbed his Moslem customs and prayers. In fact, many nonorthodox Moslems and intellectuals feel that there is nothing incompatible between the Moslem way of life and socialism and even believe the two are complementary. Furthermore, as the Moslem peoples have become better educated and find their way into the ruling elite, they use their position to move their own people into the hierarchy, crowding out the Russians. Similarly, schools of higher education in the Moslem republics give priority to natives in their admissions.[6] The Moslem population's relative lack of concern about the nationalism of Moslem peoples in general was shown in their failure to rally to the support of their brother Moslems, the Crimean Tartars, who wanted to return to their homeland. In addition, from the limited evidence available in the West, the Islamic fundamentalist revolution in Iran and continued resistance of the Afgans in the Marxist rule of Karmal and the occupation by Soviet troops has had only a limited impact on the Moslems in the Soviet Union. It is true that the Soviet leaders, after using Moslem troops in the first wave of invasion, apparently thought better of the practice and replaced them in large part with non-Moslem troops, either because they were ineffective or because it was feared that the rebellious attitudes of the Afghans might spread to the Soviet Moslems.

The situation in the Baltic and Ukrainian republics differs but it also is not conducive to launching a successful revolt against the center. In the case of the Baltic republics the population feels that joining the Soviet Union has meant a step down in the quality of life as well as in the loss of independence, which has caused deep resentment against the Russians. For the Ukraine there is the perennial resentment of being in the shadow of the big brother. Furthermore, because of the special importance of the Ukraine to the welfare of the empire, the Russian leadership is particularly sensitive to any signs of independence among the Ukrainians. An additional cause of resentment is the large Russian colonies that have migrated to these republics since the war. These colonies make insurrection extremely difficult.

In a modern authoritarian state with a well-integrated party and government organizations and extensive means of coercion, a successful rebellion is difficult if not impossible. In these cases for a revolt to succeed it is necessary to undermine gradually the legitimacy of the system and to break down the discipline of the police and the military so that they are lax in persecuting dissidents and refuse to take action against the population. Although there may be widespread discontent among some of the national groups in the Soviet Union, there is no evidence that the authority of the regime in any of the republics is in disarray. Perhaps the dramatic and sudden cutting off of relations with Moscow would make for another scenario. The top native leadership in a republic might be persuaded to defect and throw its lot with the insurrection. But is such an eventuality likely or feasible? The native leaders have been increasingly coopted into the Soviet elite and have been rewarded by the system. Although many have accepted leadership for personal or opportunistic reasons, we cannot conclude that some are not motivated by an ideological commitment to Communism. Furthermore, even the opportunist will think twice before he defects to the dissidents who would be unlikely to trust him in the long run and would seek to remove him at the first opportunity. Finally, the Russian leadership is well aware of these dangers and has adopted a thorough screening policy for picking leading cadres in all the republics. Significantly, the second secretaries of the party at the republic level are usually Russian and one of the chief tasks of the second secretary is to control appointments inside and out-side the party. Political loyalty has always been the first criterion of any appointment to a leadership post.

Another scenario for rebellion would be for a dissident group itself to have sufficient organization and leadership cadres to take over. To suc-ceed the group would also need a large cache of arms or access to arms through infiltration of the various armed services stationed in the re-public. Such a scenario has little chance in the Soviet system today. There is no evidence that the dissidents have at present any hidden arms or that they have a network that penetrates deeply into the state and party apparatus. And even though the secret police have never been able to expunge completely the dissident movements, they have for the most part kept the movements small and tenuous. One possible excep-tion is the conservative Sufi brotherhoods, particularly widespread among the Moslem people of the northern Caucasus. The brotherhoods are primarily religious organizations, committed to the Moslem way of life, that concentrate their energies on mystical and spiritual pursuits. They could become politically dangerous, but since the regime seems well aware of the potential threat, the movement is undoubtedly kept under close surveillance.[7]

One other dissident movement seems to have the potential for be-coming a ruling organization in a crisis—the Lithuanian dissidents. Not that in itself the group has either the organization or the cadres. How-ever, the Lithuanian Catholic church, a formidable organization that never really made its peace with the Communist system, is a group around which the masses could rally and that could provide the leadership of an insurrection. Except for these two organizations, the Sufi brotherhood and the Lithuanian Catholic church, there is no known independent core organization around which national dissidents could rally.

In conclusion, there is little reason to believe that a strategy of missile targeting aimed at splitting the Soviet Union into fifteen or more republics would succeed. Perhaps, in an extended conventional war that weakened Moscow's control and exacerbated the hardships and the hostility of the non-Great Russian population, it might be possible to organize rebellions—particularly if at the same time the West could aid the dissident forces through covert activities in the manner of the OSS (Office of Strategic Services), precursor of the CIA in World War II. But it is a long way from native grumblings and resentment of Moscow's imperialism to a successful rebellion, even in time of war.

DIFFERENTIATING THE COUNTER-POPULATION ATTACK

The more gruesome alternative remains, however, not simply destroying bridges but differentiating the degree of devastation on opposite sides of the bridges. If the United States kills more Great Russians and fewer minorities, perhaps this strategy will more tellingly erode the Kremlin's control over its empire.

The accuracies of new missiles surely allow more of such a targeting option than would have been possible previously. Smaller warheads can be used and can be aimed more precisely. One could, for example, leave relatively untouched the older cities of the Baltic republics of Latvia, Lithuania, and Estonia (in which the local nationalities still tend to predominate), while systematically destroying the newer suburbs inhabited more heavily by Great Russians. One could exempt the Asiatic sections of the USSR while hitting European Russia. One could exempt the Ukraine and White Russia while directing most of the attack at the Great Russian nationality from which the Politburo leadership itself has been drawn, the nationality that allegedly is a primary tool of this leadership's grip on power.

Colin Gray hints at such a strategy in his 1979 article, "The Case for a Theory of Victory":

> More to the point perhaps, identifiation of the demise of the Soviet state
> as the maximum ambition for our military activity, encourages us to attempt

to seek out points of high leverage within that system. For examples, we begin to take serious policy note of the facts that:

—The Soviet peoples as a whole have no self-evident affection for, as opposed to toleration of, their political system or their individual political leaders.

—The Soviet Union, quite literally, is a colonial empire—loved by none of its non Great Russian minority peoples.[8]

Gray's argument might refer only to the breaking of communication linkages, as we discussed earlier, and not necessarily to any deliberate ethnic differentiation in rates of homicide.

Richard B. Foster is considerably more explicit in a 1978 report of the Stanford Research Institute:

The Great Russian nation is Slavic, with a history of Pan-Slavism. Great Russia is the center of gravity of the USSR empire. The "liberation" element of a U.S. political targeting concept is in part concerned with breaking up the Soviet empire. In this concept the non-Russian republics in the USSR as well as Eastern European nations would be spared collateral damages insofar as possible with very careful targeting of military forces and bases.[9]

Equally explicit is the suggestion in an article by Bernard Albert in 1976 *Orbis* titled "Constructive Counterpower":

The purpose of the suggested attack would not be to stimulate a popular revolt, but only to encourage the local communist leadership to refrain from active cooperation with the central government in its own self-interest. In return, the United States would attack only the Soviet control apparatus and refrain from any destruction of Ukrainian values. An attack structured to damage Great Russia but not the nationality states poses an extreme threat to the central leadership, for should the war be protracted, the Ukraine might emerge as the strongest post-conflict state.[10]

The Carter administration's changes in targeting doctrine leaked to the press in the summer of 1980 involved only a partial move in this direction. The list of targets facilitated by the new accuracies and options, as installed in Presidential Directive 59, apparently included Soviet military forces, the factories critical to any early Soviet economic recovery, and the concrete bomb shelters reserved for the Soviet leadership.[11] The list was justified by arguments very much like those noted earlier, that the Soviet leadership will have to be deterred in kind, deterred by the prospects of defeat rather than by the simple punishment of all of its people.

The Presidential Directive issued by Jimmy Carter did not thus venture into the more dangerous terrain of ethnic targeting, but the risk of such a move is all too great because the same perception of Soviet motivations applies, because the enhanced accuracies of new missiles make such ethnic targeting just as much an "option." The rumblings of suggestions of this kind of option are heard now in Washington, and, as noted, such suggestions are not impossible to find in print.

At times the expectation of greater casualties among Great Russians merely extrapolates from the fact that most Soviet missile silos are located in the RSFSR, such that American warheads directed at silos (to keep them from being reloaded to fire additional rounds at the United States) would inevitably impose an additional collateral damage on the people around them. But if the ethnic differential in Soviet casualties in a nuclear war were thus more incidental than deliberate, it might still be a mistake for American planners to be welcoming it.

THE INEVITABLE MINIMUM

As with the "strategy" attached to any other weapons system, doubts may arise about how seriously to take such discussions. As greater accuracies accrue from the simple fruits of technology, could we merely be seeing the justification of such new capabilities by their project managers? Do U.S. strategic planners have to find a use for accuracy, in both the cruise missile and the MX, because the taxpayers might otherwise decide that their money has been wasted (or because these accurate missiles might otherwise be seen as nothing but a counterforce instrument directed at Soviet missile silos, i.e., as unambiguously menacing and destabilizing)?

Yet perhaps these are serious and worthwhile targeting options, approaches U.S. planners would have considered a long time ago if they had only had the means to exercise such fine choice with such high accuracy. Most Americans might prefer to punish only a portion of the adversary's population rather than punishing all of it, if indeed the guilty could be sorted out from the innocent. Those who take Soviet strategic pronouncements seriously might similarly decide that the United States in fact has a deterrence gap if it continues to rely only on the blunderbuss approaches of Mutual Assured Destruction. What if the Soviets are serious (rather than bluffing) when they pretend to care more about other things than the destruction of their cities?

It must be noted that some ethnic discrimination in targeting is natural and inevitable and has been in effect all through the nuclear age. When U.S. strategic planners spoke of the "assured destruction" of the Soviet Union and its cities, were they determined also to assure the destruction

of Budapest (our heroes of 1956) or Prague (our heroes of 1968) or Warsaw (the kinsmen of the pope, and of many Americans)? Of course not.
Viewing Eastern Europe as a set of captive nations involuntarily under
the control of Moscow, the United States might have felt driven to use
some nuclear warheads against troop concentrations and related targets
within these nations, but would have genuinely tried to avoid imposing
collateral damage on the civilians surrounding such targets. Those em-
ploying Mutual Assured Destruction targeting philosophy would con-
versely have welcomed such collateral damage within the Soviet Union
and would have moved directly to strike at the hearts of the cities.

Exempting Poland, Hungary, and Czechoslovakia from attack, it might
only then be a small step to exempting Lithuania, Latvia, and Estonia
since the U.S. government has never legally recognized the incorporation of these countries into the USSR, therefore, making them "captive
nations." But we already see the beginning of a slippery slope here, as
the differentiation of these three "Soviet Socialist Republics," along with
the Eastern European "independent states' of the Warsaw Pact, could
then slide the United States into further differentiation in favor of other
SSRs. Since these "Republics" are demarcated on ethnic grounds, the
precedent and invitation for ethnic targeting is already in place. (As an
historical aside, the U.S. army air force already has practiced some ethnic
discrimination in targeting during World War II. Prague was never
bombed, while Dresden was flattened.)

If the average American can thus discriminate between a Pole and a
Russian, or a Latvian and a Russian, the next step might be to discriminate between the Uzbek (if the average American has ever heard of an
Uzbek) and a Russian, or a Ukrainian and a Russian. These nations too
can arguably be thought of as captive, governed against their ethnic or
ideological preferences. These also can be seen as the power possessions
of the Great Russian imperialists, people whose demographic expansion
vis-à-vis the Great Russians would threaten the very power the Mos-
covites are alleged to crave. Some postwar targeting plans that have
been declassified indeed show that the U.S. air force had already adopted
part of such an analysis for the 1950s.

2. For sometime we have been looking at the Ukrainian Separatists Movement in terms of a possible air offensive against the U.S.S.R. The significance
of the Ukrainian Separatists Movement is such that Ukrainian cities have
been moved down the priority list so that they appear beyond the initial
phases of the offensive.

3. This decision will be valuable if propaganda programs are aimed at
capitalizing upon this action.[12]

The suggestions of ethnic targeting put forward recently are thus not so novel, or strange, or without precedent. It is precisely because they have some logical precedent, and some plausible logic, that they are in danger of winning a wider acceptance and a wider declaration and application. Yet the general point is that such thinking should be reined in and contained, that its further elaboration and extension would hurt, rather than help, American interests.

THE COSTS

What are the likely costs for the United States of a continued slide into the logic of ethnic targeting? There are costs in world image and in possible Soviet retaliation.

We are in fact discussing genocide as a substitute for Massive Retaliation. Even if genocide were indeed to produce fewer fatalities than old-fashioned Massive Retaliation, its sheer cold-blooded deliberation is likely to offend the moral sensitivies of much of the world, of our allies as well as the neutrals.

As a retaliation against Soviet aggression, it would be one thing if American missiles could be so pinpointed to kill only one thousand or so of the most guilty Soviet leaders (or even a hundred and forty thousand Communist leaders sometimes suggested now as another target for U.S. pinpoint accuracy). If very few innocent other Russians were killed, the world might come to see such American military planning as just and morally appropriate, somewhat analogous to the execution of Nazi leaders after the Nuremburg trial.

But aiming at millions of Great Russians, only because of their ethnicity (because they are given preferential treatment in promotions to positions in the USSR, and thus may serve as part of the conspiracy that holds on to such power), would strike Europeans as behavior more typical of the defendants than the prosecutors at Nuremburg. It is genocide to choose to kill, or not to kill, simply on the basis of the likely language of the victim, rather than hitting him incidentally as part of the general assault on the nation.

A second cost in any such American trend is that the Soviets now also have accurate missiles and could soon enough contemplate some ethnic targeting of their own. Indeed, one might expect such Soviet target choice, just as one might expect the American comparisons of Moscow and Prague.

Soviet propaganda has always depicted American blacks and Spanish-speaking Americans as downtrodden groups, as victims of the capitalist system. Could Soviet missiles in any future war (especially the newer

[281]

missiles that will be so much more accurate) really be targeted without some consideration of these factors? The Soviet Union might well offer Mexico neutrality and exemption from attack in any World War III, in exchange for whatever benefits Mexico might deliver in the postwar recovery period. Would it not make sense to offer the Mexican government some similar exemption for the ethnic Mexicans within the United States, many of whom are indeed legally still nationals of Mexico?

Just as in American planning, such Soviet thinking has to be inevitable. Yet the tone of international politics will be considerably worsened if such thinking is elevated and amplified on both sides. Will we hear future discussions of how Soviet nuclear warheads are carefully aimed at Scarsdale and not at Harlem, at the San Fernando Valley and not the Spanish-speaking sections of East Los Angeles? If the world thinks such scenarios sick, it must remember that sicknesses have been contagious in the past.

SOME CONCLUSIONS

Breaking up the Soviet Union by simply cutting its internal communications and letting separate nationalisms do the job will not be so easy. The Soviet Union is certainly feeling some of the growing nationalist pressures that have spread over the globe, but Soviet leaders have been able to manage and contain these feelings by a combination of policies: permitting the limited development of national cultures, coopting more and more natives into the elite, raising living standards, isolating the population as much as possible from the outside world, crushing quickly any dissident group looking toward independence, tying all organizations (social, economic, and political) around the Communist party, and pursuing a policy of gradual assimilation.

The implementation of these policies does not mean that the Soviets have the nationality problem solved and that new problems are not developing. The very policy of coopting natives into the leadership is creating powerful native groups in the republics who want to keep the republics and their resources for themselves and discourage Russian colonists and domination. There are also serious potential problems growing out of the different rates of population growth among the nationalities, with Moslem groups growing at more than twice the rate of "Europeans" in the Soviet Union. This growth rate is arousing Russian fears about the "yellowing" of the country and is creating an oversupply of new workers in central Asia, in contrast to the growing shortage of workers in the rest of the country. Another concern is the instability of

Russia's East European satellites, particularly Poland, and the fear that the unrest could spread to the Soviet Union.

There are indeed new and continuing problems that the Soviet regime must face; but there is little reason to expect that Moscow will be unable to contain them or that native independence movements could become a threat. The Soviets have always been quick to crush any attempt by even the smallest groups to advocate national independence. The new military capabilities of U.S. missiles have not really altered the capabilities of the Soviet regime to defend itself from attempts to break up the empire.

The difficulties with a policy of differential counterpopulation attacks are somewhat more complicated. The MAD of Mutual Assured Destruction is surely already "sick," as the two nuclear superpowers have deterred each other from initiating wars by the threat of killing millions of each other's people. Yet a philosophy of ethnic targeting will strike most observers as more sick, forcing those who are aimed at, in either country, to resent the ethnicity of those who are exempted from punishment. How are the Great Russians of the USSR to respond to the American policy of sparing Lithuanians from attack? Should they program a few warheads of their own against this republic, just to restore the demographic balance that the American attack would upset? Are differing ethnic groups in the United States going to attack each other in order to deny the USSR ultimate say in who survives and who dies in a thermonuclear war?

The advantage of Mutual Assured Destruction was that it typically pretended to be "collateral damage," or "bonus damage," as part of a necessarily blunderbuss attack on the enemy's war-fighting ability. While many academic strategists long ago concluded that the real objective of any nuclear force was precisely mass homicide, the official statements of each side have never had to admit this point but could always pretend that military targets were being aimed at, with civilians suffering only incidentally in the process. Countries were thus to be attacked all at once, sharing in the miseries of this prospect together.

The choices offered by new guidance systems perhaps made it inevitable that such hypocrisy would end. As U.S. planners now have to admit, they will be killing people because they want to (since they could have avoided such killings by pinpointing military targets). Planners also now get drawn into discussions of whom they want to kill.

The accuracies of the new ballistic and cruise missile systems surely are the basic source of the problem. Where the CEP (circular error probable—the circle around the intended target within which half of one's warhead will fall) was once closer to a half mile, in the future it promises to be in the hundreds of feet. Such accuracy poses a counterforce threat of first-strike attack since a warhead falling this close to an underground silo is likely to destroy the missile inside that silo. It also poses all the other options, and other problems, we are discussing here.

What is true for United States nuclear targeting must thus be true for the Soviet side as well. The ability to aim nuclear warheads so precisely inevitably raises the question of how such an ability to discriminate will be used. The greatest current fear, of course, is that the new accuracies of Soviet missiles may be directed at the land-based missile silos of Minuteman and Titan (and then also at the silos of the MX). In making the scenario for such a partial Soviet counterforce strike plausible (the U.S. submarine-based missile force would presumably still escape attack), it is sometimes projected that the Russians would carefully aim to avoid imposing casualties on American civilians. Such a "surgically clean" use of nuclear warheads is one use to which the Soviet capabilities might be put. Another use, however, would be to kill some Americans while leaving others alive.

It does not take a particularly pernicious imagination to come up with many of these uses, for simple technological development of today's superb accuracies would almost inevitably pull imaginations in this direction—in speculation about what the adversary might do, and also in speculation about what one's own forces can do. The ability to stamp out all such speculation is simply not there. The task is rather to contain such speculation, to rein it in, lest it somehow take on a life of its own, markedly poisoning all possibilities of détente between the superpowers and perhaps weakening the American image abroad.

Rather than differentiating among the USSR's nationalities, in the past a more typical American attitude was to assume the Great Russians resented Soviet dictatorship just as much as Ukrainians or Moldavians, that all these were people to be identified with (and indeed liberated, if this could ever be accomplished without a recourse to the devastation of war). A genuine Marxist analysis would similarly not differentiate among the ethnic groups of America but rather would look forward to giving us all, black and white alike, the benefits of "socialism." It would be healthier for the balance between the two superpowers if targeting analysis were held back at this less discriminating level. It would be healthier also for the image and interests of the United States.

[14]

War Termination and
Nuclear Targeting Strategy

George H. Quester

The lists of outputs sought in strategy and arms control are often stated too statically, as presented below in table 14.1. It is now normal to note that each of these outputs may conflict with each of the others in some specific policy choice. The arbitrary classification of eight kinds of goals in table 14.1 indicates the generation of 28 (8 × 7/2) different kinds of tension about which we have to be concerned; an improvement in our national position in one category would be achieved only at the cost of a setback in another.

In this chapter I will attempt to expand considerably the range of strategic complications by adding a time dimension to the array of outputs; we must contemplate the possibility that a nuclear war has actually broken out and that some joint interest will emerge in terminating it. This will thus be an exercise in transforming the menu of important output given in table 14.1 into something more dynamic, based on the war-termination assumption that deterrence had failed and might fail again, as in table 14.2.

As with any such list, table 14.2 obviously represents a necessarily arbitrary simplification of the horizon of options that require consideration. Nonetheless, it opens up a host of important tensions and necessities for choice.

The most obvious tension, which draws much attention and indeed usually monopolize the discussion, is the tradeoff between basic deterrence and all that follows. To what extent should the United States design and construct its nuclear forces, and the uses to which they will be put, for the sole purpose of preventing nuclear war? To what extent should the United States deviate from this purpose to accomplish any of the other tasks listed?

The current American strategic debate is too often phrased in terms

Table 14.1. Considerations in strategy and arms control

A. Reduce the probability of nuclear war.	B. Reduce the probability of conventional war.	C. Reduce the peacetime costs of being prepared.
If nuclear war happens, reduce the "costs."	If conventional war happens, reduce the "costs."	Prevail politically in peacetime.
If nuclear war happens, prevail politically.	If conventional war happens, prevail politically.	

of tensions between deterring nuclear war and winning it should it happen.[1] The improved accuracies that would allow the United States to destroy Soviet missile silos in the event of a World War III would indeed help it win, but in many analyses these improved accuracies might increase the chances of such a war in the first place, by putting the Soviets in fear of an American counterforce attack.[2] If the above were the only tension, we might well come down on the side of Mutual Assured Destruction (MAD) rather than war fighting—content to forget about victory, convinced that any pursuit of options for victory would not be worth the price if the United States thereby had to threaten Soviet retaliatory forces too much with the prospect of a first strike.[3]

Yet the discussion in this chapter goes on to explore the ramifications of a different tension. Might U.S. strategic planners need to choose at certain points between strategy that deters nuclear war in the first place and strategy that contributes to terminating it once it has started? We deal here primarily with ending such a war before it has run full course, hardly a hawkish or inhuman consideration, and with keeping it from resuming quickly thereafter.

Advocates of preventing war can hardly be indifferent to terminating it. Yet the choices thereafter may be difficult, as we have to consider deploying and aiming some of the same high-accuracy missile systems that so much draw the enthusiasm of the war fighters.

A persuasive argument can thus be made that U.S. planners would best deter nuclear war by concentrating exclusively on countervalue targeting, making it clear to the Soviets that their cities will be hit in any nuclear war and that Soviet civilians will be killed (perhaps because the United States would have no other targets to aim at). It should also be made clear that the United States will pose no preemptive counterforce threat to the Soviet missile forces (i.e., that a Soviet leader will not be put into the position of "use them or lose them").[4]

Yet our exercise here assumes (not unreasonably) some risk—that such

Table 14.2. Considerations in strategy and arms control based on assumption of deterrence failure

A. Reduce the probability of nuclear war.	B. Reduce the probability of conventional war.
	    If conventional war happens, reduce the costs.
	    If conventional war happens, prevail politically.
		C. Reduce the peacetime cost of being prepared.
		    Prevail politically in peacetime.

D. If nuclear war happens, reduce the costs.
    If nuclear war happens, prevail politically.
    If nuclear war happens, avoid prolongation of the war.		

E. If nuclear war is prolonged, reduce the costs.
    If nuclear war is prolonged, prevail politically.
    If nuclear war is prolonged, avoid further prolongation.		

F. If nuclear war is terminated, avoid another resumption.
    If nuclear war is terminated, prevail politically.
    If nuclear war is terminated, reduce the costs of peacetime preparedness.		

G. If nuclear war is terminated, reduce probability of conventional war.
    If conventional war happens, reduce the costs.
    If conventional war happens, prevail politically.		

deterrence might fail. If U.S. planners want to hedge at all against such failure, they will compromise the devotion of our resources to simple deterrence. Further, they will have to make a new series of choices, as outlined in table 14.2.

Once a nuclear war has begun, great importance would need to be attached to intrawar deterrence, that is, to erecting a new set of incentives to keep the adversary from doing its worst. But such incentives conflict somewhat with trying to credibly deter nuclear war in the first place.

Such incentives also may conflict with each other in terms of the different kinds of "worst" the enemy can do. The United States would want to induce the enemy to stop shooting missiles at American cities, but also to stop any counterforce against U.S. missiles, perhaps to call back tank forces advancing on the territory and industry of Western Europe, and also to avoid resumption of such warfare after any war termination has been achieved. At points, U.S. targeting policy may work to discourage one of such forms of Soviet attack, but only at the price of being less dissuasive of another.

STRONG DOUBTS ABOUT STRAIGHTFORWARD COUNTERFORCE

If deterrence has failed and nuclear war has begun, U.S. command authorities would be concerned with limiting and stopping the killing of the American population and/or limiting and stopping the erosion of the relative U.S. power position. Would the United States achieve this goal best by using its missiles or by holding some in reserve; by hitting the enemy's cities or by hitting its missile sites; by not hitting any targets or by hitting other kinds of targets?[5]

One straightforward approach to war termination and the protection of the American people would be to completely destroy the adversary's nuclear force, that is, to win a grand military victory. This strategy might be easily executed if the adversary were India or China, but it may be impossible if the enemy is the USSR. Doing "as much as we can" against the USSR might still strike some observers as appropriate service of the mix of goals cited above; but is it really?

Discussions of the development of greater accuracies for ballistic and cruise missiles are understandably focused on their possible counterforce capabilities against land-based missile silos. "Ten kilotons on the roof does it every time," such that great reductions in missile CEPs might make it very attractive for the United States (or the USSR) to initiate a counterforce exchange between North Dakota and Siberia in some future crisis.

Yet such a straightforward counterforce use of accurate missiles swings in and out in appropriateness as we shift the time period in our matrix of policy goals. It is well understood now that such targeting, and the deployment of weapons capable of it, may be inappropriate in the prewar period since, by making the other side nervous about any U.S. preemptive intentions, the United States might increase the likelihood of war. Such targeting becomes appropriate and valuable once such a war has begun, if the two sides are indeed locked in a spasm struggle of doing as much damage as possible to each other. One could reduce the damage suffered by one's own population by keeping the other side from reloading missile launchers to fire another round, and so forth. But counterforce targeting could become inappropriate again, even after a war has broken out, if the two sides were doing less than the maximum damage to each other, if some intrawar deterrence were thus being maintained, and if each side were holding a fair amount of its nuclear destructive capability in reserve. To threaten the survivability of this reserve would be to push it into use.

Instead of eliminating the enemy's ability to wage nuclear war, a different approach thus would make it in the adversary's interest to stop shooting nuclear warheads, even if a day or week or month of nuclear war had already occurred. This strategy might entail the suspension of all hostilities, but is does not need to.[6] What needs further study is the possibility of deescalating from nuclear war to conventional war, as the conventional war continues in some parts of the world. What are the best and most meaningful ways of sending the signal that "we'll stop using nuclears if you'll stop," a "no-first-use from here on" kind of agreement? Simply stopping may not do the trick since the other side may assume that we are simply regrouping, or (worst of all) that we are out of nuclear warheads.

Discouraging the enemy from using nuclear warheads against valued American targets may thus indeed entail continuing to use nuclear warheads against the enemy, but in a very tailored way. Rather than aim at missile sites, thus creating a "use them or lose them" situation, the United States might aim to avoid enemy missile sites entirely, and also aim to avoid enemy cities, in hopes of providing more incentive to leave American cities alone.

If the damage to the civilian population could be contained (and this, as we shall discuss, is a very demanding assumption indeed), an interesting third alternative would be to aim at a genuine erosion of the Soviet basic industry, threatening the enemy's long-run military production prospects without threatening immediate strategic nuclear capability, avoiding the killing of many Soviet citizens until the enemy kills many American citizens.[7] Hopefully this strategy would convey a message that the Soviets had better hoard their missiles rather than use them, since (in the peace that is to come) Soviet assembly lines will not be able to produce any replacements for them. The United States, in short, would want to give the Soviet adversary some strategic as well as humane reasons to hold back nuclear attack.

REDUCING ADVERSARY ANTICIPATIONS OF COUNTERFORCE

But how do U.S. strategic planners develop greater missile accuracies, and the command and control that goes with them, without giving the other side the worrisome impression that its land-based missile force will be the first-priority target? As the United States acquires greater and greater precision for its nuclear warheads, it could dedicate more of them to specific industrial targets; but the same precision could impress the USSR as a threat to Soviet missile silos. Are there any ways in which the United States can deploy or configure or design or fire its missiles so that Moscow would have assurance that its missile force were not threatened? How much assurance does the United States have that Moscow itself is staying away from a launch-on-warning policy?

Part of the answer of course comes in changing the public discussion that, by the way, is largely shaped and formulated in the United States. The United States could, as a matter of government policy, cease showing concern about the prospect of a "clean" Soviet attack on Minuteman, as the winds of August do not constitute the typical pattern, and as U.S. fallout shelter programs are not reliable.

Besides ceasing to worry in public about a surgical Soviet attack on our missile forces, what else would show the Soviet Union that the United States does not propose to attack Soviet missile silos as long as the war is otherwise limited? The discussion of other targets could be brought into the open, in both public statements and the leaks in which the American system abounds. In assaying their new "multiple options," U.S. planners could (and very possibly should) avoid comparing the destruction of cities with the destruction of Soviet missile silos, stressing instead some additional options that are entirely off this spectrum.

A similar contribution to U.S. intrawar bargaining and management capability should be achievable by changes in the actual war plans. If one wished merely to destroy a dam on the Volga, for example, how could an ICBM be fired so that it was obvious from launch that the missile was not aimed at a missile complex? The paucity of numbers fired might be an important clue; a U.S. limited strategic attack against Soviet industry might be executed with small salvos fired one at a time (i.e., with no missiles in a second salvo fired until all of the first salvo had hit, thus letting the Soviet Union see what the United States was aiming at). An important theme throughout this argument will be that U.S. planners need to plan for, and think about, smaller salvos; any U.S. success at war termination and war moderation may depend upon this strategy, as the United States aims to make the best of things once World War III has begun.

Apart from the numbers, it must be possible to pick the angle of fire so that the trajectory would be maximally unlikely to be mistaken for an attack on the enemy's strategic forces. Thought should then be given to missile trajectories and to the elementary geographic facts of where Soviet missile silos are located, as compared to other targets the United States might want to be free to hit. One supposes that this calculation entails drawing a line on a map between the desired target and the missile concentrations and trying to fire from a point at a right angle to that line so that there could be no question of undershooting or overshooting.

COMPETITIVE COUNTERVALUE EXCHANGE

Applying disincentives to the outbreak of war almost always conflicts with maintaining disincentives to escalation after the war has begun. The United States scares the other side into remaining at peace by the prospects of uncontrolled escalation; but U.S. planners then must work hard, after peace has ended, to make sure that the predictions of escalation are not confirmed.

In the past the choices for U.S. nuclear targeting strategy have been reasonably portrayed along two axes—a continuum between counterforce and countervalue targeting, and another between as-rapidly-as possible rates of weapons fire and slower rates of fire. As suggested, the argument here is that counterforce and countervalue targets must be broken down more finely. If a nuclear war begins, some kinds of value targets should be hit and some should not. Some kinds of force targets should be hit, and some should not. (In particular, if the other side's nuclear forces have not yet been fired at U.S. cities but are being held in reserve, holding the U.S. population as an as-yet-unharmed hostage, the United States may well be better off not attacking these forces.)

The issue of timing similarly may have to be redefined and reexamined. Especially where the United States is inflicting damage on value targets, the crucial comparison may be between the speed at which U.S. forces are doing damage and the adversary's sense of the length of time accumulating before any return to normalcy is possible. If the United States makes return to normalcy seem too far off, it may instill in the adversary leadership a "what difference does it all make" mentality, which could lead the Soviets to fire their missiles with the intent of doing as much damage as possible to what the United States values, a result to be avoided. If the relationship of ongoing rate of damage to likely rate of recovery is not overwhelming, however, war termination (or at least war deescalation) may seem much more attractive to the other side.

Would the Japanese have surrendered as easily, and cooperated as fully, if all their cities, rather than just two, had been hit with A-bombs in August of 1945? Could it be that the limitations of U.S. capability actually helped in getting favorable war termination?

Imposing "unacceptable levels of damage" on the USSR is a widely cited benchmark for prewar deterrence because the United States wants to make the enemy's choice of war "unacceptable"; but does this benchmark remain appropriate if deterrence has failed and the United States is in the middle of a nuclear war?

Unacceptable damage during a nuclear war could all too well mean inhibition-removing damage. If U.S. planners remain interested in intrawar deterrence, concerned to give the USSR some incentive to hold back from hitting American cities, will the United States not have to hunt for some "as-yet-*not*-unacceptable" damage by which to improve its position, by which to torment and deter the Soviet national command authorities through visions of what a prolongation of the nuclear exchange could lead to? Thus, what U.S. planners need to create is some gradually accumulating damage to the USSR, the kind that would become unacceptable if it were prolonged but is not yet unacceptable as things stand.

One generally is not very persuasive by killing hostages but gets more by instead holding them under threat (to put it crudely, by torturing or at least tormenting them). The analog in nuclear war would thus be avoiding hitting the kinds of targets that are dead forever once hit (for example, people) and instead hitting the kinds of targets that bruise and hurt but that can recover somewhat and then be hit again.

An important difference in psychological impact between the conventional bombings of World War II and the thermonuclear attacks envisaged here is that the conventional bombings lent themselves to repeat attack, that is, the deed was not done all at once. The Allies had reason, therefore, to hope for surrender (i.e., for war termination), without having to destroy all of Germany or Japan in the process.

The essence of a limited use of nuclear weapons may thus be an old-fashioned contest of resolve, which sometimes is to be viewed as the game of "chicken" and sometimes as "tug-of-war." "Chicken" is slightly more apt as the analog of the political or military crisis; it is acted out prior to any use of nuclear weapons, with the threat of such use hanging over both sides if one side does not give up. The disaster both sides fear is not yet realized but draws inexorably closer if both sides remain obdurate. The Cuban Missile Crisis is an obvious example.

Somewhat different is the kind of crisis where each side is indeed already experiencing pain, where either would be better off immediately (not just hypothetically) surrendering, but would be much better off if the other side surrendered first. Vietnam is a good example, as is the prolongation of World War I after its outbreak.

The exchange of limited nuclear strikes may thus be somewhat more like the latter kind of "tug-of-war," or competition of resolve, rather than like the game of chicken. As with the trench war of 1917, or the bombings and firefights of Vietnam, the United States would be trying to show the other side in the exchanges of nuclear shots that it would be better off coming to terms and that the United States (which also would be better off) will not be the first to surrender.

In the game of chicken, nuclear war is often seen as all out, as the ultimate in destructiveness, which neither side wants to get into. If all-out nuclear war happens, if the autos collide in the teenage game of chicken, the contest of wills is over.

In the intrawar nuclear exchange planning we are discussing, however, nuclear war must not be allowed to become a total disaster. An adversary who has nothing left to lose is not going to surrender, is not going to moderate behavior, is not going to do anything except inflict the maximum possible revenge upon the United States.

Then how does one win the game of mutual torment, of mutual display of resolve? What one has to do, to repeat, is to find targets that can be hurt, but hurt in a way where the other side does not want them hurt more. Too little punishment will be ignored. Too much punishment ends the game, with the other side no longer interested in being persuaded of the needs for restraint or concession.

A first look at the contest might then conclude that the advantage will lie with the side that has the most painful instruments in reserve. If the Soviet Union has eight thousand warheads when the United States has only four thousand, the argument would go, the Soviet national command authorities will be able to call the United States's bluff more easily than the United States can call the Soviets'.

A longer contemplation of the problem might provide a different answer, however. Each side already may have much more destructive capability than it can use, particularly if we are talking only of countervalue operations. The contest then may not be one of stockpiling destructive instruments but of identifying enough painful and vulnerable targets on the other side. By analog, this might be illustrated by a feud between the Hatfields and the McCoys, where the issue was not who had the most shotguns but rather who had the most young children to be sniped at.

An exchange of nuclear retaliatory strikes will not be a contest to see who is vindicated in the history books as the toughest warrior or most astute bargainer. Rather it will be an effort at winning the best possible outcome for one's country. Great care will have to be exercised, therefore, in enunciating the retaliatory threats upon which the contest is based. If one side, for example, announces a policy of destroying two cities for each one the adversary attacks, the adversary may for reasons of preattack machismo feel driven to do the same, this still being the chicken phase of the contest, where each side is exploiting what is seen

[293]

as impending catastrophe. If both sides then feel locked into such declarations, however, they might try to go through with them if a war actually broke out, with decidedly escalatory results.

The tormenting of the Soviets by the limited use of nuclear weapons thus need not be (and should not be) to "hurt them more than they hurt us." Rather, it should be to hurt them more than they can accept, with the implication that such penalties will continue as long as they do not desist from this course. In ordinary criminal law we similarly do not punish with death someone who has caused a deadly traffic accident. More probably the person is punished with a severe fine or imprisonment, enough hopefully to make him desist from such criminal negligence in the future.

LIMITS OF THE SIGNIFICANCE OF SOVIET STRATEGIC THEORY

The Soviets thus far have little acknowledged, through their strategic pronouncements, any of the possibilities of limited strategic nuclear war or of intrawar deterrence.[8] This fact may seem discouraging when we wish to find alternatives to all-out use of nuclear weapons once a war has begun. At the same time, this fact might be encouraging in that it makes a little less likely and threatening the options and scenarios we can conceive for the possible Soviet initiation of a limited nuclear war.

The lack of a Soviet enunciated doctrine does not settle anything either way, of course, since capabilities that would be matched up with real doctrine could emerge, even if the real doctrine were never published. Some forms of initiation of a limited nuclear war that U.S. strategic planners should worry about are based on simple projections from growing Soviet capabilities, regardless of whether Russian propaganda pretends to see no prospects for limited strategic exchanges. Whatever the Soviet willingness or unwillingness to admit a contemplation of such scenarios, it would be reasonable for the United States to have considered the nature of its optimal response.

If U.S. strategic planners were contemplating initiating a nuclear war (i.e., being the first to escalate and to cross the conventional/nuclear threshold), Soviet unwillingness to help the West outline new firebreaks surely constitutes a handicap for the West. In the face of anything like a Soviet conventional invasion of Europe, this unwillingness generates an argument for using means other than nuclear escalation to bail the West out of its problems.

But what if nuclear war breaks out nonetheless, and has not yet gone to the all-out-spasm phase of maximum use of such weapons by each side? No matter what Soviet statements and pretenses have been in the past, the United States must choose to do what it finds appropriate for the moment, which presumably means reserving the possibility of limiting the exchange. To fire off a great number of warheads early on probably eliminates the possibility of mutual restraint; to hold back for a while longer leaves mutual restraint as a possibility.

How, indeed, could the Russians not have some philosophy of less-than-total nuclear war? In war no side ever bombs everything it can reach on the other side; this would be needless destruction of some of the prizes of the contest and a waste of ammunition. For a maximal military victory, Soviet effort aimed at crippling the U.S. strategic potential would have to be a carefully thought-out and executed attack.

The Soviets, in their public discussions of war, have been reluctant to admit the possibility of special kinds of restraint—in which each side holds back some of its destructive power simply because the other side is doing the same. At times the Soviets have pretended to believe that any war will escalate; more typically, they have claimed to be convinced that every nuclear war would quickly break through any pattern of mutual restraint.

Thus for the moment we have a minor paradox in that Americans can identify attractive limited-strategic-nuclear-war options for the Soviet Union to exploit with its new missile capabilities in the near future, while the Soviet Union persists in claiming that no such limited strategic wars are possible. This might seem to support the view that the Soviet Union indeed suffers from some blind spots in strategic analysis. Or it might suggest that the USSR does not feel itself yet so well endowed with politically usable strategic warfare hard-target options.

Is it possible that the Soviet Union does not understand the strategy of intrawar bargaining? The mere fact that the Soviets have acquiesced in conventional limited-war contests, with each side indeed continually restraining itself, shows that they surely understand the logic involved. Limited nuclear war is possible; for the Soviets to be unaware of this fact would mean that much of what they have done to date makes absolutely no sense.

Such limited nuclear war may indeed be likely (as opposed to certain) to escalate, at least unless important steps are taken to keep it under control; but this notion is something many Americans also believe. If one indeed accepted a high likelihood of escalation, one might conclude that all thought of intrawar bargaining, war termination, and limited nuclear options should be shelved, as we simply resign ourselves to the hope that the inevitable mess of a nuclear war will keep it from happening in the first place. Our assumption here, however, has been that such escalation is not yet unbearably likely, that there is a real opportunity cost if we pass up the chance to achieve a better outcome through alterations of the nuclear targeting plans.

TOWARD MORE RATIONAL FORMS OF ECONOMIC TARGETING

It is probably self-evident by now that the United States should not use its strategic nuclear forces, if World War III should break out, against any targets simply because "we had nothing better to do with them." Yet the pre-PD-59 emphasis on "attacking the Soviet economy" often had a flavor of this, as the United States planned to set back the Soviet economy "as much as possible," inflicting a great number of civilian casualties in the process, as collateral damage.[9]

Such a countereconomy formulation may in fact simply have amounted to a euphemism in place of an explicit endorsement of countervalue retaliatory policies. Attacking the enemy's economy is an assault on the enemy's capability rather than a punishment related to the enemy's intentions, and thus such an assault conforms more to the traditional morality of what is allegedly permissible in war. The argument here is that more serious consideration should be given to new forms of economic targeting, in the context of war limitation and war termination, after the nuclear threshold has been crossed.

If a countereconomy attack can be carried through without inflicting substantial casualties on the civilian population, this could indeed be a useful tormenting device for imposing the will of the U.S. National Command Authorities (NCA) on the Soviet leadership. Thought should thus be given to the forms of targeting that would impose high economic cost on the USSR without touching the civilian population, in effect listing economic targets in descending order of propinquity to population centers. A Soviet nuclear power plant might, for example, already be located remote from urban centers because of the inherent fears of accidents; thus it would be a perfect target to strike at in this regard.

The points raised earlier about a gradual (rather than all-at-once) attrition of industrial capacity will remain in effect, as one wants to maximize the motivational impact of potential damage rather than the damage itself. Closely linked to avoiding too much permanent damage to the USSR would be targeting intended to make the Soviet Union dependent on the outside world, perhaps on the United States itself, for some key bottleneck resource imports after a truce.[10] If war termination is the U.S. goal—on political terms desirable for the U.S., with a reasonable assurance that the war will not resume quickly—which would be better: a 50 percent destruction of the Soviet economy, with the prospect of recovery only after a long delay, or the surgical extraction of some input upon which 50 percent of the Soviet economy depends, an input that the United States could supply?

What is wanted ideally is a situation in which the USSR comes to need U.S. cooperation badly—cooperation in withholding further bombings, cooperation in delivering recovery supplies.

The kind of target that would lend itself to such a short-term disruptive attack might thus be a port through which the bulk of some import passed. Similarly, it might be some large oil-storage or oil-producing facility. Dams are often mentioned, but dams may take longer to rebuild than is optimal for these calculations.

The ability to rebuild is not inherently crucial here. The same effect could be achieved with permanent damage to one or two of what amount to a series, with the logical implication that the worst has not happened yet, but can happen if concessions are not made.

Hitting national parks or other cultural monuments remote from population centers is sometimes suggested. This strategy is analogous to the terrorist's technique, when holding an airliner full of passengers, of shooting just one passenger to show the government involved that the terrorist is serious.

If Soviet investments in civil defense were to come close to approximating what some Americans fear, the paradoxical result would make many such U.S. targeting tactics easier. Suppose that the Soviet Union indeed evacuated its cities during some crisis, allegedly as part of showing its resolve for a coming contest of will. Would not the empty cities make precisely the kind of economic targets the United States wants, allowing the United States, with relatively cleaner conscience and relatively greater confidence in intrawar bargaining, to destroy part of one city on one day, another part on the next, part of another city on the third day, and so on, until the Soviets elected to cease whatever the United States so strenuously objected to?

To extend our analogy with the temporary reduction of GNP, the most valuable deterrent with regard to the enemy's population may be difficult to extract from the weapons the United States has, namely to stun or incapacitate the Soviet people temporarily without killing them. This strategy conforms to that of the terrorist when he takes over an airplane full of people. It is what some forms of chemical warfare have sometimes promised in the past.

The United States is unlikely to get into strategic war planning for the use of delayed-action biological warfare, with it holding the leverage of necessary antidotes and immunizations as a bargaining chip. But the United States should aim for the logical equivalent in its use of nuclear weapons against Soviet industry and/or the fringes of Soviet urban areas.

[297]

If the United States must thus get close to inflicting damage on the Soviet population base, attention should be devoted to the kinds of attacks that would, instead of killing the urban masses, put the Soviet government on a "short leash" in regard to a longer-term threat to food, water, or medical care. The object would again be to put the Soviet leadership into the position of having everything to gain by coming to terms with the United States as soon as possible. "Everything to gain" means, of course, that the United States has avoided inflicting most of the permanent loss.

Much alarm has been generated in the U.S. strategic community about the possible resurgence of a Soviet civil defense effort.[11] But the opposite side of the coin needs to be explored more fully—namely, whether the development of such an effort, perhaps even with the evacuation of Soviet cities, might not actually offer the United States more effective intrawar deterrence and compellence options. The United States might feel more free to destroy Kiev if all the inhabitants had been evacuated. The United States might similarly find more ways to torment and inconvenience the Soviet people and regime because the evacuation put people into an inherently uncomfortable situation.

"Making normalcy more attractive" may thus have to be the goal, rather than making normalcy impossible to return to. The United States is hardly lacking in experience with this kind of logic. The only real difficulty is probably that such experience has all come at the non-nuclear level. The B-52 bombings of North Vietnam illustrate this strategy. The U.S. aim throughout was to torment rather than to kill—that is, to give Hanoi a continuing reason to come to terms. The North Vietnamese investment in civil defense made the U.S. task easier rather than harder, allowing the U.S. bombing to set back the economic development plans of the Communist regime without killing nearly as many civilians.

Indeed, bombing probably succeeded in producing a war termination in this case. What produced a new outbreak, as Hanoi conquered the South, was not any mismanagement of the strategic-bombing tool but the decisions of Congress, made in the shadow of Watergate, to circumscribe the authority of the executive branch to continue with or to resume such bombing attacks.

DEESCALATION AND NUCLEAR WAR TERMINATION

The normal view of nuclear war termination is that it is something we automatically wish to accomplish as quickly as possible, by victory or by negotiation, with other considerations decidedly secondary to this one. Yet the menu sketched at the outset of this chapter suggests some important alternative considerations, not the least being that we would want to discourage another outbreak of nuclear war in the near future.

What would be the impact of the first round of nuclear war on the likelihood of future rounds? The predictions here go in opposite directions, based on differing lines of argument. After witnessing the enormous and appalling destruction from this first use of nuclear weapons in anger since 1945, many of us might assume that all the nuclear weapons states would be much more adverse to such operations in the future. The real experience of seeing burnt flesh, and avoiding radioactive contamination, would replace the abstract calculations with which we typically now work.

But there are reasons for worry in the opposite direction. With the precedent of using nuclear weapons in combat, each side would have less tendency to assume that the other side would persist in a conventional warfare mode. It took a long time after Nagasaki for the idea to take hold that using nuclear weapons in warfare was beyond the pale. It would take quite a while once more, after terminating a nuclear war, for the same idea to become real again.

The process of limiting a war has always depended somewhat on the exploitation of track records of restraint. As Thomas Schelling has pointed out, to have not used poison gas at all since the outbreak of a war serves as a powerful signal that one will not use such gas today, or tomorrow either.[12] To have used it yesterday for the first time, however, makes such a nonuse signal much more difficult to send, for some precious time would now have to elapse as a new pattern of nonuse was again developed.

For the termination of a nuclear war, or for a termination or limitation of the use of nuclear weapons in such a war, it is likely that much more explicit forms of communication will be needed—messages sent in the clear by sentences, rather than by demonstrations in practice. The composition and formulation of such offers of new mutual restraint might thus be an important advance task since the time constraint when they need to be delivered can become urgent.

The burden of conveying such messages might of course be reduced somewhat if more advanced thought is given to the targets against which the United States will direct nuclear attacks, to endow them with some kind of self-limited and self-containing nature. If, for example, the United States is responding to a Soviet attack on one of its cities, it might well be tempted to retaliate against one Soviet city; but the city should be chosen so that the pairing of the two is fairly obvious, with the accompanying message being that the United States proposes to stop the nuclear exchange after the retaliation has been inflicted.

The casualties suffered in round one of a nuclear war, moreover, may not always discourage further warfare. Sometimes the cry for revenge and compensation drives people and governments to be even more war minded thereafter. From what we know of limited war at the conventional level (a considerably more slow-moving and less deadly affair), the tendency is for such wars to escalate over time, as lines of mutual restraint are deliberately or inadvertently erased in the fighting of the war, as the ongoing costs put the governments and masses on each side more in the mood to escalate, to get revenge, and to win compensation for early losses. Deescalations of limited wars, while not impossible to find, are rarer by comparison.

War termination in a conventional war can of course come by total victory, and it has come with total restoration of peace, as a cease fire or a peace treaty becomes accepted.

How easy would it be to deescalate a nuclear war to the conventional level? Would it be easier to move all the way down to an across-the-board peace, with no more firing for the moment of even conventional rounds? An important study might indeed be to sort out the historical examples that exist of such partial as compared to total deescalations, to see which pattern appears more promising.

Thus many reasons exist to expect that the process of deescalation from nuclear to non-nuclear war will be beset with difficulties. The exchange of nuclear attacks is itself likely to be a nerve-jarring experience, leaving both sides less equipped for the fine tuning that the imposition of a mutual restraint entails. At a certain point, the discussion of war termination and intrawar deterrence thus would have to shift from the "rational model" calculations of costs and gains and contingent options to the impact of nuclear escalation and nuclear barrages on the nerve endings and internal coherence of the decision-making systems involved. Will the national command authorities involved be so agitated by the awesome casualties of even a limited nuclear exchange that they will be incapable of watching for, and perceiving, evidence of restraint from the other side, or suggestions of deescalation and additional restraint?

One can attempt to "harden" the electronic communications and command facilities, but how does one "harden" the human beings involved? No matter how many advance exercises, briefings, and simulations are employed, the atmosphere after a first use of nuclear weapons in anger would be decidedly abnormal, with abnormal behavior thus to be predicated in response.

Of course this prediction amounts to a powerful argument against becoming involved in the fighting of a nuclear war in the first place, but that is not our subject here. As we contemplate how best to prepare for policy, should such a war happen, and how best to end it, a much more substantial preparation of decision makers for the basic atmosphere of a nuclear war might be a very wise investment. While it may be easy to have an advance discussion as we are having here, of the actual gains, costs, and choices that will be faced in such a war, the disorientation, depression, and general upset that will accompany the war are far more difficult to outline on paper.

Some of the U.S. decisions on nuclear targeting and war termination thus must depend on what can be predicted about discouraging repetitions of the war outbreak. There are many analogs in the termination of conventional wars, only some of which will be relevant to the nuclear case. Will peace persist longer if the United States behaves as a "generous winner," or if it shows some vindictiveness toward the end? Will generosity and restraint be seen as a sign of weakness, tempting the other side to go to the brink more often in the subsequent months and years of peace, or would they be accepted magnanimously, making peace more stable and secure?

The mix of impact and results has never been easy to sort out. Should the Prussians under Bismarck have pulled out of France more rapidly, or less rapidly, in 1871 if they wanted to head off French revanche? Should Israel have withdrawn immediately from the Sinai desert after defeating Egypt in 1967?

In the nuclear context, the tough questions will be whether to terminate the war, or at least the nuclear phase of the war, with as restrained a last round as possible, or whether to add a certain "spite" salvo to remind the other side that it should be grateful for the deescalation.

In all the years in which we have escaped the use of nuclear weapons in battle, the United States has manipulated the possibility of such use to achieve deterrence of conventional war as well. For countries like West Germany and South Korea, as well as for more secure areas like Japan and Britain, the implicit American message has been that any conventional Soviet attack might produce an escalation to nuclear war. The strategy may well have worked despite a continual debate in the United States about whether threats of Massive Retaliation are credible, and so forth.

If the United States was so unfortunate as to fight a round of nuclear war, and so fortunate as to terminate it after the first round, it would still not be indifferent to whether this "extended deterrence" of conventional aggressions by the other side had been enhanced, or eroded, or left the same.

Thus no shortage of paradox can be found in the sorting of choices that have to be made here. The United States will be striving to terminate a nuclear war as soon as possible after deterrence has failed. At the same time it will be striving to retain a deterrent for the postwar atmosphere (i.e., to behave during a short burst of nuclear war so as to support some of the bluff and image that will be needed for deterrence later).

To behave "rationally" while the war is going on may be more than a little inconsistent with the threats made in the original (unsuccessful) effort at deterring Soviet aggression. But such rational behavior may also occasionally be inconsistent with what is ideal for discouraging a resumption of war.

This paradox complicates all the more the targets the United States should look for. The United States needs to hit targets that encourage the other side to hold back the worst it can do, but also targets that encourage the other side to stop military aggression completely. Yet U.S. targeting must also be chosen to give an impression of still further devastation to come if the other side had not desisted in time. Nuclear wars, as we are fighting them, will thus be a blend of chicken and tug-of-war since we are concerned with both ending the war and setting useful precedents to discourage future wars.

The analog to this strategy may be some of the bloody offensives launched at the very end of the Korean War as negotiations for ending that conflict were virtually completed—offensives intended more to teach the opposite side a lesson about the future than to change the terms of the immediate peace. One should not be surprised, therefore, if a city on either side is destroyed gratuitously just as a nuclear armistice is agreed upon. Planners should give some thought in advance as to what the appropriate response to such action would be.

A FEW CONCLUSIONS

If one had to name a central deficiency of the current nuclear strategic targeting strategy, it would be that the rate of fire projected in advance for such wars would typically be too high for the optimal exploitation or salvaging of the scenarios we can anticipate. Even where the pretense is one of limited and carefully orchestrated war, the damage that will be done and the panic that will be instilled in the other side are greater than they should be. This excess is largely due to a combination of the philosophical attitudes sketched out above. We have been too much governed by an assumption that when deterrence fails, nothing else matters; we also too often conclude that, when war breaks out, considerations of winnowing down the enemy's capabilities must come ahead of affecting his intentions.

If one is going to be at all serious about the moderation and termination of a nuclear war, two interrelated conclusions seem plausible. The United States will have to fire its missiles at a slower rate, and (not at all incompatible with this) the United States will want to hold back a larger reserve of strategic forces as a back-up threat to guarantee Soviet behavior.

These conclusions bring us at last to the fundamental issues of what kinds of strategic forces to procure—the ultimate base from which war conduct and war outcome are always likely to flow. What kinds of capabilities and accuracies does the United States want to possess? What kinds might it instead be a dangerous embarrassment to possess simply because, in intrawar bargaining or war termination situations, they might push our adversary into the very behavior we wish to avoid? What kinds of capabilities, if they do not threaten to stampede the Soviets into bad behavior, still amount to a diversion from what the U.S. needs the most?

Improving the accuracy of U.S. missile warheads presumably lets U.S. planners hit more often what they are aiming at, and spare what they are trying to avoid hitting, which usually will be of advantage in an intrawar bargaining situation. One possible disadvantage has been mentioned numerous times—that such accuracy might pose the frightening threat of an effective American counterforce disarming strike. Such a threat would be diffused if the enemy were to deploy missiles in more secure environments, for example, on board submarines. The risk will also be reduced if the scale of carefully aimed nuclear attacks is kept low enough so that the Soviets could know that a disarming counterforce strike was not in prospect, and if the U.S. NCA otherwise signals that it is not its intention to put the Soviets into a ''use them or lose them'' situation.

A more serious disadvantage of acquiring higher accuracies would arise if it came at the budgetary price of delaying the enhancement of the survivability of our own land-based missiles, and their back-up systems, and their connected command, control, and communications system.

An elementary explanation for anticipating unreasonably high rates of U.S. missile fire may indeed be that U.S. missiles are simply not expected to have prolonged survivability as a reserve force after the outbreak of a war because incoming Soviet missile warheads can destroy them (or because the infrastructure upon which they depend for command and control, or simple ability to fire, would erode as a war rolled on, even if the missile silos were not struck directly). In short, the United States may itself be feeling too much in a ''use them or lose them'' situation; the United States may conclude that its land-based missiles must be fired early. Yet all the dictates of concern for possible war termination, and the maximization of American national interests after a nuclear war has broken out, argue that important categories of Soviet targets should be avoided, with the potential for their later destruction held in reserve.

If some U.S. strategic force strength thus inherently had to be of the variety that too early loses its punch, U.S. planners might then want to find targets for these warheads far away from those Soviet hostages whom they want to keep alive; or the planner might decide to dispense with the use of these missile warheads altogether, "losing them" instead of "using them."

Perhaps the most salient procurement recommendation that emerges is that more effort should be channeled toward increasing the fraction of the U.S. strategic nuclear forces that can survive for long periods of time as a strategic reserve force, without any significant degradation of command and control, without any urgency that early use is required if there is to be any use at all.

Current projects for the MX follow-on to the Minuteman force stress both the enhancement of missile survivability against Soviet counterforce attack and the enhancement of the accuracy of U.S. missiles against Soviet targets. The first is unquestionably desirable. The second, as noted, has some advantages in offering more target options, with the prospect of sparing the targets the United States does not wish to hit, but can also be disquieting to the Soviets for the counterforce capability it may seem to give the United States.

Leaving aside for the moment the argument that U.S. missile accuracy could be undesirable in its own right, clearly some tradeoffs could be made; the same money could be spent either for greater survivability or for great accuracy in U.S. missile systems but not for both. The thrust of the argument is that more such input should be channeled, when such choices arise, toward force survivability.

If a nuclear war is to be terminated, it would have to be limited in some meaningful sense while it is fought. If it is to be limited or terminated, greater accuracies in missile and bomber delivery systems would assuredly be of some value, but even more important would be greater prior deliberation on U.S. targeting and hostage taking.

Much could have been done in this regard, and still can be done, even without the substantial increases in accuracy. If the improvements in accuracy of the MX had to be abandoned because the system posed too much of a threat to Soviet missile silo survivability (or because the U.S. need to make its own forces more survivable dictated a submarine or airborne basing mode that degraded U.S. missile accuracy), the United States might still be able to develop a limited targeting policy consistent with the prospect of termination of a nuclear war after it has started. Even with CEPs of a half mile or more, there would be ways to punish the USSR while maintaining an active Soviet interest in terminating the punishment.

Advocates of "winning" a nuclear war have placed great stress on the need for imaginative thinking in contemplating the target base of the Soviet Union. Advocates of terminating such a war should be encouraged to join in this exercise with similar imagination and zest. Preventing the outbreak of such a war in the first place still commands the highest priority, but preventing its continuation into a second day or a second week might also merit a peace prize or two.

Contributors

Desmond Ball is head of the Strategic and Defence Studies Centre at the Australian National University, Canberra. He has been a research fellow at the Center for International Affairs at Harvard University and a research associate at the International Institute for Strategic Studies in London. He was a consultant to the Rand Corporation from March 1981 to January 1982. The author of some eighty academic monographs and articles on nuclear strategy, nuclear weapons, national security decision-making, and Australia's defense policy, his most recent books are *Politics and Force Levels: The Strategic Missile Program of the Kennedy Administration* (University of California Press, Berkeley, 1980) and *A Suitable Piece of Real Estate: American Installations in Australia* (Hale & Iremonger, Sydney, 1980). He is editor of *Strategy and Defence: Australian Essays* (George Allen & Unwin, Sydney, 1982). His monographs include *Deja Vu: The Return to Counterforce in the Nixon Administration* (California Seminar on Arms Control and Foreign Policy, Santa Monica, Calif., December 1974); *Can Nuclear War Be Controlled?* (Adelphi Paper No. 169, International Institute for Strategic Studies, London, Autumn 1981); and *Targeting for Strategic Deterrence* (Adelphi Paper No. 185, International Institute for Strategic Studies, London, Summer 1983).

David T. Cattell is professor of political science at the University of California, Los Angeles (UCLA). He is author of *Leningrad: A Case Study of Soviet Urban Government* (Praeger, New York, 1968) and coauthor with Richard Sisson of *Comparative Politics: Institutions, Behavior, and Development* (Mayfield Publishing, Palo Alto, Calif., 1978).

Lawrence Freedman is professor and head of the Department of War Studies at King's College London, University of London. Born in

Tynemouth, England, in 1948, he was educated at the Whitley Bay Grammar School and at the universities of Manchester, York, and Oxford. He then held research positions at Nuffield College, Oxford, and at the International Institute for Strategic Studies before becoming head of policy studies at the Royal Institute of International Affairs. He was appointed to the chair of war studies in April 1982. In addition to many articles on defense and foreign policy, Lawrence Freedman is author of *U.S. Intelligence and the Soviet Strategic Threat* (Macmillan, London, 1977); *Britain and Nuclear Weapons* (Macmillan, London, 1980); and *The Evolution of Nuclear Strategy* (St. Martin's Press, New York, 1981). He is also editor of *The Troubled Alliance: Atlantic Relations in the 1980s* (St. Martin's Press, New York, 1983).

Colin S. Gray is president of the National Institute for Public Policy, Washington, D.C. He has previously been assistant director of the International Institute for Strategic Studies in London and the director of national security studies at the Hudson Institute in New York. He is the author of numerous publications, including *The Soviet-American Arms Race* (Saxon House, Westmead, Farnborough, 1976); *The Geopolitics of the Nuclear Era: Heartland, Rimlands, and the Technological Revolution* (Crane, Russak & Company, New York, 1977); *The Future of Land-Based Missile Forces* (Adelphi Paper No. 140, International Institute for Strategic Studies, London, Winter 1977); *Strategy and the MX* (Heritage Foundation, Washington, D.C. 1980); *The MX ICBM and National Security* (Praeger, New York, 1981); *Strategic Studies and Public Policy: The American Experience* (University Press of Kentucky, Lexington, 1982); and *The American Military Space Policy: Information Systems, Weapon Systems, and Arms Control* (Abt Books, Cambridge, Mass., 1982).

Michael Kennedy received his Ph.D. in Economics from Harvard University in 1974 and subsequently taught in the Department of Economics at the University of Texas. Currently, he is with the Economics Department of the RAND Corporation, where he is working on national security issues, particularly strategic defense.

William T. Lee is an employee of the Defense Intelligence Agency. From 1972 to 1981 he was a consultant on Soviet military and economic matters. He was an employee of the Stanford Research Institute from 1964 to 1972 and of the Central Intelligence Agency from 1951 to 1964. He has published numerous articles and studies on Soviet military affairs and is the author of *The Estimation of Soviet Defense Expenditures, 1955–75* (Praeger, New York, 1977).

Kevin N. Lewis is a member of the Washington office staff of the Rand Corporation, specializing in areas relating to defense policy and budget planning. He has also been an instructor at the Johns Hopkins University School of Advanced International Studies. In addition to writing a number of Rand reports, he has published articles in *Scientific American, Survival, U.S. Naval Institute Proceedings,* and *Orbis,* among others. A book by Lewis, entitled *Planning America's Nuclear Forces, 1945–1980,* is forthcoming.

Frederic S. Nyland is currently a program engineering manager in the Operations Analysis Department of the Space and Electronics Systems Division, Martin Marietta Aerospace, Denver, Colo. He is involved in a variety of projects, including analyses of the survivability and utility of space-based lasers, the use of ELF communications with strategic submarines, and the use of space systems in support of strategic nuclear forces. Nyland was an analyst at the Rand Corporation from 1960 to 1981, during which time he wrote more than one hundred reports, papers, and working notes, including *Estimating Bomber Penetration and Weapons Effectiveness* (December 1973); *Earth-Penetrating Weapons for Attacking Hard Targets* (December 1974); *Standoff Air Attacks against Ships* (October 1979); *Shooting at Satellites in Synchronous Orbit and Beyond* (April 1981); *Problems and Prospects for Battle Management: The Empty Silo Problem* (September 1970); *Aspects of the HARDSITE Defense of Minuteman* (December 1971); *On the Utility of Information in Missile Duels* (August 1969); and *Some Operational Considerations of an Orbiting Space Station* (December 1964).

George H. Quester is chairman of the Department of Government and Politics at the University of Maryland, where he teaches courses in international politics and defense policy. Prior to coming to the University of Maryland, he taught at Cornell University, Harvard University, UCLA, and the National War College. He is author of *The Politics of Nuclear Proliferation* (Johns Hopkins University Press, Baltimore, 1973); *Offense and Defense in the International System* (Wiley, New York, 1977); *Deterrence before Hiroshima: The Airpower Background of Modern Strategy* (Wiley, New York, 1966); and *Nuclear Diplomacy: The First Twenty-Five Years* (Dunellen, New York, 1970).

Bennett Ramberg is a research fellow at the Center for International and Strategic Affairs, University of California, Los Angeles. He was earlier a research fellow at Stanford University's Arms Control Program and Princeton University's Center of International Studies. Ramberg's publications include *Global Nuclear Energy Risks: The Search for Preventive Med-*

icine (Westview, Boulder, Colo., 1985); *Nuclear Power Plants as Weapons for the Enemy: An Unrecognized Military Peril* (University of California Press, Berkeley, 1984); *Globalism vs Realism: International Relations' Third Debate* co-edited with Ray Maghroori (Westview, Boulder, Colo., 1982); *Destruction of Nuclear Energy Facilities in War: The Problem and the Implications* (Lexington Books, Lexington, Mass., 1980); and *The Seabed Arms Control Negotiations: A Study of Multilateral Arms Control Conference Diplomacy* (University of Denver, 1978).

Jeffrey Richelson is a professor in the School of Government and Public Administration at the American University, Washington, D.C. He has previously been a research associate at the Center for International and Strategic Affairs, University of California, Los Angeles, and a strategic analyst at Analytical Assessments Corporation, Marina del Rey, California. He is the author of numerous books and articles on nuclear targeting policy, Soviet decision making, intelligence operations, and social choice theory. His articles include "PD-59, NSDD-13, and the Reagan Strategic Modernization Program," *Journal of Strategic Studies*, June 1983, and "The Keyhole Satellite Program," *Journal of Strategic Studies*, June 1984. He is also author of *The U.S. Intelligence Community* (Ballinger, Cambridge, Mass., 1985) and *Sword and Shield: The Soviet Intelligence Apparatus* (Ballinger, Cambridge, Mass., 1985).

David Alan Rosenberg wrote chapter 2 while assistant professor of history at the University of Houston in 1982–83. He is currently a senior fellow at the Strategic Concepts Development Center of National Defense University, Washington, D.C. He was born in New York in 1948 and was educated at the American University, Washington, D.C., and the University of Chicago. He has taught at the University of Wisconsin—Milwaukee, written a history of navy long-range planning for the Office of the Secretary of the Navy, and completed a history of the U.S. navy's early strategic nuclear plans and policy for the deputy chief of naval operations (plans, policy, and operations). His publications include articles in *International Security, Journal of American History, Bulletin of the Atomic Scientists, Naval War College Review, Pacific Historical Review*, and *Reviews in American History*; and chapters in *Airpower and Warfare* (1978) and *The Chiefs of Naval Operations* (1980). He is currently completing a history of U.S. plans, policies, and capabilities for nuclear war from 1945 through the 1960s and a biography of Adm. Arleigh A. Burke. He is a naval reserve officer and a member of the International Institute for Strategic Studies.

David S. Yost is an associate professor at the U.S. Naval Postgraduate

School, Monterey, California. His publications on international security affairs have appeared in *Survival*, *Orbis*, *World Politics*, *International Security*, *Armed Forces and Society*, *Current History*, *The World Today*, *Comparative Strategy*, *Europa-Archiv*, *Défense Nationale*, and *Strategic Review*, among other journals in the United States, Britain, France, and West Germany. He is author of *European Security* and the *SALT Process* (Washington Paper No. 85, Sage Publications, Beverly Hills, 1981) and of *France's Deterrent Posture and Security in Europe*, Adelphi Papers nos. 194 and 195 (International Institute for Strategic Studies, London). He is also editor of *NATO's Strategic Options: Arms Control and Defense* (Pergamon Press, New York, 1981). He was a National Endowment for the Humanities/International Affairs Fellow of the Council on Foreign Relations and a NATO Research Fellow during the 1984–85 academic year. He will be a fellow in international security studies at the Woodrow Wilson International Center for Scholars, Smithsonian Institution, in 1986.

Notes

1. Toward a Critique of Strategic Nuclear Targeting

1. Harold Brown, *Department of Defense Annual Report Fiscal Year 1980* (Washington, D.C., 1979), p. 78.

2. For a fuller discussion of the relationship between these three elements of U.S. strategic nuclear policy, see Desmond Ball, *Developments in U.S. Strategic Nuclear Policy under the Carter Administration* (ACIS Working Paper No. 21, Center for International and Strategic Affairs, University of California, Los Angeles, February 1980).

3. See John Edwards, *Super Weapon: The Making of MX* (W. W. Norton, New York, 1982), pp. 67–68. See also Fred Kaplan, *The Wizards of Armageddon* (Simon & Schuster, New York, 1983), pp. 370–371.

4. James R. Schlesinger, "Uses and Abuses of Analysis," in Senate Committee on Government Operations, *Planning, Programming, Budgeting* (Washington, D.C., 1970), p. 133.

5. Ibid.

6. For a more comprehensive critique of the possibility of controlling the escalation process, see Desmond Ball, *Can Nuclear War Be Controlled?* (Adelphi Paper No. 169, International Institute for Strategic Studies, London, Autumn 1981).

7. See Desmond Ball, "Soviet Strategic Planning and the Control of Nuclear War," *Soviet Union/Union Soviétique* 10, pts. 2–3 (1983), especially pp. 203–204.

8. Desmond Ball, "Soviet ICBM Deployment," *Survival* 22, no. 4 (July-August 1980), 167–170.

9. Director of Central Intelligence, *Soviet Civil Defense* (Central Intelligence Agency, NI 78–100003, July 1978), p. 8; and Harold Brown, *Department of Defense Annual Report Fiscal Year 1981* (Washington, D.C., 1980), p. 78.

10. Ibid.

11. General Brown to Senator William Proxmire, 3 February 1977, reprinted in *Survival* 19, no. 2 (March/April 1977), 77; and *Aviation Week & Space Technology*, 7 February 1977, p. 16.

12. Cited in Edgar Ulsamer, "The USSR's Military Shadow Is Lengthening," *Air Force Magazine*, March 1977, p. 42.

13. U.S. Arms Control and Disarmament Agency (ACDA), *Effectiveness of Soviet Civil Defense in Limiting Damage to Population* (ACDA Civil Defense Study Report No. 1, ACDA, Washington, D.C., 16 November 1977), p. 20.

14. Colin S. Gray, "Soviet Strategic Vulnerabilities," *Air Force Magazine*, March 1979, p. 64.

15. Anthony H. Cordesman, *Deterrence in the 1980s: Part 1—American Strategic Forces and Extended Deterrence* (Adelphi Paper No. 175, International Institute for Strategic Studies, London, Summer 1982), p. 41.

16. Leon Sloss, draft notes, no date, p. A-3.

17. Henry S. Rowen, "The Evolution of Strategic Nuclear Doctrine," in Lawrence Martin, ed., *Strategic Thought in the Nuclear Age* (Heinemann, London, 1979), p. 137.

18. *Statement of Secretary of Defense Robert S. McNamara before the House Armed Services Committee on the Fiscal Year 1966–70 Defense Program & 1966 Defense Budget*, 18 February 1965, mimeo, p. 39.

19. See Russell T. Nichols, *"Two Theories of Bombing"* (Rand Corporation, Santa Monica, Calif., unpublished note, 6 July 1949).

20. U.S. House Armed Services Committee, *Hearings on Military Posture and H.R. 6722* (Washington, D.C., 1973), p. 499.

21. Cited in Joint Committee on Defense Production, *Civil Preparedness Review, Part II: Industrial Defense and Nuclear Attack* (Washington, D.C., 1977), p. 8.

22. Harold Brown, *Department of Defense Annual Report Fiscal Year 1979* (Washington, D.C., 1978), p. 55.

23. Brown, *Department of Defense Annual Report Fiscal Year 1980*, p. 77.

24. U.S. Arms Control and Disarmament Agency (ACDA), *The Effects of Nuclear War* (ACDA, Washington, D.C., April 1979), pp. 16–17.

25. U.S. Congress, Office of Technology Assessment, *The Effects of Nuclear War* (Croom Helm, London, 1980), pp. 100–101.

26. Bernard Brodie, *Strategy in the Missile Age* (Princeton University Press, Princeton, 1965), p. 136.

27. Brown, *Department of Defense Annual Report Fiscal Year 1981*, p. 140.

28. House Appropriations Committee, *Department of Defense Appropriations for 1980* (Washington, D.C., 1979), pt. 3, p. 105.

29. House Appropriations Committee, *Department of Defense Appropriations for 1977* (Washington, D.C., 1976), pt. 1, p. 152.

30. See Robert L. Gallucci, *Neither Peace nor Honor: The Politics of American Military Policy in Vietnam* (Johns Hopkins University Press, Baltimore, Md., 1975), chap. 4.

31. Robert Jervis, *The Logic of Images in International Relations* (Princeton University Press, Princeton, 1970), p. 216.

32. Caspar W. Weinberger, *The Potential Effects of Nuclear War on the Climate: A Report to the United States Congress* (Washington, D.C., 1985), p. 2.

2. *U.S. Nuclear War Planning, 1945–1960*

An earlier version of this chapter was presented at the session "Nuclear Targeting and Strategic Policy" at the 78th Annual Meeting of the American Political Science Association, Denver, Colorado, 2–5 September 1982. It presents in abbreviated form the findings of a study, "The Origins of Overkill, Nuclear Weapons, and American Strategy, 1945–1960," presented at the U.S. Military Academy History Symposium on the Theory and Practice of American National Security, 1945–1960, which took place 17–18 April 1982, and published both in the proceedings of that conference, edited by Norman Graebner, and in *International Security* 7 (Spring 1983).

1. Eisenhower's decision is described in two documents: Andrew Goodpaster, Memorandum of Conference with the President (hereafter cited as MCP), 11 August 1960, dated 13 August 1960, in Staff Notes, August 1960– ,folder 3, box 51, DDE Diary, Ann C. Whitman file, Dwight D. Eisenhower Papers as President (hereafter cited as ACWF, EPP), Dwight D. Eisenhower Library, Abilene, Kansas (hereafter cited as DDEL); and Adm. Arleigh Burke, rough draft Memorandum for the Record, Subject: Meeting with the President on SecDef's Proposal to turn Targetting and the Preparation of Single Integrated Operational Plan over to SAC, 11 August 1960, in NSTL/SIOP Briefing folder, Adm. Arleigh A. Burke

Papers (hereafter cited as AAB), Operational Archives, Naval Historical Center, Washington, D.C. (hereafter cited as NHC).

2. Portions of the NSTAP are quoted or described in Message, CNO to CINCLANTFLT, CINCUSNAVEUR, R201933Z November 1960, NSTL/SIOP Messages, Exclusives and Personals, AAB, NHC; Memorandum, Op-06C to Op-00, Subject: CNO Discussions regarding NSTL/SIOP with Generals Lemnitzer, Decker, and Spivy on 9 Nov., with Enclosure Precis re Army participation in the NSTL/SIOP dated 1 November 1960, BM00211-60, 8 November 1960; Special Edition, Flag Officers Dope, 4 December 1960; and Memo for the Record, October 1960, all in Memorandums and Letters (NSTL) folder, AAB, NHC. History and Research Division, Headquarters, Strategic Air Command, *History of the Joint Strategic Target Planning Staff: Background and Preparation of SIOP-62* (partially declassified history released by the declassification branch, Joint Secretariat, Joint Chief of Staff, in April 1980), p. 14. Seventy-nine airmen and civilians were among the 219 SAC personnel assigned to JSTPS.

3. This information is derived from material contained in Special Edition, Flag Officers Dope, 4 December 1960; Memorandum, Rear Adm. C. V. Ricketts (Op-60) to Op-00, Op-60 BM-0001028-60, Subject: JCS 2056/189, The Initial NSTL & SIOP, 22 November 1960; Memorandum, Arleigh Burke for General Lemnitzer, Op-00 Memo 00683-60, Subject: NSTL/SIOP, 22 November 1960; Memo, Rear Adm. Paul Blackburn, Op-60C, to Op-00, BM-000222-60, Subject: Message Traffic between CINCs and CNO, comments concerning, with Enclosures 1 and 2 summarizing messages; Resume of NSTL-SIOP Briefing, Offutt AFB, 28 September 1960, attached to Op-60C to Op-00, BM-000167-60, 29 September; and Joint Strategic Target Planning Agency, Memorandum for the Record, Subject: Minutes of 1st Meeting of the Policy Committee, B-76824, 14 September 1960, all in Memorandums and Letters (NSTL) folder, AAB, NHC; and Message, to RBEP with JCS, Report of Preliminary Review of SIOP-62, 182250Z November 1960; Cable, Brig. Gen. J. A. Spivy, USA, JCS Liaison Group Offutt, to JCS for director, Joint Staff, Subject: 11th Weekly Activity Report—14th Meeting of Policy Committee, 15–16, 19 November 1960; Message, CNO to CINCPACFLT, CINCLANTFLT, CINCUSNAVEUR, 0051/06 November 1960; and Message, CINCLANT to CNO, from Vice Adm. Fitzhugh Lee for Rear Admiral Blackburn, Subject: JSTPS Progress, 2031Z/22 October 1960, all in NSTL/SIOP Messages folder, AAB, NHC. Covering nuclear delivery capability and government and military control centers were 599 DGZs; 151 covered the urban-industrial base. This comprised the Minimum NSTL. There were also 227 defensive DGZs, and 65 "other" DGZs for a total NSTL of 1,042. Cable, Spivy to JCS, 19 November 1960.

4. This command structure is discussed in greater detail in Frank G. Klotz, "The U.S. President and the Control of Strategic Nuclear Weapons" (D. Phil. diss., Oxford University, 1980). Earlier, more general accounts include Ernest R. May, ed., *The Ultimate Decision: The President as Commander in Chief* (George Brazilier, New York, 1960); Richard F. Haynes, *The Awesome Power: Harry S. Truman as Commander in Chief* (Louisiana State University Press, Baton Rouge, 1973); and Douglas Kinnard, *President Eisenhower and Strategy Management: A Study in Defense Politics* (University Press of Kentucky, Lexington, 1977). On the role of the secretary of defense, the best recent study is Douglas Kinnard, *The Secretary of Defense* (University Press of Kentucky, Lexington, 1980).

5. The basic structure of U.S. war planning is described in Robert D. Little, *Organizing for Strategic Planning: The National System and the Air Force* (USAF Historical Division Liaison Office, Washington, D.C., 1964; declassified with deletions, 1975); George F. Lemmer, *The Air Force and the Concept of Deterrence, 1945–1950* (USAF Historical Division Liaison Office, Washington, D.C., 1963; declassified with deletions, 1975); idem, *The Air Force and Strategic Deterrence, 1951–1960* (Office of Air Force History, Washington, D.C., 1967; declassified with deletions, 1980); and James F. Schnabel, Kenneth W. Condit, and Walter S. Poole, *The History of the Joint Chiefs of Staff: The Joint Chiefs of Staff and National Policy,* vol. 1: *1945–1947,* vol. 2: *1947–1949,* vol. 4: *1950–1952* (Michael Glazier, Wilmington, Del.,

1979, 1980). The JSCP/JSOP structure is mandated in JCS Policy Memo 84, Joint Program for Planning, 14 July 1952, and its revisions of 27 July 1955 and 8 April 1960, in CCS 381 (11-29-49) Secs. 3 and 24, and CCS 3100, Plans (13 April 1959) respectively, all in Record Group 218, Papers of the United States Joint Chiefs of Staff, Modern Military Branch, U.S. National Archives (hereafter cited as JCS).

6. The work of strategic theorists is best described in Bernard Brodie, *The American Scientific Strategists* (Rand Corporation, Santa Monica, Calif., Paper P 2979, October 1964); idem, *War and Politics* (Macmillan, New York, 1973), especially chap. 10; Colin Gray, *Strategic Studies and Public Policy: The American Experience* (University Press of Kentucky, Lexington, 1982); and Bruce L. R. Smith, *The Rand Corporation: Case Study of a Non Profit Advisory Corporation* (Harvard University Press, Cambridge, 1966).

7. The best studies of this process are Lawrence Freedman, *U.S. Intelligence and the Soviet Strategic Threat* (Westview Press, Boulder, Colo., 1977); and John Prados, *The Soviet Estimate: U.S. Intelligence Analysis and Russian Military Strength* (Dial Press, New York, 1982).

8. David Alan Rosenberg, "U.S. Nuclear Stockpile, 1945 to 1950," *Bulletin of the Atomic Scientists* 38 (May 1982), 25–30; idem, "American Atomic Strategy and the Hydrogen Bomb Decision," *Journal of American History* 66 (June 1979), 62–87.

9. Rosenberg, "U.S. Nuclear Stockpile," 26–29.

10. The texts and circumstances surrounding the issuance of NSC-30 and NSC-20/4 are documented in U.S. Department of State, *Foreign Relations of the United States* (hereafter cited as *FRUS*), *1948*, vol. 1, *General: The United Nations* (Washington, D.C., 1976), pp. 589–669.

11. Rosenberg, "U.S. Nuclear Stockpile," pp. 26–29; idem, "American Atomic Strategy," pp. 68–75; Harry Borowski, *A Hollow Threat: Containment and Strategic Air Force Power before Korea* (Greenwood Press, Westport, Conn., 1982), pp. 162–184.

12. Notes for discussion with General Vandenberg, 4 November 1948, Diary folder, box B–64, Curtis LeMay Papers, Manuscript Division, Library of Congress (hereafter cited as LC); Briefing on Exercise "Dualism" conducted by Col. John A. Armstrong, 9 December 1948, A/AE (1948) 354.2 Exercise Dualism, Record Group 341, Papers of the Chief of Staff of the United States Air Force, Modern Military Branch, National Archives (hereafter cited as CSAF).

13. Rosenberg, "U.S. Nuclear Stockpile," pp. 27–30; JCS 1952/8, 25 August 1949, CCS 373 (10-23-48) Sec. 5, JCS; Prados, *Soviet Estimate*, pp. 24–30; Alfred Goldberg, ed., *History of Headquarters, USAF, 1 July 1950 to 30 June 1951* (Department of the Air Force, Washington, D.C., 1955), p. 7; James M. Erdman, "The Wringer in Postwar Germany: Its Impact on United States–German Relations and Defense Policies," in Clifford L. Egan and Alexander W. Knott, eds., *Essays in Twentieth Century Diplomatic History Dedicated to Professor Daniel M. Smith* (University Press of America, Washington, D.C., 1982), pp. 159–191.

14. Rosenberg, "American Atomic Strategy," pp. 64–71; Air Plan for MAKEFAST, 10 October 1946, PO 381 (10 September 1946), CSAF; Robert Frank Futrell, *Ideas, Concepts, Doctrine: A History of Basic Thinking in the U.S. Air Force, 1907–1964*, 2 vols. (Aerospace Studies Institute, Maxwell Air Force Base, Ala., 1971), 1: 218; JCS 1952/1, 21 December 1948, CCS 373 (10-23-48) Sec. 1, JCS.

15. JCS 2056/7, 12 August 1950, with Decision, 15 August 1950, CCS 373.11 (12-14-48) Sec. 2, JCS.

16. Entry, General LeMay's Diary, 23 January 1951, Diary 3, 1951 folder, box B-64, Curtis E. LeMay Papers, LC.

17. Ibid; Walter S. Poole, History of JCS, 4: 165–167; JCSA 2056/47, 13 May 1953, with Decision, 27 May 1953, CCS 373.11 (12-14-48) Sec. 11, JCS.

18. Nuclear production increases are described in Richard G. Hewlett and Francis Duncan, *History of the United States Atomic Energy Commission*, vol. 2, *Atomic Shield, 1947–1952*

(Pennsylvania State University Press, University Park, Pa., 1969), pp. 181–184, 362–375, 521–532, 547–568. Stockpile size is estimated in David Alan Rosenberg, "A Smoking, Radiating Ruin at the End of Two Hours: Documents of American Plans for Nuclear War with the Soviet Union, 1954–1955," *International Security* 6 (Winter 1981/82), 3–38; William M. Arkin, Thomas B. Cochran, and Milton M. Hoenig, "The U.S. Nuclear Stockpile," *Arms Control Today* 12 (April 1982), 1–2; and is estimated for 1952–54 in Memorandum, 2 November 1951, with page with figures labeled "Atomic Conf. Finletter's Office 11/2/51," Diary Notes folder, Dan A. Kimball Papers, box 2, Harry S. Truman Library.

19. Information on nuclear weapons design is drawn from the following sources: Rosenberg, "U.S. Nuclear Stockpile," pp. 27–28; Office of Public Affairs, U.S. Department of Energy, Nevada Operations Office, *Announced United States Nuclear Tests, July 1945 through December 1981*, NVO–209 (Rev. 2) January 1982; JCS 1823/8, 6 November 1948; JCS 1823/11, 20 December 1948; and JCS 1823/35, 30 November 1950, all in CCS 471.6 (8-15-45) Secs. 12 and 20, JCS (declassified, with deletions, December 1976 and August 1980); Lee Bowen, *History of the Air Force Atomic Energy Program*, vol. 4, *The Development of Weapons* (USAF Historical Division History, Washington, D.C., 1955; declassified, with deletions, June 1981), 1–143; Table appended to letter, Robert H., Duff, Office of Classification, U.S. Department of Energy, to David A. Rosenberg, 4 December 1980; Herbert York, *The Advisors: Oppenheimer, Teller, and the Superbomb* (W. H. Freeman, San Francisco, 1976); Affidavit, Dimitri A. Rotow, 3 May 1979, in *United States of America vs. The Progressive, Inc.* (copy courtesy of Aaron Meyers, Esq.); and Charles Hansen, "U.S. Nuclear Bombs," *Replica in Scale* 3 (January 1976), 154–159.

20. Bowen, *Air Force Atomic Energy*, 4: 174–233; JCS 1823/35; York, *Advisors*, 82–87. Yield possibilities in boosted weapons are discussed in David Holloway, "Research Note: Soviet Thermonuclear Development," *International Security* 4 (Winter 1979/80), 192–197; and in JCS 1823/34, 1 November 1950, CCS 471.6 (8-15-47) Sec. 20, JCS.

21. Memorandum for the President, 17 January 1952, summarizing meeting of NSC Special Committee on Atomic Energy with the president, 16 January 1952, Expansion of the Fissionable Material folder, NSC-Atomic file, president's secretary's file, Harry S Truman Papers, Harry S Truman Library, Independence, Missouri (hereafter cited as PSF, HSTL). The bootstrapping dynamic was described in author's interview with John P. Coyle, veteran navy operations analyst, Washington, D.C., 29 March 1978.

22. JCS 1800/164, 6 September 1951, CCS 370 (8-19-45) Sec. 34, JCS.

23. Poole, *History of JCS*, 4: 79–131.

24. Ibid., pp. 175–177; JCS Policy Memorandum 84, 14 July 1952.

25. NSC-68, "United States Objectives and Programs for National Security," 14 April 1950, Department of State, *FRUS, 1950*, vol. 1, *National Security Affairs: Foreign Economic Policy* (Washington, D.C., 1977), pp. 281–282.

26. On Eisenhower's nuclear background, see in particular Rosenberg, "U.S. Nuclear Stockpile," pp. 27–28; JCS 1725/2, 12 March 1947, CCS 004.04 (11-4-46) Sec. 3, JCS; Maj. Gen. K. D. Nichols USA (Ret.) to David A. Rosenberg, 27 October 1980; Oral History, Gen. Lauris Norstad, Interview by Thomas Soapes, 11 November 1976, DDEL, 6–29, 39–42; Senior Officers Debriefing Program, Conversations between Gen. Andrew J. Goodpaster, Col. William D. Johnson, and Lt. Col. James C. Ferguson, 29 January 1976, pp. 56–57; 25 February 1976, pp. 6–14, U.S. Army Military History Research Collection, U.S. Army Military History Institute, Carlisle Barracks, Pa. (hereafter cited as USAMHI).

27. Memorandum, C. E. Wilson to the chairman, JCS, Subject: Transfer and Deployment of Atomic Weapons, 24 June 1953, in JCS 2019/62, 25 June 1953, CCS 471.6 (8-15-45) Sec. 39, JCS; Andrew J. Goodpaster, MCP, 13 January 1961, dated 17 January 1961, AEC, December 1960–January 1961, vol. 3, folder 6, subject series, alphabetical subseries, White House Office, staff secretary (hereafter cited as WHO-SS, DDEL).

28. NSC 162/2, Review of Basic National Security Policy, 30 October 1953, NSC Papers, Modern Military Branch, National Archives (hereafter cited as NSC-MMB).

29. Holloway, "Soviet Thermonuclear Development," pp. 192–197.

30. Glenn Snyder, "The New Look of 1953," in Warner R. Schilling et al., *Strategy, Politics, and Defense Budgets* (Columbia University Press, New York, 1962), pp. 407–409; Maj. Gen. Robert M. Lee, USAF, Memorandum for the Chief of Staff, U.S. Air Force, 21 August 1953, Subject: The Coming National Crisis, Top Secret File (1), 1952–57, subject file, box 121, Nathan F. Twining Papers, LC; Gen. Matthew B. Ridgway, Memorandum for the Record, 17 May 1954, Historical Record, 15 January to 30 June 1954 Folder, box 30, Matthew B. Ridgway Papers, USAMHI; Memorandum, Dwight Eisenhower to John Foster Dulles, 8 September 1958, DDE Diary, August–September 1958, folder 2, box 3, ACWF-EPP, DDEL; NSC 5440/1, 28 December 1954; approved as Basic National Security Policy in NSC 5501, 6 January 1955, NSC-MMB.

31. A. J. Goodpaster, MCP, 22 December 1954, ACW Diary Dec. 1954 (2) folder, ACW Diary series, box 3, ACWF-EPP, DDEL; Draft Special N.I.E., 11–8–54: Probable Warning of Soviet Attack on the U.S. Through Mid–1957, 10 September 1954, SNIE 11-8-54 folder, box 47, White House Office, special assistant for national security affairs (hereafter cited as WHO-SANSA), DDEL.

32. Document 1: Memorandum, Op–36C to Op–36, Subject: Briefing given to the representatives of all services at SAC Headquarters, Offutt Air Force Base, Omaha, on 15 March 1954; and introduction in Rosenberg, "A Smoking, Radiating Ruin," pp. 3–28; U.S. Department of Energy, *Announced U.S. Nuclear Tests*, p. 4.

33. Brodie, *War and Politics*, 394n; Alfred Goldberg, *A Brief Survey of the Evolution of Ideas about Counterforce* (Rand Corporation, Santa Monica, Calif., Memorandum RM–5431-PR, October 1967, revised, March 1981), pp. 8–12; George F. Lemmer, *Air Force Strategic Deterrence*, pp. 55–57; Final Report, Project VISTA, "A Study of Ground and Air Tactical Warfare with Especial Reference to the Defense of Western Europe," California Institute of Technology, Pasadena, Calif., 4 February 1952, Modern Military Branch, National Archives, pp. xxi-xxviii, 138–142, 165–192; Red Line Message, Personal to Vandenberg from Norstad, 7 December 19521, Red Line Messages, 1 May–31 December 1951 folder, Vandenberg Papers, LC.

34. "Comments on WSEG #10 for General Twining," n.d. (ca. early 1954), Ready file, General Twining (1954), box 120, Nathan Twining Papers, LC; Briefing of WSEG Report No. 12, "Evaluation of An Atomic Offensive in Support of the Joint Strategic Capabilities Plan," 8 April 1955, published as document 2 in Rosenberg, "A Smoking, Radiating Ruin," pp. 29–38.

35. JCS 2056/75, 10 November 1955, with Decision, 18 November 1955; JCS 2056/71 12 April 1954; JCS 2057/47, 18 October 1954, in CCS 373.11 (12-14-48) Secs. 24, 23, and 20 respectively, JCS; Nathan Twining to Curtis LeMay, 9 June 1955; LeMay to Twining, 18 June 1955; and Twining to LeMay, 22 July 1955, Twining folder, box B-60, LeMay Papers, LC; CSAFM 284-55, 7 October 1955, appended to JCS 2057/32, 7 October 1955, CCS 381 (12-1-47) Sec. 5, JCS; Maxwell Taylor, *The Uncertain Trumpet* (Harper & Row, New York, 1959), pp. 23–46.

36. NSC 5602/1, Basic National Security Policy, 15 March 1956, NSC 5602/1, Basic National Security Policy folder, NSC series, Policy Papers subseries, box 17, WHO-SANSA, DDEL, pp. 1–11.

37. "Meeting the Threat of Surprise Attack," Report to the President by the Technological Capabilities Panel of the Science Advisory Committee, Office of Defense Mobilization, 14 February 1955, Technological Capabilities Panel of the S.A.C., 14 February 1955 folder, subject series, alphabetical subseries, box 11, WHO-SS, DDEL, vol. 1, pp. 10–22, 31–46; vol. 2, pp. 50–71, 73–111.

38. James R. Killian, Jr., *Sputniks, Scientists, and Eisenhower* (MIT Press, Cambridge, 1977), pp. 68–93.

39. Holloway, "Soviet Thermonuclear Development," pp. 192–197; 23 January 1956, Robert Ferrell, ed., *The Eisenhower Diaries* (W. W. Norton, New York, 1981), 311–312.

40. Document 2 in Rosenberg, "A Smoking, Radiating Ruin," pp. 29–38; A. J. Goodpaster, MCP, 10 February 1956, in Joint Chiefs of Staff, January–April 1956, folder 2, subject series, Defense Department subseries, box 4, WHO-SS, DDEL; Prados, *Soviet Estimate*, pp. 43–50.

41. A. J. Goodpaster, MCP, 4 November 1957, dated 6 November 1957, Science Advisory Committee, November 1957–April 1958, folder 3, subject series, alphabetical subseries, box 23, WHO-SS, DDEL: NSC 5724, "Deterrence and Survival in the Nuclear Age," Report to the President by the Security Resources Panel of the Science Advisory Committee, 7 November 1957, in Gaither Report, November 1957–January 1958; folder 2, ibid., box 13; Appointments, 9 November 1957, November 1957, folder 2, ACW Diary, box 9, ACWF-EPP-DDEL.

42. NSC 5602/1, 15 March 1956. The JCS debates over these questions are contained in CJCS (Military Strategy and Posture) files of JCS chairman Arthur Radford's office files, JCS; A. J. Goodpaster, MCP, 10 February 1956; and CCS 381 (11-29-49) Sec. 30, JCS.

43. NSC 5602/1, 15 March 1956. The 1956 authorization is noted in Arthur W. Radford, Memorandum for the Secretary of Defense, Subject: Department of Defense Report on the Status of U.S. Military Programs as of 31 December 1956, CCS 381, U.S. (1-31-50) Sec. 68, JCS. The April 1956 date is based on the titles of documents 16 to 22 on Withdrawal Sheet in "AEC Policy on Use of Atomic Weapons," Briefing Notes subseries, NSC series, box 1, WHO-SANSA, DDEL. The evidence of later advance authorizations is found in B. L. Austin, Memorandum for Chairman, JCS, DM-03-58, 27 March 1958, Subject: Status of the "Instructions for the Expenditure of Nuclear Weapons under Special Circumstances," CCS 471.6 (8-15-45) Sec. 111, JCS; Memorandums, James S. Lay, Jr., to the secretaries of state and defense, Subject: Policy Regarding Use of Atomic Weapons, 19 March, and 2, 9, 23 April 1958; Memorandum, Gordon Gray to General Goodpaster, 15 December 1958, discussing proposed Executive Order; undated page containing chronology of developments regarding Instructions for the Expenditure of Nuclear Weapons from 17 February 1959 through 18 May 1960; and Thomas S. Gates to the president, 5 June 1959, all in AEC-Policy on Use of Atomic Weapons Folder, box 9, WOH, Project Cleanup, DDEL; also withdrawal sheet of documents, ibid., and withdrawal sheets of documents in Atomic Weapons, Presidential Approval, and Instructions for Use Of, folders 1–5; and Atomic Weapons, Correspondence and Background for Presidential Approval, Policy re Use, folders 2–6, both in NSC series, subject subseries, box 1, SHO-SANSA, DDEL; and Instructions to Commanders, folders 1–5, subject series, alphabetical subseries, box 14, SHO-SS, DDEL.

44. A. J. Goodpaster, MCP, 7 November 1957, following NSC Meeting, Military Planning, 1958–61, folder 3, subject series, Defense Department subseries, box 6, WHO-SS, DDEL; Robert Cutler, Memorandum for the President, Subject: SAC Concentration in U.S. and reaction Time, 25 October 1957, Robert Cutler 1956–67, folder 1, Administration series, box 11, ACWF-EPP, DDEL.

45. Briefing for the President, SAC Operations with Sealed Pit Weapons, in Defense Department, vol. 2, folder 9, July 1958, box 1, Defense Department subseries; A. J. Goodpaster, MCS, 27 August 1958, dated 29 August 1958, in Atomic Energy Commission, vol. 7, folder 4, August–September 1958, box 3, alphabetical subseries, both in subject series, WHO-SS, DDEL.

46. Memorandum, chief of staff, USAF, to the JCS, on Launching of the Strategic Air Command Alert Force, CSAF M-72-58, 10 March 1958, enclosed in JCS 1899/398, 10 March

1958, in CCS 381, U.S. (5-23-46) Sec. 95, JCS. JCS deliberations on airborne alert are in CCS 3340, Strategic Air and ICBM Operations, 10 September 1959, JCS; Futrell, *Ideas, Concepts, Doctrine,* pp. 578–582; and Historians Office, Headquarters, Strategic Air Command, *Development of Strategic Air Command* (Headquarters, Strategic Air Command, Omaha, Neb., 1976), pp. 67–77.

47. Futrell, *Ideas, Concepts, Doctrine,* p. 551; Strategic Air Command Progress Analysis, 1 November 1948–31 December 1956, box B-100, LeMay Papers, LC, pp. 65–69; Prados, *Soviet Estimate,* pp. 30–37, 75–126; Lemmer, *Air Force Strategic Deterrence,* pp. 56–59.

48. Curtis E. LeMay, Memorandum for the Chief of Staff, USAF, Subject: USAF Tasks and Objective Force Structure (1959–1970), 5 May 1959, with Tabs A through E appended, approved by the chief of staff, 12 May 1959, Air Force Council folder; Jacob E. Smart, Decision, Subject: USAF Tasks and Objective Force Structure (1959–70), 15 May 1959, Air Force Council Decisions, 1959 Notebook, both in box 25, Thomas D. White Papers, LC.

49. Curtis E. LeMay, Memorandum to the Chief of Staff, USAF, Subject: The Threat, 2 March 1960, with paper enclosed, approved by General White, 2 March 1960, Air Force Council folder 1, January–June 1960, box 36, White Papers, LC.

50. A. J. Goodpaster, Memorandum for Adm. Arthur W. Radford, 29 February 1956, Joint Chiefs of Staff, January–April 1956, folder 2, subject series, Defense Department, box 4, WHO-SS, DDEL.

51. Interview with John P. Coyle, 29 March 1978. Coyle was a major navy analyst on Project BUDAPEST. BUDAPEST is also mentioned in Coyle's brief unclassified 1978 paper, "Biography of a Strategic Concept," courtesy John Coyle. JCS concerns regarding large nuclear weapons are noted in DM-221-57, 9 July 1957, Memorandum for General Eddleman et al., Subject: Use of Large Weapons, CCS 471.6 (8-15-45) Sec. 9C, JCS; and Memorandum, Nathan Twining to chairman, JCS, 8 May 1957, Subject: Studies of Large Yield Weapons, subject file, top secret file, 1952–57, folder 4, box 122, Twining Papers, LC. The date of BUDAPEST is noted in Chairman, JCS, Daily Log, 29 August 1957. Diary of CJCS Notebook, 8/15/56–12/31/57, box 6, ibid.

52. For background on navy thinking on nuclear strategy, see David Alan Rosenberg, "American Postwar Air Doctrine and Organization: The Navy Experience," in Alfred F. Hurley and Robert C. Ehrhardt, eds., *Air Power and Warfare: The Proceedings of the 8th Military History Symposium, U.S. Air Force Academy, October 18–20, 1978* (Washington, D.C., 1979), pp. 245–278; Berend D. Bruins, "Navy Bombardment Missiles to 1960," (Ph.D. diss., Columbia University, 1981). On Burke's philosophy, see David Alan Rosenberg, "Arleigh Albert Burke," in Robert William Love, Jr., *The Chiefs of Naval Operations* (Naval Institute Press, Annapolis, 1980), pp. 263–319.

53. See Naval Warfare Analysis Group Study 1, Introduction of the Fleet Ballistic Missile into Service, forwarded by Rear Adm. Roy L. Johnson to the chief of naval operations, Serial 007 P93, 30 January 1957, and written by John P. Coyle. NAVWAG 1 was declassified in March 1980 by the Office of the Chief of Naval Operations. On Polaris development in general, see Richard G. Hewlett and Francis Duncan, *Nuclear Navy, 1946–1962* (University of Chicago Press, Chicago, 1974), pp. 220–270; and Harvey M. Sapolsky, *The Polaris System Development: Bureaucratic and Programmatic Success in Government* (Harvard University Press, Cambridge, 1972).

54. Arleigh Burke, CNO Speech-Discussion, Defense Policy Seminar, Harvard University, 24 March 1960, AAB, NHC, 9–10; Arleigh Burke, CNO Personal Letter No. 5 to Retired Flag Officers, Subject: Pertinent Information, Summary of Major Strategic Considerations for the 1960–70 Era, Navy folder, box 28, White Papers, LC. Burke's thinking was built on such papers as Rear Adm. Roy L. Johnson, Memorandum for the Distribution List, Subject: Adaptation of a National Military Posture to the Era of Nuclear Parity: A Suggested Navy Posture, Serial 0008 P93, 3 December 1957, with paper, same subject, appended, A-16-10 folder, 1957, Strategic Plans Division Papers, NHC; JCS 2056/143, 22

December 1959, containing navy Memorandum, 30 September 1959; declassified with deletions, August 1980, 3205, Target Systems (17 August 1959); Memorandum, James S. Russell to the secretary of defense, Subject: Statement of Navy Views on the Concept of Employment and Command Structure for the Polaris Weapons System, Serial 000182 P60, 5 May 1959, CCS 4720, Intermediate Range (5 January 1959) Group II, both JCS. See also Rosenberg, "Arleigh Albert Burke," pp. 292–295.

55. SM-12-58, 4 January 1958, Memorandum for General Twining et al., Subject: SM-910-57 of December 1957, and Army Flimsy, 26 December 1957, Subject: JCS 1844/242, Atomic Annex to the Joint Strategic Capabilities Plan, both in CCS 373.11 (12-14-48) Sec. 38, JCS. Information on the "Alternative Undertaking" is also based on other documents in the same place; JCS 1844/242, 2 December 1957, declassified with many deletions by the Directorate of Freedom of Information and Security Review, Office of the Secretary of Defense (hereafter cited as OSD-FOI); and interview with John P. Coyle, 29 March 1978. The JSCP Annex C was approved 9 April 1958, DM-136-58, 23 April 1958, Memorandum for General Eddleman et al., Subject: Operational Implications of the Use of Surface Burst Nuclear Weapons, CCS 471.6 (10-16-46) Sec. 24, JCS.

56. Gordon Gray, Memorandum of Conversation with the President, 19 November 1958, dated 22 November 1985, Meetings with the President, 1958, folder 1, Special Assistant series, presidential subseries, box 3, WHO-SANSA, DDEL.

57. NSC Action no. 2009, Record of Action by the National Security Council at its 387th meeting, held on 20 November 1958 (approved by the president on 1 December 1958), declassified copy provided by National Security Council, 1980.

58. Gordon Gray, Memoranda of Conversation with the President, Monday, 16 February 1959, dated 18 February 1959; and Thursday, 26 February 1959, dated 28 February 1959, Meetings with the President, 1959, folder 6, Special Assistant series, presidential subseries, box 4, WHO-SANSA, DDEL. The Hickey committee tasking is contained in Gen. Nathan F. Twining, Memorandum for Lt. Gen. Thomas F. Hickey, Net Evaluation Sub Committee, CM-305-59, 20 February 1959, Subject: Approval of Relative Merits from the Point of View of Effective Deterrence of Alternative Retaliatory Efforts, CCS 3070, Grand Strategy, 20 February 1959, JCS. The JCS debates on these taskings are contained in the same place.

59. Transcript, Admiral Burke's conversation with Admiral Russell, 11 November 1960, Transcripts & Phone Cons (NSTL) folder, AAB, NHC; Brief Summary of Comparative Data, NESC 2009 and NTSDBs, dated 29 August and 7 September 1960, Memorandums and Letters (NSTL) AAB, NHC.

60. A. J. Goodpaster, MCP, 5 May 1960, dated 7 May 1960, Joint Chiefs of Staff, folder 8, September 1959–May 1960, subject series, Defense Department subseries, box 4, WHO-SS, DDEL; A. J. Goodpaster, MCP, 6 April 1960, Defense Department, vol. 4, folder 3, March–April 1960, subject series, Defense Department subseries, box 2, WHO-SS DDEL. See also the president's comments on Polaris in A. J. Goodpaster, MCP, 18 March 1960, dated 26 March 1960, ibid. On Eisenhower's thinking, see A. J. Goodpaster, MCP, 21 November 1959, dated 2 January 1960, Defense Department, vol. 4, folder 1, January 1960, subject series, Defense Department subseries, box 2 WHO-SS, DDEL; A. J. Goodpaster, MCP, 5 November 1959, dated 6 November 1959, Staff Notes, November 1959, folder 3, DDE Diary, box 45, ACWF-EPP, DDEL; A. J. Goodpaster, MCP, 16 November 1969, dated 2 December 1959, Budget Military, FY 62, folder 2, subject series, Defense Department subseries, box 3, WHO-SS, DDEL.

61. JCS 1620/250, 28 April 1959, CCS 4720, Intermediate Range (5 January 1959) Group 2, JCS; Arleigh Burke, Memorandum for all DCNOs, Subject: SAC Control of the FBM, Op-00 Memo 0529-58, 8 December 1958, originator's file, AAB, NHC; *Washington Star*, 17 April 1959; JCS 1620/254, 2 May 1959, CCS 4720, Intermediate Range (5 January 1959) Group 2, JCS. See also Rosenberg, "Arleigh Albert Burke," pp. 302–304.

62. JCS 2056/131, 20 August 1959, declassified with deletions, 1980, CCS 3205, Target

Systems (17 August 1959) JCS. See also Strategic Air Command, *History of the JSTPS*, pp. 6–11.

63. A. J. Goodpaster, MCP, 6 July 1960, Staff Notes, July 1960 folder, DDE Diaries, box 51, ACWF-EPP, DDEL; Thomas Gates to Brig. Gen. A. J. Goodpaster, 10 August 1960, with draft memorandum to the JCS and TABS B and C, in Defense Department vol 4–7, August 1960 folder, box 2, Defense Department subseries, subject series, WHO-SS, DDEL.

64. Untitled memorandum, dated 11 August 1960, appended to A. J. Goodpaster, MCP, 13 August 1960. This was a typed, unsigned version of Admiral Burke's arguments. The original handwritten and first typed drafts of this memorandum are contained in NSTL/SIOP Briefing folder, AAB, NHC.

65. A. J. Goodpaster, MCP, 13 August 1960.

66. Ibid.

67. Message, CNO to CINCPACFLT, CINCLANTFLT, CINCUSNAVEUR, 0051/06 November 1960; Special Edition, Flag Officers Dope, 4 December 1960.

68. Precis, appended to Memorandum Op-06C to Op-00, BM-00211-60, 8 November 1960.

69. Message, CINCPAC to RBEP with JCS, Report of Preliminary Review of SIOP-62, 182250Z January 1951, NSTL/SIOP Messages folder, AAB, NHC.

70. Message, CINCLANT to CNO, Subject: JSTPS Progress, 2031Z/22 October 1960.

71. Message, CNO to CINCLANTFLT, CINCPACFLT, CINCUSNAVEUR, R 2019337Z November 1960; Memorandum Arleigh Burke to Rear Admiral Blackburn, Subject: Political Aspects of the SIOP, Series 0653-60, 9 November 1960, in originator's file, AAB, NHC.

72. George B. Kistiakowsky, *A Scientist at the White House* (Harvard University Press, Cambridge, 1976), pp. 396, 399–400, 405–407, 413–416; Transcript, telephone conversation, Admiral Burke and Kistiakowsky, 24 October 1960, Transcripts and Phone Cons (NSTL) folder, AAB, NHC.

73. Kistiakowsky, quoted in Transcript, Admiral Burke's conversation with Admiral Russell, 11 November 1960.

74. Transcript, Admiral Burke's conversation with Captain Aurand, 25 November 1960, in Transcripts & Phone Cons (NSTL) folder, AAB, NHC.

3. *The Development of the SIOP, 1960–1983*

1. U.S. Senate, Armed Services Committee, *Study of Airpower* (Washington, D.C., 1956), p. 170.

2. Ibid., pp. 168–173.

3. Frank G. Klotz, "The U.S. President and the Control of Strategic Nuclear Weapons," (D. Phil. diss., Oxford University, 1980), p. 261.

4. Ibid., pp. 261–262.

5. Ibid., p. 262.

6. "Joint Strategic Target Planning Staff Gives President 'Packaged Plans' for Nuclear Strike," *Army, Navy, Air Force Journal and Register* 100 (24 August 1963), 20–21.

7. History and Research Division, Headquarters, Strategic Air Command, *History of the Joint Strategic Target Planning Staff: Background and Preparation of SIOP–62* (sanitized copy declassified by OJCS, 21 April 1980), p. 15.

8. Desmond Ball, *Deja Vu: The Return to Counterforce in the Nixon Administration* (California Seminar on Arms Control and Foreign Policy, Santa Monica, Calif., December 1974), pp. 10–11.

9. David Alan Rosenberg, "The Origins of Overkill: Nuclear Weapons and American Strategy, 1945–1960," *International Security* 7, no. 4 (Spring 1983), 6.

10. Ibid., p. 55.

11. Ball, *Deja Vu*, pp. 10–11.

12. Rosenberg, "Origins of Overkill," p. 62.

13. Ibid.

14. *International Herald Tribune*, 9 May 1978.

15. Ball, *Deja Vu*, p. 11.

16. For a fuller discussion of the developments in strategic nuclear policy during the Kennedy administration, from which much of this section is derived, see Desmond Ball, *Politics and Force Levels: The Strategic Missile Program of the Kennedy Administration* (University of California Press, Berkeley, 1980), chap. 9.

17. See Alfred Goldberg, *A Brief Survey of the Evolution of Ideas about Counterforce* (Rand Corporation, Santa Monica, Calif., RM–5431-PR, October 1967), p. 25.

18. House Appropriations Committee, *Department of Defense Appropriations for 1963* (Washington, D.C., 1962), pt. 2, p. 13.

19. Cited in William W. Kaufmann, *The McNamara Strategy* (Harper & Row, New York, 1964), pp. 74–75.

20. Cited in Fred Kaplan, " 'New Look' From the Pentagon," *Inquiry* 22 (September 1980), 10.

21. Kaufmann, *McNamara Strategy*, pp. 114–120.

22. Office of the Secretary of Defense, *Memorandum for the President Recommended FY 1964-FY 1968 Strategic Retaliatory Forces*, 21 November 1962, p. 14.

23. Cited in Henry Trewhitt, *McNamara: His Ordeal in the Pentagon* (Harper & Row, New York, 1971), p. 115.

24. *Newsweek*, 9 April 1962, p. 32.

25. Senate Armed Services Committee, *Military Procurement Authorization, Fiscal Year 1964* (Washington, D.C., 1963), pp. 40–41.

26. Senate Armed Services Committee and Senate Appropriations Committee, *Military Procurement Authorization, Fiscal Year 1966* (Washington, D.C., 1965), p. 43.

27. *Statement of Secretary of Defense Robert S. McNamara before the House Armed Services Committee on the Fiscal Year 1966–70 Defense Program and 1966 Defense Budget*, 18 February 1965, p. 39.

28. *Statement of Secretary of Defense Robert S. McNamara before a Joint Session of the Senate Armed Services Committee and the Senate Subcommittee on Department of Defense Appropriations on the Fiscal Year 1968–72 Defense Program and 1968 Defense Budget*, 23 January 1967, p. 39.

29. Ball, *Deja Vu*, p. 16.

30. Ibid., pp. 16–17.

31. Ibid., p. 17.

32. David Landau, *Kissinger: The Uses of Power* (Houghton Mifflin, Boston, 1972), pp. 141, 258.

33. Fred Kaplan, *The Wizards of Armageddon* (Simon & Schuster, New York, 1983), p. 365.

34. Ibid., p. 366.

35. Henry Kissinger, *The White House Years* (Weidenfeld & Nicholson, London, 1979), pp. 216–217.

36. Ibid., p. 217.

37. Richard Nixon, *U.S. Foreign Policy for the 1970s: A New Strategy for Peace*, Report to the Congress of 18 February 1970 (Washington, D.C., 1970), p. 122.

38. Michael Getler, "On the Other Hand, Mr. President?" *Armed Forces Management*, April 1970, p. 23.

39. Richard Nixon, *U.S. Foreign Policy for the 1970s: Building for Peace*, Report to the Congress of 25 February 1971 (Washington, D.C., 1971), pp. 170, 173.

40. Kissinger, *White House Years*, p. 127.

41. Lynn Etheridge Davis, *Limited Nuclear Options: Deterrence and the New American Doctrine* (Adelphi Paper No. 121, International Institute for Strategic Studies, London, Winter 1975–76), p. 3.

42. William Beecher, "Major War Plans Are Being Revised by White House," *New York Times*, 5 August 1972, pp. 1, 9.

43. House Armed Services Committee, *Hearings on Military Posture and H.R. 1872* (Washington, D.C., 1979), pt. 3, book 1, pp. 8, 12–13; House Appropriations Committee, *Department of Defense Appropriations for 1975* (Washington, D.C., 1974), pt. 1, p. 499.

44. Jack Anderson, "Not-So-New Nuclear Strategy," *Washington Post*, 12 October 1980, p. C–7.

45. See for example, Senate Foreign Relations Committee, *US-USSR Strategic Policies* (top secret hearing held on 4 March 1974; sanitized and made public on 4 April 1974), pp. 18–19.

46. *Washington Post*, 12 October 1980, p. C–7.

47. Ibid.

48. Senate Armed Services Committee, *Department of Defense Authorization for Fiscal Year 1979* (Washington, D.C., 1978), pt. 8, p. 6280; House Armed Services Committee, *Hearings on Military Posture and H.R. 1872*, pt. 3, book 1, pp. 6–26.

49. Ibid., p. 11.

50. Ibid., pp. 15, 25.

51. Senate Armed Services Committee, *Fiscal Year 1977 Authorization for Military Procurement, Research and Development, and Active Duty, Selected Reserve and Civilian Personnel Strengths* (Washington, D.C., 1976), pt. 2, p. 6422; House Appropriations Committee, *Department of Defense Appropriations for 1977* (Washington, D.C., 1976), pt. 8, p. 30; House Appropriations Committee, *Department of Defense Appropriations for 1980* (Washington, D.C., 1979), pt. 3, p. 878; House Armed Services Committee, *Hearings on Military Posture and H.R. 1872*, pt. 3, book 1, pp. 6–26.

52. House Appropriations Committee, *Defense of Defense Appropriations for 1978* (Washington, D.C., 1977), pt. 2, p. 212. See also *Los Angeles Times*, 2 February 1977, p. 1.

53. House Appropriations Committee, *Defense Appropriations for 1980*, pt. 3, p. 167.

54. Donald H. Rumsfeld, *Annual Department of Defense Report Fiscal Year 1978* (Washington, D.C., 1977), p. 77.

55. See William R. Van Cleave and W. Scott Thompson, eds., *Strategic Options for the Early Eighties: What Can Be Done?* (National Strategy Information Center, New York, 1979), p. 121.

56. See, for example, Michael P. Kennedy and Dennis E. Smallwood, *Recovery Model: Initial Analysis* (Rand Corporation, Santa Monica, Calif., WM-10141-DNA, March 1978).

57. *Air Force Magazine*, September 1978, p. 26.

58. Rowland Evans and Robert Novak, "Nuclear 'Blockbuster,' " *Washington Post*, 27 January 1977, p. A–24.

59. Lawrence J. Korb, "National Security Organization and Process in the Carter Administration," in Sam C. Sarkesian, ed., *Defense Policy and the Presidency: Carter's First Years* (Westview Press, Boulder, Colo., 1979), chap. 11.

60. See Robert G. Kaiser, "Global Strategy Memo Divides Carter's Staff," *Washington Post*, 7 July 1977; Hedrich Smith, "Carter Study Takes More Hopeful View of Strategy of U.S.," *New York Times*, 8 July 1977, p. 1; Richard Burt, "U.S. Study Asserts Russians Could Not Win Nuclear War," *International Herald Tribune*, 7–8 Janaury 1978.

61. *International Herald Tribune*, 7–8 January 1978, and Charles Mohr, "Carter Orders Steps to Increase Ability to Meet War Threats," *New York Times*, 26 August 1977, pp. 1, 8.

62. House Armed Services Committee, *Hearings on Military Posture and H.R. 1872*, pt. 3, book 1, p. 9; *Aviation Week and Space Technology*, 6 March 1978, p. 16.

63. Mohr, "Carter Offers Steps," pp. 1, 8.

64. House Armed Services Committee, *Hearings on Military Posture and H.R. 1872*, pt. 3, book 1, p. 437.

65. See testimony of William J. Perry, Senate Armed Services Committee, *Department of Defense Authorization for Appropriations for Fiscal Year 1980* (Washington, D.C., 1979), pt. 1, pp. 298–299; House Appropriations Committee, *Defense Appropriations for 1980*, pt. 3, pp. 116–117.

66. Testimony of Perry, Senate Armed Forces Committee, *Department of Defense Authorization for Appropriations for Fiscal Year 1980*, pt. 1, p. 407. See also *Air Force Magazine*, March 1979, p. 52; and "Statement of Harold Brown on the Defense Budget before the Senate Foreign Relations Committee," 19 September 1979, mimeo, pp. 19, 20.

67. See Richard Burt, "Pentagon Reviewing Nuclear War Plans," *New York Times*, 16 December 1977, p. 5.

68. Senate Foreign Relations Committee, *Nuclear War Strategy* (Washington, D.C., 1981), p. 16.

69. House Appropriations Committee, *Defense Appropriations for 1980*, pt. 3, p. 116. See also Colin S. Gray, "Targeting Problems for Central War," chap. 10 of this volume.

70. House Armed Services Committee, *Hearings on Military Posture and H.R. 1872*, pt. 3, book 1, pp. 9, 14.

71. Desmond Ball, "Counterforce Targeting: How New? How Viable?" *Arms Control Today*, 11, no. 3 (February 1981), 2, 6.

72. Harold Brown, "The Objective of U.S. Strategic Forces," Address to the Naval War College, Washington, 22 August 1980 (official text, U.S. International Communication Agency), p. 5.

73. Leon Sloss, "The Evolution of the Countervailing Strategy," May 1981, mimeo, p. 7.

74. Michael Getler, "Carter Directive Modifies Strategy for a Nuclear War," *Washington Post*, 6 August 1980, p. A-10; Richard Burt, "U.S. Stresses Limited Nuclear War in Sharp Shift on Military Strategy," *New York Times*, 6 August 1980.

75. Senate Armed Services Committee, *Department of Defense Authorization for Appropriations for Fiscal Year 1982* (Washington, D.C., 1981), pt. 7, p. 4210.

76. Tad Szulc, "The New Brinkmanship," *New Republic*, 8 November 1980, p. 21.

77. "Nuclear War Protections Ordered," *Washington Star*, 12 August 1980, p. 11.

78. Senate Foreign Relations Committee, *Nuclear War Strategy*, pp. 15–16.

79. "U.S. War Plan: Hit Russian Industry," *Los Angeles Times*, 2 February 1977, p. 1.

80. House Appropriations Committee, *Defense Appropriations for 1980*, pp. 167–170.

81. "Why C³I is the Pentagon's Top Priority," *Government Executive*, January 1982, p. 14.

82. Robert Scheer, *With Enough Shovels: Reagan, Bush, and Nuclear War* (Random House, New York, 1982), p. 12.

83. There are several references to the effect that in 1974, at the time the development of SiOP–5 was initiated, the U.S. strategic targeting plan contained more than 25,000 targets. See, for example, Senate Foreign Relations Committee, *US-USSR Strategic Policies* (Washington, D.C., 1974), p. 38. In 1979, General Ellis testified that there had been "an annual average increase in the numbers of installations included in the target list of approximately 10 percent over the past several years." Senate Armed Services Committee, *Department of Defense Authorization for Appropriations for Fiscal Year 1980* (Washington, D.C., 1979), p. 397.

84. House Appropriations Committee, *Defense Appropriations for 1980*, pt. 3, p. 878; House Armed Services Committee, *Hearings on Military Posture and H.R. 1872*, pt. 3, book 1, p. 186.

85. Senate Armed Services Committee, *Department of Defense Authorization for Appropriations for Fiscal Year 1981* (Washington, D.C., 1980), pt. 5, p. 2721.

86. Testimony of Vice Adm. Frank McMullen, then vice-director of strategic target

planning, in House Armed Services Committee, *Hearings on Military Posture and H.R. 1872*, pt. 3, book 1, p. 17–19.

87. U.S. Arms Control and Disarmament Agency (ACDA), *Effectiveness of Soviet Civil Defense in Limiting Damage to Population* (ACDA Civil Defense Study Report No. 1, Washington, D.C., 16 November 1977), pp. 18–20.

88. House Appropriations Committee, *Defense Appropriations for 1980*, pt. 3, p. 878; Senate Armed Services Committee, *Department of Defense Authorization for Appropriations for Fiscal Year 1980*, pt. 3, p. 1437; Harold Brown, *Department of Defense Annual Report Fiscal Year 1980* (Washington, D.C., 1979), p. 85.

89. Senate Armed Services Committee, *Department of Defense Authorization for Appropriations for Fiscal Year 1981*, pt. 2, pp. 544–545.

90. Jack Anderson, "U.S. Said to Prepare Mideast Options," *Washington Post*, 24 September 1980, p. C-27.

91. House Appropriations Committee, *Defense Appropriations for 1980*, pt. 3, p. 878.

92. Henry S. Rowen, "The Evolution of Strategic Nuclear Doctrine," in Lawrence Martin, ed., *Strategic Thought in the Nuclear Age* (Heinemann, London, 1979), p. 137.

93. Senate Foreign Relations Committee, *Nuclear War Strategy*, p. 18. See also R. D. Shaver and T. B. Garber, *Launch Under Attack (LUA): An Analytical Assessment of Minuteman Targeting Options* (Rand Corporation, Santa Monica, Calif., IN 24212-AF, March 1979).

94. Senate Armed Forces Committee, *Department of Defense Authorization for Appropriations for Fiscal Year 1980*, pt. 3, p. 1437.

95. Ibid.

96. Rowen, "Evolution of Strategic Nuclear Doctrine," p. 134. See also testimony of Gen. Alton D. Slay, Senate Armed Services Committee, *Fiscal Year 1977 Authorization for Military Procurement*, pt. 2, p. 6509.

4. Soviet Nuclear Targeting Strategy

This chapter draws heavily on articles from the journal of the Soviet General Staff, *Military Thought*, which has been declassified through 1973. These declassified issues are available only in translations, which were prepared by the U.S. government's Foreign Broadcast Information Service. With one or two exceptions, all other references to Soviet source materials are to the original sources, the titles of which are transliterated and translated.

1. Current U.S. MIRVed ICBMs and SLBMs are not effective against hard targets by design. For example, the current Poseidon missile does not have a stellar update component in the guidance system, which would have made it much more accurate. As currently proposed, the MX ICBM will have the combination of accuracy and yield required to attack missile silos. Whether similar proposals will be made for future SLBM designs remains to be seen.

2. Cited in Raymond L. Garthoff, *Soviet Strategy in the Nuclear Age* (Praeger, New York, 1958), p. 72.

3. Ibid., pp. 72–73.

4. Marshal V. D. Sokolovsky, ed., *Voennaia strategiia* (Military strategy) (Moscow, 1962), repeated on p. 235 of the 3d (1968) edition.

5. Ibid., 3d ed., p. 255.

6. Marshal N. Krylov, *Nedeliia* (Week) no. 36 (September 1967).

7. Maximum fatality targeting is an optimization routine that maximizes the fatalities inflicted by the Nth weapon. Such optimization routines are feasible for computer simulations, often described as analysis, but are difficult to execute with the missiles or aircraft actually deployed on either side. U.S. proponents of the Mutual Assured Destruction

(MAD) strategy have usually used the results of maximum fatality computer simulation to show the outcome of the strategy in terms of the population losses on both sides.

8. General of the Army S. P. Ivanov, "Soviet Military Doctrine and Strategy," *Military Thought*, no. 5 (1969, FDP No. 0116/69), 47. (Unfortunately, all references to the declassified issues of *Military Thought* are to English translations; the originals are not available. Even the translations are difficult to acquire.) For a more recent statement, except for the reference to the overseas adversary, see General N. A. Lomov, chief ed., *Nauchnotekhicheskii progress i revoliutsia v voennom dele* (Scientific-technical progress and the revolution in military affairs) (Moscow, 1973), pp. 138–139. Lomov's book is written by a collective of line military officers and military commissars and is the latest volume in the Officers' Library Series.

9. Cited in Ivanov, "Soviet Military Doctrine," p. 48. Soviet military writers routinely refer to this statement by Brezhnev, like earlier statements by Khrushchev, as the political guidance for seeking "victory" in a nuclear war.

10. Reprint of L. I. Brezhnev's 1967 report to the Supreme Soviet, 3–4 October 1967, in *KPSS o vooruzhennykh silakh sovetskovo soiuza: Documentary 1917–1981* (Communist Party of the Soviet Union on Armed Forces of the Soviet Union: documents, 1917–1981) (Moscow, 1981), pp. 471–480, particularly p. 479.

11. Rear Admiral V. Andreyev, "The Subdivision and Classification of Theaters of Military Operations," *Military Thought*, no. 11 (1964, FPD No. 924, 30 June 1965), 15. The acronym TVD used for convenience here is a transliteration of the Cyrillic letters. Translated, the acronym is TMO.

12. Ibid.

13. Colonel M. Shirokov, "Military Geography at the Present Stage," *Military Thought*, no. 11 (1966, FPD No. 0730), 57.

14. General Lieutenant G. Sememov and General Major V. Prokhorov, "Scientific-Technical Progress and Some Questions on Strategy," *Military Thought*, no. 2 (February 1969, FPD No. 60/69, 18 June, 1969), 23.

15. Shirokov, "Military Geography," p. 59.

16. Colonel M. Shirokov, "The Question of Geographic Influences on the Military and Economic Potential of Warring States," *Military Thought*, no. 4 (April 1968, FPD 0052/69), 36.

17. Ibid., p. 34.

18. Ibid.

19. Ibid., pp. 37–40.

20. Albert Speer, *Inside the Third Reich* (Macmillan, New York, 1970), pp. 280–283.

21. Ibid., pp. 278–279, for Speer's observations not only on the ten thousand antiaircraft guns and hundreds of thousands of troops assigned to defending German cities, but also on the consequences of air defense demands on German electronic and optical industries.

22. Shirokov, "Geographic Influences," p. 38.

23. Ibid., p. 39.

24. Ibid.

25. Ibid., p. 36. None of this is to argue that the Soviets have not considered the alternative of targeting cities and population, nor is it to argue that no senior Soviet officers have proposed such targeting. The Soviets may well have considered such alternatives but do not seem to have adopted them.

26. As the Soviet leaders frankly said to the Yugoslavs:

It is also necessary to emphasize that the services of the French and Italian CPs to the revolution were not lesser but greater than those of Yugoslavia. Even though the French and Italian CPs have so far achieved less success than the CPY, this is not due to any special qualities of the CPY, but mainly because after the destruction of the Yugoslav Partisan Headquarters by German paratroopers, at a moment when the people's liberation movement in Yugoslavia was passing through a serious crisis, the Soviet Army came to the aid of the Yugoslav people, crushed the German invader, liberated Belgrade and in this way created the conditions which were necessary to the CPY to achieve power. Unfortunately, the Soviet army did not and could not render such assistance to the French and Italian CPs. (*The Soviet-Yugoslav Dispute*, [Royal Institute of International Affairs, London, 1948], p. 51.)

This frank statement of what happened in Eastern Europe and, implicitly, what the Soviets would have done for Western Europe had they had the opportunity should not be dismissed as obsolete Stalinist rhetoric. Even today, the Soviets say essentially the same thing more subtly when they credit World War II with creating the "world socialist system." And as the postwar history of Hungary and Czechoslovakia has shown, the Red Army is prepared to "liberate" Eastern Europe more than once.

27. Colonel Ye. Rybkin, "XXV S'ezd KPSS i problema mirnogo sosush chestovaniia sotsializma i kapitalizma" (XXV Congress CPSU and the problem of the peaceful coexistence of socialism and capitalism) *Voenno-istoricheskiy zhurnal* (Military-historical journal), no. 1 (1977), 3, 4.

28. For the typical Soviet view, expressed by another articulate military commissar, that nuclear weapons are instruments of political policy like any other weapon, see Colonel S. Tiushkevich, "Razvitie ucheniia o voine i armii no opyte Velikoi Otechestvennoi Voiny" (Development of teaching on war and the army according to the experience of the Great Patriotic War), *Kommunish vooruzhennykh sil* (Communist of the Armed Forces), no. 22 (1975), 14. Tiushkevich writes: "The premise of Marxism-Leninism on war as a continuation of policy by military means remains true in a situation of fundamental changes in military affairs. The attempt of certain bourgeois ideologists to prove that nuclear missile weapons lead war outside the framework of policy and that nuclear war moves beyond the control of policy, outside the framework of policy, ceases to be an instrument of policy and does not constitute its continuation, is theoretically incorrect and politically reactionary."

29. Shirokov, "Military Geography," pp. 59, 60.

30. In Lomov, *Nauchnotekhnicheskii progress*, p. 139, the alternative objectives of nuclear targeting are given as "annihilation, destruction, neutralization," distinctions also found in *Military Thought* articles. The nature of the target probably determines the degree of damage in most cases. Thus, missiles in silos, or nuclear weapons in storage, must be annihilated or destroyed, but airfield runways do not have to be cratered as long as the aircraft are rendered inoperable and their crews killed. On the other hand, targets to be neutralized in one theater could be destroyed in another depending on the politico-military objectives of operations in the various TVDs.

31. Marshal (Aviation) S. A. Krasovskiy, ed., *Aviatsiia i kosmonavtika SSSR* (Moscow, 1968), p. 347.

32. General of the Army V. Tolubko, "Raketnye voiska strategicheskogo naznacheniia" (Strategic rocket troops), *Voenno-istoricheskii zhurnal (VIZ)*, no. 4 (1975); no. 10 (1976).

33. Ibid., no. 4, p. 54; no. 10, p. 21.

34. Ibid., no. 4, p. 54; no. 10, p. 20.

35. Ibid.

36. Ibid., no. 10, p. 20.

37. Ibid., p. 22, where Brezhnev is mentioned along with Ustinov and most of the military men previously cited, with the addition of Marshal A. M. Vasilevskiy and Marshal of Artillery N. D. Iakolev, as the political, state, and military leaders who directed missile development and the formation of the early missile units. Marshal of the Soviet Union Brezhnev achieved one-star rank as a political officer in 1943, was promoted in 1953, and made four stars in 1975. Biographic information from William F. Scott and Harriet F. Scott, *The*

Armed Forces of the USSR (Westview Press, Boulder, Colo., 1978). For Brezhnev's position as chairman of the Military Council, probably when he became general secretary in 1964, see Harriet Fast Scott, "The Soviet High Command," *Air Force* (March 1977), 52–56.

38. Tolubko, "Raketnye voisk a," no. 10, p. 21.

39. The Council of Defense has existed, under one title or another, since 1917–1918. During most and probably all of this period the council has been headed by the reigning general secretary of the Communist party, who probably approves or disapproves, funds or denies funding, for all major weapons systems development and production deployment programs. See Scott, "Soviet High Command," pp. 52–53.

40. V.I. Varofolomeyev and M. I. Kopytor, eds., *Design and Testing of Ballistic Missiles* (Moscow, 1970, JPRS 51810, 19 November 1970), pp. 11, 18.

41. If the yield/CEP plot falls on or below a kg/cm² line, then the missile system achieves 0.9 damage expectancy with two rounds against targets hardened to this degree.

42. John M. Collins, *U.S.-Soviet Military Balance: Concepts and Capabilities* (McGraw-Hill, 1980), p. 446. Collins does not list the CEP and yield for the SS-18 Mod 3 but does report the same CEP for the SS-19 Mod 2 as for the SS-18 Mod 4. This CEP is credited to the SS-19 Mod 4 inasmuch as they are contemporary modifications and the yield is assumed to be unchanged from the Mod 1.

43. I am much indebted to John Shannon of Science Applications, Inc., whose pioneering research on Soviet damage objectives is the basis for most of this section. The author, however, is solely responsible for the specific presentation in this section and its subsequent application.

44. For example, V. G. Malikov, *Shakhtnye puskovye ustanovki* (Silo launchers) (Moscow, 1971), p. 10 is typical of the treatment of damage requirements against hard targets in Soviet technical literature. Perhaps the most authoritative source for both high probability of damage and high confidence in achieving it is the *Sovietskaia Voennaia entsiklopediia* (Soviet military encyclopedia), vol. 6, p. 455, and vol. 5, p. 477. The later source also states that these damage objectives serve as the basis for calculating munitions requirements for destroying the target.

45. Collins, *U.S.-Soviet Military Balance*, p. 461; U.S. Department of Defense, *Soviet Military Power*, 2d ed. (Washington, D.C., 1983), pp. 36–37; Robert Levgolo, "Grand Illusions," *New York Times*, 5 January 1983.

46. International Institute of Strategic Studies, *The Military Balance, 1979–1980* (International Institute of Strategic Studies, London, 1980), p. 60.

47. Collins, *U.S.-Soviet Military Balance*, p. 461.

48. This estimate allows for French IRBMs and some growth in CPR deployments since 1980.

5. British Nuclear Targeting

1. Summarized from Andrew J. Pierre, *Nuclear Politics: The British Experience with an Independent Nuclear Force, 1939–1970* (Oxford University Press, London, 1972).

2. Michael Quinlan, deputy under secretary of state (policy and programmes), in House of Commons, *Strategic Nuclear Weapons Policy* (Fourth Report from the Defence Committee, Session 1980–81), p. 106.

3. Sir Charles Webster and Noble Frankland, *Strategic Air Offensive against Germany*, 4 vols. (Her Majesty's Stationery Office, London, 1961).

4. Michael Howard, "Bombing and the Bomb," in *Studies in War and Peace* (Maurice Temple Smith, 1970), pp. 145–146.

5. Margaret Gowing, *Independence and Deterrence: Britain and Atomic Energy, 1945–1952*, vol. 1: *Policy Making* (Macmillan, London, 1974), pp. 169, 170, 175, 188–189.

6. Ibid., pp. 216–217. Simpson notes that the actual American target at this time was for 400 bombs by 1953, and concludes that there may have been some U.S.-UK liaison. However, the same conclusion could have been reached by less direct methods. John Simpson, *The Independent Nuclear State* (Macmillan, London, 1983), p. 67.

7. Simpson, *Independent Nuclear State*, p. 76.

8. Gowing, *Independence*, pp. 316, 414.

9. See David Alan Rosenberg, "The Origins of Overkill," *International Security*, Spring 1983, pp. 16–18. See also Fred Kaplan, *The Wizards of Armageddon* (Simon & Schuster, New York, 1983), pp. 40–49.

10. Quoted in Gowing, *Independence and Deterrence*, 1: 437, 441–442.

11. *Hansard (Commons)*, vol. 537, 1 March 1955, col. 1897. Harold Macmillan, then defence minister, made a similar point in the same debate about the need to have "influence over the selection of targets and the use of our vital striking forces." 2 March 1955, col. 2182.

12. Robert P. Berman and John C. Baker, *Soviet Strategic Forces: Requirements and Responses* (Brookings Institution, Washington, D.C., 1982), p. 45.

13. Peter Nailor, in Jonathan Alford and Nailor, *The Future of Britain's Deterrent Force* (Adelphi Paper No. 156, International Institute for Strategic Studies, London, Spring 1980), p. 3.

14. Some Canberra bombers had been fitted with atomic bombs as early as 1954 but these had no capability to reach the Soviet heartland unless those armed with atomic bombs were deployed in Germany. Lincoln bombers, of which some 450 were built, could reach Soviet territory but would have been extremely vulnerable to Soviet air defenses. They left service in 1955. Seventy U.S. B-29s well able to attack Soviet territory were transferred to the RAF in 1970. According to Gowing, these "did not carry atomic bombs" (p. 235).

15. Pierre, *Nuclear Politics*, p. 139.

16. *Times*, 14 November 1958, quoted in Pierre, *Nuclear Politics*, p. 96.

17. Simpson, *Independent Nuclear State*, p. 110.

18. *Report on Defence: Britain's Contribution to Peace and Security, 1958*

19. Harold Macmillan, *Tide of Fortune* (Macmillan, London, 1969).

20. Andrew Brookes, *V-Force: The History of Britain's Airborne Deterrent* (Jane's, London, 1982), pp. 80–81.

21. John Baylis, *Anglo-American Defence Relations, 1939–1980: The Special Relationship* (Macmillan, London, 1981), p. 59.

22. Stewart Menaul, *Countdown: Britain's Strategic Nuclear Forces* (Robert Hale, London, 1980), p. 91.

23. Ibid., p. 113.

24. Ibid., pp. 116, 141.

25. Rosenberg, "The Origins of Overkill," p. 60.

26. Ibid., p. 62; Desmond Ball, *Targeting for Strategic Deterrence* (Adelphi Paper No. 185, International Institute for Strategic Studies, London, Summer 1983), p. 9. The NESC–2009 study reflected gradually improving intelligence, particularly from U-2 flights. However, it is clear that much was speculative. For example, there were few if any Soviet ICBM sites at that time.

27. Quoted by Pierre, *Nuclear Politics*, p. 179; Brookes, *V-Force*, p. 81.

28. It was when the decision was made to produce the much more powerful thermonuclear weapons in 1954 that the decision was made to cut the planned V-bomber force from 250 to 180. In 1957 it was decided that the force should eventually contain some 144 front-line strike aircraft, of which 104 would be the more capable Mark 2s. Brookes, *V-Force*, pp. 100, 128.

29. See Simpson, *Independent Nuclear State*, p. 254.

30. Menaul, *Countdown*, p. 115.

31. Brookes, *V-Force*, p. 102. Brookes estimates that at least 100 would have been available for war within 12 hours.

32. The warheads for Thor were American. In 1964 Leonard Beaton estimated that the British nuclear stockpile was 1,000 to 1,500 warheads. Leonard Beaton, *Would Labour Give Up the Bomb* (*Sunday Telegraph* pamphlet, 1964). A more recent estimate confirms Beaton's figures for that period and suggests that total warhead stocks since then are unlikely to have surpassed 2,000. Joseph Gallacher, *Nuclear Stocktaking: A Count of Britain's Warheads* (Bailrigg Paper on International Security, no. 5, University of Lancaster, 1982). However, Simpson suggests that "the size of the British stockpile of strategic devices has remained constant at 100–200 bombs or warheads since the early of 1960s." *Independent Nuclear State*, p. 156. Tactical devices put the numbers higher, up to 400 by the end of the 1960s and over 550 by 1982. Ibid., p. 255.

33. *Times*, 21 January 1965. It is extremely difficult to be precise about V-bomber numbers because detailed breakdowns or even overall numbers were never made public.

34. Pierre, *Nuclear Politics*, p. 186. It was reported in early 1966 that Mark I Vulcans were all to be withdrawn from Bomber Command and that 45 had been produced. See *Flying Review International*, January 1966. See Appendix to Robert Jackson, *AV10 Vulcan* (Patrick Stephen, Cambridge, 1984). Brookes gives a figure of 115 Vulcans and Victors in service. This excludes the Victors used as tankers but not those used for strategic reconnaissance; see *V-Force*, p. 152. Yet another breakdown of the composition of the V-bomber force and overall numbers is found in Robert Jackson, *V-bombers* (Ian Allan, London, 1981), and is used by Simpson, *Independent Nuclear State*, p. 297. The difficulty is that the government never released authoritative figures.

35. Pierre, *Nuclear Politics*, p. 186.

36. *Guardian*, 4 August 1960, reported ten to fifteen canceled.

37. Menaul, *Countdown*, p. 133.

38. See *Jane's All The World's Aircraft, 1961–62*.

39. Brookes, *V-Force*, p. 112.

40. Menaul, *Countdown*, p. 117.

41. Ibid., pp. 139, 160.

42. Ball, *Targeting for Strategic Deterrence*, p. 16.

43. Ibid. Ball lists them as including airfields, rail lines, rail choke points, and rail yards; Soviet MRBM and IRBM; underground command and control facilities; military headquarters; SAM sites; tank concentrations; troop concentrations and assembly points; ammunition and weapon depots; logistic support sites; POL depots; supply routes; lines of communication; bridges and mountain passes; sluices and dams; harbors; etc.

44. Alford and Nailor, *Future of Britain's Deterrent Force*, pp. 27–28.

45. According to Peter Malone, "in both allied and independent missions, the British were targeted against the Soviet homeland." He bases this assertion on the fact that the United States accepts the British definition of the nuclear forces as being "strategic" in character. *British Nuclear Deterrent*, p. 93.

46. As the agreement states, "The Prime Minister made it clear that except where Her Majesty's Government may decide that supreme national interests are at stake, these British forces will be used for the purposes of international defence of the Western Alliance in all circumstances."

47. For example, Secretary of State for Defence John Nott has stated, "in the last resort, Great Britain must be responsible for her own defences. She cannot shuffle them off on another nuclear power." *Hansard*, vol. 21, 29 March 1982, col. 25.

48. This point was made by Ian Smart in the early 1970s in the context of possible Anglo-French cooperation: "At present Britain, through the Joint Strategic Targeting Committee, has access to American information concerning potential Soviet targets, while its

general collaboration on intelligence matters with the United States can be taken to provide adequate information about Soviet ABM and anti-aircraft defences." Ian Smart, *Future Conditional: The Prospect for Anglo-French Nuclear Cooperation* (Adelphi Paper No. 78, International Institute for Strategic Studies, London, July 1971), p. 6.

49. Geoffrey Kemp, *Nuclear Forces for Medium Powers*, pt. 1: *Targets and Weapons Systems*, pts. 2 and 3: *Strategic Requirements and Options* (Adelphi Papers Nos. 106 and 107, International Institute for Strategic Studies, London, Autumn 1974), pp. II–3, I–12/13, II–4.

50. The cities in order of population would be Leningrad, Kiev, Tashkent, Baku, Kharkov, Novosibirsk, Kuybyshev, Sverdlovsk, Minsk, and Tbilisi.

51. Kemp, *Nuclear Forces for Medium Powers*, pp. II–4/5.

52. Ian Smart, *The Future of the British Nuclear Deterrent: Technical, Economic, and Strategic Issues* (Royal Institute of International Affairs, London, 1977), pp. 38, 40–42.

53. On the debate see Lawrence Freedman, *Britain and Nuclear Weapons* (Macmillan, London, 1980), chaps. 5 and 6. For more detail see Lawrence Freedman, "The Small Nuclear Powers," in David Schwartz and Ash Carter, eds., *Missile Defense* (Brookings Institution, Washington, D.C., forthcoming).

54. Quinlan, *Strategic Nuclear Weapons Policy*, p. 107.

55. *Statement on the Defence Estimates*, Cmnd. 8951-I, p. 7.

56. *The United Kingdom Trident Programme* (Defence Open Government Document 82/1, Ministry of Defence, London, 1982), p. 6.

57. *The Future United Kingdom Strategic Nuclear Deterrent Force* (Defence Open Government Document 80/23, Ministry of Defence, London, July 1980), p. 5. An attack of this sort is mentioned as a possibility in Smart, *Future Conditional*, p. 42. Also Peter Nailor argues that in the early 1960s, it was presumed that deterrence came partly from saying to the USSR that, in effect, a U.K. attack "would not only be a grievous blow in itself, but would materially weaken your capacity to withstand successfully an attack from the United States which, for the purposes of this argument, you will have to assume would be a separate sector." Alford and Nailor, *Future of Britain's Deterrent Force*, p. 4.

58. *Future United Kingdom Strategic Nuclear Deterrent Force*, pp. 5–6.

59. Quinlan, *Strategic Nuclear Weapons Policy*, p. 85.

60. Letter to the *Tablet*, 15 August 1981. The original article was published as "Preventing War," the *Tablet*, 18 July 1981.

61. For a proposal along these lines see Jonathan Alford, "The Place of British and French Nuclear Weapons in Arms Control," *International Affairs* 59, no. 4 (Autumn 1983).

6. French Nuclear Targeting

The views expressed herein are those of the author alone and not those of the Department of the Navy or any other U.S. government agency.

1. Perhaps the two most useful of several broad historical analyses are Lothar Ruehl, *La politique militaire de la cinquième république* (Fondation Nationale des Sciences Politiques, Paris, 1976), and Michael M. Harrison, *The Reluctant Ally: France and Atlantic Security* (Johns Hopkins University Press, Baltimore, 1981).

2. Lucien Poirier's most important work is *Des stratégies nucléaires* (Hachette, Paris, 1977).

3. Cf. David S. Yost, "French Defense Budgeting: Executive Dominance and Resource Constraints," *Orbis* 23 (Fall 1979), 593–597.

4. Raymond Tourrain, *Rapport d'information par la Commission de la Défense Nationale et des Forces Armées sur l'état et la modernisation des forces nucléaires françaises* (no. 1730, Assemblée Nationale, Paris, October 1980).

5. De Gaulle's press conference of 23 July 1964, cited in ibid., p. 14 (emphasis added).

Note the coincidence between the date de Gaulle foresaw for the threshold of French strategic nuclear credibility and the date of France's withdrawal from NATO's integrated military structure.

6. Poirier, *Stratégies*, pp. 192, 305.

7. See Raymond Aron's classic, *The Great Debate: Theories of Nuclear Strategy*, trans. Ernst Pawel (Doubleday, New York, 1965), pp. 100–143.

8. Giscard d'Estaing, "Allocution," *Défense Nationale*, July 1976, p. 13.

9. Pierre Mauroy, "La cohérence d'une politique de défense," *Défense Nationale*, October 1981, p. 21.

10. Guy Lewin, "La dissuasion française et la stratégie anti-cités," *Défense Nationale*, January 1980, p. 24.

11. Jeannou Lacaze, "La politique militaire," *Défense Nationale*, November 1981, p. 12.

12. Poirier, *Stratégies*, pp. 297, 321.

13. Pierre Hautefeuille, "Etude sur défense et dissuasion nucléaires (1ère partie)," *Stratégique*, no. 5 (1980), 86.

14. Parliamentary report by Jacques Cressard, summarized in *Le Monde*, 26–27 September 1980.

15. Guy Méry, "Conférence," *Défense*, no. 9 (May 1977), 20.

16. Ivan Margine, "L'avenir de la dissuasion," *Défense Nationale*, April 1978, p. 23. Margine is the pseudonym of a high Defense Ministry official.

17. Lewin, "Dissuasion française," p. 27.

18. Lewin, "L'avenir des forces nucléaires françaises," *Défense Nationale*, May 1980, pp. 17–18.

19. Tourrain, *Rapport d'information*, p. 206.

20. Pierre Riou, "La force des choses," *Défense Nationale*, July 1980, p. 17. Riou is the pseudonym of a high Defense Ministry official.

21. Gérard Vaillant, "Défense en France," *Défense Nationale*, March 1980, p. 145.

22. Raymond Barre, "La politique de défense de la France," *Défense Nationale*, November 1980, p. 12 (emphasis added).

23. Charles Hernu, "Répondre aux défis d'un monde dangereux," *Défense Nationale*, December 1981, p. 15.

24. Lacaze, "Politique militaire," p. 11 (emphasis added).

25. See Charles Ailleret, "Défense 'dirigée' ou défense 'tous azimuts,' " *Revue de Défense Nationale*, December 1967, pp. 1923–1932; Ruehl, *Politique militaire*, pp. 223, 227; and Harrison, *Reluctant Ally*, pp. 130–134.

26. Michel Debré, "La France et sa défense," *Revue de Défense Nationale*, January 1972, pp. 7–8.

27. Méry, "Conférence," p. 19.

28. Raymond Barre, "Discours prononcé au Camp de Mailly le 18 juin 1977," *Défense Nationale*, August–September 1977, p. 12.

29. Jeannou Lacaze, "Concept de défense et sécurité en Europe," *Défense Nationale*, July 1984, p. 13. The British government has also expressed interest in this basic concept: "Indeed, one practical approach to judging how much deterrent power Britain needs is to consider what type and scale of damage Soviet leaders might think likely to leave them critically handicapped afterwards in continuing confrontation with a relatively unscathed United States." (*The Future United Kingdom Strategic Nuclear Deterrent Force*, Ministry of Defense, London, July 1980, p. 5.)

30. Margine, "Avenir de la dissuasion," p. 14; Lewin, "Dissuasion française," p. 26. At the same time, official French sources have implied that the SSBN capability in itself is more than sufficient for priority target coverage; Lewin has written that "one very soon reaches a threshold beyond which the submarines would have only secondary targets to strike." Lewin, "Avenir des forces nucléaires," p. 16.

31. Riou, "Force des choses," p. 12.

32. One may speculate that France could launch twenty rather than eighteen IRBMs in that at least two of the four test silos could also be used to launch S–3s. Although Tourrain recommends that three of the four test silos be kept ready for immediate use, twenty IRBM launches would probably represent the operational maximum. While the French government has never revealed how many S–3s have been produced, no special provisions for reloading silos appear to have been made, despite test launches. Tourrain, *Rapport d'information*, p. 225.

33. Geoffrey Kemp, *Nuclear Forces for Medium Powers*, pts. 2 and 3: *Strategic Requirements and Options* (Adelphi Paper No. 107, International Institute for Strategic Studies, London, 1974), p. 20.

34. CEA experts cited in Yves Boyer, *La politique de défense nationale en France et la nouvelle majorité* (PSIS Occasional Paper No. 4F, Graduate Institute of International Studies, Geneva, November 1981), p. 24.

35. Tourrain, *Rapport d'information*, pp. 110, 129, 213, 261.

36. Jeannou Lacaze, "Politique de défense et stratégie militaire de la France," *Défense Nationale*, June 1983, p. 15.

37. Law no. 83–606 of 8 July 1983, granting approval to the military program for the years 1984–1988, *Journal Officiel*, 9 July 1983, p. 2118. The United States has approved the sale to France of four very-low-frequency transmitters for the Astarte program. For details, see *Le Monde*, 16 September 1982, p. 14.

38. Hernu, "Répondre aux défis," p. 16; Hernu article in *Le Figaro*, 30–31 January 1982.

39. Tourrain, *Rapport d'information*, p. 239.

40. *Aviation Week and Space Technology*, 25 July 1983, p. 16.

41. Lacaze, "Politique de défense," p. 16.

42. Mitterrand in *Le Monde*, 26–27 July 1981, p. 6.

43. Lacaze, "Politique militaire," pp. 13–14.

44. *Le Monde* reported on 24 June 1982 that France planned to build only four sets of sixteen M-4 SLBMs to be able to transfer the SLBMs between SSBNs for maximum deterrent effectiveness at minimal cost; only the three SSBNs at sea and the one in port for refitting yet available for a return to service on seventy-two hour alert would carry SLBMs. French interview sources disputed the accuracy of this story, noting that additional SLBMs would be required for tests, maintenance, and emergency replacements. While the maximum number of SSBNs at sea would be four, SLBMs would also be available for launching from the SSBN in port. Moreover, although the M-4 is normally launched underwater, it could readily be launched from an SSBN in port.

45. Boyer, in *Politique de défense nationale*, describes the accuracy as between that of the Poseidon and the Minuteman III Mk 12A, which are attributed 450-meters CEP and 220-meters CEP respectively in *The Military Balance, 1982–1983* (International Institute for Strategic Studies, London, 1982), p. 112.

46. Jacques Chevallier, "Les armes et les ripostes mises en oeuvre par la défense française," in *La France face aux dangers de guerre: Actes du Colloque* (Fondation pour les Etudes de Défense Nationale pour l'Association des Anciens Elèves de l'Ecole Nationale d'Administration, Paris, 1980), 1: 175–176.

47. Pierre Usunier cited in *Air et Cosmos*, 11 June 1983, p. 105.

48. Jacques Isnard in *Le Monde*, 24 June 1982, p. 33.

49. Riou, "Force des choses," p. 13.

50. Chevallier, "Armes et ripostes," p. 176.

51. Giscard d'Estaing in *Le Monde*, 28 June 1980; Yvon Bourges in *Air et Cosmos*, 23 August 1980, p. 35.

52. Présidence de la Republique, Service de Presse, Communiqué, 14 November 1981. In May 1985, General Lacaze suggested that plans for the SX were again in flux and that

possible improvements in Soviet ballistic missile defenses might lead the French to reconsider acquiring cruise missiles—though the latter would have to saturate or evade Soviet air defenses. See Lacaze, "L'avenir de la défense française," *Défense Nationale*, July 1985, pp. 18, 22–24.

53. Law no. 80–606, p. 2118.

54. Cf. David S. Yost, "Ballistic Missile Defense and the Atlantic Alliance," *International Security* 7 (Fall 1982), and idem, "European Anxieties about Ballistic Missile Defense," *Washington Quarterly* 7 (Fall 1984).

55. Kemp, *Nuclear Forces*, p. 20.

56. Alford testimony in House of Commons, Fourth Report from the Defence Committee, Session 1980–81, *Strategic Nuclear Weapons Policy* (Her Majesty's Stationery Office, London, 1981), p. 26.

57. Testimony by H. Kinloch, ibid., p. 6.

58. Michel Tatu in *Le Monde*, 26 April 1975; François de Rose in *La France face aux dangers de guerre*, 1: 407.

59. Hautefeuille, "Etude sur défense," p. 107.

60. Ibid., p. 113.

61. Lewin, "Dissuasion française," p. 28.

62. Televised interview with Yvon Bourges on 7 May 1980, in *Foreign Broadcast Information Service, Western Europe*, 9 May 1980, p. K6.

63. Guy Méry in *Le Monde*, 19 November 1980, p. 12.

64. Alexandre Sanguinetti in *Le Nouvel Observateur*, 10 September 1979.

65. Lewin, "Dissuasion française," p. 26.

66. Ibid., pp. 24, 31.

67. Barre, "Politique de défense de la France," p. 14.

68. Poirier, *Stratégies*, p. 192.

69. Lacaze, "Politique militaire," p. 12.

70. Gen. Pierre Gallois interview of 3 July 1980, cited in Lara Marlowe, "French Defense Policy since 1968" (Master of Letters thesis, Brasenose College, Oxford University, 1980), p. 145; see also Gallois in *L'Express*, 16 March 1984, p. 26.

71. Paul Edward Buteux, "The Politics of Nuclear Consultation in NATO, 1965–1974: The Experience of the Nuclear Planning Group" (Ph.D. thesis, London School of Economics and Political Science, 1978), p. 126.

72. The memorandum of 11 March 1966 appears as an appendix in Kenneth Hunt, *NATO without France: The Military Implications* (Adelphi Paper No. 32, Institute for Strategic Studies, London, 1966), pp. 22–23.

73. Lacaze, "Politique militaire," p. 10.

74. Margine, "Avenir de la dissuasion," p. 20. In July 1985 former prime minister Pierre Messmer said that France has never accepted any targeting coordination regarding her strategic nuclear forces: "Even though the United States a decade ago very much insisted on coordination, what they really wanted was to learn our target planning without telling us about their own plans." See transcript of broadcast on West German television on 16 July 1985 in *Foreign Broadcast Information Service—Western Europe*, 18 July 1985, pp. J1–J2.

75. James M. Markham, "Arms Pact Sought by Bonn and Paris: They Agree to Seek a Common Policy—France to Consult about Nuclear Strategy," *New York Times*, 23 October 1982, p. 4.

76. Konrad Seitz, "La coopération franco-allemande dans le domaine de la politique de sécurité," *Politique Etrangère*, December 1982, pp. 982–984.

77. François Mitterrand cited in *Le Monde*, 24–25 October 1982.

78. Lothar Ruehl, "Europäische Sicherheit unter atomarer Bedrohung," in Robert Picht, ed., *Das Bündnis im Bündnis: Deutsch-französische Beziehungen im Internationalen Spannungsfeld* (Severin & Seidler, Berlin, 1982), p. 95. The best analysis of these complex issues is André

Adrets, "Les relations franco-allemandes et le fait nucléaire dans une Europe divisée," *Politique Etrangère*, Autumn 1984, pp. 649–664. Adrets is the pseudonym of a former Defense Ministry official. See also David S. Yost, "Radical Change in French Defense Policy? A Review Essay," *Survival* 28 (January–February 1986).

79. Giscard d'Estaing television interview of 12 November 1975, text in *Les déclarations du Président de la République sur la politique de défense et la politique militaire, juin 1974–décembre 1976* (Ministère de la Défense, Paris, 1977), pp. 29–30.

80. *Policy, Troops, and the NATO Alliance: Report of Senator Nunn to the Senate Committee on Armed Services* (Government Printing Office, Washington, D.C., 1974), p. 3, cited in Jeffrey Record, *U.S. Nuclear Weapons in Europe: Issues and Alternatives* (Brookings Institution, Washington, D.C., 1974), p. 34.

81. See Jacques Andréani, "L'Europe, l'Otan, et la France: Les problèmes non résolus de la défense européenne," *Politique Etrangère*, Summer 1983, p. 350. Although this article represents personal views, it should be noted that M. Andréani was director of political affairs in the French Foreign Ministry at the time of its publication.

82. Lacaze has tacitly acknowledged this point in "Politique militaire," p. 12. Lacaze conceded this point more explicitly in May 1985 but referred only to improved survivability measures—harder IRBM silos and mobile delivery systems—as possible solutions; no reference to flexible targeting as a potential remedy was made. See Lacaze, "L'avenir de la défense française," p. 22.

83. Giscard d'Estaing in *Le Monde*, 19 November 1980, p. 12.

84. Barre, "Discours prononcé," pp. 226–227.

85. Barre, "Politique de défense de la France," p. 14.

86. Margine, "Avenir de la dissuasion," p. 29.

87. Giscard d'Estaing in *Le Monde*, 19 November 1980. Although some French observers have argued that the president's legal authority to order the use of nuclear weapons should be clarified (e.g., Michel Schneider in *Le Monde*, 8 December 1983, p. 13), Prime Minister Pierre Mauroy has argued that the Constitution, various laws, and the intrinsic requirements of deterrence justify the president's unique powers in this respect. Mauroy cited in *Le Monde*, 11–12 March 1984, p. 11.

88. François Maurin, "La mise en place opérationnelle de la triade stratégique (Mirage IV, SSBS Albion, SNLE) et des chaînes de contrôle," paper presented on 28 September 1984 at the colloquium "De Gaulle et la dissuasion nucléaire (1958–1969)," organized by the Institut Charles-de-Gaulle and the Université de Franche-Comté, pp. 16–17.

89. Poirier, *Stratégies*, pp. 316–319, 335.

90. Jacques Isnard in *Le Monde*, 25 September 1968.

91. Jacques Isnard in *Le Monde*, 20 May 1981.

92. For a more detailed description of the formal policy-making process and the strategic studies community in France, see David S. Yost, "Strategic and International Affairs Research in France," *Orbis* 25 (Fall 1981).

93. Giscard d'Estaing in *Le Monde*, 28 June 1980.

94. Barre, "Politique de défense de la France," p. 14.

95. Lewin, "Dissuasion française," p. 26.

96. Ibid., p. 17; Mauroy, "Cohérence d'une politique," p. 23.

97. Lacaze, "Politique militaire," p. 11.

98. Mauroy, "Cohérence d'une politique," p. 23; Hernu, "Répondre aux défis," p. 14.

99. Jacques Bonnemaison cited in *Newsweek*, 11 July 1983, p. 28; see also Bonnemaison in *L'Express*, 15 July 1983, p. 42.

100. Press conference of 24 October 1974.

101. Jacques Chirac, "Au sujet des armes nucléaires tactiques françaises," *Défense Nationale*, May 1975, p. 12.

102. Barre, "Discours prononcé," p. 14.

103. Barre, "Politique de défense de la France," p. 15.

104. Mauroy, "Cohérence d'une politique," p. 25.

105. Ibid., p. 20. Pierre Mauroy, "Vers un nouveau modèle d'armée," *Défense Nationale*, November 1982, p. 17.

106. Giscard d'Estaing in *Le Monde*, 28 June 1980.

107. Charles Hernu, "La politique et la volonté de défense," *Politique Internationale*, no. 16 (Summer 1982), 13.

108. For the Socialists, see *Le Monde*, 4 July 1985, pp. 1, 6; for the U.D.F., *Le Monde*, 15 June 1985, p. 8.

109. *Le Monde*, 28 June 1985, pp. 1–2.

110. Hernu and Isnard in *Le Monde*, 22 June 1985, pp. 1, 4.

111. Giscard d'Estaing interview of 12 February 1978, in Tourrain, *Rapport d'information*, p. 34.

112. Margine, "Avenir de la dissuasion," p. 27.

113. Gen. Claude Vanbremeersch, commander of the First Army, interview in *L'Aurore*, 4 February 1980, p. 2.

114. François Maurin, "Entretien avec le géneral Maurin," *Défense Nationale*, July 1974, p. 16.

115. Paul Arnaud de Foïard, "Autres propos sur la dissuasion nucléaire," *Défense Nationale*, May 1980, pp. 30–31 (emphasis added).

116. Giscard d'Estaing, *Déclarations*, p. 55.

117. Ministry of Defence, *United Kingdom Deterrent Force*, p. 6. With only one SSBN always at sea, the British obviously have fewer targeting options than the French.

118. This discussion of three functional roles owes a great deal to chap. 12 of Lawrence Freedman, *Britain and Nuclear Weapons* (Macmillan, London, 1980).

119. See the views of Pompidou and Debré as reported in Marc Ullmann, "Security Aspects in French Foreign Policy," *Survival*, November/December 1973, p. 263.

120. Tourrain, *Rapport d'information*, p. 316.

121. Mauroy, "Cohérence d'une politique," p. 22.

122. Jean-Louis Gergorin, "Menaces et politiques dans la décennie 1980," in *La France face aux dangers de guerre*, 1: 66, 156.

123. Poirier, *Stratégies*, pp. 301, 318.

124. Guy Méry, "Une armée pour quoi faire et comment?" *Défense Nationale*, June 1976, p. 14.

125. See Poirier, *Stratégies*, pp. 322, 334.

126. This chapter's focus on targeting-related military concerns may mislead the reader. As Raymond Aron noted some twenty years ago, France's nuclear forces serve at least five peacetime political purposes, which supplement their roles in enhancing military security: (a) guaranteeing autonomy within the Atlantic alliance; (b) providing international prestige; (c) supporting related scientific and technical research; (d) supplying the armed forces with new tasks after the loss of empire; and (e) helping to restore public confidence in France's historical destiny. Aron, *Great Debate*, pp. 104–105. For further background, including tactical nuclear forces, see David S. Yost, *France's Deterrent Posture and Security in Europe*, pt. 1: *Capabilities and Doctrine*, and pt. 2: *Strategic and Arms Control Implications* (Adelphi Papers Nos. 194 and 195, International Institute for Strategic Studies, London, Winter 1984–85).

7. *The Dilemmas of Counterpower Targeting*

1. See James R. Schlesinger, "Flexible Strategic Options and Deterrence," *Survival* 16, no. 2 (March/April 1974), 86–90.

2. U.S. House, Appropriations Committee, *Department of Defense Appropriations for 1978* (Government Printing Office, Washington, D.C., 1977), p. 212.

3. Richard Burt, "Carter Shifts U.S. Strategy for Deterring Nuclear War," *New York Times*, 19 February 1979, p. 5; Robert Kaylor, "Brown Would Widen Range of Russian Military Targets," *Washington Post*, 14 January 1979, p. A13.

4. See Fred C. Iklé, "Can Deterrence Last Out the Twentieth Century?" *Foreign Affairs* 51, no. 2 (January 1973), 267–285; Bruce Russett, "Assured Destruction of What?: A Countercombatant Alternative to Nuclear Madness," *Public Policy* 22, no. 2 (Spring 1974), 121–138; and Bernard Albert, "Constructive Counterpower," *Orbis* 20, no. 4 (Summer 1976), 343–367. My use of the term *counterpower* rather than *countercombatant* should not be taken to imply that my discussion of counterpower strictly follows Albert's rather than Russett's discussion. I simply believe the term to be more descriptive.

5. See Anthony Cave Brown, ed., *Dropshot: The American Plan for World War III against Russia in 1957* (Dial Press, New York, 1978).

6. The 25,000 figure refers to the potential targets listed in the Defense Intelligence Agency's Target Data Inventory (TDI). See U.S. Senate, Committee on Foreign Relations, *U.S.-U.S.S.R.: Strategic Programs* (Government Printing Office, Washington, D.C., 1974), p. 38.

7. Robert McNamara, Commencement Address, University of Michigan, 16 June 1962.

8. Central Intelligence Agency, *Directory of Soviet Officials*, vol. 1: *National Organizations* (Washington, D.C., 1978); Leonard Schapiro, *The Government and Politics of the Soviet Union*, 6th ed. (Vintage, New York, 1978).

9. Central Intelligence Agency, *Soviet Civil Defense* (Washington, D.C., 1978).

10. U.S. Senate, Committee on Foreign Relations, *Fiscal Year 1980 Arms Control Impact Statements* (Government Printing Office, Washington, D.C., 1979), p. 87.

11. See Jeremy Azrael, *Emergent Nationality Problems in the USSR* (Rand Corporation, Santa Monica, Calif., 1977).

12. John Lauder, "Lessons on the Strategic Bombing Survey for Contemporary Defense Policy," *Orbis* 18, no. 3 (Fall 1974), 779.

13. Colin S. Gray, "Nuclear Strategy: Toward a Theory of Victory," *International Security* 4, no. 1 (Summer 1979), 68.

14. Francis Hoeber, "How Little Is Enough?" *International Security* 3, no. 3 (Winter 1978–79), 53–73.

15. Fritz Ermarth, "Contrasts in Soviet and American Strategic Thought," *International Security* 3, no. 2 (Fall 1978), 138–155.

16. Leon Goure, *Shelters in Soviet War Survival Strategy* (Advanced International Studies Institute, Washington, D.C., 1978), p. 9.

17. U.S. Senate, Committee on Foreign Relations, *Fiscal Year 1980 Arms Control Impact Statements*, p. 87.

18. Amrom Katz, *Verification and SALT: The State-of-the-Art and the Art of the State* (Heritage Foundation, Washington, D.C., 1979).

19. See A. Amalrik, *Will the Soviet Union Survive until 1984?* (Harper & Row, New York, 1970); and John P. Dunlop, "Solzhenitsyn in Exile," *Survey* 21, no. 96 (1975).

20. Richard Foster, *The Soviet Concept of National Entity Survival* (SRI International, Arlington, March 1978), pp. 37–38.

21. Ibid., p. 58 (emphasis added).

22. For an account of past U.S. covert activity in Eastern Europe, see William R. Corson, *The Armies of Ignorance* (Dial Press, New York, 1978).

23. For a study concerning the targeting of power projection forces, see Joseph V. Braddock et al., *Determination of FOM for Use in SIOP Targeting of Soviet Conventional Military Forces Stationed in the Soviet Union* (BDM Corporation, McLean, Va., 1978).

8. *Targeting Problems for Central War*

1. Leon V. Sigal, "Rethinking the Unthinkable," *Foreign Policy*, no. 34 (Spring 1979), 39.

2. *New York Times*, 24 January 1979, p. A13.

3. Harold Brown, *Department of Defense Annual Report, Fiscal Year 1979* (Washington, D.C., 1978), p. 65.

4. Ibid.

5. Fred C. Iklé, "Can Nuclear Deterrence Last Out the Century?" *Foreign Affairs* 51, no. 2 (January 1973).

6. See Colin S. Gray, *The Geopolitics of the Nuclear Era: Heartland, Rimlands, and the Technological Revolution* (Crane, Russak for the National Strategy Information Center, New York, 1977).

7. See, for example, Senate Foreign Relations Committee, *U.S.-USSR Strategic Policies* (Washington, D.C., 1974).

8. I have developed this thesis at length in my *Nuclear Strategy and National Style* (University Press of America, Washington, D.C., 1985).

9. Senate Foreign Relations Committee, *Nuclear Weapons and Foreign Policy* (Washington, D.C., 1974), p. 160.

10. See Bernard Brodie, "The Development of Nuclear Strategy," *International Security* 2, no. 4 (Spring 1978), 79.

11. A forceful statement of this thesis is Paul H. Nitze, "Deterring our Deterrent," *Foreign Policy*, no. 25 (Winter 1976–77), 195–210.

12. See Colin S. Gray, *The MX ICBM and National Security* (Praeger, New York, 1981).

13. For a useful summary that rests upon Soviet written sources, see Joseph D. Douglass and Amoretta Hoeber, *Soviet Strategy for Nuclear War* (Hoover Institution Press, Stanford, Calif., 1979).

14. The prospects for the exercising of great discrimination in targeting are reviewed in Carl H. Builder, *The Prospects and Implications of Non-nuclear Means for Strategic Conflict* (Adelphi Paper no. 200, IISS, London, Summer 1985).

15. This discussion does not accommodate the possible ramifications of fears of a nuclear winter. See Francis P. Hoeber and Robert K. Squire, "The 'Nuclear Winter' Hypothesis: Some Policy Implications," *Strategic Review* 13, no. 3 (Summer 1985), 39–46, and Colin S. Gray, "The Nuclear Winter Thesis and U.S. Strategic Policy," *Washington Quarterly* 8, no. 3 (Summer 1985).

16. Of recent years there has been much sterile debate (exchange of assertions) over just what *was* the U.S. trump card in October 1962.

17. See Ken Booth, *Strategy and Ethnocentrism* (Croom Helm, London, 1979). A recent analysis of considerable interest is Notra Trulock III, "Weapons of Mass Destruction in Soviet Strategy" (paper presented at the Conference on Soviet Military Strategy in Europe, Oxford, 24–25 September 1984).

18. This elementary, though critically important, truism was explained with exemplary forceful clarity in Bernard Brodie, *Strategy in the Missile Age* (Princeton University Press, Princeton, N.J., 1959), pp. 296–297. What was true in 1959 remains, in this instance, true today.

19. An ASW campaign against the Soviet attack submarines that help protect SSBN deployment areas (in the far north) also would function as a threat multiplier.

20. However, it can be argued that if the United States is to lose a general war, it would be prudent to attempt to ensure that the Soviet Union lost also.

9. *On Keeping Them Down; or, Why Do Recovery Models Recover so Fast?*

1. This employment aim replaced the previous goal of destroying the "viability" of the Soviet economy promulgated by then secretary of defense Robert McNamara about a decade earlier. The objective of destroying viability, in theory, requires that the USSR be rendered incapable of satisfying, out of residual production, demands arising from surviving population and enterprises, and that stocks that do survive are insufficient to sustain the economy during its attempt to restore adequate output.

2. For some leading unclassified examples, see T. K. Jones, "The U.S.-Soviet Strategic Balance: Options and Non-Options," *Journal of International Relations*, Fall 1977; and Jones and W. Scott Thompson, "Central War and Civil Defense," *Orbis*, Fall 1978.

3. Note the importance here of *can* as opposed to *do*.

4. On the question of locating such bottlenecks, see J. Leavitt, *Analysis and Identification of Nationally Essential Industries*, vol. 1 (Institute for Defense Analysis, Washington, D.C., P–972, March 1974).

10. *Exemplary Industrial Targets for Controlled Conflict*

This analysis was performed under contract for the Federal Preparedness Agency. The judgments are those of the author and do not necessarily reflect the views of any department or agency of the U.S. government. The author is indebted to former colleagues who offered advice and assistance, namely Lois Heiser, Louis Wegner, Norman Hanunian, and Hans Heymann.

1. See *The Input-Output Structure of the US Economy, 1967* (Survey of Current Business, Interindustry Economics Division, U.S. Department of Commerce, February 1974).

2. Ibid.

3. Ibid.

4. Ibid.

5. The data on U.S. petroleum refineries and steel-producing plants are derived from *Products Pipe Line Map of the United States and Southern Canada* (American Petroleum Institute, Washington, D.C., 1973), and *Directory of Iron and Steel Works of the United States and Canada* (American Iron and Steel Institute, Washington, D.C., 1974). The data on nonferrous metal production and stockpiling are from staff of the Bureau of Mines, *Minerals Yearbook 1971* (U.S. Department of the Interior, Washington, D.C., 1971), and some special materials made available by the Office of Preparedness for this study. The data for natural gas distribution are from Maynard M. Stephens and Joseph A. Golasinski, *Vulnerability of Natural Gas Systems* (U.S. Department of the Interior and Defense Civil Preparedness Agency, Washington, D.C., June 1974), and *The National Atlas of the United States of America* (U.S. Department of the Interior, Geological Survey, Washington, D.C., 1970).

6. R. T. Pretty and D. H. R. Archer, eds., *Jane's Weapon Systems, 1973–74* (Jane's Yearbooks, London, 1974).

7. See testimony of James R. Schlesinger, in Subcommittee on Arms Control, International Law and Organization, U.S. Senate, Committee on Foreign Relations, *Briefing on Counterforce Attacks* (Washington, D.C., 1975), p. 10.

8. Samuel Glasstone, ed., *The Effects of Nuclear Weapons*, 2d ed. (U.S. Atomic Energy Commission, Washington, D.C., 1964).

9. D. C. Kephart, *Damage Probability Computer for Point Targets with P and Q Vulnerability Numbers* (Rand Corporation, Santa Monica, Calif., R-1380-PR, February 1974).

10. Maynard M. Stephens, *Vulnerability of Total Petroleum Systems* (Defense Civil Preparedness Agency, Washington, D.C., May 1973).

11. *Flood Control and Navigation Maps of the Mississippi River*, 41st ed. (Army Corps of Engineers, 1973).

11. *Population Targeting and U.S. Strategic Doctrine*

1. Nuclear Targeting Policy Review Panel, *Phase I Report* (Department of Defense, Washington, D.C., 1978).

2. Harold Brown, *Department of Defense Annual Report Fiscal Year 1979* (Washington, D.C., 1978), p. 55.

3. Bruce Bennett and James Foster, "Retaliation against the Soviet Homeland," in Richard K. Bets, ed., *Cruise Missiles: Technology, Strategy, and Politics* (Brookings Institution, Washington, D.C., 1981).

4. Giulio Douhet, *The Command of the Air* (Coward McCann, New York, 1942), p. 128.

5. Ibid.

6. Text in Charles Webster and Noble Frankland, *The Strategic Air Offensive against Germany*, vol. 4 (Her Majesty's Stationery Office, London, 1961), p. 73.

7. Ibid.

8. George Quester, *Deterrence before Hiroshima: The Airpower Background of Modern Strategy* (John Wiley & Sons, New York, 1966), p. 73.

9. Ibid., p. 112.

10. F. H. Hinsley, E. E. Thomas, C. F. G. Ransom, and R. C. Knight, *British Intelligence in the Second World War: Its Influence on Strategy and Operations*, vol. 2 (Cambridge University Press, New York, 1981), p. 258.

11. Quester, *Deterrence before Hiroshima*, p. 149.

12. David Irving, *The Destruction of Dresden* (Ballantine, New York, 1965), p. 210.

13. W. Craven and J. L. Cate, *The Army Air Forces in World War II*, vol. 5 (University of Chicago Press, Chicago, 1952), pp. 615–618.

14. Quoted in Gregg Herken, *The Winning Weapon: The Atomic Bomb in the Cold War, 1945–1950* (Vintage, New York, 1981), p. 286.

15. Aside from the historically contentious issue of whether the atomic bombings were required to produce unconditional surrender without an invasion, Michael Walzer has argued that while the bombings of Hiroshima and Nagasaki would have been justified if necessary to prevent defeat or defend the U.S., they cannot be justified on the grounds that they were required to simply allow the United States to attain its most desired objective (unconditional surrender). See Michael Walzer, *Just and Unjust Wars: A Moral Argument with Historical Illustrations* (Basic Books, New York, 1977), pp. 263–268.

16. Herken, *Winning Weapon*, pp. 196–199; David Alan Rosenberg, "U.S. Nuclear Stockpile, 1945–1960," *Bulletin of the Atomic Scientists*, May 1982, pp. 25–30.

17. Rosenberg, "U.S. Nuclear Stockpile."

18. David MacIsaac, "The Air Force and Strategic Thought, 1945–1951" (Wilson Center International Security Studies Program Working Paper, no. 8, 1979).

19. See Peter Wyden, *Day One* (Simon & Schuster, New York, 1984).

20. See John Prados, *The Soviet Estimate: U.S. Intelligence Analysis and Russian Military Strength* (Dial Press, New York, 1982).

21. Anthony Cave Brown, ed., *DROPSHOT: The American Plan for World War III against Russia in 1957* (Dial Press/James Wade, New York, 1978).

22. Letter from David Rosenberg.

23. "Strategic Implications of the Atomic Bomb," 29 August 1947, USSR Series (3-2-46), sec. 8, United States Joint Chiefs of Staff Modern Military Section, National Archives, Washington, D.C., cited by Herken, *Winning Weapon*.

24. Herken, *Winning Weapon*, p. 271.

25. Thomas H. Etzold and John Lewis Gaddis, *Containment: Documents on American Policy and Strategy, 1945–1950* (Columbia University Press, New York, 1980), pp. 343–357.

26. Herken, *Winning Weapon*, p. 291.

27. Brown, *DROPSHOT*, p. 23.

28. Aaron Friedberg, "A History of U.S. Strategic Doctrine, 1945–1980," *Journal of Strategic Studies*, 1/1980, pp. 37–71.

29. Desmond Ball, *Deja Vu: The Return to Counterforce in the Nixon Administration* (California Seminar, Santa Monica, Calif., 1974), p. 11.

30. "New Targeting Plan," *Aviation Week*, 12 December 1960, p. 25.

31. Ball, *Deja Vu*, p. 12.

32. Ibid.

33. Cited in William W. Kaufmann, *The McNamara Strategy* (Harper & Row, New York, 1964), pp. 114–120.

34. C. Johnston Conover, *U.S. Strategic Nuclear Weapons and Deterrence* (Rand Corporation, Santa Monica, Calif., 1977), pp. 13–17.

35. Ball, *Deja Vu*, p. 16.

36. Desmond Ball, "Counterforce Targeting: How New? How Viable?" *Arms Control Today* 11, no. 2 (February 1981).

37. "U.S. War Plans Call for Striking Russian Industry," *Los Angeles Times*, 2 February 1977, p. 1; House Committee on Appropriations, *Department of Defense Appropriations for 1978*, pt. 2 (Washington, D.C., 1977), p. 212.

38. House Committee on Armed Services, *Hearings on Military Posture and H.R. 6722* (Washington, D.C., 1973).

39. Desmond Ball, "Issues in Strategic Nuclear Targeting: Target Selection and Rates of Fire" (paper prepared for delivery at 1982 Annual Meeting of the American Political Science Association, Denver, Colo., 2–5 September 1982).

40. "Testimony of Admiral Stanffield Turner, DCI," in Joint Economic Committee, *Allocation of Resources in the Soviet Union and China* (Washington, D.C., 1977), p. 60; "Testimony of Vice Admiral Frank McMullen, Vice Director Strategic Target Planning, JSTPS," in House Committee on Armed Services, *Hearings on Military Posture and H.R. 1872* (Washington, D.C., 1979), bk. 1, pt. 3, p. 20.

41. Robert Galucci, *Neither Peace nor Honor* (Johns Hopkins University Press, Baltimore, 1975), pp. 93–94.

42. Joint Committee on Defense Production, *Civil Preparedness Review*, pt. 2: *Industrial Defense and Nuclear Attack* (Washington, D.C., 1977), p. 106.

43. Senate Committee on Armed Services, *Fiscal Year 1977 Authorization for Military Procurement, Research and Development, and Active Duty Selected Reserve and Civilian Personnel Strengths* (Washington, D.C., 1976), pt. 2, p. 6423.

44. "U.S. War Plans Call for Striking Russian Industry," *Los Angeles Times*, 2 February 1977.

45. Desmond Ball to author, 24 September 1984.

46. For other aspects of PD-59 and Carter administration targeting policy see Ball, "Issues in Strategic Nuclear Targeting"; and idem, "Developments in U.S. Strategic Nuclear Policy under the Carter Administration" (ACIS Working Paper No. 21, 1980).

47. William Beecher, "U.S. Drafts New N-War Strategy vs Soviets," *Boston Globe*, 27 July 1980, pp. 1, 12.

48. Brown, *Department of Defense Annual Report Fiscal Year 1979*, p. 55.

49. House Committee on Appropriations, *Department of Defense Appropriations for 1983* (Washington, D.C., 1982), pt. 4, p. 552.

50. R. H. Craver, M. K. Drake, J. T. McGahan, J. F. Schneider, and E. Swick, *The Feasibility of Population Targeting* (Scientific Applications, Inc., McLean, Va., 1978).

51. See Walzer, *Just and Unjust Wars*, chap. 17; Gregory Kavka, "Some Paradoxes of De-

terrence," *Journal of Philosophy* (1978), 285–303; Sisela Bok, *Lying: Moral Choice in Public and Private Life* (Random House, New York, 1978); Richard S. Hartigan, "Non-Combatant Immunity: Reflections on Its Origins and Present Status," *Review of Politics* (1967), 204–220.

52. Ball, "U.S. Strategic Forces: How Would They Be Used?" *International Security* 7, no. 3 (1982–83), 31–60.

53. "Protocol Additional to the Geneva Conventions of 12 August 1949, and Relating to the Protection of Victims of International Armed Conflicts," Protocol I (Geneva, July 1977).

54. Ibid.

55. *Significantly less* should be interpreted as requiring not only that the number of people killed is relatively smaller but also that the absolute numbers of fatalities are such that there is some meaningful difference in prospects for recovery. Clearly, what constitutes *significantly less* is highly subjective.

56. Spurgeon M. Keeny, Jr., and Wolfgang K. H. Panofsky, "MAD versus NUTS: Can Doctrine or Weaponry Remedy the Mutual Hostage Relationship of the Superpowers?" *Foreign Policy*, Winter 1981–82, pp. 282–304; Wolfgang K. H. Panofsky, "The Mutual Hostage Relationship between America and Russia," *Foreign Affairs* 51 (1973), 109–118; Glenn C. Buchan, "The Anti-MAD Mythology," *Bulletin of the Atomic Scientists*, April 1981, pp. 13–17.

57. Office of Technology Assessment, *The Effects of Nuclear War* (Allanheld Osmun, Montclair, N.J., 1980), p. 100.

58. C. Bruce Sibley, *Surviving Doomsday* (Shaw & Sons, London, 1977), pp. 22–23.

59. Central Intelligence Agency, *Soviet Civil Defense* (Central Intelligence Agency, NI 78-10003, Washington, D.C., July 1978), p. 2.

60. Ibid.

61. Arthur Katz, *Life after Nuclear War* (Ballinger, Cambridge, Mass., 1981), p. 314.

62. Desmond Ball, "Research Note: Soviet ICBM Deployment," *Survival* 22, no. 4 (July/August 1980), 167–168.

63. Desmond Ball, "The Soviet Target Base" (mimeo, 1981).

64. Bernard Brodie, *Strategy in the Missile Age* (Princeton University Press, Princeton, N.J., 1959), p. 156.

65. U.S. Air Force, *International Law—The Conduct of Armed Conflict and Air Operations* (Department of Defense, Washington, D.C., 19 November 1976), pp. 1–4.

66. Carl H. Builder and Morlie Graubard, *The International Law of Armed Conflict: The Implications for the Concept of Assured Destruction* (Rand Corporation, Santa Monica, Calif., R–2804-FF, January 1982).

12. *Targeting Nuclear Energy*

1. Anthony Cave Brown, ed., *DROPSHOT: The United States Plan for War with the Soviet Union in 1957* (Dial Press, New York, 1978), pp. 201–202, 289.

2. *New York Times*, 30 May 1982, pp. 1, 6; and Senate Armed Services Committee, *Department of Defense Authorization for Appropriations for Fiscal Year 1981* (Washington, D.C., 1980), pt. 5, p. 2721.

3. "Country-by-Country Status," *Nuclear Engineering International* 30 (August Supplement), 7–14.

4. Quoted in Donald McIsaac, ed., *United States Strategic Bombing Survey* (Garland, New York, 1976), p. 649.

5. McIsaac, in ibid., p. 3. See also Wilson Clark and Jake Page, *Energy Vulnerability and War: Alternatives for America* (Norton, New York, 1981), pp. 49–54.

6. Robert Jackson, *Air War over Korea* (Ian Allan, London, 1973), pp. 141–143; Walter

G. Mermes, *Truce Tent and Fighting Front* (Government Printing Office, Washington, D.C.), pp. 319–324.

7. Insight Team of the *London Sunday Times*, *The Yom Kippur War* (Doubleday, Garden City, N.Y., 1974), pp. 203–205.

8. *The Pentagon Papers* (Bantam Books, New York, 1971), pp. 502–505; U.S. Department of Defense, *United States–Vietnam Relations*, vol. 6 (Washington, D.C., 1971).

9. Theodore B. Taylor, "Reactor Safety Considerations Related to Sabotage and Wartime Bombardment of Nuclear Power Plants" (unpublished manuscript, 1968), pp. 7–9.

10. Ibid., p. 7a. There may be yet other reasons the plants are attractive targets. For example, there is no public explanation for Iraq's bombardment of Iran's unfinished facility along the Persian Gulf in 1984 and 1985.

11. Stockholm International Peace Research Institute, *Ecological Consequences of the Second Indochina War* (Almqvist & Wiksell, Stockholm, 1976), pp. 49–63.

12. Conrad V. Chester and Rowena O. Chester, "Civil Defense Implications of the Pressurised Water Reactor in a Thermonuclear Target Area," *Nuclear Applications and Technology* 9 (December 1970), 786–795; idem, "Civil Defense Implications of a LMFBR in a Thermonuclear Target Area," *Nuclear Technology* 21 (March 1974), 190–200.

13. Conrad V. Chester and Rowena O. Chester, "Civil Defense Implications of the U.S. Nuclear Power Industry during a Large Nuclear War in the Year 2000," *Nuclear Technology* 31 (December 1976), 326–338.

14. Chester and Chester, "Civil Defense Implications of the Pressurised Water Reactor," p. 787.

15. Steven Alan Fetter, "The Vulnerability of Nuclear Reactors to Attack by Nuclear Weapons" (Bachelor of Science in Physics thesis, Massachusetts Institute of Technology, Department of Physics, Cambridge, Mass., May 1981), p. 81.

16. Demetrios L. Basdekas, "Nuclear Power: A Strategic Vulnerability and Its Assymetries" (unpublished manuscript, 1980); David M. Ericson, Jr., et al., *Interaction of Electromagnetic Pulse with Commercial Nuclear Power Plant Systems*, NUREG/CR–3069 and SAND82–2738/2 (U.S. Nuclear Regulatory Commission, Washington, D.C., 1983).

17. Chester and Chester, "Civil Defense Implications of the U.S. Nuclear Power Industry," p. 331.

18. Chester and Chester, "Civil Defense Implications of an LMFBR," p. 191.

19. For elaboration see Steve Fetter and Kosta Tsipis, "Catastrophic Nuclear Radiation Releases" (Program in Science and Technology for International Security, Department of Physics, Massachusetts Institute of Technology, Cambridge, Mass., Report No. 5, September 1980); idem, "Catastrophic Releases of Radioactivity," *Scientific American* 244 (April 1981), 41–47; Bennett Ramberg, *Destruction of Nuclear Energy Facilities in War: The Problem and the Implications* (Lexington Books, Lexington, Mass., 1980), chap. 2.

20. "Country-by-Country Status," *op. cit.*, pp. 14–15.

21. Central Intelligence Agency, *USSR Summary Map—Population* (Central Intelligence Agency, Langley, Va., April 1974).

22. Central Intelligence Agency, *West Germany—Population* (Central Intelligence Agency, Langley, Va., 400470, May 1972).

23. Leon Gouré, *War Survival in Soviet Strategy: USSR Civil Defense* (Center for Advanced International Studies, Miami, Fla., 1976).

24. Philip R. Pryde, "Nuclear Energy in the Soviet Union," *Current History* 77 (October 1979), 115–118, 135.

25. Fred Kaplan, "The Soviet Civil Defense Myth," *Bulletin of the Atomic Scientists* 34 (March 1978), 14–20; idem, "Soviet Civil Defense: Some Myths in the Western Debate," *Survival* 20 (May–June 1978), 113–120.

26. For a list of these facilities see B. M. Jasani, "Nuclear Fuel Fabrication Plants" and

"Nuclear Fuel Reprocessing Plants," in Stockholm International Peace Research Institute, *Nuclear Proliferation Problems* (MIT Press, Cambridge, Mass., 1974), pp. 70–98; and "Country-by-Country Status," pp. 7–15.

27. Ibid., 13–14. For mixed oxide fuel fabrication facilities, see Jasani, "Nuclear Fuel Fabrication," pp. 84–85.

28. Chester and Chester, "Civil Defense Implications of the U.S. Nuclear Power Industry," pp. 337–338.

29. Richard A. Falk, "Environmental Warfare and Ecocide: A Legal Perspective," in Richard A. Falk, ed., *The Vietnam War and International Law: The Concluding Phase* (Princeton University Press, Princeton, N.J., 1976), p. 290.

30. "Protocol Additional to the Geneva Conventions of 12 August 1949, and Relating to the Protection of Victims of International Armed Conflicts (Protocol I)" (mimeo, Diplomatic Conference on the Reaffirmation and Development of International Humanitarian Law Applicable to Armed Conflicts, Geneva, 1977), pp. 37–39.

31. United Nations, Committee on Disarmament, *Report of the Committee on Disarmament* (General Assembly, Official Records, Thirty-sixth Session, Supplement No. 27, United Nations, N.Y.: A/36/37, 1981), pp. 66–74. See in particular Sweden's proposal, "Memorandum Submitted by the Delegation of Sweden on Certain Aspects of a Convention Prohibiting Radiological Warfare" (United Nations Committee on Disarmament, Geneva, CD/RW/WP-19, 16 March 1981). As of the time of this writing, September 1985, no progress has been made in the Committee toward a convention prohibiting attacks on reactors and support installations.

32. Bennett Ramberg, *Nuclear Power Plants as Weapons For the Enemy: An Unrecognized Military Peril* (University of California Press, Berkeley, Calif., 1984).

33. Chester and Chester, "Civil Defense Implications of the U.S. Nuclear Power Industry," pp. 329–330.

34. *Nucleonics Week*, 28 July 1977.

35. For elaboration see Ramberg, *Destruction of Nuclear Energy Facilities in War*, pp. 132–134.

13. *Ethnic Targeting: Some Bad Ideas*

1. See, for example, William Schneider and R. J. Milefsky, *Regionalization of the USSR* (BDM Corporation, McLean, Va., 1978).

2. Bernard Brodie, *Strategy in the Missile Age* (Princeton University Press, Princeton, N.J., 1964), p. 136.

3. Helene Carrere d'Encausse, *Decline of an Empire: The Soviet Socialist Republics in Revolt* (Harper Colophon Books, New York, 1981), pp. 191f.

4. Ibid., pp. 224f.

5. Ibid., pp. 212f.

6. Rasma Karklins, "Nationality Power in Soviet Republics: Attitudes and Perceptions," *Studies in Comparative Communism*, Spring 1981, pp. 70–93.

7. Alexandre Bennigsen, "Muslim Conservative Opposition to the Soviet Regime: The Sufi Brotherhoods in the North Caucasus," in Jeremy R. Azreal, ed., *Soviet Nationality Policies and Practices* (Praeger, New York, 1978), pp. 334f.

8. Colin S. Gray, "Nuclear Strategy: The Case for a Theory of Victory," *International Security* 4, no. 1 (Summer 1979), 68.

9. Richard B. Foster, *The Soviet Concept of National Entity Survival* (SRI International, Arlington, Va., 1978), p. 62.

10. Bernard S. Albert, "Constructive Counterpower," *Orbis* 19, no. 2 (Summer 1976), 362.

11. See William Beecher, "U.S. Drafts New N-war Strategy vs. Soviets," *Boston Globe*, 27 July 1980, p. 1; and Richard Burt, "New Nuclear Strategy: An Inevitable Shift," *New York Times*, 7 August 1980, p. 3.

12. RG 341, Modern Military Branch, U.S. National Archives, Entry 214, Files 2-5800 to 2-5899.

14. *War Termination and Nuclear Targeting Strategy*

1. For an example, see Colin Gray, "Nuclear Strategy: A Case for a Theory of Victory," *International Security* 4, no. 1 (Summer 1979), 54–87.

2. Advocates of systems like the MX sometimes attempt to escape the choice by contending the Soviets would never thusly initiate a war out of fear of American attack but only as part of a premeditated aggression; the American ability to win World War III is thus contended to serve handsomely to deter it as well.

3. See Herbert Scoville, Jr., *MX: Prescription for Disaster* (MIT Press, Cambridge, Mass., 1981).

4. See Wolfgang Panofsky, "The Mutual-Hostage Relationship between America and Russia," *Foreign Affairs* 52, no. 1 (October 1973), 109–118.

5. For useful discussions of the termination of a nuclear war, see Herman Kahn, William Pfaff, and Edmund Stillman, *War Termination: Issues and Concepts* (Hudson Institute, Croton-on-Hudson, New York, 1968). See also Edmund Stillman, "Civilian Sanctuary and Target Avoidance Policy in Thermonuclear War," and Herman Kahn, "Issues of Thermonuclear War Termination," in William T. R. Fox, ed., "How Wars End," *Annals of the American Academy of Political and Social Science* 392 (November 1970), 116–132, 133–172. For a recent analysis, see Edward C. Luck, "Deterrence Theory and Nuclear War Endings," in Stuart Albert and Edward C. Luck, *On the Endings of Wars* (Kennikat Press, Port Washington, N.Y., 1980), pp. 25–43. For earlier treatments, see Klaus Knorr and Thornton Read, eds., *Limited Strategic War* (Praeger, New York, 1962), and Paul H. Backus, "Finite Deterrence, Controlled Retaliation," *United States Naval Institute Proceedings* 85, no. 673 (March 1959), 23–31. For a broader analysis, see Fred C. Iklé, *Every War Must End* (Columbia University Press, New York, 1971).

6. For some ideas on deescalation from nuclear war to conventional war, see Herman Kahn, *On Escalation: Metaphors and Scenarios* (Praeger, New York, 1965), pp. 230–243.

7. Some imaginative lists of targets within the Soviet Union are presented in Herman Kahn, *On Thermonuclear War* (Princeton University Press, Princeton, N.J., 1960). See also John B. Shewmaker and Mary R. Tietz, *Retaliatory Issues for the U.S. Strategic Forces* (Congressional Budget Office, Washington, D.C., 1978).

8. For discussions of the likely nature of actual Soviet nuclear strategy, see Benjamin Lambeth, "Selective Nuclear Operations and Soviet Strategy," in Johan Holst and Uwe Nerlich, eds., *Beyond Nuclear Deterrence: New Aims, New Arms* (Crane Russak, New York, 1977), pp. 79–104; and Dimitri Simes, "Deterrence and Coercion in Soviet Policy," *International Security* 5, no. 3 (Winter 1980–81), 80–103.

9. For discussions of the 1980 "changes" in U.S. nuclear targeting strategy, see Desmond Ball, "PD-59: A Strategic Critique," *F.A.S. Public Interest Report*, October 1980; and Richard Burt, "New Nuclear Strategy: An Inevitable Shift," *New York Times*, 13 August 1980, p. 3.

10. For interesting variations on economic targeting, see Edmund D. Bronner, *Targeting the Political Economy of the Soviet Union USSR* (Rand Corporation, Santa Monica, Calif., 1976).

11. For an example, see Leon Goure, *War Survival in Soviet Strategy* (University of Miami, Coral Gables, Fla., 1976).

12. See Thomas C. Schelling, *The Strategy of Conflict* (Harvard University Press, Cambridge, Mass., 1960), especially pp. 75–77.

Bibliography

1. Early U.S. Targeting Plans, 1945–1960

Ball, Desmond J. *Deja Vu: The Return of Counterforce in the Nixon Administration*. Santa Monica, Calif.: California Seminar on Arms Control and Foreign Policy, 1974.
——. *Politics and Force Levels: The Strategic Missile Program of the Kennedy Administration*. Berkeley: University of California Press, 1980.
——. "Targeting for Strategic Deterrence," Adelphi Papers No. 185. London: International Institute for Strategic Studies, 1983.
Brown, Anthony Cave, ed. *DROPSHOT: The American Plan for World War III against Russia in 1957*. New York: Dial Press, 1978.
Etzold, Thomas, and Gaddis, John Lewis. *Containment: Documents on American Policy and Strategy, 1945–1950*. New York: Columbia University Press, 1978.
Friedberg, Aaron L. "A History of U.S. Strategic 'Doctrine,' 1945 to 1980." *Journal of Strategic Studies* 3:3 (1980), 37–71.
Herken, Gregg. *The Winning Weapon: The Atomic Bomb in the Cold War, 1945–1950*. New York: Random House, 1981.
Kanzelberger, Michael W. *American Nuclear Strategy: A Selective Analytical Survey of Threat Concepts for Deterrence and Compellence*. Santa Monica, Calif.: Rand Corporation, 1979.
Kaplan, Fred. *The Wizards of Armageddon*. New York: Simon & Schuster, 1983.
MacIsaac, David. "The Air Force and Strategic Thought 1945–1951." Wilson Center International Security Studies Program Working Paper, no. 8, 1979.
Rosenberg, David A. "American Atomic Strategy and the Hydrogen Bomb Decision." *Journal of American History* 66 (June 1979), 62–88.
——. "The Origins of Overkill: Nuclear Weapons and American Strategy, 1945–1960." *International Security* 7:4 (Spring 1983), 1–71.
——. "A Smoking Radiating Ruin at the End of Two Hours: Documents on American Plans for Nuclear War with the Soviet Union, 1945–1955." *International Security* 6:3 (Winter 1981–82), 3–38.
——. *Toward Armageddon: The Foundations of American Atomic Strategy*, forthcoming.
Rowen, Henry. "The Evolution of Strategic Nuclear Doctrine." In Lawrence Martin, ed., *Strategic Thought in the Nuclear Age*. London: Heinemann, 1979.
Strategic Air Command, History and Research Division. *History of the Joint Strategic Target Planning Staff: Background and Preparation of SIOP-62*. Offutt, Neb.: Strategic Air Command, 1962.
Wells, Samuel F. "The Origins of Massive Retaliation." *Political Science Quarterly* 96:1 (1981), 31–52.

2. U.S. Targeting Plans, 1961–1977

Ball, Desmond J. *Deja Vu: The Return of Counterforce in the Nixon Administration*. Santa Monica, Calif.: California Seminar on Arms Control and Foreign Policy, 1974.

———. *Politics and Force Levels: The Strategic Missile Program of the Kennedy Administration.* Berkeley: University of California Press, 1980.

Beecher, William. "Major War Plans Are Being Revised by White House." *New York Times* 5 August 1972, pp. 1, 9.

Enthoven, Alain C. "1963 Nuclear Strategy Revisited." In Harold P. Ford and Francis X. Winters, S.J., eds., *Ethics and Nuclear Strategy.* Maryknoll: Orbis, 1977.

Finney, John W. "U.S. Says It Is Retargeting Some Missiles under a New Strategic Concept." *New York Times*, 11 January 1974, p. 6.

Friedberg, Aaron L. "A History of U.S. Strategic 'Doctrine' 1945 to 1980." *Journal of Strategic Studies* 3:3 (1980), 37–71.

Johnson, Oswald. " 'New' U.S. Nuclear Policy: Just a Footnote in Politics?" *Los Angeles Times*, 10 September 1980, pp. 1, 10.

Kahan, Jerome. *Security in the Nuclear Age: Developing U.S. Strategic Arms Policy.* Washington, D.C.: Brookings Institution, 1975.

Kaufmann, William W. *The McNamara Strategy.* New York: Harper & Row, 1974.

Lambeth, Benjamin S., and Lewis, Kevin L. "Economic Targeting in Nuclear War: U.S. and Soviet Approaches." *Orbis*, Spring 1983, 127–149.

Mandelbaum, Michael. *The Nuclear Question: The United States and Nuclear Weapons, 1946–1976.* New York: Cambridge University Press, 1979.

Pringle, Peter, and Arkin, William. *SIOP: Nuclear War from the Inside.* London: Sphere, 1983.

U.S. Congress. House. Committee on Appropriations. *Department of Defense Appropriations for FY 1975.* Pt. 1. Washington, D.C., 1974.

———. *Department of Defense Appropriations for FY 1977.* Pt. 8. Washington, D.C., 1976.

———. *Department of Defense Appropriations for FY 1978.* Pt. 2. Washington, D.C., 1977.

———. Committee on Armed Services. *Hearings on Military Posture and H.R. 1872.* Pt. 3, bk. 1. Washington, D.C., 1979.

"U.S. War Plan Calls for Striking Russian Industry," *Los Angeles Times*, 2 February 1977, pp. 1, 9.

3. Current Targeting Doctrine

Anderson, Jack. "U.S. Strategic Targets Include China." *Washington Post*, 3 October 1980, p. C14.

Ball, Desmond J. "Development in U.S. Strategic Nuclear Policy under the Carter Administration." ACIS Working Paper No. 21. UCLA, 1980.

Beecher, William. "U.S. Drafts New N-War Strategy vs. Soviets." *Boston Globe*, 27 July 1980, pp. 1, 12.

Burt, Richard. "Carter Said to Back a Plan for Limiting Any Nuclear War." *New York Times*, 6 August 1980, pp. 1, 6.

———. "Carter Shifts U.S. Strategy for Deterring Nuclear War." *New York Times*, 10 February 1970, p. 5.

———. "New Nuclear Strategy: An Inevitable Shift." *New York Times*, 7 August 1980, p. A-3.

———. "The New Strategy for Nuclear War: How It Evolved." *New York Times*, 13 August 1980.

———. "Pentagon Reviewing Nuclear War Plans." *New York Times*, 16 December 1977, p. A-5.

———. "U.S. Moving toward Vast Revision of Its Strategy on Nuclear War." *New York Times*, 30 November 1978.

Getler, Michael. "Administration's Nuclear War Policy Stance Still Murky." *Washington Post*, 10 November 1982, p. A24.

——. "Carter Directive Modifies Strategy for a Nuclear War." *Washington Post*, 6 August 1980, p. 10.

Halloran, Richard. "Pentagon Draws Up First Strategy for Fighting a Nuclear War." *New York Times*, 30 May 1982, pp. 1, 6.

Johnson, Oswald. 'New' U.S. Nuclear Policy: Just a Footnote in Politics? *Los Angeles Times*, 10 September 1980, pp. 1, 10.

Kaylor, Robert. "Brown Would Widen Range of Russian Military Targets." *Washington Post*, 14 January 1979, p. A13.

Leitenberg, Milton. "Presidential Directive (P.D.) 59: United States Nuclear Weapons Targeting Policy." *Journal of Peace Research* 4:18 (1981), 309–317.

Middleton, Drew. "SAC Chief Is Critical of Carter's New Nuclear Policy." *New York Times*, 7 September 1980, p. 5.

Pringle, Peter, and Arkin, William. *SIOP: Nuclear War from the Inside.* London: Sphere, 1983.

Scheer, Robert. "Pentagon Plan Aims at Victory in Nuclear War." *Los Angeles Times*, 15 August 1982, pp. 1, 23.

U.S. Congress. House. Committee on Armed Services. *Hearings on Military Posture and H.R. 1872.* Pt. 2, bk. 1. Washington, D.C., 1979.

——. Senate. Committee on Armed Services. *Department of Defense Authorization for Appropriations for FY 1979.* Pt. 9. Washington, D.C., 1978.

——. *Department of Defense Authorization for Appropriations for FY 1980.* Pt. 3. Washington, D.C., 1979.

——. *Department of Defense Authorization for Appropriations for FY 1981.* Pt. 5. Washington, D.C., 1980.

——. *Department of Defense Authorization for Appropriations for FY 1982.* Pt. 7. Washington, D.C., 1981.

"U.S. Plans New Atomic Strategy." *Baltimore Sun*, 6 August 1980, p. 1.

Weintraub, Bernard. "Pentagon Reviewing Strategic Posture." *New York Times*, 1 December 1977, p. A21.

——. "Pentagon Seeking Shift in Nuclear Deterrent Policy." *New York Times*, 5 January 1979, p. A5.

——. "U.S. Is Reassessing Its Strategy for Meeting Soviet Nuclear Strike." *New York Times*, 14 May 1977, pp. 1, 9.

Wood, David. "U.S. Strategy Misunderstood Officials Say." *Los Angeles Times*, 6 June 1982, p. 4.

4. *Issues in Targeting*

Adelman, Kenneth. "Beyond MAD-ness." *Policy Review*, Summer 1981, pp. 77–85.

Albert, Bernard S. "Constructive Counterpower." *Orbis* 20 (1976), 343–366.

Arkin, William M. "Why SIOP-6?" *Bulletin of the Atomic Scientists*, April 1983, pp. 9–10.

Backus, P. H. "Finite Deterrence, Controlled Retaliation." *United States Naval Proceedings* 85 (1959), 23–29.

Bailey, Martin J. "Deterrence, Assured Destruction, and Defense." *Orbis* 16 (1972), 683–695.

Baker, John C., and Berman, Robert P. "Evaluating Counterforce Strategy." *New York Times*, 22 February 1974.

Ball, Desmond J. "PD-59: A Strategic Critique." *F.A.S. Public Interest Report*, October 1980, pp. 5–6.

——. "Can Nuclear War Be Controlled?" Adelphi Paper No. 163. London: International Institute for Strategic Studies, 1981.

——. "Counterforce Targeting: How New? How Viable?" *Arms Control Today* 11:2 (February 1981).

——. "Targeting for Strategic Deterrence." Adelphi Paper No. 185. London: International Institute for Strategic Studies, 1983.

——. "U.S. Strategic Forces: How Would They Be Used?" *International Security* 7:3 (Winter 1982/83), 31–60.

Bennett, Bruce, and Foster, James. "Strategic Retaliation against the Soviet Homeland." In Richard Betts ed., *Cruise Missiles: Technology, Strategy, and Politics,* pp. 137–172. Washington, D.C.: Brookings Institution, 1981.

Beres, Louis René. "Presidential Directive 59: A Critical Assessment." *Parameters* 11 (1981), 19–28.

——. "Tilting toward Thanatos: America's 'Countervailing' Nuclear Strategy." *World Politics,* October 1981, pp. 25–46.

Black, Edwin F. "Presidential Directive 59: The Beginning of a Nuclear Strategy." *U.S. Naval Institute Proceedings,* January 1981, pp. 93–94.

Bower, Michael. "Controlled Thermonuclear War." *New Republic,* 30 July 1962.

Brodie, Bernard. "The Development of Nuclear Strategy." *International Security* 3 (1978), 65–83.

——. *Strategy in the Missile Age.* Princeton, N.J.: Princeton University Press, 1978.

Brown, Harold. "The Objective of U.S. Strategic Forces." Address to the Naval War College. Washington, D.C., 20 August 1980.

Brunner, Edmund D. *Targeting the Political Economy of the USSR.* Santa Monica, Calif.: Rand Corporation, 1976.

Buchan, Glenn C. "The Anti-MAD Mythology." *Bulletin of the Atomic Scientists,* April 1981, pp. 13–17.

Builder, Carl H. "Why Not First-Strike Counterforce Capabilities?" *Strategic Review,* Spring 1979, pp. 32–39.

Burt, Richard. "A New Order of Debate on Atomic War." *New York Times,* 17 August 1980, p. E4.

Buzzard, A. W. "Massive Retaliation and Graduated Deterrence." *World Politics* 8 (1956), 228–237.

Carter, Barry. "Nuclear Strategy and Nuclear Weapons." *Scientific American,* May 1974, pp. 20–31.

"Command and Control: Use It or Lose It?" *F.A.S. Public Interest Report* 33 (October 1980).

Comptroller General. *Countervailing Strategy Demands Revision of Strategic Force Acquisition Plans.* Washington, D.C.: Government Accounting Office, 1981.

Conover, C. Johnston. *U.S. Strategic Weapons and Deterrence.* Santa Monica, Calif.: Rand Corporation, 1977.

Corddry, Charles W. "Clearing Up a Cloudy Issue." *Baltimore Sun,* 24 August 1980, p. K2.

Curl, Richard L. "Strategic Doctrine in the Nuclear Age." *Strategic Review,* Winter 1975.

Davis, Lynn. "Limited Nuclear Options: Deterrence and the New American Doctrine." Adelphi Paper No. 10. London: International Institute for Strategic Studies, Spring 1975.

Douglass, Joseph D. "U.S. Strategy for General Nuclear War." *International Security Review* 5:3 (1980), 287–315.

Feld, Bernard T. "A Policy for Doom." *New York Times,* 19 August 1980.

Foster, Richard B. "From Assured Destruction to Assured Survival." *Comparative Strategy* 2 (1980), 53–74.

——. "One Prolonged Nuclear War." *International Security Review* 6 (1981–1982), 497–518.

Garwin, Richard. "Launch Under Attack to Redress Minuteman Vulnerability." *International Security,* Winter 1979–80, pp. 117–139.

Goldberg, Alfred. *A Brief Survey of the Evolution of Ideas about Counterforce.* Santa Monica, Calif.: Rand Corporation, October 1976.

Goldhamer, Herbert. "The U.S.-Soviet Strategic Balance as Seen from London and Paris." *Survival* 19 (1977), 202–207.

Gray, Colin S. "Dangerous to Your Health: The Debate over Nuclear Strategy and War." *Orbis* 25 (Summer 1982), 327–349.

Green, Phillip. *Deadly Logic: The Theory of Nuclear Deterrence.* Columbus: Ohio State University Press, 1966.

Greene, Wade. "Rethinking the Unthinkable." *New York Times Magazine,* 15 March 1981, pp. 15ff.

Greenwood, Ted, and Nacht, Michael L. "The New Nuclear Debate: Sense or Nonsense." *Foreign Affairs* 52 (1974), 761–780.

Guertner, Gary L. "Strategic Vulnerability of a Multinational State: Deterring the Soviet Union." *Political Science Quarterly* 96:2 (1981), 209–223.

Hoeber, Francis P. "How Little Is Enough?" *International Security* 3 (1978–79), 53–73.

Housman, Damian. "What the President Means Is . . ." *National Review,* 31 October 1980, pp. 1332–1333.

Howard, Michael E. "On Fighting a Nuclear War." *International Security* 5:4 (1981).

Hughes, G. Phillip, and Neu, C. R. *U.S. Strategic Nuclear Forces: Deterrence Policies and Procurement Issues.* Washington, D.C.: Congressional Budget Office, 1977.

Iklé, Fred C. "Can Nuclear Deterrence Last Out the Century?" *Foreign Affairs* 51 (1973), 267–285.

Intriligator, Michael D. "The Debate over Missile Strategy." *Orbis* 11 (1968), 1138–1139.

"It has to Deter." *The Economist,* 16 August 1980, pp. 9–10.

Jarvenpaa, Pauli. "Flexible Nuclear Options: New Myths and Old Realities." Cornell University Peace Studies Program Occasional Paper No. 7, 1976.

Jervis, Robert. *The Illogic of American Nuclear Strategy.* Ithaca, N.Y.: Cornell University Press, 1983.

——. "Why Nuclear Superiority Doesn't Matter." *Political Science Quarterly,* Winter 1979–80, pp. 617–633.

Kahan, Jerome. *Security in the Nuclear Age: Developing U.S. Srategic Arms Policy.* Washington, D.C.: Brookings Institution, 1975.

Kahn, Herman. *On Thermonuclear War.* Princeton, N.J.: Princeton University Press, 1960.

——. *Thinking about the Unthinkable.* New York: Horizon Press, 1962.

Kaplan, Fred. "Going Native without a Field Map: The Press Plunges into Limited Nuclear War." *Columbia Journalism Review,* January/February 1981, pp. 23–29.

——. " 'New' Look from the Pentagon." *Inquiry,* September 1980.

Keeny, Spurgeon M., Jr., and Panofsky, Wolfgang K. H. "MAD versus NUTS: Can Doctrine or Weaponry Remedy the Mutual Hostage Relationship of the Superpowers?" *Foreign Affairs,* Winter 1981/82, pp. 287–304.

Knorr, Klaus, and Read, Thornton, eds. *Limited Strategic War.* New York: Praeger, 1962.

Lauder, John A. "Lessons of the Strategic Bombing Survey for Contemporary Defense Policy." *Orbis* 18 (1974), pp. 770–780.

Lewis, Kevin N. *Lessons of the Strategic Bombing and the Thermonuclear Breakthrough: An Example of Disconnected Defense Planning.* Santa Monica, Calif.: Rand Corporation, 1981.

——. *Nuclear Weapons Policy, Planning, and War Objectives: Toward a Theater-Oriented Deterrent Strategy.* Santa Monica, Calif.: Rand Corporation, 1982.

——. *U.S. Strategic Force Planning: Restoring the Links between Strategy and Capabilities.* Santa Monica, Calif.: Rand Corporation, 1982.

Martin, Laurence. "Changes in Strategic Doctrine: An Initial Interpretation." *Survival,* July/August 1974, pp. 158–164.

[353]

May, Michael. "Some Advantages of a Counterforce Deterrence." *Orbis* 14 (1970), 270–283.

Mossberg, Walter S. "Fighting a Nuclear War." *Wall Street Journal*, 27 August 1980, p. 14.

Neu, C. R. *Economic Models and Strategic Targeting*. Santa Monica, Calif.: Rand Corporation, 1976.

Nitze, Paul. "Assuring Strategic Stability in an Era of Detente." *Foreign Affairs* 54 (1976), 207–232.

———. "Atoms, Strategy, and Policy." *Foreign Affairs* 34 (1956).

Nunn, Jack H. "Termination: The Myth of the Short, Decisive Nuclear War." *Parameters*, December 1980, pp. 36–41.

Panofsky, Wolfgang K. H. "The Mutual-Hostage Relationship between America and Russia." *Foreign Affairs* 51 (1973), 109–118.

Payne, Keith B. "Deterrence, Arms Control, and U.S. Strategic Doctrine." *Orbis*, Fall 1981, pp. 747–769.

Payne, Keith B.; Conover, C. Johnston; and Bennett, Bruce William. *Nuclear Strategy: Flexibility and Stability*. Santa Monica, Calif.: California Seminar on Arms Control and Foreign Policy, 1979.

Powers, Thomas. "Choosing a Strategy for World War III." *Atlantic Monthly*, November 1982, pp. 82–110.

———. *Thinking About the Next War*. New York: Signet, 1983.

Quester, George H. "Ethnic Targeting: A Bad Idea Whose Time Has Come." *Journal of Strategic Studies* 5:2 (June 1982), 228–235.

———. *New Alternatives for Targeting the Soviet Union*. Marina del Rey, Calif.: Analytical Assessments Corporation, 1979.

Ramberg, Bennett. *Destruction of Nuclear Energy Facilities in War*. Lexington, Mass.: Lexington Books, 1980.

Rathjens, George. "Flexible Response Options." *Orbis* 18 (1974), 667–688.

Rathjens, George, and Ruina, Jack. "Nuclear Doctrine and Rationality." *Daedalus*, Winter 1981, pp. 179–187.

Ravenal, Earl C. "Counterforce and Alliance: The Ultimate Connection." *International Security* 6:4 (1982), 26–43.

"Rethinking the Unthinkable." *Time*, 25 August 1980, pp. 31–32.

Richelson, Jeffrey T. "The Dilemmas of Counterpower Targeting." *Comparative Strategy* 2 (1980), 223–237.

Robinson, Clarence A. "Carter Strategic Policy under Scrutiny." *Aviation Week and Space Technology*, 11 August 1980, pp. 21–23.

Rosecrance, Richard. "Strategic Deterrence Reconsidered." Adelphi Paper No. 116. London: International Institute for Strategic Studies, 1975.

Rosenbaum, Ron. "The Subterranean World of the Bomb." *Harper's*, March 1978, pp. 85–105.

Rowen, Henry S. "The Need for an Analytical Framework." *International Security* 1 (1976), 130–146.

Russett, Bruce. "Assured Destruction of What?: A Countercombatant Alternative to Nuclear MADness." *Public Policy* 22 (1974), 121–131.

Salomon, Michael D. "New Concepts for Strategic Parity." *Survival* 19 (1977), 255–262.

Schelling, Thomas C. "Controlled Response and Strategic Warfare." Adephi Paper No. 19. London: International Institute for Strategic Studies, 1965.

Scoville, Herbert, Jr. "Flexible Madness?" *Foreign Policy* 15 (1974), 167–177.

Shewmaker, John B., and Tietz, Mary R. *Retaliatory Issues for U.S. Strategic Nuclear Forces*. Washington, D.C.: Congressional Budget Office, 1978.

Siegal, Leon V. "Rethinking the Unthinkable." *Foreign Policy* 34 (1979), 35–51.

Slocombe, Walter. "The Countervailing Strategy." *International Security* 5:4 (1981).

[354]

Snow, Donald. "Current Nuclear Deterrence Thinking." *International Studies Quarterly* 23 (1979), 445–486.
———. *The Nuclear Future: Toward a Strategy of Uncertainty*. Birmingham: University of Alabama Press, 1983.
———. *Nuclear Strategy in a Dynamic World: American Policy in the 1980s*. Birmingham: University of Alabama Press, 1981.
Snyder, Jack. *Rationality at the Brink: The Role of Cognitive Processes in Failures of Deterrence*. Santa Monica, Calif.: Rand Corporation, 1977.
Soulé, Robert R. *Counterforce Issues for the U.S. Strategic Nuclear Forces*. Washington, D.C.: Congressional Budget Office, 1978.
Steinbrunner, John. "Beyond Rational Deterrence: The Struggle for New Conceptions." *World Politics* 28 (1976), 223–245.
———. "Nuclear Decapitation." *Foreign Policy* 45 (1981–82), 16–28.
Strauch, Ralph E. *Information and Perception in Limited Strategic Conflict: Some U.S. and Soviet Differences*. Santa Monica, Calif.: Rand Corporation, 1976.
Thaxton, Richard. "Directive Fifty-nine." *The Progressive*, October 1980, pp. 36–37.
U.S. Congress. House. Committee on Appropriations. *Department of Defense Appropriations for FY 1975*. Pt. 1. Washington, D.C., 1974.
———. *Department of Defense Appropriations for FY 1977*. Pt. 8. Washington, D.C., 1976.
———. *Department of Defense Appropriations for FY 1978*. Pt. 2. Washington, D.C., 1977.
———. *Department of Defense Appropriations for FY 1980*. Pt. 3. Washington, D.C., 1979.
———. Committee on Armed Services. *Hearings on Military Posture and H.R. 1872*. Pt. 3, bk. 1. Washington, D.C., 1979.
———. Senate. Committee on Foreign Relations. *Briefing on Counterforce Attacks*. Washington, D.C., 1974.
———. *Nuclear War Strategy*. Washington, D.C., 1981.
Utgoff, Victor. "In Defense of Counterforce." *International Security* 6:4 (1982), 44–60.
Van Cleave, William, and Barnett, Roger W. "Strategic Adaptability." *Orbis* 17 (1974), 665–676.
Wadsworth, James. "Counterforce." *Saturday Review*, 28 July 1962.
Wagstaff, Peter. "An Analysis of the City Avoidance Theory." *Stanford Journal of International Studies* 7 (1972), 162–172.
Walkowicz, T. F. "Counterforce Strategy." *Air Force*, February 1955.
Westervelt, Donald R. "The Essence of Armed Futility." *Orbis* 18:3 (1974), 680–705.

5. Soviet Strategy and Perceptions

Arnett Robert L. "Soviet Attitudes toward Nuclear War: Do They Really Think They Can Win?" *Journal of Strategic Studies* 2 (1979), 172–191.
Austin, Anthony. "Moscow Expert Says U.S. Errs on Soviet War Arms." *New York Times*, 25 August 1980, p. 2.
Ball, Desmond. "Soviet Strategic Planning and the Control of Nuclear War." *Soviet Union/Union Sovietique*, 1983.
Clark, Magnus. *The Nuclear Destruction of Britain*. London: Croom Helm, 1981.
Corddry, Charles W. "Soviet Illusion Blamed for New Nuclear Plans." *Baltimore Sun*, 11 August 1980, p. 8.
"Do the Russians Ponder Nuclear Victory?" *F.A.S. Public Interest Report*, October 1980, pp. 6–7.
Douglass, Joseph D., Jr. "Soviet Nuclear Strategy in Europe: A Selective Targeting Doctrine." *Strategic Review* 5 (1977), 19–32.

Douglass, Joseph D., Jr. and Hoeber, Amoretta M. *Soviet Strategy for Nuclear War*. Stanford: Hoover Institution Press, 1979.

Ermarth, Fritz. "Contrasts in American and Soviet Strategic Thought." *International Security* 3 (1978), 138–155.

Frank, Lewis Allen. *Soviet Nuclear Planning: A Point of View of SALT*. Washington, D.C.: American Enterprise Institute, 1977.

Garthoff, Raymond L. "Mutual Deterrence and Strategic Arms Limitation in Soviet Policy." *International Security*, Winter 1979–80, pp. 117–139.

Goure, Leon; Kohler, Foy D.; and Harvey, Mose L. *The Role of Nuclear Forces in Current Soviet Strategy*. Coral Gables, Fla.: Center for Advanced International Studies, 1974.

Hanson, Donald W. "Is Soviet Strategic Doctrine Superior?" *International Security* 7:3 (Winter 1982/83), 671–683.

Holman, Paul. "Deterrence vs. War Fighting: The Soviet Preference." *Air Force Magazine*, March 1981, pp. 50–54.

Kime, Steven. "The Soviet View of War." In Graham D. Vernon, ed., *Soviet Perceptions of Peace and War* (Washington, D.C.: NDU Press, 1981).

Lambeth, Benjamin. "Selective Nuclear Operations and Soviet Strategy." In Johan J. Holst and Uwe Nehrlich, eds., *Beyond Nuclear Deterrence: New Aims, New Arms*. New York: Crane, Russak, 1977.

———. "Uncertainties for the Soviet War Planner." *International Security* 7:3 (Winter 1982/83), 139–166.

Lee, William T. "Soviet Military Capabilities." In Graham D. Vernon, ed., *Soviet Perceptions of War and Peace*. Washington, D.C.: NDU Press, 1981.

———. "Soviet Nuclear Targeting Strategy and SALT." In Steven Rosefielde, ed., *World Communism and the Crossroads*. Boston: Martinus Nijhoff, 1980, pp. 55–58.

Leebaert, Derek, ed. *Soviet Military Thinking*. Boston: Allen & Unwin, 1981.

Lockwood, Jonathan Samuel. *The Soviet View of U.S. Strategic Doctrine: Implications for Decision Making*. New Brunswick, N.J.: Transaction, 1983.

MccGwire, Michael. "Soviet Strategic Weapons Policy, 1955–1970." In Michael MccGwire, Ken Booth, and John McDonnell, eds., *Soviet Naval Policy: Objectives and Constraints*. New York: Praeger, 1975.

McConnell, James. "Soviet and American Strategic Doctrines: One More Time." Center for Naval Analyses Professional Paper 271, January 1980.

Miller, Mark E. "Soviet Strategic Thought: The End of an Era?" *International Security Review* 5:4 (1980–81).

Millett, Stephen M. *Soviet Perceptions of Nuclear Strategy and Implications for U.S. Deterrence*. Columbus, Ohio: Battelle, 1981.

Papp, Daniel S. "Soviet Perceptions of the Strategic Balance." *Air University Review* 32:2 (1981), 12–35.

Pipes, Richard. "Why the Soviet Union Thinks It Could Fight and Win a Nuclear War." *Commentary*, July 1977.

Ra'anan, Uri. "Soviet Strategic Doctrine and the Soviet-American Global Contest." *Annals of the American Academy of Political and Social Science* 457 (September 1981).

Richelson, Jeffrey T. "Soviet Strategic Doctrine and Limited Nuclear Operations: A Metagame Analysis." *Journal of Conflict Resolution* 23 (1979), 326–336.

Scott, William F., and Scott, Harriet Fast. "Soviet Perceptions of U.S. Military Strategies and Forces." In Graham D. Vernon, ed., *Soviet Perceptions of Peace and War*. Washington, D.C.: NDU Press, 1981.

Sienkiewicz, Stanley. "SALT and Soviet Nuclear Doctrine." *International Security* 2 (1978), 84–100.

Snyder, Jack L. *The Soviet Strategic Culture: Implications for Limited Nuclear Operations*. Santa Monica, Calif.: Rand Corporation, 1977.

Sokolovsky, V. C. *Soviet Military Strategy*. New York: Crane, Russak, 1975.

Soll, Richard. "The Soviet Union and Protracted War." *Strategic Review* 8 (1980), 15–28.

"Soviets Rail against New U.S. Targeting Doctrine." *Soviet World Outlook*, 15 September 1980, p. 4.

Spielmann, Karl F. *Political Utility of Strategic Superiority: A Preliminary Investigation into the Soviet View*. Arlington, Va.,: Institute for Defense Analyses, 1979.

——. *Prospects for a Soviet Strategy of Controlled Nuclear War: An Assessment of Some Key Indicators*. Arlington, Va.: Institute for Defense Analyses, 1976.

Strauch, Ralph E. *Information and Perception in Limited Strategic Conflict: Some U.S. and Soviet Differences*. Santa Monica, Calif.: Rand Corporation, 1976.

Trofimieko, Henry A. "Changing Attitudes toward Deterrence." ACIS Working Paper No. 25. UCLA, 1980.

——. "Counterforce: Illusion of a Panacea." *International Security* 5:4 (1981).

U.S. Congress. House. Committee on Armed Services. *Hearings on Military Posture and H.R. 1872*. Pt. 3, bk. 1. Washington, D.C., 1979.

6. The Targeting Process

Conant, Frank D., and Irons, James V. *Determination of Figures of Merit for Use in SIOP Targeting of Soviet Conventional Military Forces Stationed in Russia*. McLean, Va.: BDM Corporation, 1978.

Dalkey, N.; Helmer, O.; and Thompson, F. B. *Report on a Preliminary Systems Analysis for Strategic Targets*. Santa Monica, Calif.: Rand Corporation, 1953.

Durbin, E. P. *Choosing Weights for Strategic Targets*. Santa Monica, Calif.: Rand Corporation, 1977.

"Joint Strategic Targeting Planning Staff Gives President 'Package Plans' for Nuclear Strikes." *Army, Navy, Air Force Journal and Register* 100 (24 August 1963), 20–21.

Mariska, Mark D. "The Single Integrated Operational Plan." *Military Review*, March 1972, pp. 31–39.

Middleton, Drew. "SAC Chief Is Critical of Carter's New Nuclear Plan." *New York Times*, 7 September 1980, p. 19.

O'Malley, Jerome F. "JSTPS: The Link between Strategy and Execution." *Air University Review* 28:4 (1977), 38–46.

Rowen, Henry. "Formulating Strategic Doctrine." In *Report of the Commission on the Organization of the Government for the Conduct of Foreign Policy*. Appendix K. Washington, D.C.: Government Printing Office, 1975.

U.S. Congress. Senate. Committee on Armed Services. *Department of Defense Authorization for Appropriations for FY 1980*. Pt. 6. Washington, D.C.: 1970.

——. *Department of Defense Authorization for Appropriations for FY 1982*. Pt. 7. Washington, D.C., 1981.

7. Morality and Targeting

Alexander, Lawrence A. "Self-Defense and the Killing of the Non-Combatants: A Reply to Fullinwinder." *Philosophy and Public Affairs* 5 (1976), 408–415.

Anscome, G. E. M. "War and Murder." In Walter Stein, ed., *Nuclear Weapons and Christian Conscience*. London: Merlin, 1961.

Bennett, John C., ed. *Nuclear Weapons and the Conflict of Conscience*. New York: Charles Scribner's, 1962.

Bennett, Jonathan. "Whatever the Consequences." *Analysis* 26 (1965), 86–87.

Bibliography

Bok, Sissela. *Lying Moral Choice in Public and Private Life*. New York: Random House, 1978.

Brandt, Richard. "Utilitarianism and the Rules of War." *Philosophy and Public Affairs* 1 (1972), 145–165.

Builder, Carl H., and Graubard, Morlie H. *The International Law of Armed Conflict: Implications for the Concept of Assured Destruction*. Santa Monica, Calif.: Rand Corporation, 1982.

Collier, Ellen C. "International Law on the Use of Nuclear Weapons and the United States Position." Congressional Research Service Report No. 19-29F, 6 February 1979.

Corden, Pierce S. "Ethics and Deterrence: Moving Beyond the Just-War Tradition." In Harold P. Ford and Francis X. Winters, S.J., eds., *Ethics and Nuclear Strategy*. Maryknoll: Orbis, 1977.

Davies, Kim. "Killing People Intentionally by Chance." *Analysis* 41:3 (1981), 156–160.

Duff, R. A. "Intentionally Killing the Innocent." *Analysis* 34 (1973), 16–19.

Ford, Harold P., and Winters, Francis X., S.J. *Ethics and Nuclear Strategy*. Maryknoll: Orbis, 1977.

Ford, John C. "The Hydrogen Bombing of Cities." In William J. Nagle, ed., *Morality and Modern Warfare*. Baltimore: Helicon Press, 1960.

———. "The Morality of Obliteration Bombing." *Theological Studies* 5 (1944), 261–309.

Fullinwider, Robert K. "War and Innocence." *Philosophy and Public Affairs* 5 (1975), 90–97.

Geddess, Leonard. "On the Intrinsic Wrongness of Killing Innocent People." *Analysis* 33 (1973), 93–97.

Hartigan, Richard S. "Non-Combatant Immunity: Its Scope and Development." *Continuum* 3 (1965).

———. "Non-Combatant Immunity: Reflections on Its Origins and Present Status." *Review of Politics* 29 (1967), 204–220.

Kavka, Gregory S. "Some Paradoxes of Deterrence." *Journal of Philosophy* 75 (1978), 285–303.

Kenny, Anthony. "Postscript: Counterforce and Countervalue." In Walter Stein, ed., *Nuclear Weapons and Christian Conscience*. London: Merlin, 1961.

Levin, Michael. "The Case for Torture." *Newsweek*, 7 June 1982, p. 13.

Levinson, Sanford. "Responsibility for Crimes of War." *Philosophy and Public Affairs* 2 (1973), 244–273.

Markus, R. A. "Conscience and Deterrence." In Walter Stein, ed., *Nuclear Weapons and Christian Conscience*. London: Merlin, 1961.

Mavrodes, George I. "Conventions and the Morality of War." *Philosophy and Public Affairs* 4 (1974), 117–131.

Murphy, Jeffrie G. "The Killing of the Innocent." *The Monist* 57 (1973), 527–550.

Nagel, Thomas. "War and Massacre." *Philosophy and Public Affairs* 1 (1972), 123–144.

Nagle, William. *Morality and Modern Warfare*. Baltimore: Helicon Press, 1960.

Nozick, Robert. *Anarchy, State, and Utopia*. New York: Basic Books, 1974.

O'Brien, William V. *Nuclear War, Deterrence, and Morality*. New York: Newman Press, 1967.

Ramsey, Paul. *War and the Christian Conscience*. Durham, N.C.: Duke University Press, 1961.

Russett, Bruce. "A Countercombatant Deterrent? Feasibility, Morality, and Arms Control." In Sam Sarkesian, ed., *The Military Industrial Complex: A Reassessment*. Beverly Hills, Calif.: Sage, 1972.

Stein, Walter, ed. *Nuclear Weapons and Christian Conscience*. London: Merlin, 1961.

Wasserstrom, Richard A., ed. *War and Morality*. Belmont, Calif.: Wadsworth, 1970.

Wohlstetter, Albert. "Bishops, Statesmen, and Other Strategists on the Bombing of Innocents." *Commentary* 75 (6 June 1983), 15–35.

Index

Library of Congress Cataloging-in-Publication Data
Main entry under title:

Strategic nuclear targeting.

  (Cornell studies in security affairs)
  Bibliography: p.
  Includes index.
  1. Targeting (Nuclear strategy)—Addresses, essays, lectures.　I. Ball, Desmond.　II. Richelson, Jeffrey.　III. Series.
U263.S76　1986　　　358'.39　　　85–48195
ISBN 0–8014–1898–4